Lecture Notes of the Institute for Computer Sciences, Social Informatics and Telecommunications Engineering 339

More information about this series at http://www.springer.com/series/8197

Shuai Liu · Guanglu Sun · Weina Fu (Eds.)

e-Learning, e-Education, and Online Training

6th EAI International Conference, eLEOT 2020
Changsha, China, June 20–21, 2020
Proceedings, Part I

Springer

Editors
Shuai Liu
Human Normal University
Changsha, China

Weina Fu
Hunan Normal University
Changsha, China

Guanglu Sun
Harbin University
Harbin, China

ISSN 1867-8211 ISSN 1867-822X (electronic)
Lecture Notes of the Institute for Computer Sciences, Social Informatics and Telecommunications Engineering
ISBN 978-3-030-63951-8 ISBN 978-3-030-63952-5 (eBook)
https://doi.org/10.1007/978-3-030-63952-5

This Springer imprint is published by the registered company Springer Nature Switzerland AG
The registered company address is: Gewerbestrasse 11, 6330 Cham, Switzerland

Preface

We are delighted to introduce the proceedings of the 6th edition of the 2020 European Alliance for Innovation (EAI) International Conference on e-Learning e-Education and Online Training (EAI eLEOT 2020). This conference has brought together researchers, developers, and practitioners from around the world who are leveraging and developing information technology for educational modernization, such as artificial intelligence and big data. The theme of eLEOT 2020 was "Education with New Generation Information Technology."

The technical program of eLEOT 2020 consisted of 62 full papers, including 2 invited papers in oral presentation sessions at the main conference tracks. The conference tracks were: Track 1 – Education based Information Technology; and Track 2 – New Generation Information Technology in Education. Aside from the high-quality technical paper presentations, the technical program also featured two keynote speeches. The two keynote speakers were Prof. Yu-dong Zhang from the School of Informatics, University of Leicester, UK, who was the fellow of IET (FIET), the senior member of IEEE and ACM, and the 2019 recipient of "Highly Cited Researcher" by Web of Science; as well as Prof. Gautam Srivastava from the Department of Mathematics and Computer Science, Brandon University, Canada, who was the senior member of IEEE and popularly known in the field of data mining and big data, with more than 60 high-quality publications.

Coordination with the steering chair, Prof. Imrich Chlamtac, Bruno Kessler Professor, University of Trento, Italy, was essential for the success of the conference. We sincerely appreciate his constant support and guidance. It was also a great pleasure to work with such an excellent Organizing Committee team and we thank them for their hard work in organizing and supporting the conference. In particular, the Technical Program Committee (TPC), led by our TPC co-chairs, Dr. Fei Lang from Harbin University of Science and Technology, China, and Prof. Lei Chen from Georgia Southern University, USA, who completed the peer-review process of technical papers and made a high-quality technical program. We are also grateful to the conference manager, Barbora Cintava, for her support and all the authors who submitted their papers to the eLEOT 2020 conference.

We strongly believe that the eLEOT conference provides a good forum for all researchers, developers, and practitioners to discuss all science and technology aspects that are relevant to new technologies in education. In particular, all of us believe it is the right time to introduce new technologies for online education since COVID-19 is attacking the world. We also expect that future eLEOT conferences will be as successful and stimulating as indicated by the contributions presented in this volume.

October 2020

Shuai Liu
Guanglu Sun
Weina Fu

Organization

Steering Committee

Imrich Chlamtac	University of Trento, Italy

Organizing Committee

General Chair

Guanglu Sun	Harbin University of Science and Technology, China

TPC Chair and Co-Chairs

Shuai Liu	Hunan Normal University, China
Fei Lang	Harbin University of Science and Technology, China
Lei Chen	Georgia Southern University, USA

Sponsorship and Exhibit Chair

Jiazhong Xu	Harbin University of Science and Technology, China

Local Chair

Wensheng Tang	Hunan Normal University, China

Workshops Chair

Suxia Zhu	Harbin University of Science and Technology, China

Publicity and Social Media Chair

Ao Li	Harbin University of Science and Technology, China

Publications Chairs

Zhaojun Li	Western New England University, USA
Huiyu Zhou	University of Leicester, UK

Web Chairs

Jing Qiu	Harbin University of Science and Technology, China
Weina Fu	Hunan Normal University, China

Posters and PhD Track Chair

Rafi Judgal	Harbin University of Science and Technology, China

Panels Chair

Xiaochun Cheng	Middlesex University, UK

Technical Program Committee

Dan Sui	California State Polytechnic University, Pomona, USA
Jianfeng Cui	Xiamen University of Technology, China
Arun Kumar Sangaiah	Vellore Institute of Technology, India
Lei Ma	Beijing Polytechnic University, China
Wei Wei	The University of Texas at Dallas, USA
Shuai Yang	Changchun University of Technology, China
Ruolin Zhou	Western New England University, USA
Yongjun Qin	Guilin Normal College, China
Gihong Min	Pai Chai University, South Korea
Xuanyue Tong	Nanyang Institute of Technology, China
Jinming Wen	Centre national de la recherche scientifique, France
Yanning Zhang	Beijing Polytechnic University, China
Khan Muhammad	Sejong University, South Korea
Lili Liang	Harbin University of Science and Technology, China
Carlo Cattani	Tuscia University, Italy
Xinyu Liu	Hunan Normal University, China
Zheng Pan	Horizon Robotics Co. Ltd, China
Shuai Liu	Hunan Normal University, China
Shuai Wang	Hunan Normal University, China
Jiesheng He	Hunan Normal University, China
Jing Qiu	Harbin University of Science and Technology, China
Yun Lin	Harbin Engineering University, China
Chengyan Li	Harbin University of Science and Technology, China
Weina Fu	Hunan Normal University, China
Jian Luo	Hunan Normal University, China

Contents – Part I

Education Research with Information Technology

Contents – Part II

Education Research with Information Technology

Empirical Research on the Creative Design Talents Cultivation of Sino-Foreign Cooperative Education Project in Local Engineering Universities

Li Yuan and Zhu Tiejun(✉)

Anhui Polytechnic University, Wuhu 241000, China
ztj@ahpu.edu.cn

Abstract. At present, China's higher education has stepped into a deepening stage of international development. As the main force to provide high-quality international applied talents for serving the local economic construction, it is the trend for local engineering universities to set up and implement Sino-foreign cooperative education projects that meet their school running positioning and professional characteristics. This paper taking the undergraduate education project of visual communication design jointly held by Anhui Polytechnic University and Bridgeport University as an example, this paper analyzes in detail the framework, operation management, curriculum system and practice platform of international design application-oriented innovative talents cultivation mode, and points out the existing problems, and puts forward countermeasures and solutions. Through empirical research, it provides useful exploration and reference for the talents cultivation of design Sino-foreign cooperative education projects in Local Engineering Colleges.

Keywords: Local engineering universities · Internationalization · Creative design · Talents cultivation · Sino-foreign cooperative education project · Empirical research

1 Introduction

At present, China's higher education, under the guidance of the country's in-depth promotion of education internationalization strategy, has shown a more and more open attitude and has been deeply practiced in many fields. In recent years, Sino-foreign cooperative education has become an important part of China's higher education because of its flexibility in the form of school running, internationalization of educational resources, intersection of teaching system, integration of educational environment and diversification of educational management. Statistics in June 2019 show that China's "Sino-foreign cooperative education institutions and projects have reached 2,431, including more than 800 Chinese universities, more than 700 foreign universities, 33 countries and regions, and about 600,000 Chinese students" [1].

S. Liu et al. (Eds.): eLEOT 2020, LNICST 339, pp. 3–15, 2020.
https://doi.org/10.1007/978-3-030-63952-5_1

"Among them, in order to establish the goal of international talents cultivation and the standards and models in line with international standards, the purpose of which is to enable students not only to adapt to the needs of China's social development, but also to adapt to the needs of international competition and regional economic integration" [2]. Internationalization, application and innovation have become the demand standard for talents in the international community under the background of economic globalization. The implementation of Sino-foreign cooperative education projects are based on the introduction of foreign high-quality education resources, the cultivation of international application-oriented innovative talents as the foundation, and provide a solid and powerful talent guarantee for the country in the fierce international competition in the future. This paper takes the undergraduate education project of visual communication design jointly held by Anhui Polytechnic University and Bridgeport University as an example, analyzes the experience, practice, existing problems and countermeasures of the project in the training mode of international applied innovative talents in design, and summarizes the current talents cultivation achievements of the project. It provides beneficial exploration and concrete practice for the talents cultivation of design Sino-foreign cooperative education projects in local engineering universities.

2 Background and Problems

Project structure layout needs further scientific and effective integration. The undergraduate education project of visual communication design is the first Sino-foreign cooperative education project approved by the department of education of Anhui Province. It started enrollment in September 2014. Although the operation mode and talents cultivation plan of the project have been investigated and demonstrated for many times, there will inevitably be some differences in the actual operation process, and the project introduces relevant innovation mechanisms such as the introduction of MOOCs in the process of the talents cultivation, so its overall structure and implementation path need to be tested and further scientific and effective integration.

The introduction of international educational resources still needs to be strengthened. Although the project has achieved diversification and effective pertinence in the introduction of international resources, compared with the Sino-foreign cooperative education projects in coastal provinces, the introduction of international education resources is still relatively weak, and for the characteristics of visual communication design, students' contact with the design cutting edge and design fashion still needs to be expanded.

Therefore, design personality development courses and independent innovation courses need to be enhanced. The core elements of the cultivation of design talents are the expansion of design individuality and design innovation. The international cultivation mechanism of Sino-foreign cooperative talents needs to be strengthened in this aspect. At present, although the project integrates more international courses and practical courses in the curriculum system, however, there is a lack of design personality development courses, independent innovation courses, design team cooperation training courses, design inspiration inspiring courses and brainstorming courses. There are great differences in living habits, teaching methods and concepts between China and foreign countries. Therefore, both domestic and foreign teaching need to integrate and improve, learn from each other, and make students adapt to different teaching modes more quickly.

The characteristics of Sino-foreign cooperative education determine that its talents cultivation mode, teaching process and management mode are different from those of other majors. Whether students can successfully achieve the set goals in China, successfully adapt to the learning and living environment during their stay abroad, and finally become excellent international applied innovative talents, can not be separated from tracking supporting and guarantee mechanism. Although a series of methods have been put forward in the aspects of curriculum system integration, faculty guarantee, practice platform construction, innovative employment, etc., the project still lacks in the construction of deep-seated detailed supporting guarantee mechanism, such as optimizing the talents cultivation process, controlling the real-time development trend of students and correcting the deviation of goals.

3 Empirical Research

As one of the few local engineering universities in Anhui Province, Anhui Polytechnic University undertakes the task of delivering a large number of high-quality international applied talents and serving the local economic construction. Therefore, the current situation and its own responsibilities and positioning require the university to vigorously introduce foreign high-quality education resources, develop and implement a batch of high-quality and high-level Sino-foreign cooperative education projects. Through all-round international cooperation and exchange, we can improve the level of education, teaching and management, cultivate more high-quality international applied talents, and better serve the local economic and social development. At the same time, Anhui Polytechnic University is also actively improving some inevitable problems in the project of Sino-foreign cooperation.

In order to further promote the international exchange and cooperation in education of Anhui Polytechnic University, and further implement the open school running strategy of Anhui Polytechnic University, with the goal of learning from and drawing on the advanced educational concepts, teaching methods, unique school running modes and experience of American universities, realize the benign interaction and common growth of the teaching management and curriculum system of the two universities, promote talents cultivation mode and teaching reform, speed up the establishment of high-level application-oriented university, constantly strengthen the external exchange and contact between teachers and students, expand the international vision, and improve the international level and comprehensive strength of school education, after a long-term in-depth research and multiple rounds of dialogue and exchanges with the University of Bridgeport in the United States, Anhui Polytechnic University has successfully implemented the undergraduate education project of visual communication design in cooperation with the University of Bridgeport.

3.1 Cultivation Model Framework

Firstly, in terms of talents cultivation framework, the project mode advocates "to cultivate specialized talents with international design culture vision, understanding Chinese design culture characteristics, adapting to the design requirements of the digital era, and integrating traditional design skills and modern digital media application technology" [3]. On the one hand, through domestic education, improve students' understanding of traditional art and culture and carry out training of contemporary design thinking; On the other hand, through overseas study, broaden students' horizons, promote students to understand the latest achievements and development information of art design at home and abroad, enhance students' cross-cultural communication ability, and pay attention to the acquisition of design innovation ability and scientific research ability (Fig. 1).

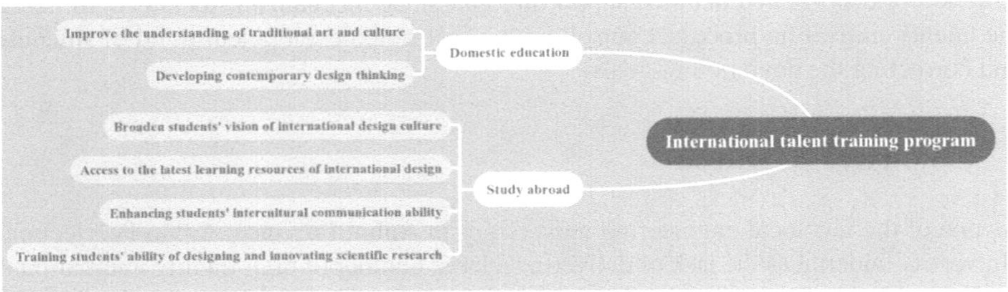

Fig. 1. The mind map of international talent cultivating plan

Secondly, in the specific operation mode, the project adheres to the quality concept of Sino-foreign cooperative education as the guide, "quality construction has become a distinct theme in the new stage of Sino-foreign cooperative education", [4] focuses on the quality construction of Sino-foreign cooperative education, and strengthens the process control of teaching quality; takes the quality standard of talents cultivation as the main line, creates the overall development of students' quality and skills; creates a good international learning atmosphere for students by deeply introducing and integrating high-quality international resources and allocating teaching curriculum system with characteristics; builds a diversified communication platform and practice base of international design culture and expands the international channels for students' employment. Therefore, Anhui Polytechnic University, through the Sino-foreign cooperative education project, not only promotes the talents cultivation and the internationalization of education and teaching, but also further promotes the construction of art and design disciplines, so as to provide strong support for the effective improvement of the school running strength and level.

3.2 Operation Management

In Line with the University's Goal of Cultivating High-Quality International Applied Talents. After 85 years of accumulation, Anhui Polytechnic University has formed a structure of coordinated development of science, culture, management, economics, law, art and other disciplines. In many disciplines and specialties, it has not only accumulated rich experience in running schools, but also formed a group of disciplines and specialties that support each other. The conditions of experiment and practice training, the campus environment and the construction of campus culture have been significantly enhanced, and talents cultivation has been carried out with the continuous improvement of quality and the general recognition of the society. The initial employment rate of undergraduates has remained above 95% for many years, ranking among the best in Anhui Province. In 2014, it was awarded “Anhui University Innovation and entrepreneurship education demonstration university” and “Top 50 universities with typical employment experience of National Graduates” (Fig. 2).

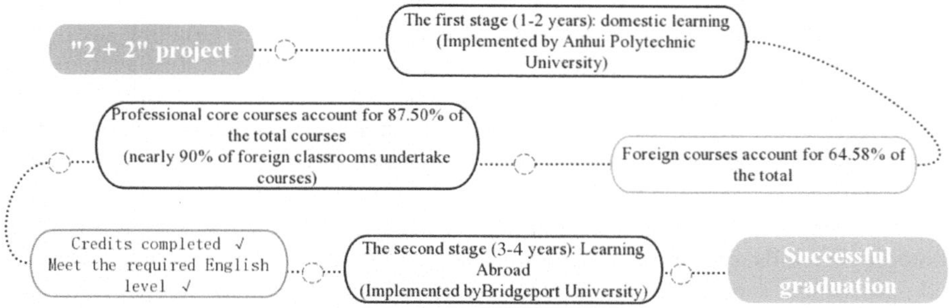

Fig. 2. Flow chart of “2 + 2” project

These achievements are due to the guiding ideology of Anhui Polytechnic University is clear. It adheres to the school running concept of “building the school with quality, strengthening the school with talents, and developing the school with characteristics and harmony”. With the goal of cultivating high-quality international applied talents, it always takes open school running as an important policy for the development of the school, adapts to the requirements of the internationalization of higher education, innovates the talents cultivation mode, and further optimizes the talents cultivation plan, provides more diversified choice space for students’ growth and personalized development, including Sino-foreign cooperative education projects, improves students’ comprehensive quality and international social adaptability, adheres to the connotative development road of strengthening characteristics, and provides talent support for social development and local economic construction.

Characteristics of Curriculum System. In order to give full play to its greatest advantages, the project takes “2 + 2” as the school running form, that is, the first stage courses recognized by both parties in the education and teaching plan and will be implemented by Anhui Polytechnic University, and the students who have completed the required credits and meet the requirements of English level will enter the second stage courses of Bridgeport University in the third year. In the cultivation plan of the first two years, the foreign curriculum introduced by the project accounts for 64.58% of the total curriculum of the project; the professional core curriculum introduced accounts for 87.50%; the teaching hours of the professional core curriculum undertaken by the teachers of foreign educational institutions account for nearly 90%.

“To build an international application-oriented curriculum system that conforms to the characteristics and reality of art majors is the key of the international application-oriented talents cultivation mode of art majors. This mode will build a scientific and effective international application-oriented curriculum system that integrates general education, language skills, comprehensive literacy, professional knowledge, practical training and other modules" [5]. Therefore, in the formulation of the cultivating plan and the construction of the curriculum system, the project builds a distinctive educational content and teaching system that integrates general education platform, discipline professional education platform, professional direction module, practical education platform and comprehensive education platform. Among them, general education platform mainly includes humanities and Social Sciences, Natural Sciences (Mathematics), language skills (English), computer information technology and physical education; Discipline professional education platform includes design basis, professional basic theory and professional core courses; Professional direction module includes thematic courses at all levels of visual communication design direction; Practical education platform is divided into basic education practice training and professional education practice training, including entrance education, military training, social practice, productive labor, photography skills, design services, advertising and public relations, business practice and professional forums; Comprehensive education is a communication platform integrating ideological and cultural quality education, academic and scientific activities, literary and artistic activities, sports activities, volunteer activities and other rich educational activities. In addition, the project also highlights the principle of multi-disciplinary integration of art, design and cultural industry management. With the purpose of cultivating students' design thinking ability, design understanding ability, design integration ability and design realization ability, it has formed an international curriculum system and distinctive characteristics of interdisciplinary of "transnational education, combination of learning, research, and social service" (Fig. 3).

International Applied Curriculum System

Characteristic education content	Specific courses included				
General Courses Platform	Humanities and Social Sciences	Natural Science (Mathematics)	Language skills (English)	Computer information technology	Sports
Discipline professional education platform	Design basis	Professional basic theory	Professional core courses		
Professional direction module	Special courses of visual communication design direction at all levels				
Practical education platform	Practical training of basic education	Professional education practice training			
Comprehensive education platform	Ideological and cultural quality education	Academic research activities	Literary activities	Sports activities	Volunteer activities

Fig. 3. International Applied Curriculum System

Diversity and Pertinence of Introducing High Quality Resources. "The main goal of Sino-foreign cooperative education is to introduce foreign high-quality educational resources, and strive to cultivate talents who can adapt to economic globalization, information globalization, international awareness, international exchanges and competitiveness" [6]. From the initial setup and construction, close connection and communication, to operation and implementation, the project will introduce high-quality international resources as the core factor of project operation, and pay special attention to its diversity and pertinence. In addition to the above mentioned integration of domestic and foreign curriculum systems, the introduced diversity also includes the reference of educational concepts in foreign countries, the introduction of foreign original textbooks, the recruitment of foreign teachers, the promotion of international MOOCs and the application of international teaching methods, and so on. In order to achieve the main goal, the university has actively expanded its own development space, introduced more high-quality teaching resources, and improved the teaching mode.

"The 'high quality' of educational resources is relative to specific organizations and projects, and the criteria are not unique and absolute. In fact, different types and levels of Sino-foreign cooperative education institutions and projects have different needs for 'quality education resources'" [7]. It is true that the school's orientation, management mode, students and teachers' level and ability, differences in disciplines and specialties, and differences in the project's running form and training mode all affect the understanding, evaluation, absorption and maximization of the effectiveness of high-quality resources. According to the nature of running a local engineering university, at the beginning of the connection demonstration, the project is a targeted docking of Bridgeport University in the United States, which not only has a high reputation and quality of running a school, but also has a very close professional positioning. It is a Sino-foreign cooperative project for design. The University of Bridgeport is also characterized by its design specialty, which has been certified by the National Association of Arts and design institutes of the United States. Aiming at the positioning of visual communication design specialty, Bridgeport University has established cooperative relations with nearly 100 universities and institutions in more than 80 countries and regions, and has a smooth and multiple channel to obtain the latest development trends in the field of visual communication design. In addition, the university's geographical location is superior. It's only an hour's drive from the financial and economic center and fashion design capital of New York. No matter its professional teachers or other professional resources can closely integrate the design frontier of the United States and the world, but also provide a broad platform and the best stage for the project students to study in the United States.

Pay Attention to the Key Role of the Construction of International Teaching Staff in the Talent Cultivation of the Project. "In Sino-foreign cooperative education, a considerable part of the courses need to be taught in foreign languages, emphasizing bilingual teaching of professional courses, while the teaching materials generally adopt the original English textbooks supporting the project" [8]. In addition to the foreign teachers specially employed by the project, the faculty of Anhui Polytechnic University is still the main force of the project implementation and talent cultivation, therefore, the teachers with rich professional knowledge and innovation awareness, as well as international professional quality and foreign language skills become the key factors in the process of project teaching quality and talent cultivation control. In this regard, Anhui Polytechnic University bases on the overseas cooperation resources and contact channels, and takes the Sino-foreign cooperative education project as the platform to build an international teaching staff of the project. First, it vigorously supports and takes incentive measures to encourage professional teachers to go abroad for further study, especially overseas colleges and universities. Since the implementation of the project, about 5 professional teachers go to famous foreign universities for further study every year; Secondly, the double track mechanism of cultivation and introduction is implemented to actively introduce high-level talents studying abroad to work in the university. At present, the project has gathered a group of high-level talents studying abroad and returning home and undertakes specific teaching and management work; Thirdly, with the help of project platform, a project agreement has been reached with Bridgeport University of the United States. The Bridgeport University is responsible for providing the required number of qualified and experienced teachers to teach for the project and also assisting Anhui Polytechnic University to implement the internship required by the project. In addition, the US side also undertakes the task of receiving professional training, which will be implemented in the United States, for professional teachers of Anhui Polytechnic University in every year. Till now, eight teacher training sessions and four management staff training sessions have been carried out and reached significant training achievements. Fourth, through the establishment of an international cooperation research base and a teacher's studio in the Chinese side university, the teachers and students of the project can participate in the exchange and cooperation based on the international platform without leaving campus. Now, Anhui Polytechnic University has a design art research base jointly established with Sejong University in South Korea and a teacher's studio jointly established with Bridgeport University in the United States.

Build a Diversified Communication Platform and Practice Base of International Design Culture. The project is based on the goal of training international applied innovative talents of design in local engineering universities. Guided by deepening the construction of talent innovation system and deeply integrating local economic development, it strives to build a diversified communication platform, practice base and innovation environment of international design culture, and focuses on training students' design practice ability, independent innovation ability and skill application ability. First, deepen and make full use of existing overseas cooperation resources and vigorously expand new channels. At present, the project guides and encourages students to actively participate in various activities, such as art exchange, academic discussion, study and tour camp, cultural experience and practical training program, which have been carried out by the university with the United States, South Korea, Thailand, Taiwan and other places and are expanding constantly. While experiencing and appreciating foreign diversified design culture and practical exchange, it also helps students to learn the living environment and cultivate the ability of communication, cooperation and independence, and then adapt to study abroad in advance; Secondly, as mentioned above, the international cooperative research base and teachers' studio established by the university are used to provide domestic international teaching and research platform for project students; Thirdly, actively hold design exhibitions and art performances cooperated with overseas universities, so as to promote the multiple collision and burst of students' design inspiration, as well as the cultivation of team cooperation and innovation awareness. For example, each year, both universities carry out joint exhibition of students' design works based on project platform. "The exhibition will build an information exchange platform for colleges and universities at home and abroad to achieve the goal of full exchange, mutual discussion and mutual enlightenment, and realize a new design leap, which will not only help to open up academic horizons and integrate diversified creative ideas, but also provide opportunities for the innovation and transformation of art design achievements in colleges and universities in Anhui Province, and help local economic development" [9]; The fourth is to highlight the specific practice of application-oriented talents cultivation mode, "art and design major is an application-oriented major, and it also cultivates application-oriented talents with strong practical ability and skills" [10]. Therefore, Anhui Polytechnic university expands the practice base in an all-round way and forms a practice system covering the whole process of talents cultivation, so as to comprehensively strengthen the practical ability of students. Now, Anhui Polytechnic University owns a national off-campus practical education base, and School of Arts has a number of teaching practice bases, social practice bases and innovation and entrepreneurship education platforms, a provincial key research base of Humanities and Social Sciences, a design and art research center, and a scientific research platform for university-enterprise cooperation of art design has been created by making full use of the advantages of Wuhu national advertising industrial park close to the campus. It has built a new platform for the close integration of production, learning and research between teachers and students.

3.3 Countermeasures and Suggestions

Control and Adjust the Project Operation Process and Implementation Plan in Real Time. In order to effectively deal with the deviation between the original plan and structure layout and the actual operation process, the project should formally establish a real-time monitoring operation mechanism, through the multi-dimensional real-time management system, combined with daily teaching, after-school activities, assessment and evaluation, external feedback and social response, to control the project operation process in real time, find problems and adjust them in time, effectively guarantee the optimal and most efficient project structure system.

Introduce Social Forces to Deepen the Development of International High-Quality Resources and Optimize the Allocation. On the one hand, in view of the advantages that local engineering universities have in close contact with local economy and society, the project should make full use of and actively mobilize social forces, contact and introduce high-quality international resources of local society, and jointly build a resource sharing platform. On the other hand, it should increase investment in education funds, and optimize the allocation and timely deployment of education resources, such as in some professional core courses or quality training course, "small class" teaching can be carried out. Through the deep interaction of teachers and students in a small range, while cultivating their active learning and in-depth thinking, the teaching content, form and method can also be adjusted accordingly, so as to give full play to the flexibility and maximum utilization of educational resources allocation.

Establish a Perfect Project Self-evaluation System as Soon as Possible. China's Ministry of Education promotes the evaluation mechanism of Sino-foreign cooperative education institutions and projects, which is conducive to the improvement of the quality and the guiding use of international resources. At the same time, it promotes the self-discipline of schools and the supervision of social forces through government supervision, so as to gradually form a good trend of scientific development. According to the evaluation document of Sino-foreign cooperative education issued by China's Ministry of Education, "based on the self-evaluation of each school, on-site investigation and evaluation shall be organized by random sampling and other methods." Therefore, the project should establish a perfect self-evaluation system as soon as possible in strict accordance with the indicators at all levels determined by the government evaluation of Sino-foreign cooperative education, and take the way of regular evaluation to find out problems, analyze causes, rectify deficiencies, and promote improvement. At the same time of improving the ability of running project and highlighting the professional characteristics, it is more conducive to the cultivation of high-quality talents, the improvement of school reputation and the expansion of project influence. In addition, "the project partner should also establish a long-term mechanism of self-control and evaluation, and put forward a perfect quality standard system and an excellent internal quality evaluation system, so as to ensure high-quality education and teaching" [11].

Design and Innovate the Content and Form of Curriculum, and Promote the Innovation of Students with the Influence of Self Innovation. On the basis of ensuring the quality of teaching, in order to better promote the acquisition of innovation ability in the cultivating of design talents, the project should creatively innovate in the content and form of the course. Based on the students' learning state, learning comprehension, learning interest and the plasticity of innovation ability, it can set up some innovation courses or innovation processes in the existing courses with appropriateness and pertinence. Without setting any existing course objectives, the students can set and complete their own learning through independent consultation. During this learning period, teachers give guidance and instruction and set up assessment tasks with innovation as the requirements, so as to fully meet the students' desire for innovation and the leading desire of classroom teaching, so as to thoroughly generate the internal driving force of their learning and endless ideas of innovation design, and shape and cultivate their "soft power", that is, "the attraction and appeal of talents themselves", in the innovative curriculum dominated by students [12].

In-depth Consideration and Introduction of Humanized and Scientific and Effective Student Development Tracking Supporting Guarantee Mechanism. In view of the dynamic operation of the project, it needs to control the whole process, and pays close attention to the growth and development of students and the process of talent cultivation [13]. In order to better grasp the development trends of students and the real-time state of learning psychology, it is suggested that on the one hand, "joint meeting system, joint teaching guidance committee, unified teaching implementation procedures, joint teaching supervision committee and unified teaching quality evaluation system and so on, should be implemented with the participation of students in the whole process," [14] on the other hand, it introduces the early warning mechanism of students' potential learning crisis, teacher-student interview system, learning and psychological problems appointment guidance system, regular learning effect and problem-solving experience sharing theme activities, real-time data analysis and feedback mechanism of students' learning and various activities, and other closely tracking supporting guarantee mechanisms, so as to provide meticulous humanistic care, promote the healthy growth of students, and guarantee the quality of talents cultivation with scientific and effective mechanism system [15].

3.4 Achievements in Talents Cultivation

The Sino-foreign cooperative education project itself is an innovative form of education and teaching [16]. It not only integrates international high-quality resources, but also brings new learning experience to students with its new education concept and education mode. In addition, the status and influence of the first Sino-foreign cooperative education project is its advantage. Anhui Polytechnic University strives to build it into a representative Sino-foreign cooperative education demonstration project. With great efforts in education, teaching, teachers, management, etc. the project has made some achievements in talents cultivation since its successful enrollment in September 2014, which are shown in the following aspects: first, the impact of project is constantly expanding, because the visual communication design is an advantageous specialty in both universities, strong combination, the social response of the project is high. In the questionnaire of students' comprehensive situation, students have a high degree of recognition for it, and it is generally believed that the integrated training program and curriculum system design between China and the United States are reasonable; Secondly, through the data analysis collected by the questionnaire, the professional level of students has been significantly improved, which is highly praised for the introduction of American teachers to teach courses and their teaching methods, and at the same time, the self-confidence of students has been enhanced, the self-evaluation and analysis are objective and accurate, and the students can be aware of their strengths and weaknesses, and have specific ideas and plans for future personal development; Thirdly, the best mode of talents cultivation for design Sino-foreign cooperative education projects is to bring students a wide range of feelings, contacts, participation, experience and involvement in international design cutting-edge and design fashion, to bring students excellent and innovative design ideas and design practice of a broad international platform [17]. Through the introduction of rich international high-quality resources and the construction of domestic and foreign skill practice platform and social application platform, students' social performance and comprehensive ability are significantly enhanced. Data analysis results show that the comprehensive quality training program (including listening to academic lectures and participating in various extracurricular activities) has a high degree of participation, with an annual average of about 280 people (about 35 students for one batch of this project). Meanwhile, it actively participates in various events organized by university and social organizations, with an annual average of about 150 people. Students actively participate in volunteer activities. Some students also participate in skills training of social organizations and overseas study tours organized by the university. In the activity, the students' application ability has been improved significantly. They also share their learning and life experience abroad with the public, and show their learning results, so that more students can feel the advantages and characteristics of this project more intuitively.

4 Conclusion

At present, the implementation of international cooperative education has become an important means of internationalization of higher education [18]. Anhui Polytechnic University Visual Communication Design Sino-US cooperation undergraduate education project actively implements the national education internationalization development strategy, around the national policy goal orientation and the local economic demand, constructs the international application-oriented innovative talents cultivation mode in line with the school running orientation of the local engineering university and the actual development of design majors. In the aspects of multi-dimensional strengthening of quality construction, diversified introduction and integration of high-quality international resources, characteristic allocation of teaching curriculum system, cultivation and introduction of international teachers, and creation of a diversified exchange platform and practice base for international design culture, it provides beneficial exploration and specific practice for the talents cultivation of Sino-foreign cooperative education project in local engineering universities.

Acknowledgement. This work is supported in part by 2018 Anhui provincial quality engineering project "Sino-foreign cooperation training project" (2018zwpy001) and Zhongjiang scholar talent project.

References

1. Information Times Homepage. http://www.xxsb.com/content/2019-06/25/content_54873.html. Accessed 9 Aug 2019
2. Xue Xiaoqiang, F.: Methods, significance and value of Sino-foreign cooperative education in cultivating applied talents. Vocat. Educ. Res. **3**, 56–57 (2008)
3. Zongping, F.: Research on the teaching quality assurance mechanism in Sino-foreign cooperative education. Jiangsu High. Educ. **01**, 76–78 (2015)
4. Jinhui, L., Liu Mengjin, F.: On the quality construction of Sino-foreign cooperative education. Educ. Res. **10**, 72–78 (2013)
5. Tiejun, Z., Ye Guixia, F.: Research on the construction strategy of international applied talents cultivation mode for art majors. J. Bengbu Univ. **2**(1), 111–114 (2013)
6. Jiaofeng, G., Chen Hongyu, F.: Problems and countermeasures in the teaching of Sino-foreign cooperative education. J. Changsha Univ. **3**, 125–126 (2007)
7. Yan Xiao, F.: Influencing factors and basic principles of introducing foreign high-quality education resources into Sino-foreign cooperative education. Jiangsu High. Educ. **1**, 120–122, 155 (2014)
8. Zongdeng, Z., Hongying, Z., Liu Zhi, F.: On the problems and countermeasures of Sino-foreign cooperative education of art and design. Design **2**, 155–156 (2014)
9. Anhui Polytechnic Universitynetwork. http://www.ahpu.edu.cn/s/1/t/173/f2/06/info61958.htm. Accessed 10 Sept 2019
10. Niu Yanan, F.: Practical research on application-oriented talents cultivation mode of art design major in Sino-foreign cooperative education project. Art Technol. **3**, 374–381 (2014)
11. Zhou Chaocheng, F.: Analysis of Three frameworks for quality assurance in Sino–foreign cooperative education project. Chin. Educ. Soc. **4**, 97–107 (2009)

12. Liwen, D., David, F.: Strategies to improve the "soft power" of applied undergraduate talents cultivation. J. Hebei Normal Univ. Sci. Technol. **11**, 83–86 (2012)
13. Dong Xiaomei, F.: Discussion on cultivation mode of international applied innovative talents in local engineering universities. Innov. Entrep. Educ. **3**(2), 72–75 (2012)
14. Qiongdan, M., Liang Yueqiao, F.: Research on the evaluation of students' learning satisfaction of Chinese foreign cooperative education project. High. Educ. Forum **4**, 111–114124 (2020)
15. Fei, Z., Huang Yingjie, F.: Research on the development of Chinese foreign cooperative institutions and professional projects of 42 first-class universities in China. Heilongjiang High. Educ. Res. **38**(5), 35–41 (2020)
16. Gong Jian, F.: Main problems and improvement path of Chinese foreign cooperative education in local universities. J. Yichun Univ. **4**, 121–125 (2020)
17. Li Zongmin, Du Jianhui, F.: research on quality assurance strategy of Chinese foreign cooperative undergraduate education based on results. Educ. Internationalization **11**, 129–133 (2018)
18. Zhang Qian, F.: Reflections on the diversified management of Chinese foreign cooperative education in colleges and universities. Contemp. Educ. Pract. Teach. Res. **2**, 106–107 (2020)

Evaluation Model of Case Teaching Effect of Engineering Cost Based on Data Mining

Xiao Qi-rong(✉)

Department of Architectural Engineering,
Dazhou Vocational and Technical College, Dazhou 635001, China
xienxue4111@163.com

Abstract. Aiming at the problem that the traditional teaching effect evaluation model of engineering cost case is less comprehensive, a teaching effect evaluation model of engineering cost case based on data mining is designed. Based on data mining, the evaluation data of teaching effect of engineering cost cases are mined, a series of relevant data are analyzed and obtained by using the method of data mining process, and the clustering analysis of evaluation data is realized by using the typical k-means algorithm. According to the result of cluster analysis, the evaluation index system of teaching effect of engineering cost cases is designed based on the ability indexes in the professional ability system of engineering cost students. Based on the analytic hierarchy process (AHP), the hierarchical structure of the evaluation model of project cost case teaching effect is established, the evaluation matrix is constructed, the weight vector is calculated, and the construction of the evaluation model of project cost case teaching effect is realized through consistency test. In order to prove that the evaluation benchmark of the teaching effect evaluation model of engineering cost case based on data mining is comprehensive, the traditional teaching effect evaluation model of engineering cost case is compared with the model, and the experimental results show that the evaluation benchmark of this model is comprehensive.

Keywords: Data mining · Project cost · Case teaching · Effect evaluation model

1 Introduction

The engineering cost specialty is a practical specialty. Students of this major should have the practical operation skills to determine and control the project cost when they graduate, and the determination and control of the project cost are realized through the preparation and review of the project budget, final accounts, bill of quantities and pricing according to the professional knowledge they have learned, the construction engineering drawings, the construction engineering quota and other technical data. Because case teaching can make students truly become students, it can enhance students' perceptual knowledge, improve students' knowledge application ability, deepen students' understanding of practical work of engineering cost specialty, shorten the time for students to adapt to work, and

S. Liu et al. (Eds.): eLEOT 2020, LNICST 339, pp. 16–28, 2020.
https://doi.org/10.1007/978-3-030-63952-5_2

enhance students' confidence in mastering knowledge and skills [1]. Therefore, case teaching is an effective way to improve students' practical skills.

There are two types of teaching procedures that can be used to teach cases: you can review the theoretical knowledge before teaching the case, or you can directly teach the case. Reviewing the theoretical knowledge before teaching the case refers to reviewing the theoretical knowledge involved in the case before teaching the case, which is helpful to help students recall the lost theoretical knowledge, so as to improve students' understanding and acceptance of the case, and then improve case teaching Effect. This teaching procedure conforms to the law of cognition that human beings understand things from the shallow to the deep, and also conforms to the law of loss of human memory [2]. Case direct teaching refers to teaching plan. Before the implementation of case teaching, we have learned the necessary theoretical knowledge. Therefore, in the case teaching stage, it is not necessary to review the theoretical knowledge involved in the case [3]. The content of case teaching of engineering cost includes case teaching of preparing construction drawing budget, case teaching of engineering quantity list valuation, and case teaching of engineering quantity list valuation. In the case of preparing construction drawing budget, the teaching should be organized according to the specific steps of the construction drawing budget preparation. In the case of engineering quantity list preparation, the teaching should be organized in strict accordance with the requirements of GB50500-2003D and the specific steps of the engineering quantity list. The core content of the valuation is to determine the comprehensive unit price and measure item price of each sub-project [4]. In order to evaluate the teaching effect of engineering cost case teaching, a model of teaching effect evaluation of engineering cost case based on data mining is proposed.

2 Design a Model for Evaluating the Effect of Engineering Cost Case Teaching Based on Data Mining

2.1 Cluster Analysis of Evaluation Data

Based on data mining, the evaluation data of project cost case teaching effect is mined. Using the method of data mining process, a series of relevant data are analyzed and obtained. The typical k-means algorithm is used to realize the clustering analysis of evaluation data [5]. First, collect the evaluation data related to the project cost case teaching, that is, according to the teaching effect of the project cost case teaching, according to the specific 20 evaluation items under the five first level indicators in the teaching evaluation table, score in turn (5 points for each item, full score).

Then carry out data preparation processing, including data cleaning and data conversion. Data cleaning refers to: cleaning up the vacant values, smooth noise data, and outlier data in the engineering cost case teaching evaluation data, and finally retained 300 complete evaluation data [6]. Data conversion refers to: there are 20 evaluation items in the teaching evaluation form, and clustering of all 20 items is unnecessary. Therefore, the data in the evaluation form is reorganized from the five first-level evaluation indicators. The values of the five primary indicators are equivalent to the sum of the scores of the secondary indicators [7]. After the conversion, we converted the 20 assessment items into the following five aspects: "teaching quality", "teaching content", "teaching method", "class effect", and "teaching management". We can use these five aspects as representative indicators to complete data clustering on the five attributes of the collected 300 data samples.

Then carry out data mining to obtain data samples, as shown in Table 1.

Table 1. Data samples

Teaching quality	Content of courses	Teaching method	Classroom effect	Teaching management
22	26	28	9	5
24	25	26	7	4
20	24	24	8	4
24	28	27	8	5
20	21	23	6	3
22	24	25	7	4
22	25	24	6	4
22	26	24	7	
…	…	…	…	…

For cluster analysis of data samples, using the k-means algorithm, first select L data from n data as the initial cluster center. Then the other remaining objects are assigned to the corresponding clusters by class, and the classification is based on the similarity with the cluster center. Finally, the corresponding average value of each cluster center is obtained by calculation, and the process is repeated to obtain the standard measure function of final convergence to complete the task. In the actual calculation process, the 300 sample data is divided into three cluster numbers L, and these three cluster numbers respectively represent three levels of "satisfactory", "basic satisfaction" and "dissatisfaction".

The specific implementation of the algorithm needs to input sample data first: in Notepad, input the data in Table 2 according to the format of Table 3, and the sample data waiting to be input is stored in the data. Dat file.

Table 2. Input data

Serial number	Input data	Interpretation
1	Numlist = 300	300 samples
2	Numopt = 5	The number of attributes is 5
3	NumCluster = 3	The number of clusters is 3

Table 3. Data input format

Numlist	–	Sample size(int)
Numopt	–	Number of attributes(int)
Numcluster	–	Number of clusters K(int)
list[1,1]	...list[1,Numopt]	sample 1(real)
list[2,1]	...list[2,Numopt]	sample 2(real)
...	...	...
List[numlist,1]	...list[numlist,numopt]	sample N(real)

The general process of clustering is like this. The main () function is used as the main function, in which the initclusters () function is first used to input the sample data, then the runkmeans () is called, and distributesamples (), FindClosestcluster (), EucNorm () are called in runkmeans () internally. Assign each object in the function to the nearest cluster, and then calculate the new center point of each cluster by calling calcnewclustercenters() and recalculating. When there is no change in the cluster center, write the cluster flag convflag as 1, and the whole clustering process is completed. If the cluster center is still changing, we need to repeat the above process.

The clustering results are shown in Table 4.

Table 4. Clustering results

	Teaching quality	Content of courses	Teaching method	Classroom effect	Teaching management
Satisfied	23.83	26.83	27.6	7.83	4.33
Basic satisfaction	21.25	23.69	24.25	6.19	4.06
Dissatisfied	15.33	19	19	4.67	3

Among them:

Cluster l (satisfactory), 72 samples in total, accounting for:

$$72/300 = 24\% \tag{1}$$

Cluster 2 (basically satisfactory), 192 samples in total, accounting for:

$$192/300 = 64\% \tag{2}$$

Cluster 3 (unsatisfactory), with a total of 36 samples, accounting for:

$$36/300 = 12\% \tag{3}$$

2.2 Construction of Evaluation Index System

Based on the cluster analysis results of the evaluation results of engineering cost case teaching results, and combined with the various capacity indicators designed in the professional competence system of engineering cost major students, an engineering evaluation index system of engineering cost case teaching effects was designed [8] (Table 5).

Table 5. First level indexes of evaluation index system

	Serial number	First level index
Evaluation index system of project cost case teaching effect	1	Basic ability
	2	Core competence
	3	Development ability

Among them, the secondary indicators corresponding to the basic capacity are shown in Table 6.

Table 6. Secondary indicators corresponding to basic capacity

	Serial number	Two level index
Evaluation index system of project cost case teaching effect	1	Technical capacity of building foundation
	2	Preliminary understanding of project management
	3	Ability to apply relevant laws and regulations
	4	Basic knowledge of relevant economic theory and financial technology
	5	Basic ability synthesis

The secondary indicators corresponding to core competencies are shown in Table 7.

Table 7. Secondary indicators corresponding to core competence

	Serial number	Two level index
Evaluation index system of project cost case teaching effect	1	Project investment and financing management ability
	2	Project feasibility study and evaluation
	3	Preliminary engineering measurement capability
	4	Preliminary engineering pricing capacity
	5	Preliminary investment estimation capability
	6	Preliminary ability to prepare bidding documents
	7	Preliminary ability to evaluate bids
	8	Preliminary ability to prepare and select contract documents
	9	Preliminary ability in cost management, payment management and change management
	10	Preliminary ability to communicate with customers
	11	Preliminary procurement management ability of the project
	12	Preliminary ability of project settlement and final account preparation
	13	Preliminary ability in accounting and auditing of construction unit
	14	Preliminary contract management capability
	15	Preliminary post project evaluation

The secondary indicators corresponding to development capacity are shown in Table 8.

According to the teaching effect evaluation index, the design of the questionnaire is carried out with the engineering cost major as the research object. The questionnaire gives full consideration to the ability measurement mentioned in the evaluation index, and quantifies each evaluation index one by one. The corresponding answers of each ability are divided into five levels, respectively: A. good; B. good; C. better; D. in general;

Table 8. Secondary indicators corresponding to development capacity

	Serial number	Two level index
Evaluation index system of project cost case teaching effect	1	Project resource management
	2	customer relationship management
	3	Multi project management
	4	Enterprise strategic management
	5	LCC life cycle cost management
	6	VM value management
	7	Dispute management
	8	Claim management
	9	Integrated management

E. Difference is calculated and calculated according to the score corresponding to the grade [9].

2.3 Construction of Evaluation Model of Project Cost Case Teaching Effect

According to the evaluation index system of project cost case teaching effect, the evaluation model of project cost case teaching effect is constructed. Firstly, the hierarchy structure of the evaluation model of project cost case teaching effect is established based on the analytic hierarchy process, then the judgment matrix is constructed, the weight vector is calculated, and finally the consistency is checked to realize the construction of the evaluation model of project cost case teaching effect Jian.

The analytic hierarchy process requires a systematic analysis of the scope, the factors involved, and the relationships between the factors involved in the model, establishing the goals to be achieved by the model, the criteria for evaluation, and the index system, while creating the corresponding hierarchical structure. The hierarchical structure of the construction cost case teaching effect evaluation model established by the analytic hierarchy process is composed of the following three levels: the highest level of the predetermined target of the problem-the target layer; the middle layer that affects the target achievement criteria-the rule layer; The bottom layer-the measures layer [10]. Then use the analytic hierarchy process to make corresponding choices and adjustments to the hierarchy. When selecting the evaluation index system to determine the order of the index weights, the first 2 or 3 hierarchies can be used. When selecting a decision plan, alternatives must be added Scheme layer.

According to the hierarchical substructure, the judgment matrix is constructed as follows: the criterion, that is, each element with downward membership relation is regarded as the first element of the judgment matrix, placed in the upper left corner, and then the elements belonging to it are arranged in the first column and the first row. The usual method to fill in the judgment matrix is to repeat the question to the expert as the filling person for many times. According to the criterion of judgment matrix, the elements are compared in pairs, important elements are selected, and their importance is evaluated.

The importance degree is assigned according to 1–9 in the importance scale value table. The importance scale value is shown in Table 9.

Table 9. Importance scale values

Serial number	Factor ratio factor	Quantization value
1	Equally important	1
2	Slightly important	3
3	More important	5
4	Strongly important	7
5	Extremely important	9
Intermediate value of two adjacent judgments 2, 4, 6, 8		

The necessary mathematical methods are used to rank the judgment matrix filled by experts. That is to calculate the weight vector, which refers to the relative weight of each factor in each judgment matrix against its criterion. Some methods for calculating the weight vector are the sum method: in a consistent judgment matrix, after normalizing each column, the desired weight is obtained. For a non-consistent judgment matrix, the normalized result of each column is only approximate to the corresponding weight, and the arithmetic average of this vector needs to be used as the final weight. The corresponding formula is:

$$W_i = \frac{1}{n}\sum_{j-1}^{n} \frac{a_{ij}}{\sum_{k-1}^{n} a_{kl}} \tag{4}$$

Among them, W_i is the final weight; j is the number of columns; k is the number of normalizations; a_{ij} is the result of normalization of each column; a_{kl} is the vector consistency threshold.

Finally, check the consistency of the judgment matrix: calculate $C.I.$ according to the one-time index:

$$C.I. = \frac{\lambda\text{max} - n}{n - 1} \tag{5}$$

Among them, λ_{max} represents the maximum value of the index.

Secondly, the average random consistency index $R.I.$ corresponding to the table is specified, and its standard value table is shown in Table 10.

Table 10. Standard value table

Serial number	Matrix order	*R.I.*
1	1 order	0
2	2 order	0
3	3 order	0.58
4	4 order	0.90
5	5 order	1.12
6	6 order	1.24
7	7 order	1.32
8	8 order	1.41
9	9 order	1.45
10	10 order	1.49

Again, calculate and determine the consistency ratio $C.R.$:

$$C.R. = \frac{C.I.}{R.I.} \tag{6}$$

When $C.R.$ is less than 0.1, the consistency of the judgment matrix is considered to meet the requirements; when $C.R.$ is greater than 0.1, the judgment matrix cannot be accepted and does not meet the consistency requirements, and the judgment matrix must be revised.

3 Evaluation of Teaching Effect

3.1 Experimental Design of Teaching Effect Evaluation

In the hardware environment of intel (R) corei5-24003.6 CPU, 4 GB memory and 5400 rpm hard disk, the evaluation model of engineering cost case teaching effect based on data mining is used to evaluate the engineering cost case teaching effect. For the students of engineering cost major in a university, the evaluation experiment of engineering cost case teaching effect is carried out, and the number of students and gender ratio of the major are shown in Table 11.

Obtain the teaching evaluation data of the engineering cost case teaching course of this specialty as experimental data, and use the experimental data to evaluate the teaching effect of the engineering cost case teaching of this specialty engineering cost case teaching course.

In order to ensure the effectiveness of the experimental results, the traditional teaching effect evaluation model of engineering cost cases is compared with the data mining-based teaching effect evaluation model of engineering cost cases designed in this paper. In the process of evaluating the teaching effect of engineering cost cases, the comprehensive data of the evaluation benchmark of each evaluation model are obtained and

Table 11. Number of students in this major and sex ratio

	Male	Female
Freshman	338	229
Sophomore	168	194
Junior	369	220
Senior	390	124
Total	1265	767
Proportion (%)	62.32	37.75

compared. Among them, the traditional teaching effect evaluation model of engineering cost case includes the evaluation model of teaching effect of engineering cost case based on gray level assignment, whitening function and evaluation gray class.

3.2 Analysis of Experimental Results

The comprehensive experimental results of the evaluation benchmark based on the gray level evaluation of the construction cost case teaching effect evaluation model are shown in Fig. 1.

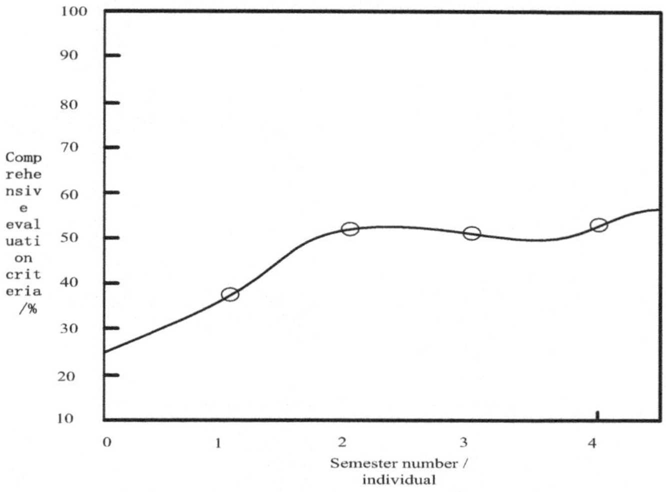

Fig. 1. Comprehensiveness of evaluation benchmark of grey level evaluation model

The comprehensive experimental results of the evaluation benchmark based on the whitening function of the evaluation model of the teaching effect of the engineering cost case are shown in Fig. 2.

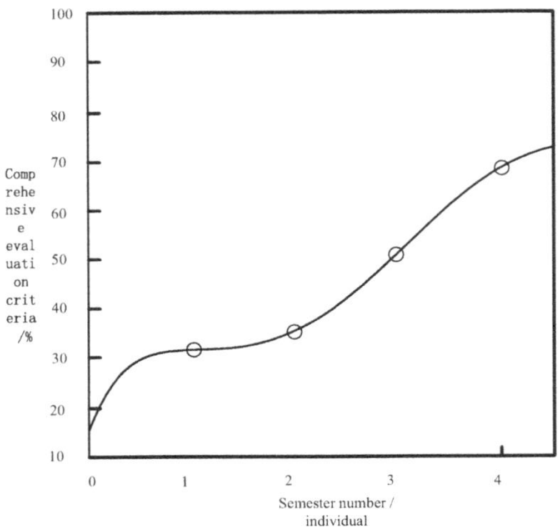

Fig. 2. Comprehensive evaluation criteria of whiteness function evaluation model

The comprehensive experimental results of the evaluation benchmark of the teaching effect evaluation model of engineering cost cases based on the evaluation grey class are shown in Fig. 3.

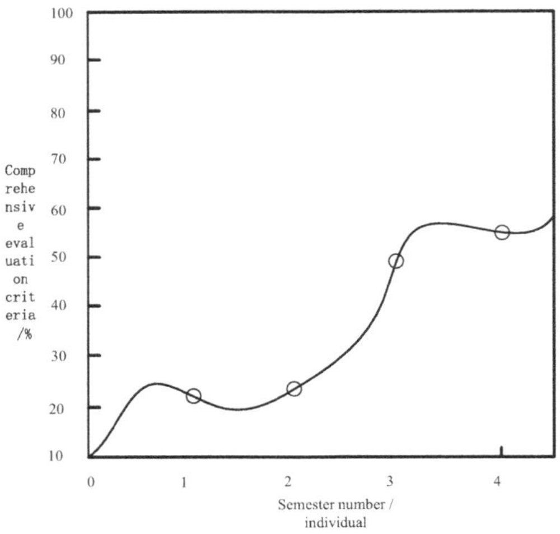

Fig. 3. Comprehensiveness of the evaluation criteria for the gray model

The comprehensive experimental results of the evaluation benchmark of the project cost case teaching effect evaluation model based on data mining are shown in Fig. 4.

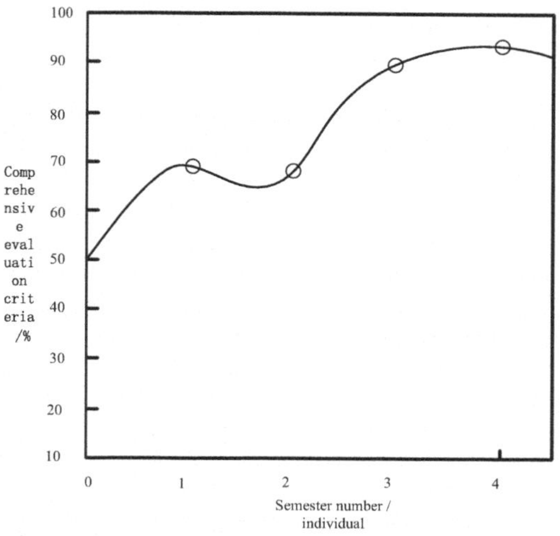

Fig. 4. Comprehensive evaluation criteria of the design model of this paper

According to the comprehensive experimental results of the evaluation benchmarks in the figure above, it can be seen that the comprehensiveness of the evaluation benchmarks of the engineering cost case teaching effect evaluation model based on data mining is higher than the traditional engineering cost case teaching effect evaluation model.

4 Concluding Remarks

The evaluation model of project cost case teaching effect based on data mining can analyze the specific factors that affect the teaching quality, and use association rule analysis to deeply mine the key factors that determine the teaching quality, find the specific influencing factors, and find a strong theoretical and practical basis for improving the teaching quality in the future.

5 Fund Projects

2018GGJCKT193 Research on the Reform of Talent Training System from the Perspective of Key Competence of Higher Vocational Colleges

References

1. Yadong, T., Boxin, H., Yuqin, D., et al.: Three-dimensional prostate tumor model based on a hyaluronic acid-alginate hydrogel for evaluation of anti-cancer drug efficacy. J. Biomater. Sci. Polym. Ed. **28**(14), 1–23 (2017)
2. Luo, X., Zhao, H., Liao, Y., Li, X.: Evaluation of the methods for quantifying particle wash-off loadings in urban impervious surfaces at small scales. Environ. Sci. Pollut. Res. **25**(7), 6969–6979 (2017). https://doi.org/10.1007/s11356-017-1018-7

3. Jiang, L.-J., Zhang, S.-M., Li, C.-W., et al.: Roles of the Nrf2/HO-1 pathway in the anti-oxidative stress response to ischemia-reperfusion brain injury in rats. J. Eur. Rev. Med. Pharmacol. Sci. **21**(7), 1532–1540 (2017)
4. Paweł, R., Marcin, Ż., Andrzej, P., et al.: Evaluation of the prognostic value of LMR, PLR, NLR, and dNLR in urothelial bladder cancer patients treated with radical cystectomy. J. Eur. Rev. Med. Pharmacol. Sci. **22**(10), 3027–3037 (2018)
5. Zhou, X., Sun, B., Wu, S., Zhang, X., Liu, Q., Xiao, Y.: Evaluation on self-healing mechanism and hydrophobic performance of asphalt modified by siloxane and polyurethane. J. Wuhan Univ. Technol. Mater. Sci. Ed. **34**(3), 630–637 (2019). https://doi.org/10.1007/s11595-019-2097-8
6. Janie, B., Kathryn, A., Joan, H., et al.: What factors contribute to postabortion contraceptive uptake by young women? A program evaluation in 10 countries in Asia and sub-Saharan Africa. J. Glob. Health Sci. Pract. **5**(4), 644–657 (2017)
7. Shen, Z.-H., Zhao, K.-M., Du, T.: HOXA10 promotes nasopharyngeal carcinoma cell proliferation and invasion via inducing the expression of ZIC2. J. Eur. Rev. Med. Pharmacol. Sci. **21**(5), 945–952 (2017)
8. Tahar, S., et al.: Large-scale geographic patterns of mercury contamination in Morocco revealed by freshwater turtles. J. Environ. Sci. Pollut. Res. Int. **25**(3), 2350–2360 (2017). https://doi.org/10.1007/s11356-017-0643-5
9. Anthony, W., Arto, G., Anthony, W.: A motivational model of physical education and links to enjoyment, knowledge, performance, total physical activity and body mass index. J. Sports Sci. Med. **16**(3), 318–327 (2017)
10. Goldenberg, A., Cohen-Chen, S., Goyer, J.P., Dweck, C.S., Gross, J.J., Halperin, E.: Testing the impact and durability of group malleability intervention in the context of the Israeli-Palestinian conflict. J. Proc. Natl. Acad. Sci. US **115**(4), 696–701 (2018)

Data Analysis of Cost Engineer Qualification Examination System Based on Data Analysis

Xiao Qi-rong(✉)

Department of Architectural Engineering, Dazhou Vocational and Technical College, Dazhou 635001, China
xienxue4111@163.com

Abstract. In order to improve the throughput performance of the cost engineer's practice qualification simulation test system, on the basis of ensuring the normal functioning of the system, data analysis technology is used to optimize the design of the simulation test system. Refit the memory and microprocessor in the hardware system separately, and install remote communication equipment to ensure the real-time transmission of test data. Based on the completion of the hardware device connection, the system's human-computer interaction interface is designed, and the system database information is improved from various aspects such as test questions and candidate information. Based on the hardware equipment and database, the software functions of the cost engineer qualification examination system are realized from the aspects of system role, examination process, and score. Through the system test experiment, it is found that the average throughput of the system is high under the condition of ensuring the running function of the examination system.

Keywords: Data analysis · Cost engineer · Qualification examination · Mock examination · Examination system

1 Introduction

Cost engineer refers to the professional engineer of engineering economy who is authorized by the state to operate after registration, specially accepts the designation, entrustment or employment of a certain department or unit, and is responsible for and assists in the valuation, pricing and management of project cost, so as to safeguard its legitimate rights and interests. The state implements the practice qualification system of cost engineer in the field of engineering cost. All units and departments engaged in the construction, design, construction, engineering cost consulting, engineering cost management, etc. of engineering construction activities must have professional technical personnel with the qualification of cost engineer in the positions of valuation, evaluation, examination, control and management [1]. At present, among the engineering cost practitioners in our country, there are generally problems such as low professional quality, narrow scope of knowledge and single professional ability. Therefore, in recent

S. Liu et al. (Eds.): eLEOT 2020, LNICST 339, pp. 29–42, 2020.
https://doi.org/10.1007/978-3-030-63952-5_3

years, to a certain extent, it is necessary to relax the entry requirements, so that more people are qualified to participate in the exam, and do a good job of pre-exam training, so that as many people as possible in a short time to better system learning engineering cost management professional knowledge, is very necessary. The pre examination training, which has been carried out in an all-round way throughout the country, is also more suitable for the development requirements at this stage. The cost engineer qualification examination belongs to the scope of the national unified planning professional and technical personnel qualification system, and has passed the national unified examination, obtained the cost engineer qualification certificate, and registered professional and technical personnel engaged in construction project cost business activities [2]. The Ministry of personnel and the Ministry of construction are jointly responsible for the policy formulation, organization and coordination, qualification examination, registration, supervision and management of the national cost engineer qualification system. We will adopt a unified national program, proposition and organization. In principle, it is held once a year. The Ministry of construction is responsible for the formulation of examination outline, the compilation of training materials and proposition, the unified planning and organization of pre examination training and other related work. The training work shall be carried out in accordance with the principle of separation from the examination and voluntary participation. The personnel department is responsible for reviewing examination outlines, examination subjects and questions, and organizing or authorizing the implementation of various examination tasks. Work with the Ministry of Construction to supervise, inspect, guide and determine eligibility criteria. At present, the qualification requirements for the cost engineer qualification examination are a college graduate, a bachelor, a second degree or a master's degree or a doctoral degree major in engineering cost, engineering economics, and engineering, and they are qualified to apply for the engineering cost business. Those who have obtained the qualification certificate may apply for initial registration within one year from the date of issue of the qualification certificate. The traditional test format is to specify the test time, and notify all candidates to focus on a unified test environment, distribute test papers for cost engineer qualifications, hire professionals to review the test papers, get the test scores of the candidates, and then determine whether the candidates have Professional qualification of cost engineer. However, the traditional examination form has the problems of a long examination period and a long marking period. As a result, candidates of the quarrel cost engineer qualification examination need to take a long time to obtain a practice qualification certificate.

For this qualification designed the simulation test system, the operation principle of the system is mainly use data analysis and transmission technique, the results of the student's answer to system server, and compared with the standard answer in the system database, and the final exam score results, compared with the traditional test model, simulated test system can shorten the test cycle. Cost engineer qualification at this stage the research achievements of simulation test system includes the examination system based on ASP technology, the examination system based on Java technology, and the examination system based on.net technology, however, when there is a lot of examinee in the examination system online at the same time, the system easy to appear the phenomenon of information deviation and caton, introducing data analysis technology for cost engineer qualification mock exam system optimization design.

Data analysis refers to the process of using appropriate statistical analysis methods to analyze a large number of collected data, extract useful information and form conclusions, and then make a detailed study and summary of the data [3]. This process is also the support process of the quality management system. In practice, data analysis can help people to make judgments in order to take appropriate action. This technology is applied to the practice qualification simulation system, which can not only ensure the examination function of the system, but also improve the throughput of the system, so as to support a large number of candidates to take online examinations at the same time, and improve the application efficiency of the examination system.

2 Hardware System Design for Practicing Qualification Examination

In order to ensure the educational, scientific, and easy-to-use of the cost engineer qualification examination, we strive to make it a high-quality learning software. In the process of system design and implementation, it is inevitable that advanced learning theory guidance and science Method guide. Under the theory of autonomous learning and interaction theory, from the hardware system, system interface, database and software functions to achieve the optimization design of the traditional cost engineer qualification examination system. After analyzing the requirements of the examination system, the overall design architecture of the system is determined, as shown in Fig. 1.

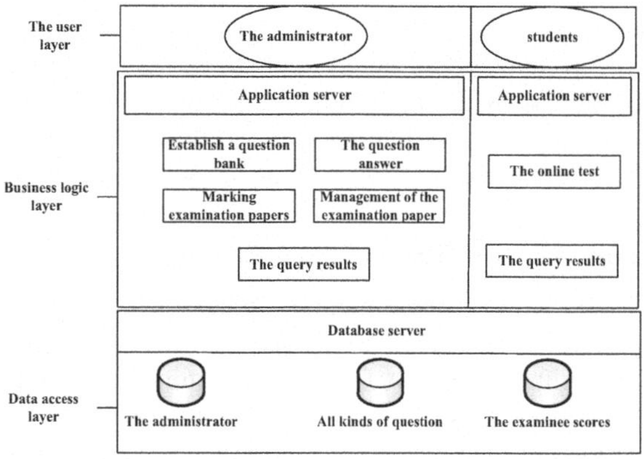

Fig. 1. Overall architecture of the mock test system

As can be seen from the figure, the entire cost engineer qualification examination system is mainly divided into three levels of structure, namely the user layer, business logic layer, and data access layer. The user level is mainly the role of teacher and student. The business logic layer includes the teacher's main business to establish classes, set up question banks, review test papers, manage test papers, and query results. Student's main business online examination, results query [4]. The data access layer mainly includes the administrator database, various question banks, test scores, and test classes. According to the overall architecture of the system, on the basis of the traditional mock examination system, the hardware environment is modified, and the connection structure of the hardware equipment is shown in Fig. 2.

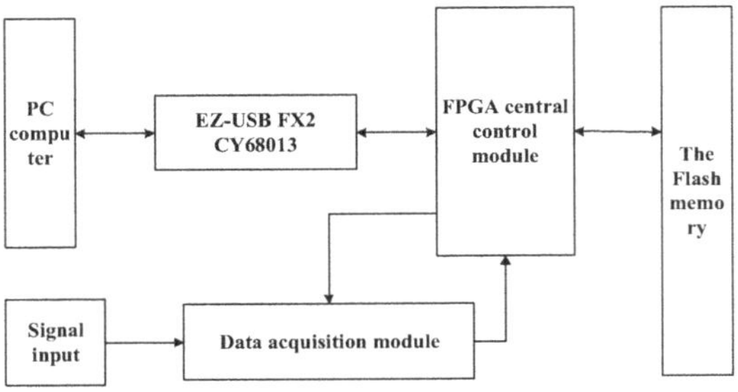

Fig. 2. System hardware equipment connection structure diagram

2.1 Memory

The storage module of the system includes SDRAM and ROM. In the embedded system, ROM is a kind of memory that can be erased by electricity and information will not be lost after power failure. It is used to store program code, constant table and some user data that need to be saved after power failure. SDRAM is the memory of the system, it does not have the characteristics of power down to keep data, but its access speed is much faster than the memory. It is mainly used as the running space, data and stack area of the program in the system. When the system starts, the CPU first reads the startup code from the reset address. After the initialization of the system, the program code is transferred in to run to improve the running speed of the system. The system uses 32M * SDRAM and 64M NAND flash to complete the design of system memory circuit.

2.2 Data Communication and Transmission Equipment

CPM module is a 32-bit RISC communication processor (CP) specially optimized for serial communication. It has a separate ROM and stores its own microcode, which can provide a flexible and complete solution for devices requiring communication capability, while reducing system frequency and energy consumption [5]. CPM supports multi-channel communication and can handle a variety of low-level protocols. By applying the communication transmission equipment to the simulation test system of cost engineer qualification, the system operation interruption caused by communication failure can be reduced.

2.3 Microprocessor

The PowerPC processor core was selected as the microprocessor device for the mock exam. The PowerPC core model MPC850 uses a fully static design. Its integer access operations are directly performed by hardware. Its integer processing unit uses a full 32-bit internal bus and 32-bit. The hardware architecture has two instruction access queues, four instruction prefetch queues, and a six instruction cache. A 32-bit external operand instruction can be executed in one bus cycle, and there are 32 32-bit pass registers internally used as source and destination operands. The MPC850 integrates an MMU unit, a 2 KB instruction cache, and a 1 KB data cache. The MMU unit provides eight data and instruction TLBs, which can support multiple page sizes. Its instruction cache and data cache are two-way group cascade, which can be physically addressed, replaced by the LRU principle, and can be locked on a row basis to prevent important instructions or data from being replaced.

3 Human-Computer Interaction Design of Practice Qualification Simulation Examination System

The simulation test interface of the cost engineer's professional qualification needs to highlight the majesty of the test and meet the professional characteristics of the cost engineer [6]. When designing the system's interpersonal interaction interface, choose a color that matches the professional characteristics, such as white and blue. In addition, the test system administrator needs to enter a lot of basic information when entering candidates, so the interface design should fully consider the convenience of the system administrator when entering data, such as when viewing a large data page, up and down scroll bars and left and right The scroll bar should be fixed to the right and bottom of the page to facilitate checking of the entered data, and the system should always check the data format when entering the data to avoid errors when storing in the database. In order to fully reflect the human-computer interaction function of the simulation test system for the cost engineer's professional qualification, the user interface, the test main interface, and the submission interface are designed separately. The mouse and keyboard can be used on different interfaces to achieve Input and modification of interface content.

4 Database Design of Practice Qualification Examination System

The question management module is the most critical part in the system design process, it realizes the division, analysis and definition of the question database data, plays a crucial role in the efficiency of the system development and even the success or failure of the system. The system USES SQLServer 2005 to generate the corresponding database based on the designed data model. Database in the early design with Access to design the field, to the late release, imported into the SQL database. Program calls, calling SQL database data.

4.1 User Information Database

The user information database stores the information of all examinees, including the examinee's name, student number, examination permit number, gender, photo and examination result. The basic format of user information database table in the simulation test system is shown in Table 1.

Table 1. User information table

The field name	The data type	Whether null is allowed or not	Primary key	Describe
User_ID	int	no	A primary key	The user id
User_Name	Varchar(20)	no	no	The user name
User_Password	Varchar(20)	no	no	password
User_RealName	Varchar(20)	no	no	Real name
User_Sex	bit	no	no	gender
User_Role	int	no	no	The user types
User_RegisterTime	DateTime	no	no	Registration time
User_LoginTime	DateTime	no	no	Landing time
User_LoginNum	int	no	no	Log in number

4.2 Cost Engineer Qualification Examination Questions Bank

The cost engineer simulation qualification test question library includes a variety of question types such as filling in blanks, multiple choice questions, and judgment questions. A variety of cost engineer qualification qualification test questions are synthesized to obtain the test question bank construction results. The test paper information structure is shown in Table 2.

Table 2. Test Paper information form

The field names	The data type	Fields that
uuid	Character_carying	Unique code, primary key
name	Character_carying	Name of test paper
Subject_id	Character_carying	Said subject number, foreign key
papertype	Character_carying	The group type
totalscore	integer	Test scores
totaltime	integer	Total test time
sort	integer	Paper display order

Record the content of the questions, answer the questions correctly, and establish the time of the questions. The correct answers can be written in multiple semicolons, which can be matched with multiple answers filled in by students in the program [7]. For the record of adding time, you can know when this question is established, which is good for updating and consulting the test questions. The longer the time is, the more test questions the examinee has taken. When the time reaches a certain program, the test questions of a certain period can be cleaned up.

4.3 Database Relational Connections

In addition, data information such as the scoring mechanism of practice qualification test for cost engineer should be input into the database according to the prescribed format, and the connection between database tables should be realized according to the logical relationship shown in Fig. 3.

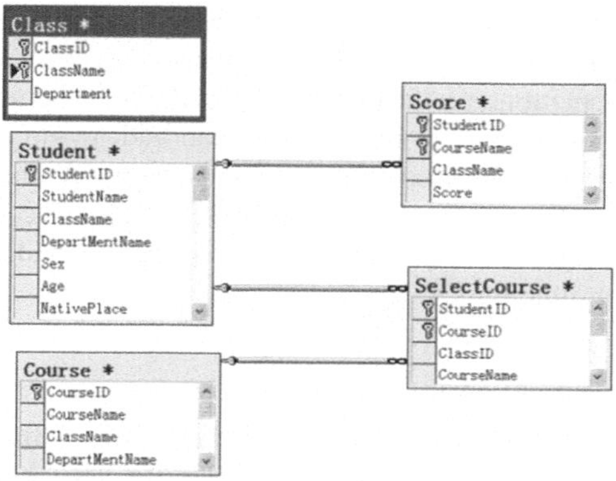

Fig. 3. Database logical relationship diagram

5 Functional Design of Practice Qualification Simulation Exam Software System

According to the needs analysis of the cost engineer's practice qualification simulation examination system, the functions of the examination system can be divided into three categories: online examination function, simulation exercise function and examination management function. Therefore, the design of software system functions can also be divided into three major functions. The modules include: an online examination function module, a simulation exercise function module, and an examination management function module. In the online exam function module, students can take the exam, modify information, and view grades, etc. In the simulation exercise function module, after successfully logging in to the system, students can perform simulation exercises before the exam and view the answer to the test questions; in the exam management function module In the administrator, the administrator can manage the related information of the exam, including student management, test question management, test paper management, exercise settings, subjective question scoring, score management, and system management [8]. In the process of practical application and operation of the simulation examination system of cost engineer's professional qualification, different roles have different rights and functions. Therefore, from the perspective of system administrator and examinee, we can simulate the actual process of the simulation examination of cost engineer's professional qualification and realize the software system functions of the simulation examination.

5.1 Role Function Design

5.1.1 Function Design of Management End

An administrator role is a user with advanced administrator privileges, all of which are granted by the system. Can use the test bank maintenance function, view and modify all the test questions can manage the marking of teachers and candidates information, add, modify and delete all the user information to be able to test paper development and maintenance of the test paper, with test paper review and performance management function of the use of authority. In short, the user master and control of all the test information administrator operating platform can achieve the management and protection of examinee information and teachers information, can add, modify or delete examinee users and teachers users. The examination system has higher requirements on data confidentiality and strict restrictions on user rights and functions. According to the system demand analysis, the system mainly realizes user management and user rights allocation and other management functions.

5.1.2 Functional Design of Examinee End

The function structure of examinee end mainly includes several function modules, such as personal information, simulation test, score query, etc. The personal information of candidates refers to the management of personal account information, such as password, contact information, etc. The function of simulation test is to promote the learning effect and improve the examinee's ability to take the test by means of simulation training. The simulation test environment is consistent with the real test environment, and the examinee can be familiar with and adapt to the test environment and rhythm through the simulation test. In addition, the online examination function collects the information of students' examination papers in real time through data transmission and analysis, and scores the final examination papers submitted, so as to obtain the simulated examination results of cost engineer's professional qualification.

5.2 Simulated Online Exam Function

The simulated test taker's behavior process during the simulation test of the cost engineer's qualifications, respectively, by determining the test content, generating test papers, and analyzing and saving the test paper data, realize the online test function of the test system.

5.2.1 Determine the Content of the Exam

There are four subjects in the qualification examination of cost engineer, which are: knowledge related to project cost management, determination and control of project cost, construction engineering technology and measurement, and case analysis of project cost [9]. At present, in addition to the case analysis of engineering cost, the subjective test question form of the case is adopted, the other subjects all adopt the objective test question form of single choice and multiple choice. In combination with the relevant questions of each subject mentioned above, the test questions are stored in the database in the same way, and the relevant procedures are applied to ensure that the front-end interface can retrieve the data of exam content and questions in the database in real time.

5.2.2 Test Paper Generation and Management

The simulation test module mainly realizes the function of extracting questions from the question bank, generating test papers and statistics of wrong questions. Therefore, the examination module is composed of three parts: the extraction of questions, the composition of test papers and the statistics of wrong questions. The process of composing the test paper is shown in Fig. 4.

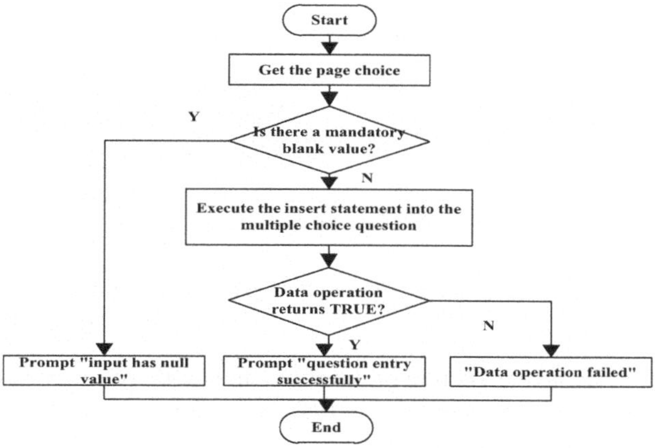

Fig. 4. Flow chart of test question entry and test paper formation

5.2.3 Test Data Saving and Analysis Function

During the operation of the system, it will involve the processing of data. Data will flow during the processing. Data flow analysis is to analyze the flow of data and express the results of the analysis in the form of a flowchart to facilitate design Personnel for system development. Data flow analysis is essentially a record of the direction of data flow and data processing flow during system operation. The purpose of data flow analysis is to analyze the flow of related data in the system. Through analysis, problems are found. Usually, these problems include: the data flow is not smooth during the operation of the system, and the same data is in the system. The types before and after do not match, and there is an unreasonable situation in the related data processing during the system operation [10]. The purpose of the analysis is to find many problems in the data and solve them. There are many reasons for these problems, and no matter which one causes them, the ultimate purpose of data flow analysis remains the same. It is to expose as many possible problems in the system as possible at this stage and then solve them accordingly. The specific analysis processing structure is shown in Fig. 5.

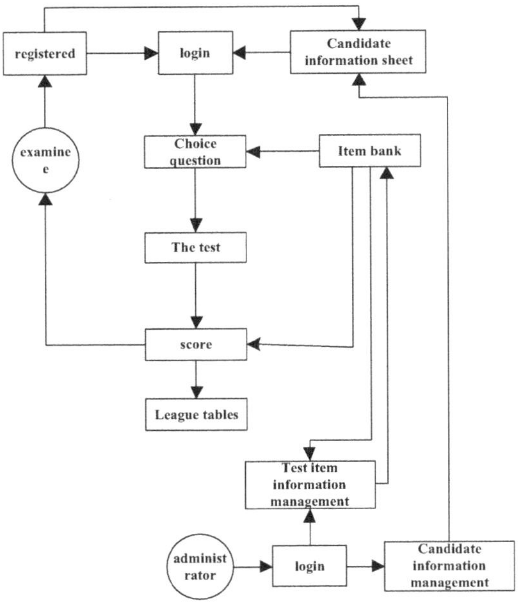

Fig. 5. Data analysis technology processing test data

Based on the processing structure of the above-mentioned data analysis technology, the input information of the candidates in the examination system is collected in real time, and the answer papers are submitted.

5.3 Statistical Scoring Function

The cost engineer qualification examination system can use the scoring statistics function to count the overall evaluation results of the candidates. When the grading teacher checks the candidate's results through the statistical scoring module of the candidate's online examination system, the online examination system will calculate the total score according to the following formula. Complete the calculation of all individual candidates.

$$score = N_x \times \eta_x + N_p \times \eta_p + N_t \times \eta_t + S_j \tag{1}$$

In the formula, N_x, N_p, and N_t are the correct numbers of multiple choice, judgment, and blank questions in the test paper, and η_i is the score corresponding to different question types. When an online formal exam candidate submits an answer or the test time is exhausted, the system will automatically submit the examination paper. The browser will judge the answer based on the answer made by the candidate. And use the test results announcement function to facilitate candidates query.

6 Test of the Simulation Examination System for the Qualification of Cost Engineer

Software testing is a necessary step to ensure the quality of software. Generally, software testing needs to occupy most of the time of software development in order to find the potential errors and problems of software. After the coding of the program design and the necessary interface design, the overall test can be started. According to the test sequence, first of all, a set of test cases including general input, critical input, error input and other data input conditions should be conceived according to the various situations and possible problems encountered in the use of the simulation test system for the professional qualification of police cost engineer. Input these test cases into the program one by one, observe whether there is an error in the operation of the cost engineer qualification simulation test system or whether there is a good fault-tolerant mechanism for illegal input, so that the designer can better improve the program to meet the needs of users. In the process of the system test experiment, the traditional simulation test system was used as the comparison system, and the system's function and performance were tested respectively, so as to prove the effectiveness and practicability of the system based on data analysis.

6.1 System Development and Test Environment

The development of the simulation examination for the qualification of cost engineer is developed in the web environment. Test the database deployment to not affect the data call speed. On SQL Server 2005, the program is deployed on another server. Local access is through the intranet and on the browser. Use two computers with good performance, one is installed with SQL Server database, and then attach the database in the system. Another deployment program page, the program calls the database directly. The distribution network, for aspect testing, is directly tested on the external network. As long as other users can access the Internet, they can directly log in the Internet IP to enter the system page. Contact 100 system users at the same time, and be able to log in to the system to take the exam at the same time. The specific environment is described as: hardware environment: the CPU of the client computer should be above 1 GHz, the memory of the computer is not less than 128 MB, the screen resolution is above 1024 * 768 The server needs a CPU with a main frequency above 1 GHz, no less than 512 MB of memory, and a hard disk capacity of no less than 40 GB. Software environment: Operating system: Windows XP SP3, development tools: Microsoft Visual Studio 2005, Web server: IIS 5.1, database: Microsoft SQL server 2005.

6.2 System Function Test

On the exam interface of practice test for cost engineer, input relevant information according to the normal answering process, observe the realization of system function.

Through the statistics of the system operation results, the comparison results about the system function tests are obtained, as shown in Table 3.

From the test results in the table, it can be seen that both test systems can successfully pass the function test of user login and password modification, but in the test process

Table 3. Comparison results of system function tests

Testing tasks	The test content	Traditional system test results	Design system test results
Change the password	Change your password and log in again	Through	Through
The user login	20 bits for username and 20 bits for password	Through	Through
Edit question information	Update question information	Update 322 questions	Update 345 questions
Examinee user submit test questions	Examinee user completes the test paper, submit the test question function	Successful after 3 submissions	Submit once and succeed
Examinee user query score information function	The examinee user inquires the result information function after the teacher marks the paper	The output result	The output result

of updating test questions, the number of design system updates is 23 more than the traditional system. In the data submission process of the test system, the success rate of the traditional system is 33.3%, while the success rate of the design system is 100%.

6.3 System Performance Testing

The performance test of the system is mainly used to test the throughput of the system. Under the test environment of two test systems, 100 examinees are controlled to be online at the same time, and the background data of the system is retrieved. The system designed in this paper, the online test system based on LoadRunner proposed in [11] and the man-machine dialogue teaching and test of medical image proposed in [12] are observed Test the concurrent data of the system and draw a comparison curve about the system throughput, as shown in Fig. 6.

It can be seen from the figure that with the gradual increase of the number of online people, the throughput of the three kinds of examination systems is gradually increasing. However, the average throughput of the online examination system based on LoadRunner proposed in literature [11] and the medical image human-computer dialogue teaching and examination system proposed in literature [12] are 70% and 78% respectively, while the designed cost engineer professional capital based on data analysis. The average throughput of the grid simulation test system is 85%. Compared with the traditional system, the throughput of the system designed in this paper is higher.

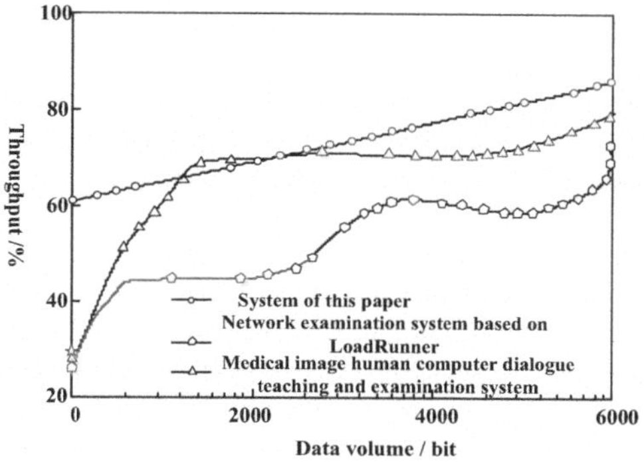

Fig. 6. System throughput performance comparison curve

7 The Conclusion

Since the introduction of the cost engineer qualification examination system, although it has been improved and improved, with the development of the project cost industry, it still needs to be adjusted to meet the new needs. In accordance with the qualification examination system of cost engineer, this paper uses data analysis technology to optimize the design of examination system, completes the hardware design of the system through memory, microprocessor and data communication transmission equipment, inputs and modifies the interface content through human-computer interaction, and completes the system software design from the aspects of system role, examination process and score According to the hardware and software of the system, the simulation examination system of cost engineer qualification is finally completed. Through the experiment, it is proved that the design of this paper can improve the throughput and application performance of the system, which lays the foundation for the qualification examination of cost engineer.

8 Fund Projects

2018GGJCKT193 Research on the Reform of Talent Training System from the Perspective of Key Competence of Higher Vocational Colleges.

References

1. Al Amin, M., Greenwood, J.: The examination system in Bangladesh and its impact: on curriculum, students, teachers and society. Lang. Test. Asia **8**(1), 1–18 (2018). https://doi.org/10.1186/s40468-018-0060-9
2. Zhou, Y., Sun, H., Macario, A., et al.: The American board of anesthesiology staged examination system and performance on the written certification examination after residency. J. Anesth. Analg. **129**(5), e159–e162 (2019)
3. Al-Hawari, F., Alshawabkeh, M., Althawbih, H., et al.: Integrated and secure web-based examination management system. J. Comput. Appl. Eng. Educ. **1**, 994–1014 (2019)

4. Inga, S., Jenset, K., Klette, K., Hammerness, G.: Teacher education in practice around the world: an examination of teacher education coursework in teacher education programs in Finland, Norway, and the United States. J. Teach. Educ. **69**(2), 184–197 (2018)
5. Abdel-Rahim, H.Y., Stevens, D.E.: Information system precision and honesty in managerial reporting: a re-examination of information asymmetry effects. J. Account. Organ. Soc. **64**, 42 (2018)
6. Toshiaki, S., Hiroyuki, K., Hayato, H., et al.: Packet transport network recovery system with examination of data transmission quality. Int. J. Reliab. Qual. Saf. Eng. **27**, 2050007 (2019)
7. Asghar, Z.B., et al.: Performance of candidates disclosing dyslexia with other candidates in a UK medical licensing examination: cross-sectional study. Postgrad. Med. J. **94**(1110), 198–203 (2018)
8. Stevenson, R.D.M., Siddall, A.G., Turner, P.J.F., Bilzon, J.L.J.: Validity and reliability of firefighting simulation test performance. J. Occup. Environ. Med. **61**(6), 479–483 (2019)
9. Francisca, S., Melgarejo, M., Virtudes, T., Milán, T., Vera, C., et al.: Cognitive function and fatigue from cardiopulmonary resuscitation effort in health care professionals: a simulation test. J. Emergencias **30**(3), 205–206 (2018)
10. Sanaz, T., Madjid, A., Tooraj, D., et al.: Design of a safety cost estimation parametric model in oil and gas engineering, procurement and construction contracts. J. Saf. Sci. **106**, 35–46 (2018)
11. Zhang, Y.H.: Performance test practice of network test system based on LoadRunner. Comput. Knowl. Technol. **21**, 106–108 (2019)
12. Shi, Y., Zhu, Y.S., Zhao, Y., et al.: The teaching and examination system of human-computer dialogue in medical imaging is constructed based on post competence. Chin. Med. Educ. Exp. J. **19**(02), 230–233 (2020)

Performance Evaluation of Integrated Circuit Industry Talent Training Based on BP Neural Network

Xia Jing[1(✉)] and Wang Hong-Gang[2]

[1] The Research Institute of Informatization and Industrialization Integration, China Academy of Information and Communications Technology, Beijing 200001, China
xjing20@tom.com

[2] College of Marxism, Fuyang Normal University, Fuyang 236037, China

Abstract. The assessment and evaluation of talent work is a comprehensive evaluation of talent quality, performance and talent value. Many years of talent management practice shows that the introduction of scientific talent evaluation system is the premise of effective development of talent resources and the foundation of personnel work. Based on this, a comprehensive evaluation method of training performance of integrated circuit industry talents based on BP neural network is proposed. On the basis of determining the number of layers and neurons in each layer of BP network, the selection of samples and original values is completed according to the performance data of talent training in integrated circuit industry, and the evaluation model is established with the help of data processing. The experimental results show that the BP neural network can fully absorb the judgment experience of experts and the practical guidance of human resource management, and has a good evaluation effect. It is not only beneficial for enterprises to evaluate scientific and technological talents more scientifically and reasonably, but also provides decision-making basis for human resource management. Secondly, BP neural network is used to evaluate the scientific and technological talents of enterprises. The evaluation process is more simple and quick, and the evaluation results of scientific and technological talents are more scientific and accurate.

Keywords: BP neural · Integrated circuit industry · Personnel training · Comprehensive performance evaluation

1 Introduction

As we all know, the circuit industry cluster can promote the development of national economy, especially the local economy, and the huge economic benefits it has created have attracted worldwide attention. In recent years, under the background of the trend of economic globalization, municipal governments around the world are actively advocating the development of circuit industry clusters. However, not all circuit industry clusters can develop healthily. Therefore, how to determine management concepts and methods to better manage the clusters has become an urgent task for the managers of

S. Liu et al. (Eds.): eLEOT 2020, LNICST 339, pp. 43–54, 2020.
https://doi.org/10.1007/978-3-030-63952-5_4

circuit industry clusters [1]. If enterprises want to occupy a place in the fierce market competition and adapt to economic globalization, networking and integration, they need to face up to the performance evaluation of talent training in the integrated circuit industry. How to make circuit industry sales staff create fair or harmonious benefits under the conditions of fairness and harmony, the most important thing is to implement a comprehensive and systematic performance evaluation of circuit industry sales staff. Mobilize its enthusiasm and creativity to train many excellent employees for integrated circuit companies, and form a team that can compete with other industries in the increasingly fierce market competition environment. After the construction of a thorough and systematic performance evaluation system, based on the dedication of the employees of IC industry sales positions to the company, the composition and integrity of objective and rigorous reward systems can fully mobilize the activity level of employees and improve their job satisfaction. Effectively improve the work level and efficiency of employees, enable the sales department to work closely with other departments, improve the overall competitiveness of the company and the same industry, achieve standardized management in the enterprise, and finally strive to obtain the target benefits. Recycling is conducive to the long-term development of enterprises. If the contribution of the individual employee is ignored, for example, some employees have the same post, but due to the different arrival time, there will be differences in skills and resources. If the evaluation is conducted according to the same performance evaluation standard [2], the actual performance level of each employee will be reduced, and the result is that the overall work efficiency will be reduced, from which we can draw the conclusion that the performance evaluation will affect human resources Decision making has an important impact. If the employee's business performance appraisal is not standardized, the most important resolutions will not know who to follow, and there will be no basis for specifying goals, which will make the resolutions have no goals and no way to start, such as salary adjustment, post promotion, etc. Generally speaking, performance evaluation is the basis to ensure the normal operation of the enterprise. Fair, effective and systematic performance evaluation can motivate employees to the greatest extent, and ultimately maximize the reasonable benefits of the enterprise to achieve its goals.

Because of this, more and more integrated circuit companies have begun to attach importance to performance evaluation and implement performance appraisal of employees in various departments and positions in integrated circuit enterprise management. However, many integrated circuit companies that implement performance evaluation have been stuck on the overall performance of performance assessment in recent years, and they have paid less attention to the performance evaluation of individual employees. In fact, no matter from the perspective of employees' personal interests or from the perspective of the overall interests of integrated circuit companies, performance evaluation is very important. Performance evaluation is an effective standard and objective standard for measuring all practical activities [3]. Performance evaluation is necessary and important for any organization. The lack of performance evaluation will lead to the blindness of cluster governance, and if there is no appropriate performance evaluation system, it will not be able to feed back the information to the relevant departments, can not make a correct judgment on the status of cluster governance, so it is difficult to accurately adjust and improve the development strategy of the cluster. Therefore, it is of great significance to establish a comprehensive, objective and applicable integrated circuit industry talent training performance evaluation method, and analyze and evaluate the implementation effect of the cluster development strategy through the measurement results. As a popular intelligent optimization algorithm in recent years, BP neural network has been successfully applied in signal processing, computer network, process control, speech recognition, pattern recognition and data compression. As an attempt, this paper will use BP neural network to establish a comprehensive performance evaluation model on the basis of determining the performance evaluation index system of integrated circuit industry talent training, and determine the weight through continuous training of learning samples, in order to avoid the limitations of traditional evaluation methods, so as to provide a new idea for the comprehensive evaluation of integrated circuit industry cluster talent training performance Road and direction.

2 Performance Evaluation of Integrated Circuit Industry Talent Training Based on BP Neural Network

2.1 Determination of Layers of BP Network

According to Kosmogorov's theorem, [4], under the premise of a certain reasonable construction and reasonable weight, in fact, a 3-layer BP network can converge to all fuzzy and complicated mappings with arbitrary accuracy. If the hidden layer is configured Too much will converge too slowly, resulting in a slower learning rate. A single hidden layer can cope with most occasions, and it is also for the purpose of saving time and cost and improving efficiency. Therefore, the number of hidden layers in the IC industry talent training performance evaluation model is determined to be 1. From the above, it is based on the BP neural network. The performance evaluation model of the sales department of the integrated circuit industry of the network includes a three-layer topology structure of an input layer, a hidden layer, and an output layer.

2.2 Determine the Number of Neurons in Each Layer

The number of neurons in the input layer is determined by the dimensions of the input layer. According to the structure of the integrated circuit enterprise employee performance evaluation system, it contains a total of 21 dimensions, including collaboration capabilities, motivation, innovation capabilities, and work results. The input layer dimension n is determined to be 21.

The number of neurons in the output layer is actually determined by the results of the actual output layer. In the process of evaluating the model, the results are integrated by all the performance indicators of the integrated circuit industry talent training, and the objective performance evaluation results are obtained. If the objective performance evaluation results of the integrated circuit industry sales department employees can be taken as the output signal [5], then the number of neurons in the output layer is 1. The output results of the model, i.e. the grades and evaluation results of the performance appraisal of the integrated circuit industry talent training, are shown in Table 1 below.

Generally speaking, the number of neurons in the hidden layer is explained by the arrival boundedness of approximation function and the fluctuation of function itself. In

Table 1. Performance evaluation grades and results

Performance grade	Very poor	Range	Same as	Preferably	Beyond compare
Evaluation findings	0–0.2	0.20–0.4	0.40–0.6	0.60–0.8	0.80–1
Total points (TP)					

fact, the number of excess or less neurons is not desirable for the establishment of the model. Although more neurons can bring greater benefits to the hidden layer (performance) [6], in reality, it can only promote the continuous extension of training time. Although the performance has been improved, it is more difficult to use accurate expressions to reveal the number of neurons in the hidden layer. After repeated verification of the expressions and multiple experiments on the target, we found the empirical formula:

$$s = (n + m)^{\frac{1}{2}} \tag{1}$$

It is very convenient to determine the number of neurons in the hidden layer. This article refers to this formula to determine the number of neurons in the hidden layer: n and m are 21 and 1, respectively (mentioned in the determination of the number of network layers above), and the number is about 4. The topological structure of the IC industry talent training assessment model is shown in Fig. 1.

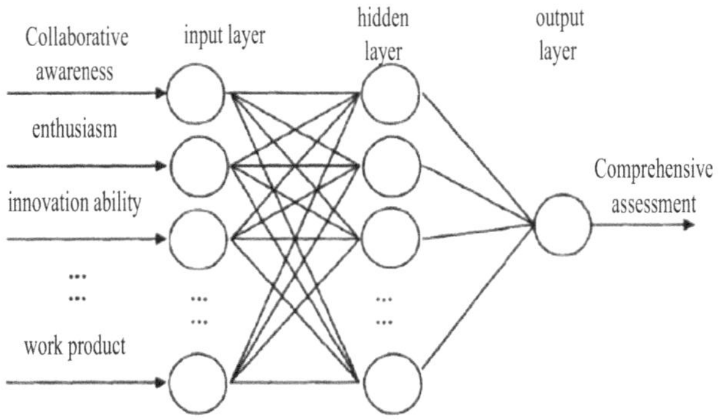

Fig. 1. Topological structure of the IC industry talent training performance evaluation model

2.3 Select Sample

After the number of neurons is determined, the number of samples is directly selected. For each factor index, they are usually able to divide it according to the index grade [7], use the method required by the model, then select comprehensively, and carry out standardized evaluation, or find a special person to evaluate, and finally get the evaluation value of the performance evaluation index of talent training in the integrated circuit industry. In this paper, for the purpose of obtaining satisfactory sample data, when processing the data, methods such as standardized evaluation can get satisfactory scores according to the reference standard of index grade, and then normalize the scores; for the method of finding a special person to evaluate, the method of taking the average value or the method of square root is generally used to sort the data.

2.4 Select Original Value

The determination of the sample is to obtain the original value. Since the main content of this article is a nonlinear relationship, the selection of the original value is related to whether the BP algorithm can converge or achieve a local minimum [8]. If the original value is selected too large, in reality it can only promote the training time continuously, but it cannot accurately output the output layer. Therefore, this article will carefully screen in the original value selection process. The initial weight usually needs to choose a small and easy to calculate random number, so as to ensure that the hidden layer as far as possible when the superposition state value of all neurons is infinitely close to zero, basically ensure that any neuron falls within the scope of the maximum derivative of the transfer function. In general, the selection of the original value is usually a random number between 0 and 1. In this article, the initial value is selected as 1.

2.5 Data Processing

The data processing involved in the comprehensive evaluation of the talent training performance of the integrated circuit industry mainly includes data correction and normalization processing [9].

Data correction. In the process of data collection, when observing the original data, it was found that individual indicators of a small number of indicators showed negative numbers, such as the negative growth rate of net profit. The processing method of this article is to convert negative indicators to 0 and continue to participate in subsequent data processing.

Normalized processing. Before modeling, the sample data should first be isotropic and dimensionless, so that it can be converted into a summable and comparable data sequence. In this paper, the standardization method of deviation is used to linearly transform the initial sample data. It is converted to [0, 1]. The formula is as follows:

Positive indicators:

$$x^* = \frac{x - x_{\min}}{x_{\max} - x_{\min}} \tag{2}$$

Reverse index:

$$x^* = 1 - \frac{x - x_{\min}}{x_{\max} - x_{\min}} \tag{3}$$

In the formula, max is the maximum value of the sample data, and min is the minimum value of the sample data.

Moderate indicators: for the current ratio, asset liability ratio, accounts receivable turnover ratio and inventory turnover ratio, refer to 2017 According to the standard value of enterprise performance evaluation formulated by SASAC in, SASAC assumes that these moderate indicators meet the judgment standard of positive indicators, so this paper also processes the data according to the positive indicators, that is, the current ratio is not large enough to reduce the profitability of the enterprise, the asset liability ratio is not large enough to cause the enterprise debt repayment crisis, and the receivable turnover ratio is not large enough to indicate the enterprise credit policy Too tight, affect the degree of sales performance; inventory turnover rate is not large enough to the extent of the risk of out of stock and other assumptions (Table 2).

Table 2. Index classification

Type	Index	Influence
Positive indicators	Basic earnings per share, Net interest rate on equity, Cost, cost, profit Operations Ratio of liabilities to net gold flows, Total asset turnover, Total asset growth rate, net margin Growth rates, Investment in safe production R & D investment as a proportion of operating income, on opolize Interest, Comprehensive utilization of waste water, Social unit per unit Contributions	Determine the division of performance and specific values to facilitate the overall performance of talent
Inverse indicators	Integrated circuit production million tons of mortality, Total energy consumption	
Moderate indicators	Current ratio, Ratio of assets to liabilities turnover of receivables, inventory turnover ratio	

2.6 Establish an Evaluation Model

BP neural network model adopts the three-layer model commonly used now, namely input layer, hidden layer and output layer. The input level represents the performance evaluation index system of personnel training (if qualitative index is advanced, normalization processing is advanced, and then input), the number of input nodes should be 12, and the result of talent training performance is taken as the output of the model, and the output result should correspond to the evaluation result [10]. In this paper, the evaluation results of talent training performance in the integrated circuit industry are divided into five grades: very poor, poor, general, good and good, which are represented by five dimensional unit vector. That is to say, when the output result is [0, 0, 0, 0, 1], the performance result of IC industry talent training is good; when the output structure is [0, 0, 0, 1, 0], the performance result of IC industry talent training is good; when the output result is [0, 0, 1, 0, 0], the performance of IC industry talent training is average; when the output result is [0, 1, 0, 0, 0], the performance of IC industry talent training is average When the output result is [1, 0, 0, 0, 0, 0], the performance result of IC industry talent training is very poor. Therefore, the output node of BP neural network model is 5.

Step 1: Determine the basic parameters of the BP neural network model and build a neural network model for talent assessment. Each connection weight w_{ij}, v_{jt} and thresholds θ_j, γ_j are given random values in the interval (-1, 1). A random set of input and target vectors $X_k = \left(a_1^k, a_2^k, \ldots, a_n^k\right)$ and $Y_k = \left(s_1^k, s_2^k, \ldots, s_n^k\right)$ are provided to the network.

Step 2: Calculate the input s_j of each neuron in the middle layer using the input sample w_{ij} connection weight $X_k = \left(a_1^k, a_2^k, \ldots, a_n^k\right)$ and the threshold value θ_j, and then use s_j to calculate the output b_j of each neuron in the middle layer through the transfer function.

$$s_j = \sum_{i=1}^{n} w_{ij}a_i - \theta_j, \quad j = 1, 2, \ldots, p \tag{4}$$

$$b_j = f(s_j), \quad j = 1, 2, \ldots, p \tag{5}$$

Step 3: Calculate the output l_t of each unit of the output layer using the output b_j, connection weight v_{jt}, and threshold γ_j of the intermediate layer, and then use the transfer function to calculate the vector C_t of each unit of the output layer.

$$l_t = \sum_{i=1}^{p} v_{jt}b_j - \gamma_t, \quad t = 1, 2, \ldots, p \tag{6}$$

Step 4: Using the target vector $Y_k = \left(y_1^k, y_2^k, \ldots, y_q^k\right)$ and the real output value C_t of the network, calculate the error d_t^k of each neuron in the output layer as:

$$d_t^k = \left(y_t^k - C_t\right)C_t(1 - C_t), \quad t = 1, 2, \ldots, q \tag{7}$$

Step 5: Use the connection weight v_j^t, the error d_t of the output layer, and the output b_j of the intermediate layer to calculate the error e_j^k of each unit of the intermediate layer as:

$$e_j^k = \left[\sum_{t=1}^{q} d_t v_{jt}\right] b_j(1 - b_j) \tag{8}$$

Step 6: Use the generalized error d_t^k of each neuron in the output layer and the output b_j of each unit in the middle layer to modify the connection weight v_j^t and the threshold γ_t.

Step 7: Use the error value e_j^k of each neuron in the middle layer and the input $X_k = (a_1, a_2, \ldots, a_n)$ of each unit in the input layer to modify the connection weight w_{ij} and the threshold θ_j.

Step 8: select the next learning sample to provide to the established neural network, and execute step 2 until the training sample is completed. Thirdly, input and target samples randomly from all learning samples, and execute step 2 until the global error is less than the preset error value, that is, network convergence.

Step 9: Use the actual value of the performance evaluation index for integrated circuit industry personnel training as the input value of the trained BP neural network model. The model will use the trained weights and thresholds for calculation, and finally output the results of personnel training performance evaluation.

3 Experiment and Analysis

3.1 Experiment Preparation

In order to better see the superiority of the method proposed in this paper, the BP neural network will be trained through the actual sample data, and the performance evaluation model of the integrated circuit industry talent training constructed above will be analyzed. Select the CA company's scientific and technological talents as samples to compare the methods in this paper with the traditional methods. Among the 100 valid sample data obtained in this paper, 90 samples are randomly selected for network training and standardization.

3.2 Model Training

The 100 samples are randomly divided into two parts: 90 samples are used for BP neural network learning and training, and the remaining 10 samples are used for network feasibility testing. The 90-sample network training is mainly programmed with MATLAB software. The 17 index data of the enterprise scientific and technological talent evaluation obtained above are filtered and standardized to form an input sample matrix. The expected output of the network is the comprehensive evaluation level of each scientific and technological talent. The training of BP neural network is realized through programming. Based on this, the accuracy of the results of talent evaluation using the network is verified through a certain number of test samples, so as to realize the intelligent evaluation of scientific and technological talents. The function net tra n Param is selected to train the neural network. In this paper, the target error accuracy is 0.001 and the maximum number of iterations is 5000. Ninety training samples were randomly selected to input BP neural network for learning and training.

Referring to the above, the value range of hidden layer neurons is 5 to 14, and experiments are performed in order, and then selected based on network training errors and network training times. After repeated experiments, it was found that when the number of hidden layers of the BP neural network was 12, the training of the network tended to the most stable state and the error accuracy was also the highest. According to the output of MATLAB software, Table 3 is obtained.

The following is the corresponding network training error diagram when the number of hidden layer neurons is 6, 12 and 13:

It can be seen from the three network training error graphs in Fig. 2, 3, and 4 that when the number of neurons in the hidden layer is selected as 6 and the network iterates to the maximum number, the network still does not converge and fails to reach the preset

Table 3. MATLAB software output results

Number of hidden layer neurons	Network training error (Performance)	Frequency of training (Epochs)
5	0.000999999	4287
6	0.00148852	No convergence
7	0.000999964	4532
8	0.000998532	2597
9	0.000998873	3447
10	0.000999987	3449
11	0.00129335	No convergence
12	0.000997344	2204
13	0.000998051	2427
14	0.00102218	No convergence

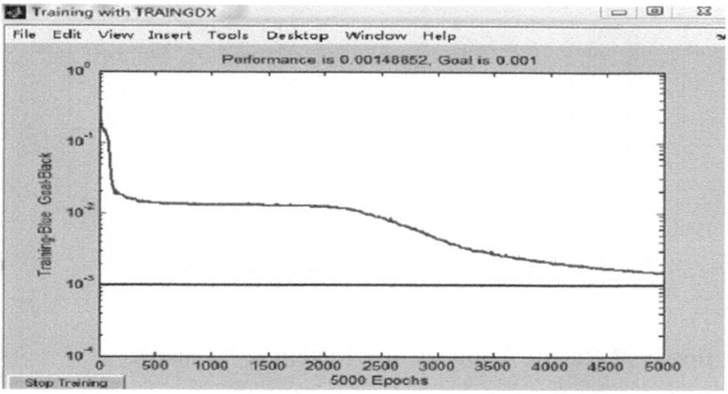

Fig. 2. Six neurons in the hidden layer

target error accuracy. The target error of 12 neurons in the hidden layer is 0.000997344, which needs to be iterated 2204 times. When the number of neurons in the hidden layer is 13, the number of iterations is 2427 epochs, but the error accuracy is worse than that when the number of neurons in the hidden layer is 12. Therefore, the number of hidden layer neurons of BP neural network constructed in this paper is 12. Neural network for these 90 After continuous learning, training and associative memory of training samples, the complex corresponding relationship between the evaluation standard of scientific and technological talents and the evaluation level of competence in the enterprise has been formed, which can correctly identify the characteristics of the input sample data, thus giving the corresponding output results, realizing the automatic processing of the evaluation index data of scientific and technological talents in the enterprise, with better practicability.

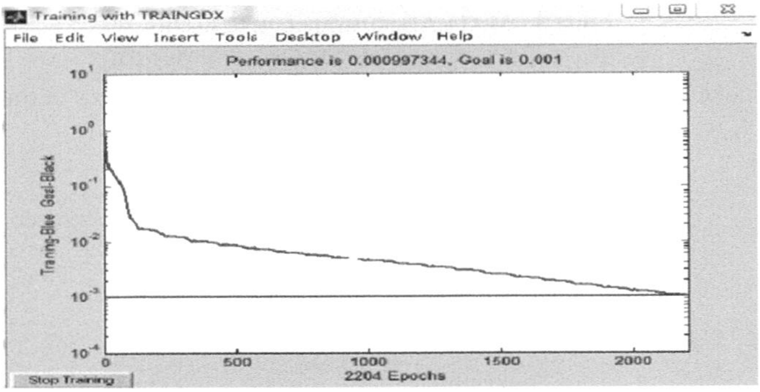

Fig. 3. 12 neurons in the hidden layer

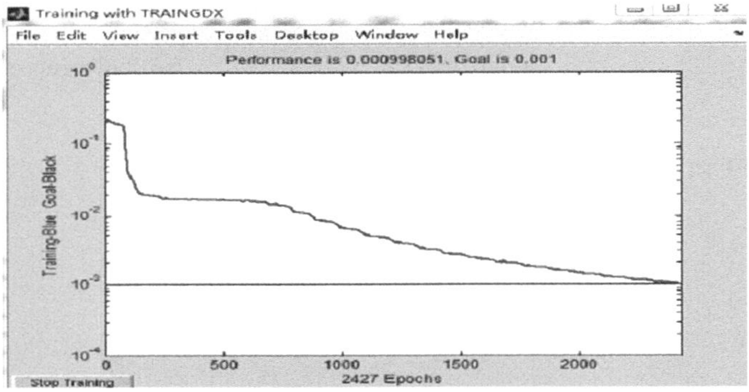

Fig. 4. 13 neurons in the hidden layer

3.3 Verification and Result Analysis of BP Neural Network

Ten sets of data are randomly selected as samples of the verification network and input into the previously trained BP neural network. Calculate the error between the expected output and the actual output to verify the feasibility and accuracy of the network, and test whether the BP neural network model learned earlier can scientifically and accurately evaluate corporate scientific and technological personnel. The simulation test using Matla software sim function is as follows: After the remaining 10 sets of sample data are standardized, they are input into the trained BP neural network for simulation test. According to the simulation output value of MATLAB software, the expected output is compared with the actual output. Finish drawing Table 4.

By using the BP neural network model with highly nonlinear mapping function to reflect the comprehensive performance level of integrated circuit industry talent training, only the basic data needs to be input into the computer, and the trained network model will automatically generate results after calculation. The whole process is simple and easy, especially without the need to determine the weight manually, thus greatly reducing the uncertainty in the traditional evaluation process It improves the accuracy of evaluation results. Therefore, the application of BP neural network model to the evaluation of the

Table 4. Expected results and actual results of BP neural network

Sample book	Actual output value	Corresponding evaluation grade	Desired output	Corresponding evaluation grade	Fractional error
1	2.0668	Same as	2	Same as	3.23
2	2.9544	Preferably	3	Preferably	1.54
3	2.9561	Preferably	3	Preferably	1.49
4	1.9753	Same as	2	Same as	1.25
5	2.0337	Same as	2	Same as	1.66
6	4.0279	Beyond compare	4	Beyond compare	0.69
7	3.1045	Preferably	3	Preferably	3.37
8	2.9036	Preferably	3	Preferably	3.32
9	1.1688	Very poor	1	Very poor	14.44
10	2.8636	Preferably	3	Preferably	4.76

training performance of integrated circuit industry talents will provide a new research idea and direction for its comprehensive performance evaluation method.

The experimental results show that the BP neural network constructed in this paper can fully absorb the judgment experience of experts and the actual guidance of human resource management of enterprises, and has a good evaluation effect. Not only is it helpful for enterprises to evaluate scientific and technological talents more scientifically and reasonably, it also provides decision-making basis for human resource management. Secondly, the use of BP neural network for enterprise scientific and technological personnel evaluation, the evaluation implementation process is simpler and faster, and the scientific and technological personnel evaluation results are more scientific and accurate. According to the evaluation results obtained by the BP neural network model, it has certain guiding significance for the selection and introduction of talents.

4 Conclusion

According to the error between each expected network output result and the actual result, it can be seen that the relative error between only one sample output result and the expected result is large, and the relative error between the actual output and the expected output of the rest samples is small, all within 5%. It shows that the BP neural network can absorb and memorize the thinking and experience of experts in the evaluation of scientific and technological talents, and the result of talent evaluation is more accurate. In addition, BP neural network has a strong nonlinear mapping function. Through training, it can learn and memorize the rules between given input and output, effectively overcome the defects of traditional evaluation methods, and weaken the influence of subjective factors as much as possible. The accuracy of evaluation results is high.

5 Conclusion

This paper analyzes the integrated circuit industry talent training performance evaluation method based on BP neural network, and evaluates the integrated circuit industry talent training performance through BP neural network. Through the establishment of BP neural network model for talent training performance evaluation, only the normalized value of talent training performance evaluation index is input into the trained model, the results can be generated automatically, and the process is simple. The weight of the index does not need to be determined artificially, which improves the objectivity and scientificity of the performance of talent training in the integrated circuit industry. Therefore, the application of neural network model in the field of performance evaluation of talent training in the integrated circuit industry can be regarded as a new attempt and development direction.

References

1. Jingchun, F., Huaai, H., Yao, Y., et al.: Comprehensive security risk factor identification for small reservoirs with heterogeneous data based on grey relational analysis model. Water Sci. Eng. **12**(4), 330–338 (2019)
2. Malkawi, A.M., Meertens, R.M., Kremers, S.P.J., Sleddens, E.F.C.: Dietary, physical activity, and weight management interventions among active-duty military personnel: a systematic review. Mil. Med. Res. **6**(3), 242–253 (2019)
3. Weiyang, J., Xiaoliang, H., Manyun, Z.: Research of personnel operational ability evaluation of large-scale complex equipment. Int. J. Plant Eng. Manage. **24**(3), 129–139 (2019)
4. Li, F., et al.: Investment environment assessment and strategic policy for subjects of federation in Russia. Chin. Geogra. Sci. **29**(5), 887–904 (2019). https://doi.org/10.1007/s11769-019-1051-1
5. Zhengben, D., Xingchen, H., Haoran, C.: Cost-benefit analysis of land development projects based on fuzzy comprehensive evaluation model. Asian Agric. Res. **11**(6), 12–14 (2019)
6. Yan, C., Haojun, Y., Jiuhua, X., et al.: Recent advances in hole making of FRP/metal stacks: a review. Trans. Nanjing Univ. Aeronaut. Astronaut. **36**(3), 361–375 (2019)
7. Lichi, Y.: Evaluation of urban development quality based on the connotation of high-quality development: a case study of Guangdong Province. J. Landscape Res. **11**(2), 83–89+94 (2019)
8. Zhang, W., Wang, M., Le, B.: Modeling and experiment on contact stiffness and accuracy analysis of ball linear guide feed unit. J. Harbin Inst. Technol. (New Ser.) **26**(1), 30–41 (2019)
9. Guo, Q., Fan, S., Xu, R., Cheng, X., Zhao, G., Yang, J.: Spindle thermal error optimization modeling of a five-axis machine tool. Chin. J. Mech. Eng. **30**(3), 746–753 (2017). https://doi.org/10.1007/s10033-017-0098-0
10. Xinhua, Z., Min, Z., Yuming, W., et al.: Interplanetary physics in mainland China. J. Space Sci. **38**(5), 665–693 (2018)

The Satisfaction Evaluation Model of Course Resources of Automobile Maintenance Major Based on Big Data

S. Lu and Y. Zhou(✉)

Chongqing Vocational College of Transportation, Chongqing 402247, China
jiangljbian@163.com

Abstract. When the conventional course resource satisfaction evaluation model is used to evaluate the automobile maintenance major, the reliability of satisfaction evaluation is low due to the large volume of data. Therefore, a big data-based satisfaction assessment model for the automobile maintenance major is proposed. Based on the loading of teaching satisfaction relationship and sample quantification, the introduction of big data analysis technology, and the use of regression equations for big data evaluation, achieved a comprehensive evaluation of the satisfaction of course resources for automobile maintenance majors. The experimental data shows that the reliability of the proposed model is 15.73% higher than that of the conventional model, and the evaluation accuracy is higher.

Keywords: Big Data · Car maintenance course resources · Satisfaction evaluation

1 Introduction

Curriculum resources are divided into three types: on-campus curriculum resources, off-campus curriculum resources, and information-based curriculum resources, based on the Outline of Basic Education Curriculum Reform (Trial). The "Outline of Basic Education Curriculum Reform (Trial)" clearly states: "Actively develop and rationally use various curriculum resources inside and outside the school, schools should give full play to the role of libraries, laboratories, specialized classrooms and various teaching facilities and practice bases; extensive The use of off-campus libraries, museums, exhibition halls, science and technology museums, factories, rural areas, military and scientific research institutions, as well as rich natural resources; actively use and develop information-based curriculum resources. " For this reason, it is necessary to actively evaluate the satisfaction of Cheng resources, especially some professional courses. Based on the big data technology, this article builds a complete evaluation model based on the automobile maintenance major.

Therefore, to strengthen the development and utilization of curriculum resources is not only one of the important contents of the new curriculum reform, but also the

S. Liu et al. (Eds.): eLEOT 2020, LNICST 339, pp. 55–66, 2020.
https://doi.org/10.1007/978-3-030-63952-5_5

necessary conditions for the realization of the new curriculum reform. It is one of the important principles for the development of curriculum resource evaluation model to change the traditional teaching concept and highlight the students' learning subject status. The development of an excellent evaluation model of curriculum resources is conducive to the cultivation of students' learning mode of "independence, cooperation and exploration", the transformation of students' passive learning status, and the realization of quality education, which requires the change of the traditional concept that teachers are the center of teaching activities, and also puts forward higher requirements for teachers in the new era. Developing a curriculum resource evaluation model suitable for students and popular with them will be more conducive to the realization of teaching objectives, including the cultivation of knowledge and skills, process and methods, emotional attitude and values.

2 Build a Satisfaction Evaluation Model of Course Resources of Automobile Maintenance Major Based on Big Data

Curriculum resources refer to the source of curriculum elements and the necessary and direct conditions for implementing the curriculum. The structure of curriculum resources includes on-campus curriculum resources and off-campus curriculum resources. In addition to textbooks, there are teachers, students, and teachers. Students and students have different experiences, life experiences and different experiences, learning methods, and teaching strategies. They are very valuable and very direct curriculum resources. Activities on campus are also important curriculum resources. Off-campus curriculum resources mainly include off-campus libraries, science and technology museums, museums, network resources, rural resources, and family resources. Combined with the automobile maintenance major, the main factors affecting the satisfaction assessment of course resources for the automobile maintenance major are divided into two categories, as shown in Fig. 1:

2.1 Loading of Teaching Satisfaction Relationship and Sample Quantification

The major of automobile maintenance is a subject that trains the ability of automobile inspection, operation, maintenance and technical management, and has the basic knowledge and professional skills required by the professional post (Group) and the high-quality technical talents preliminarily trained by automobile maintenance engineers. It is highly dependent on curriculum resources. According to the factors influencing the satisfaction evaluation of curriculum resources of Automobile Maintenance Specialty in Fig. 1, the evaluation factors of curriculum resources satisfaction are formulated as shown in Table 1:

According to the satisfaction evaluation factor, the establishment of the teaching satisfaction sample management framework mainly includes seven processes: pre-operation and maintenance, handover and maintenance, operation and maintenance service content, operation and maintenance evaluation, operation and maintenance service object, application system operation stage, and application and operation evaluation stage. Pre-operation and maintenance is to determine the key operation and maintenance procedures

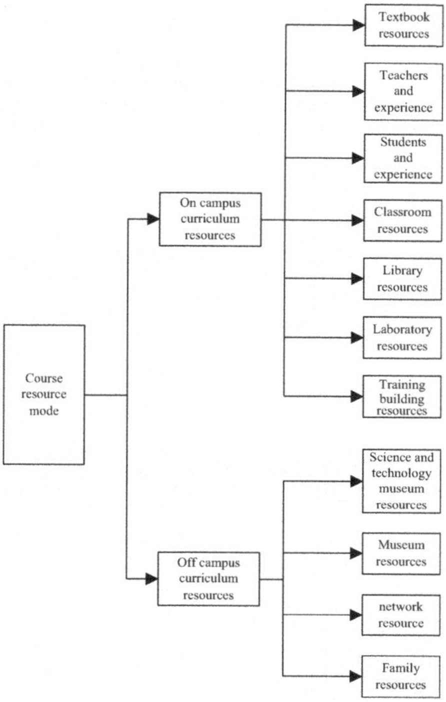

Fig. 1. Factors affecting the satisfaction evaluation of automobile maintenance curriculum resources

and collection methods according to the automatic operation and maintenance strategy, and conduct real-time statistics and data analysis on the evaluation factors of automobile maintenance professional satisfaction. Hand over operation and maintenance is according to the scope of business, the configuration of automotive maintenance professional environment. The main contents of the operation and maintenance service include investigation and evaluation service, routine operation service, response support service, optimization and improvement service, and change release service. According to different service conditions, the big data container computing platform is evaluated. Samples were quantified according to the automatic operation and maintenance strategy to eliminate the influence of thought factors.

The teaching satisfaction sample management framework is run using an automated operation and maintenance strategy, and the automated operation and maintenance strategy is a key program for cloud computing platform automated operation and maintenance. It mainly includes two parts of data collection and data monitoring. The data collection process is to determine the message queue through the data collection program, use Storm and Hadoop to analyze the implementation results [1], and cache it in the query system to implement the data (Fig. 2).

According to the collection and monitoring of automobile maintenance professional satisfaction evaluation factor data, the monitoring process mainly includes discovery

Table 1. Evaluation factors of curriculum resource satisfaction

Course resource mode	Mark sequence number	Parameters and contents
On campus curriculum resources	1	Textbook resources
	2	Teachers and experience
	3	Students and experience
	4	Classroom resources
	5	Library resources
	6	Laboratory resources
	7	Training building resources
Off campus curriculum resources	8	Science and technology museum resources
	9	Museum resources
	10	network resource
	11	Family resources

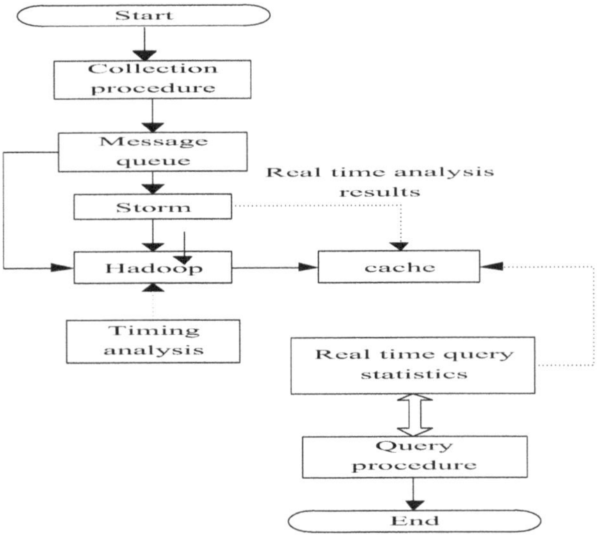

Fig. 2. Schematic diagram of data acquisition process

and record, classification and analysis, investigation and analysis, and temporary repair measures, among which the investigation and analysis is based on the form of knowledge base for analysis. Classification and analysis are carried out in the form of linear function. Based on the obtained data records, the threshold value of a function is constructed. If the data falls within the threshold range, it is defined as the same category; otherwise, if the data falls outside the threshold range, it is defined as different categories. The threshold value calculation formula of the function is shown in formula (1):

$$S = \sum Qt - \lim_{I \to 0} Ut \tag{1}$$

In the formula, Q represents the size of the analysis data; U represents the data type; t represents the system response time [2].

2.2 Introduction of Big Data Analysis

Big data analysis has the characteristics of large data volume, fast analysis speed, multiple analysis types and high analysis value [3], which is widely used in different algorithms, operation and maintenance. In order to improve the reliability of automatic operation and maintenance, big data analysis technology is introduced. Establish the teaching satisfaction sample management framework, make use of the big data analysis results to guide the operation of the framework, actively evaluate the professional satisfaction of automobile maintenance, and improve the data stability and data accuracy [4].

How to use qualitative analysis method and quantitative analysis method to identify the quantification in evaluation factors has always been an important research area. At the same time, it is also an important research area for complex evaluation models. To this end, this article mainly from the direction of automobile maintenance, further researches on the big data of the automobile maintenance professional course resource satisfaction evaluation algorithm, at the same time also conducted the LeaderRank algorithm and PageRank algorithm feasibility study, and the LeaderRank algorithm on Hadoop and GraphLab A simple data structure design. It is found through research that Hadoop has higher LeaderRank value efficiency than GraphLab in computing network vertices, and also shows a relatively high scalability when facing large-scale evaluation models [5].

As we all know, there are many methods to evaluate the importance of nodes in the evaluation model. In this paper, we mainly study the topological structure of automobile maintenance specialty. Including global attribute, local attribute, random walk and other directions. The local characteristics mainly consider the information of the vertex neighbors, the relationship between the vertex and its neighbors, and the information of the vertex itself, etc. these indexes are relatively simple to calculate, and their time complexity is relatively low, so they are more suitable for large-scale evaluation models.

The traditional LeaderRank algorithm is usually implemented on a single machine, and massive network data cannot be completed by a single machine. Therefore, a LeaderRank algorithm based on cloud computing is designed as an evaluation based on the cloud computing platform. The basic algorithm of model fast data association algorithm [6].

In the LeaderRank algorithm, you first need to establish a Ground Node to join the network, and establish a two-way connection with other Vertex in the figure. To make it as convenient as possible, on the GraphLab platform, the addition of Ground Node vertices is performed during the graph loading process; while in Hadoop, we add the ground node addition to the data preprocessing stage based on the input of the algorithm. Second, for each vertex in the graph, the Ground Node is initialized to 0, and the other vertices in the network are initialized to 1. Then update each vertex according to the relevant data. After reaching the steady state, the LeaderRank value of each vertex is obtained [7].

Hadoop in the leaderank algorithm is basically the same as that in graphlab, but there is a big difference in the way of calculating the leaderank value of each vertex [8]. As shown in Table 2, Table 2 shows the steps of leaderank algorithm.

Table 2. LeaderRank algorithm steps table

Algorithm steps	Content	Concrete measure
Step 1	Map stage	Further build the output data according to the existing data, and transfer it to the reduce stage at the same time
Step 2	Reduce stage	Analyze the output data of map phase according to the formula, and calculate the leaderank value of each vertex at the same time
Step 3	Iteration stage	Take the data output in the reduce phase as the input data, and continue to perform the operations in the map phase and the reduce phase according to the number of iterations
Step 4	Gather stage	Collect leaderank value and its ratio to its output
Step 5	Apply stage	Further update the data based on the data collected in the gather phase, and save the leader rank value of the previous iteration.

According to the above idea, we need to define a vertex data structure in Hadoop, which includes the id number of the vertex, the list of neighbors pointed to by the vertex, the LeaderRank value of the last iteration, the current LeaderRank value, and the number of neighbors pointed by the vertex. As shown in Eq. 1, Eq. 1 is the LeaderRank iterative formula.

$$LR_{i,t+1} = \sum_{(j,i)=E} LR_{j,t} d_{j,t} \tag{2}$$

In the formula, $LR_{i,t+1}$ is the LeaderRank value calculated by the vertex i in the $i+1$ iteration, where $d_{j,t}$ is the degree of the vertex i. On this basis, the obtained LeaderRank value is brought into the algorithm to obtain the final data.

2.3 Using Regression Equation to Evaluate Big Data

Relying on the analysis of big data, obtain the data package of the evaluation model, and filter the information of useless information resources. Assume that in the big data mode, the data package in the management system has one attribute Y and the Y attribute also has multiple constraints, X_1 、 $X_2 \ldots X_n$, respectively. The filter function expression constructed is as follows:

$$f(x) = \prod_{n=1}^{n} \left(\frac{K \cdot (X_1 + X_2 \cdots X_n)}{Y}\right) 2^{t+1} \tag{3}$$

In the formula, K is the data information weight coefficient corresponding to the Y attribute ($0 < K < 1$); t is the data processing time, and the unit is s. The filtered data information will be compiled and transcoded according to the general data coding principles to prepare for the ship information data preprocessing [9].

Compiling and transcoding are to ensure that data resources can be reasonably allocated in the shortest time. The designed data information preprocessing process is shown in Fig. 3.

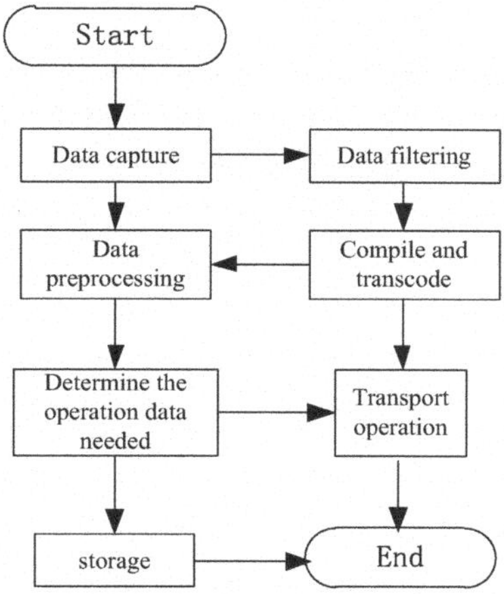

Fig. 3. Data information preprocessing process

After completing the information data capture and preprocessing, the algorithm structure of the information system is optimized. Let A represent the data in the information management system, i represents the number of operations of the data, Ymax represents the maximum value of the data operations, and Ymin represents the minimum value of the data operations. The conventional information system algorithm structure, based on the relationship between A, i, Ymax, Ymin, performs successive calculations, which makes the calculation process too cumbersome, resulting in weak data information processing capabilities in the system.

After the algorithm structure is optimized, although the data processing operation is still performed according to the relationship between A, i, Ymax, and Ymin, the relationship is processed, and the relationship expression formed is shown in Eq. 4.

$$A = \frac{\sum_{i=0}^{i} Ki^{b} + \sum_{i=0}^{i} Y\max - Y\min}{(Y\max - Y\min)^{2}} \tag{4}$$

In the formula, μ is the iteration coefficient of the number of operations on the data, λ is a measure between Ymax and Ymin, and b is a natural variable. The simple and clear relational formula formed after the conversion completes the optimization of the algorithm structure [10].

The regression equation expression of data information in big data mode is shown in Eq. 5.

$$F = d(x_i, x_j) = \sum_{k=1}^{m} \left[(x_j - x_i) d\mu^2 \right]^{\frac{1}{2}} \tag{5}$$

In the formula, x_i and x_j represent system operations i to j data information; t represents operation processing time i to j data; d represents the correlation consumption coefficient of operation processing.

2.4 Realize the Comprehensive Evaluation of the Satisfaction Degree of the Course Resources of the Automobile Maintenance Specialty

After the regression equation is determined by formula 3, the satisfaction of course resources is determined by the objective function. Determine the course resource satisfaction process as shown in Fig. 4.

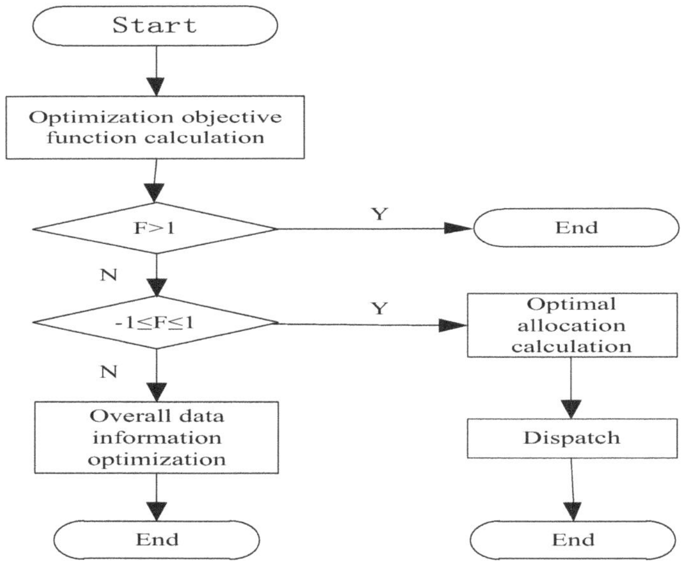

Fig. 4. Simulation flow chart of fast update strategy calculation

In fact, the data in the course resources of automobile overhaul is dynamic, changing with time, and obtained through continuous filtering and pre-processing. Therefore, the processed data is used for comparison, i.e. Formula 3, Formula 4 and Formula 5 are integrated, and the update strategy is selected through the calculation results. The calculation formula after integration is as follows:

$$F = \frac{Af(x)}{\sum_{k=1}^{m} \left[(x_j - x_i) d\mu^2 \right]^{\frac{1}{2}}} \tag{6}$$

When $F > 1$, it indicates that its satisfaction is positive and optimistic.
When $-1 \leq F \leq 1$, it means that its satisfaction is average and average.
When $F < -1$, it means that its satisfaction is negative and pessimistic.

Based on the loading of teaching satisfaction relationship and sample quantification, the introduction of big data analysis technology, and the use of regression equations for big data evaluation, achieved a comprehensive evaluation of the satisfaction of course resources for automobile maintenance majors.

3 Simulation Test Experiment

In order to verify the effectiveness of the model based on big data, the satisfaction evaluation model of automotive maintenance course resources proposed in this paper. The reliability evaluation verification of satisfaction evaluation is conducted, and the conventional course resource satisfaction evaluation model is used as the comparison object for experimental verification. The reliability evaluation analysis of satisfaction evaluation is performed by using the form of simulation test.

3.1 Experiment Preparation

In order to ensure the scientificalness of the reliability experiment of the satisfaction evaluation and strictly control the independent variables and other influencing factors, the comparative analysis was carried out by means of simulation experiment. The finite element analysis software ANSYS 18.0 was used in the simulation experiment. This reliability simulation experiment of satisfaction evaluation adopts Windows7 flagship operating system, 2 GB video memory and 8 GB running memory as the carrier of simulation software. Different experimental data types are set, and the proportion of experimental data and the size of experimental data volume are determined, as shown in Table 3.

Table 3. Data preparation for reliability comparison experiment of satisfaction evaluation

Project	Parameter	Remarks
Parameters of simulation equipment	Windows 7 ultimate operating system	2 GB of video memory and 8 GB of running memory
Test data volume	2 GB ~ 22 GB	Linear change
Types of experimental data	Text, image and video of automobile maintenance course resources	Quantity ratio 1:1:1

3.2 Experimental Process and Result Analysis

According to the determination of the satisfaction evaluation reliability comparison test data preparation table, construct a simulation experiment model, conduct simulation experiments, control the change of different types of data volume, and obtain the reliability evaluation reliability under different data volume conditions. Proceed as follows:

(1) Pre-process the simulation data prepared for the experiment, and arrange the data of each test unit in the way of text, image, video and audio, 1:1:1;
(2) Linear loading test data (2 GB ~ 22 GB);
(3) Correctly operate the simulation software, obtain the linear experimental results, and record them in a unified chart. Finally, the reliability comparison results of satisfaction evaluation are obtained, as shown in Table 4.

Table 4. Reliability comparison results of satisfaction evaluation

Test data volume	Reliability of satisfaction evaluation	
	Evaluation model of satisfaction degree	Conventional satisfaction evaluation model
2 GB	98.7%	95.1%
6 GB	95.7%	90.5%
10 GB	92.4%	82.5%
14 GB	89.4%	75.3%
18 GB	88.7%	62.1%
22 GB	86.4%	51.4%

According to the comparison results of satisfaction evaluation reliability, it can be concluded that under the condition of different amount of data, the proposed satisfaction evaluation model of automobile maintenance curriculum resources based on big data is more reliable than that of the conventional curriculum resources. Through variance calculation, the standard variance of the proposed satisfaction evaluation model is 4.24, and the standard variance of the conventional satisfaction evaluation model is 15.36. The relative range of the proposed model is 13.39%, and that of the conventional model is 57.39%. Through the data calculation, it is further proved that the proposed satisfaction evaluation model has higher stability under the condition of different vehicle maintenance test data.

Analyze the data as a whole. There are significant differences in the reliability of satisfaction evaluation between the two conventional curriculum resource satisfaction evaluation models. The proposed conventional curriculum resource satisfaction evaluation model has a higher reliability of satisfaction evaluation, while the conventional curriculum resource satisfaction evaluation model varies with the amount of data. Increased, the reliability of satisfaction evaluation decreased.

According to the experimental results, the statistical results show that the reliability of the satisfaction evaluation model based on big data is 91.88%. The reliability of the satisfaction evaluation model is 76.15%. As a result, the reliability of the proposed curriculum resource satisfaction evaluation model based on big data is 15.73% higher than that of the conventional curriculum resource satisfaction evaluation model.

In order to further verify the effectiveness of the model in this paper, the evaluation accuracy of the course resource satisfaction evaluation model of Automobile Maintenance Specialty Based on big data and the conventional course resource satisfaction evaluation model is analyzed, and the comparison results are shown in Fig. 5.

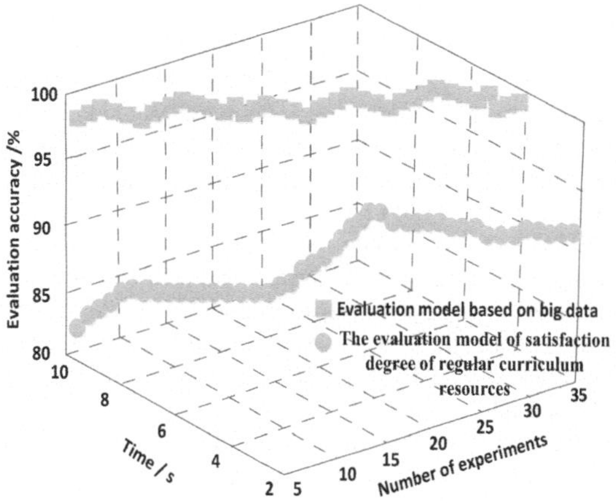

Fig. 5. Comparison results of evaluation accuracy of two models

According to Fig. 5, the evaluation accuracy of the course resource satisfaction evaluation model of Automobile Maintenance Specialty Based on big data is up to 98%, while that of the conventional course resource satisfaction evaluation model is up to 92%, which shows that the evaluation accuracy of the course resource satisfaction evaluation model of Automobile Maintenance Specialty Based on big data designed in this paper is higher than that of the conventional course resource satisfaction evaluation model High price accuracy.

4 Conclusion

This paper proposes a curriculum resource satisfaction evaluation model based on big data for automotive maintenance majors. Based on the loading of teaching satisfaction relationship and sample quantification, the introduction of big data analysis technology completes the construction of a curriculum resource satisfaction evaluation model. In order to verify the validity of the model, simulation experiments were performed. The experimental data showed that the proposed evaluation model has high reliability. It is hoped that the research in this paper can provide a theoretical basis for the evaluation of curriculum resource satisfaction. However, this model does not consider the time-consuming problem. In the next study, the shortest time is used to evaluate the satisfaction of automobile maintenance professional curriculum resources, and to ensure the accuracy of the evaluation.

References

1. Xie, Y., Yi, W., Zhang, L., et al.: Evaluation of a logistic regression model for predicting liver necroinflammation in hepatitis B e antigen-negative chronic hepatitis B patients with normal and minimally increased alanine aminotransferase levels. J. Viral Hepatitis **26**(S1), 42–49 (2019)
2. Pinto, I. Jack, C. Hewitson, B.:Process-based model evaluation and projections over southern Africa from coordinated regional climate downscaling experiment and coupled model intercomparison project phase 5 models. Int. J. Climatol. **38**(11) (2018)
3. Gupta, P. Mehlawat, M.K. Mahajan, D.: Data envelopment analysis based multi-objective optimization model for evaluation and selection of software components under optimal redundancy. Ann. Oper. Res. **1**, 1–24 (2018)
4. Bo, L., Yi-Fan, Z., Bei-Bei, Z., Xian-Qing, W.: A risk evaluation model for karst groundwater pollution based on geographic information system and artificial neural network applications. Environ. Earth Sci. **77**(9), 1–14 (2018). https://doi.org/10.1007/s12665-018-7539-7
5. Shimo, T. Hosoki, K. Nakatsuji, Y. et al.: A novel human muscle cell model of Duchenne muscular dystrophy created by CRISPR/Cas9 and evaluation of antisense-mediated exon skipping. J. Hum. Genet. **63**(3), 365–375 (2018)
6. Izawa-Ishizawa, Y., Imanishi, M., Zamami, Y., et al.: Development of a novel aortic dissection mouse model and evaluation of drug efficacy using in-vivo assays and database analyses. J. Hypertens. **37**(1), 1 (2018)
7. Do, S.H., Jo, S.H., Roh, J.S., Im, H.J., Park, H.B., Batchelor, B.: Reductive dechlorination of DNAPL mixtures with Fe(II/III)-L and Fe(II)-C: evaluation using a kinetic model for the competitions. Sci. Total Environ. **624**(15), 872–877 (2018)
8. Rasmussen, P.M., Secomb, T.W., Pries, A.R.: Modeling the hematocrit distribution in microcirculatory networks: a quantitative evaluation of a phase separation model. Microcirculation **25**(3), e12445 (2018)
9. Jin, X., Bighamian, R., Hahn, J.O.: Development and in silico evaluation of a model-based closed-loop fluid resuscitation control algorithm. IEEE Trans. Biomed. Eng. **PP**(99), 1 (2018)
10. Odle, B., Reinbolt, J., Forrest, G., Dyson-Hudson, T.: Construction and evaluation of a model for wheelchair propulsion in an individual with tetraplegia. Med. Biol. Eng. Comput. **57**(2), 519–532 (2018). https://doi.org/10.1007/s11517-018-1895-z

Evaluation Method of Multimedia Art Teaching Courseware Playback Effect Based on Data Envelopment Analysis

Yong-ji Zhou(✉) and Shou-qing Lu

Chongqing Vocational College of Transportation, Chongqing 402247, China
xuxuxu124005@163.com

Abstract. In the current information age, multimedia courseware has become the mainstream teaching method in Colleges and universities. Whether the application of teaching means is reasonable directly affects the teaching cost and teaching effect of the school. Based on this, this paper puts forward the evaluation method of multimedia art teaching courseware playing effect based on DEA. Firstly, the vector of evaluation subject, evaluation index and its index weight is determined, and a reasonable and scientific evaluation index system of multimedia courseware is constructed. Under this guidance, the comprehensive judgment grade and ranking are completed. The experiment shows that the evaluation method proposed in this paper has higher effectiveness compared with the traditional evaluation method. It can obtain more real and reliable data in the effect of playing courseware and the use experience of teachers and students, and improve the evaluation accuracy of playing effect of multimedia art teaching courseware.

Keywords: Data envelopment · Multimedia · Art teaching courseware · Playing effect

1 Introduction

Since 2001, China issued the outline for the development of educational informatization in the Tenth Five Year Plan and fully implemented the "school to school" project, a great wave of educational informatization construction has been set off all over the country, and substantial progress has been made in funding, construction scale, software and hardware platform, application promotion and other aspects [1]. China's education information construction is entering a period of rapid development. In the process of educational information construction, our government has always paid close attention to educational information as a government behavior, as an important strategy to promote educational reform and development. China's education informatization is changing from construction to application, and "from construction to application, to promote development by application" is the theme of China's education informatization at this stage. To promote development by application, it is necessary to drive application by performance evaluation. In the aspect of performance evaluation of educational informatization, both at home and abroad are in the exploratory stage.

S. Liu et al. (Eds.): eLEOT 2020, LNICST 339, pp. 67–75, 2020.
https://doi.org/10.1007/978-3-030-63952-5_6

The performance evaluation of education informatization is a relatively difficult matter. On the one hand, because education informatization is not only a dynamic development process, but also a problem of multiple inputs and multiple outputs, its output is not easy to measure with quantitative indicators. On the other hand, there is no mature theoretical guidance and suitable measurement methods and measurement tools in this field, coupled with the rapid changes in the field of education informatization, so the performance evaluation of education informatization has become a very important and considerable concern for everyone. As a combination of teaching and technology, multimedia teaching has been recognized by the teaching community for its vivid teaching style, colorful teaching content, and scientific and comprehensive teaching strategies. As the main tool of multimedia teaching, multimedia courseware has become the key to affect the effect of classroom teaching. Under the dual guidance of social demand and education policy, multimedia teaching emerges as the times require, and has been widely used and recognized by all kinds of schools. However, in the process of actually using multimedia teaching, the advantages of multimedia technology have been brought into play due to the influence of traditional teaching concepts, teachers' educational technology capabilities, and multimedia courseware making technology. Multimedia courseware, with its powerful functions, has stimulated people's passion for knowledge. Its rich content, vivid pictures, clever link combinations, colorful presentation effects, and its ease of learning and ease of use have quickly become indispensable tools for the development of modern education. Multimedia courseware is the main form of multimedia teaching. The quality of multimedia courseware production directly affects the quality of multimedia teaching. First of all, we should make clear the concept of multimedia. In the field of computer, multimedia refers to a variety of media that represent information, usually including: text, graphics, images, audio, video, animation, etc. The so-called multimedia technology is to use computer technology to carry out interactive comprehensive processing and control of text, graphics, voice, image and other information media, establish logical relations, and integrate them into a system with interactivity. Multimedia courseware is a CAI teaching software designed and developed by using multimedia technology. In terms of implementation technology, multimedia courseware is a kind of multimedia software that uses multimedia technology to deal with information media such as text, picture, sound and image interactively and comprehensively to express teaching content. In terms of courseware content, it is guided by teaching theory and learning theory, uses the method of system theory, and reasonably selects and designs teaching information according to the characteristics of teaching objectives and teaching objects Media and organic combination to form an optimized teaching structure of a teaching system. However, in the actual classroom teaching, with the increase of the utilization rate of multimedia courseware, there are also many problems. In order to understand the actual situation of multimedia courseware teaching and truly grasp the current status of the effectiveness of multimedia courseware in classroom teaching applications, based on this, put forward Research on Evaluation Method of Multimedia Art Teaching Course Playing Effect Based on Data Envelopment Analysis.

2 Evaluation Method of Multimedia Art Teaching Courseware Playback Effect Based on Data Envelopment Analysis

Data envelopment analysis (DEA) solves the above problems. It is an efficiency evaluation method used to evaluate the relative effectiveness (called DEA effectiveness) between the same departments. It was established by a. charnes and w.w. cooper in 1978 and can be widely used in performance evaluation.

2.1 Determine the Evaluation Subject

This article uses a combination of self-evaluation and other evaluations when evaluating teaching effects. The evaluation of the teaching effect is carried out from two aspects, one is the evaluation of the teachers in the class, and the other is the evaluation of the students [4]. The evaluation factors of teaching effect are divided into two parts: one is the evaluation factor set of teachers in the curriculum, which is used for the evaluation of teachers by students and tutors; the other is the evaluation of students' peers (including their own evaluation). Because there are many evaluation factors, the principal component analysis method can be used to find the main factors that are not related, as shown in the Fig. 1.

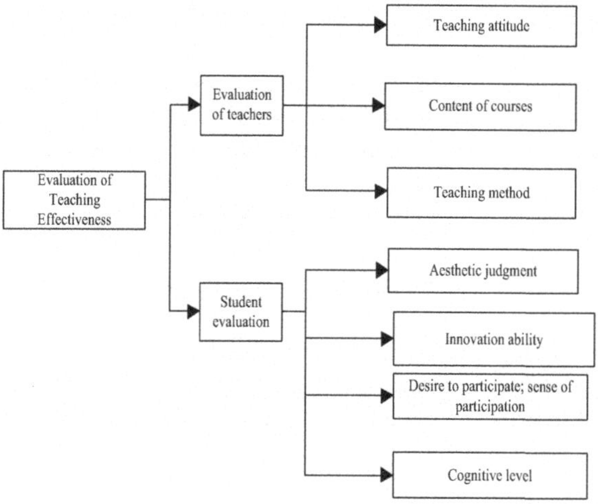

Fig. 1. Set of factors for evaluating teaching effects

The evaluation of the whole teaching effect is divided into three parts, so the main body of the evaluation is composed of students, teachers and leaders in charge.

2.2 Determine the Evaluation Index and Its Weight

Generally speaking, the importance of each indicator is different. In order to reflect the importance of each indicator, Assign a weighting factor a_i to each indicator f_i and satisfy $a_1 + a_2 + \ldots a_n = 1$ [5]. The determination of the weight set is an important step, it will directly affect the final result. Generally, the collective experience judgment method, expert consultation method, and analytic hierarchy process can be adopted, and different methods can be selected according to specific situations.

First of all, data envelopment analysis is used to measure the past situation of each evaluation object, and the index obtained can reflect the strength of the evaluation object to a certain extent, as its initial condition, this index is called the reference index; the current situation is measured by the same method, and the index obtained is called the current index [6]. The array of the reference index and the current index is called the index state of the measurement object. Let x_j be the reference index of the j th evaluation object, and y_j be the current index of the evaluation object, where $x_j \in E_1$, the array $\left(x_j, y_j\right)$ is called the index status of the j th evaluation object.

Let us observe that the index state of each evaluation unit is $\left(x_j, y_j\right), j = 0, 1, 2, \ldots\ldots n$, and:

$$T = \left\{ (x, y) \sum_{j=0}^{n} \lambda_j y_j \leq y, \sum_{j=0}^{n} \lambda_j \geq 0, j = 0, 1, 2, \ldots\ldots n \right\} \tag{1}$$

The exponential state set consisting of the above exponent states $\left(x_j, y_j\right), j = 0, 1, 2, \ldots\ldots n$, where $(x_0, y_0) = (0, 0)$ is. The exponential state set T is obviously a convex set, that is, if $(x^n, y^n) \in T$, then $\left(\lambda x' + (1 - \lambda)x^n, \lambda y' + (1 - \lambda)y''\right) \in T$. Among them, $0 \leq \lambda \leq 1$.

From this, we can establish the above possible set of exponential states.

After the indicators are obtained, the relevant weights can be calculated according to the rating of the comments and their membership vectors, which are:

$$V = \{V_1, V_2, V_3, V_4\} \tag{2}$$

$$E = (0.9, 0.7, 0.5, 0.3) \tag{3}$$

In the formula: V represents the level of student's cognitive ability, that is, the teacher's comments on the students, which are represented by good, good, average, and poor respectively; E represents the attribute vector of the evaluation index status

2.3 Establish Evaluation Matrix

Firstly, a questionnaire [7] is designed, which includes the evaluation form for students and teachers in charge, and the evaluation form for students (including mutual evaluation between students). The evaluation of students is mainly the evaluation of their recent learning., Is a process of vertical comparison [8], analyzing its recent improvement through learning. With the further development of multimedia courseware teaching, it is not difficult to see that many unreasonable uses have deviated from the purpose of multimedia courseware teaching, entered the misunderstanding, and failed to play its unique functions. The specific contents of the questionnaire analysis are as follows:

(1) Technical evaluation. Technical evaluation includes five aspects: interface design, courseware interaction, opening and expansion, media auxiliary function, and material quality. Except for media material, students are not satisfied with other technical evaluation indexes of multimedia courseware evaluation;
(2) Scientific level. Scientific evaluation includes five aspects: scientific advancement, scientific rationality, text and graphics, scientific content and scientific design. Students are not very satisfied with the three aspects of scientific advancement, scientific rationality, text and graphics. It can be seen that the multimedia courseware of colleges and universities lacks the advanced nature first, that is, it cannot reflect the advanced results of introducing advanced scientific research and teaching research at home and abroad;
(3) Usability evaluation satisfaction. Usability evaluation includes user guidance, operation and use, software operation and software performance. Students are not satisfied with the first two, that is, there are no effective user guide manual, computer operation interface, operation steps and convenience;
(4) Educational evaluation and artistic evaluation. Educational evaluation includes: teaching adaptability, structural rationality, cognitive regularity, vivid interest, and evaluation feedback. Artistic evaluation includes audio and video materials, reading volume, dubbing effects, and style consistency.

Then the two tables are summarized according to each evaluation factor, and the evaluation matrix is as follows:

$$R_{ij} = \frac{N_{ij}}{N} \tag{4}$$

Where N_{ij} is the number of comments V_j obtained by the i index f_i, and N is the number of people. Each row of the matrix adds up to 1.

2.4 Constructing a Reasonable and Scientific Evaluation Index System of Multimedia Courseware

In accordance with the principle of constructing multimedia courseware evaluation index system, the five dimensions of the summarized courseware evaluation are specifically detailed, and then constitute the following multimedia courseware evaluation index system.

Here we use the evaluation score interval variation division. The evaluation level is divided into five levels. We make the following statements for these five levels.

Level 1: indicates that the teaching software not only has the basic characteristics of teaching software, but also has considerable flexibility and intelligence in all aspects. It provides learners with very reasonable and friendly learning support and learning mechanisms, which can effectively achieve high The learning effect and help to promote student creativity and truly realize the educational advantages of computers. The comprehensive comments given by such teaching software should be: excellent, worthy of promotion, and analysis, to promote the development of computer-aided teaching.

Level 2: it means that the teaching software has the expected basic characteristics of the teaching software, and has quite strong flexibility in some aspects. At the same time, it has the unique features that other teaching software does not have, and has a breakthrough effect. It should be a relatively good teaching software.

Level 3: It indicates that the teaching software has the basic production goals of the desired teaching software, such as high interface presentation quality, good teaching software reliability, and teaching software that can overcome the teaching difficulties of ordinary teaching methods, but this teaching software lacks the corresponding flexibility., There is no particularly obvious unique point, the comprehensive comment given by such teaching software should be: acceptable and can be promoted in a small range, while pointing out the defects of this teaching software, with a view to further improvement.

Level 4: indicates that the teaching software deviates from the ideal state it should achieve. For example, the learning mechanism provided needs to be further explored, the quality of information presentation needs to be further improved, no personalized teaching measures have been taken, and every link of software development has not been in place, but the software itself has its merits. The comprehensive conclusion given by such teaching software should be: put forward This paper puts forward the quality objectives and teaching objectives that should be achieved by the teaching software after the change. At present, this software is not acceptable, and it is the most evaluated after the change.

In the implementation of courseware effect evaluation, we should pay attention to three evaluation elements, the evaluation subject (evaluator), the evaluation type, and the evaluation object (teaching software). We divide evaluators into four categories: teaching experts, technical experts, practical experts, and learners. These four types of evaluators each have their own expertise, so different types of evaluators will have different evaluation authority for different evaluation types, so different types of evaluators should have different weights in different evaluation types. . A teaching expert is often proficient in all aspects of teaching. He can scientifically evaluate the effectiveness of the teaching function of teaching software and give a more scientific score. The technical expert is mainly familiar with computer technology, and he will give a more reasonable score in technical evaluation than other evaluators. Practice experts are familiar with the entire process of software compilation, and have also done research in education and computer technology. Therefore, practice experts have a more even distribution of weights in process evaluation, technology evaluation, and education function evaluation. According to age, knowledge background, learning environment and the times of contacting Cai, the evaluation of teaching software will produce different evaluation results. For example, a learner who has never been in contact with a computer uses the teaching software for the first time. When learning, there may be a sense of curiosity, so their evaluations are higher, so learners' three different types of evaluation in teaching software are often unreliable. We do not require them to conduct a systematic evaluation of teaching software, but they can reflect the learning effects produced by teaching software.

2.5 Comprehensively Determine the Grade and Sort

The calculation of the decision level first requires the use of formula $S = W \cdot R$ to calculate the comprehensive evaluation vector [9]. Adjust the value so that the sum is 1.

Among them: W indicates the teacher's teaching weight index, which is the highest value; R indicates the student's awareness of participation throughout the class.

Calculate the comprehensive priority according to formula $N = S \cdot E^T$ [10].

Among them, N represents the final judgment level, and T represents the number of students. Art teaching activities belong to art teaching, and the quality of teaching effect can not be simply reflected in the test paper, which has certain fuzziness. In this paper, the use of data envelopment analysis to evaluate the effect of multimedia art teaching for students can not only determine the level of teaching effect, but also quantitatively see the degree of belonging to the level, which has achieved good results in practical application.

3 Experiment and Analysis

In order to better see the effectiveness of the design method in this paper, it is specially compared with the traditional evaluation method.

3.1 Experiment Preparation

Based on the above theory, a new teaching evaluation method is developed, and an empirical study on this method is carried out. The data in this paper are all from the art teaching group report card of the basic teaching and Research Office of Shaanxi art college, including the average score of the final art examination of the first semester of 2009–2010 academic year and the average score of the art examination of the corresponding classes. Table 1 It is the original data table (the real name of the teacher has been hidden in the table), and it is sorted according to the current scores of the final examination of the first semester. Using the evaluation method of multimedia art teaching courseware playback effect based on DEA designed in this paper, the playback effect value of these 9 teachers' multimedia art teaching courseware is calculated, which represents the evaluation index of teachers' teaching effect, and the ranking of teachers' teaching effect is listed in Table 2 according to the index.

Table 1. Current scores and ranking of classes taught by teachers

Name of teacher	Class	Art test results	Current accomplishments	Current performance ranking
A	Art Management 1	82.56	78.89	1
B	Art Management 2	83.66	76.23	2
C	Oil Painting 1	73.63	73.52	3
D	Oil Painting 2	90.24	69.72	4
E	Ink Painting 1	82.25	69.42	5
F	Ink Painting 2	82.21	61.25	6
G	Sketch 1	76.12	60.28	7
H	Sketch 2	77.36	59.25	8
I	Sketch 3	72.63	56.39	9

Table 2. Teaching effect value and new ranking

Name of teacher	Class	Effect value of this method	New orders	Original order	Changes in order
A	Art Management 1	95.55%	2	1	−1
B	Art Management 2	91.23%	3	2	−1
C	Oil Painting 1	99.85%	1	3	+2
D	Oil Painting 2	77.26%	7	4	−3
E	Ink Painting 1	83.79%	4	5	+1
F	Ink Painting 2	74.50%	9	6	−3
G	Sketch 1	79.19%	5	7	+2
H	Sketch 2	76.59%	8	8	0
I	Sketch 3	77.64%	6	9	+3

3.2 Result Analysis

According to the different results of the two tables, the evaluation method of multimedia art teaching courseware playback effect based on data envelopment analysis effectively eliminated the effect of the difference in initial conditions. Different, the ranking of 8 teachers has changed, making the evaluation of teaching management evaluation more objective and persuasive. In the example, there are fewer input indicators and output indicators, so the teaching effect value evaluation system obtained is relatively simple. In actual applications, the input and output indicators can be increased accordingly to obtain more real and reliable data.

In order to further verify the effectiveness of the method in this paper, the evaluation accuracy of the proposed evaluation method of the playing effect of multimedia art teaching courseware based on DEA is compared and analyzed with that of the traditional

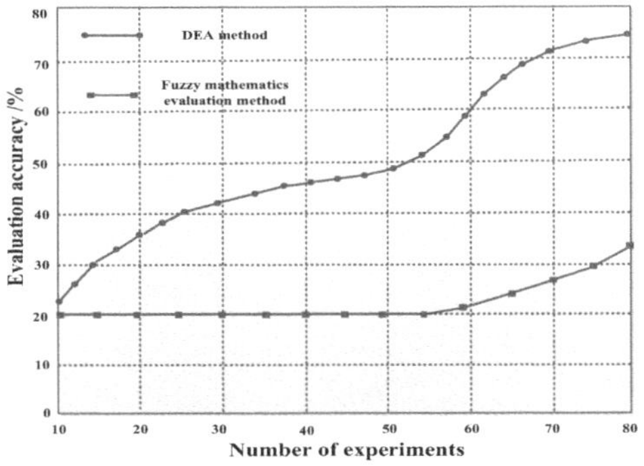

Fig. 2. Comparison results of evaluation accuracy

evaluation method of the playing effect of multimedia art teaching courseware based on fuzzy mathematics, and the comparison results are shown in Fig. 2.

As can be seen from Fig. 2, the evaluation accuracy of DEA based evaluation method is as high as 74%, while that of fuzzy mathematics based evaluation method is as high as 34%, indicating that the evaluation effect of this method is good.

4 Concluding Remarks

In view of the poor evaluation results of the traditional multimedia art teaching courseware, this paper puts forward the evaluation method based on data envelopment analysis. With the help of different evaluation subjects' visual perception of use, and with the help of the determination of comprehensive evaluation vector, the effect of courseware playing is evaluated one by one. Teaching evaluation is only a means, the purpose is for teachers to better improve the quality of teaching. Through the empirical analysis of the above example, this method can evaluate the teaching quality of each teacher more fairly and reasonably, and comprehensively consider the initial differences of students' scores before entering school. The teacher can also find the differences and analyze the reasons from them, which is conducive to the better development of teaching management activities, the improvement of the evaluation accuracy of multimedia art teaching courseware playback effect, and the multimedia teaching Learning provides a theoretical basis.

References

1. Weichao, L.: A probe into mathematics teaching model in secondary vocational schools based on microcourse learning. Vocat. Skills **19**(1), 78–81 (2020)
2. Luwei, C.: Practice and analysis of multimedia application in mental health education courses in colleges and Universities. Curriculum Educ. Res. **22**(4), 192 (2020)
3. Meiling, Z., Zhaozhao, L.: Discussion on the effectiveness of multidimensional and innovative mathematics teaching in colleges and Universities. Think Tank Age **34**(21), 188–189 (2019)
4. Yi, L., Yunlong, L., Chundong, Z., Shengyong, Y., Youquan, B.: Application of visual expression in biochemistry multimedia teaching. Basic Med. Educ. **21**(5), 395–397 (2019)
5. Hao, Y.: Application of multimedia technology in college assisted teaching in new period. Comput. Prod. Circ. **21**(7), 259 (2019)
6. Yuanyuan, L., Fangfang, L.: Measurement and Countermeasures of multi - media classroom teaching in colleges and Universities: a case study of Lv liang college. China Mod. Educ. Equip. **26**(13), 18–20 (2019)
7. Jie, H.: Research on quality standard system of multimedia courseware in higher vocational colleges. Contemp. Educ. Pract. Teach. Res. **45**(11), 17–18 (2019)
8. Shuting, J.: Application of multimedia in criminal law teaching. J. Anhui Univ. Technol. (Soc. Sci.) **36**(2), 84–86 (2019)
9. Yang, Z.: Research on design of multimedia assisted teaching system based on author - ware software. Autom. Technol. Appl. **38**(11), 54–57 (2019)
10. Chunwoo, L.: Discussion on multi - media application strategy of ideological and political theory course in colleges and Universities. J. Liaoning Univ. Technol. (Soc. Sci. Edn.) **21**(6), 126–129 (2019)

Design of Teaching Platform for Visual Programming of Industrial Robot Based on PBL and Multimedia

Peng Cheng(✉)

Chongqing Vocational College of Transportation, Chongqing 402247, China
xujnexujeng@163.com

Abstract. Aiming at the problem of poor load capacity in the traditional teaching platform of industrial robot visual programming, the teaching platform of industrial robot visual course based on PBL and multimedia is designed. This paper designs the teaching mode based on PBL mixed multimedia, realizes the communication of teaching data by using MVC framework, designs the authority management function of teaching platform according to the idea of unified authority management, considers the burden of multiple people on the platform at the same time, allocates reasonable transmission bandwidth for users, and completes the overall design of teaching platform. The experimental results show that: compared with the traditional teaching platform, the design of industrial robot visual teaching platform based on PBL and multimedia has stronger load capacity, and the platform is suitable for practical projects.

Keywords: Multimedia · Industrial robot · Visual programming · Teaching platform

1 Introduction

Industrial robot is a multi joint manipulator or multi degree of freedom machine device facing the industrial field. It can automatically perform work, and it is a kind of machine that realizes various functions by its own power and control ability [1]. It can accept the command of human beings or run according to the pre arranged program. Modern industrial robots can also act according to the principle program formulated by artificial intelligence technology [2]. With the development of information technology, industrial robots have been able to learn from the environment. Many problems in human life can be solved by industrial robots. Therefore, industrial robots have been widely used. Most of the development platforms for industrial robot applications are based on the text programming language to write the code, so as to achieve a variety of robot control [3]. Therefore, the study of visual programming for industrial robots is a trend that can not be ignored.

Modern educational technology plays an extremely important role in education. In recent years, the development of user learning puts forward higher requirements for the

S. Liu et al. (Eds.): eLEOT 2020, LNICST 339, pp. 76–87, 2020.
https://doi.org/10.1007/978-3-030-63952-5_7

design of teaching platform. With the rapid development of society, national education is becoming more and more popular and informative, and visual programming teaching platform plays an important role in the national education system [4]. In particular, the large-scale application of mobile Internet and mobile media technology provides support for the teaching environment that can be applied to mobile devices.

With the rapid development of network technology in the direction of cross belt, high-speed and multimedia, people pay more and more attention to the construction of corresponding curriculum resources, and the advantages of education resources are more and more important [5–7]. The authenticity of PBL design task, emphasizing and practicing learning with complex background and meaningful problem situation, solving problems through learners' independent exploration and cooperative learning, which is the hidden problem behind the formation of scientific knowledge, and improving students' ability of problem-solving and independent learning [8].

At the same time of using PBL teaching mode to change teaching, for the problem of poor platform load capacity in traditional visual programming teaching platform, in the design of industrial robot visual programming teaching platform based on PBL and multimedia, the remote transmission bandwidth is allocated to improve the load capacity of teaching platform.

2 Design of Visual Programming Teaching Platform for Industrial Robot

2.1 Design a Teaching Model Based on PBL and Multimedia

PBL teaching method is more advanced. It is a teaching mode based on problems, with students as the main body and in the form of group discussion. Combining PBL teaching mode with multimedia technology, the teaching platform of industrial robot visual programming based on PBL and multimedia is designed.

PBL teaching mode emphasizes problem-solving as the center. Compared with "experimental" learning methods and discovery learning methods, PBL believes that the integration of a wide range of subjects or topics should be the direction and focus of learning, more emphasis on the role of social team interaction and collective cooperation, and more emphasis on the support and guidance of teachers' strength.

Design multimedia courseware. Multimedia courseware is composed of text, pictures, tables, sound, video and other factors. The biggest feature of PBL teaching is that there is no need to present the teaching knowledge one by one. So PBL multimedia courseware should be streamlined. According to the case script prepared by the teacher, the content involved in each scene is made into a multimedia courseware with a unified template, making full use of the sound, image, animation, video and other functions brought by the multimedia technology. Difficult-to-understand materials such as examinations and treatment methods are made into easy-to-understand multimedia materials [9]. This process is by no means a list of text and auxiliary examinations. From a psychological perspective, students do not like a large amount of text accumulation. At this time, we will match the text with sound effects or animation effects to improve student attention and avoid students. Visual fatigue. Avoid lengthy video content, extract key content as much as possible, and control the time for about a minute. The multimedia courseware will be supplemented after the course feedback.

Combining multimedia courseware with PBL teaching mode, the basic teaching framework is as follows (Fig. 1).

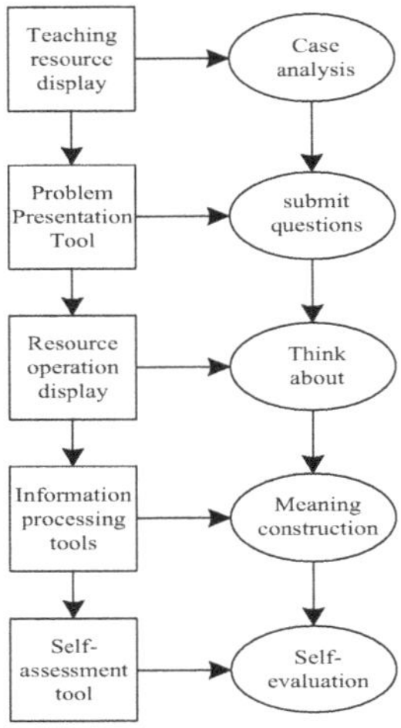

Fig. 1. Teaching framework of multimedia combined with PBL

The above teaching design is a process of optimizing teaching resources and teaching framework. It is a systematic planning process that uses systematic methods to analyze teaching problems, determine teaching objectives, establish problem-solving strategic plans, try out teaching applications, evaluate trial results and revise design plans. Because the main learners of network teaching are personalized learners, the significance of network teaching is mainly reflected in the design and development of network teaching resources.

The design of network teaching is based on a systematic approach and based on the relevant theories of learning and teaching. Through the analysis of teaching content and teaching objectives, it determines the teaching resource development model, the control method of teaching information, and the interaction between certain teaching situations And feedback methods, so as to provide learners with network resources for distance learning and provide some effective learning strategy selection methods [10].

The teaching design of the visual programming teaching platform for industrial robots is mainly to create and guarantee a good environment and learning conditions for network learning, which is conducive to the optimization of the network learning process. Teaching goals, teaching resources, teaching strategies, and teaching evaluation are the four basic elements of teaching design. Therefore, the teaching design of visual programming teaching platform must solve three main problems: clear "What do students want to learn?" Goal orientation; what kind of teaching resources and strategies should be provided to achieve certain learning objectives, that is, to solve the problems of resources and strategies; how to evaluate the learning effect of students?

2.2 Realization of Teaching Data Communication

The teaching platform interacts with the data according to the MVC framework and the specified communication format. The view organization submits the parameters in the specified format to the controller. After receiving the request, the controller parses the request and passes the parameters to the model. The model receives the parameters for data processing, The processing result is returned to the controller, which organizes the result into the specified data format and transmits it to the view to complete the data interaction.

The specific implementation of each module interaction of the platform is shown in Fig. 2. When users access code classification page or online integrated development environment through web browser, the request will be submitted to httpserver controller, which will directly return the corresponding web page file after receiving the request.

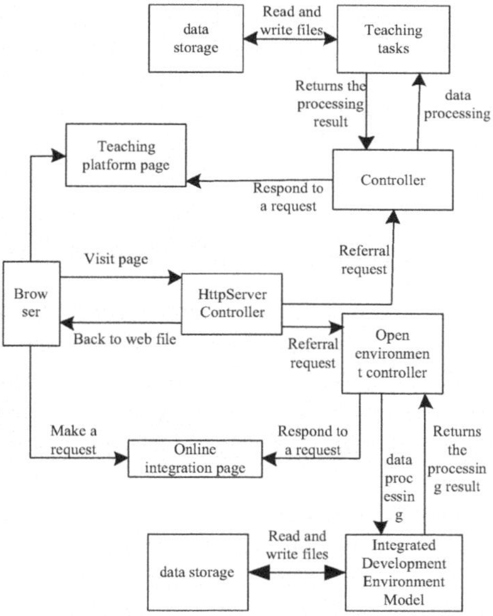

Fig. 2. Data interaction diagram

When the user submits the request in the teaching task page, the front-end script first organizes the request data into JSON format and submits the request to the httpserver controller through Ajax. After receiving the request, the controller parses the specific path and parameters of the request. It is found that the request is from the teaching task page, so the parsed parameters are transferred to the controller, After receiving the request information, the controller specifies a specific function for processing according to the specific request path, and passes parameters to the function. This function calls the corresponding model, here is the integrated development environment model. After the model receives the specific data, it calls the corresponding function. The module performs data processing and returns the processing result to the controller. The controller organizes the model's processing result into a specific json data format and returns it directly to the page. After the page script receives the returned result, the result is parsed and the corresponding fields are parsed. Display to the corresponding area.

When users submit code compilation, code running and other requests in the online integrated development environment page, the script organizes the data required by the request into the specified JSON data format, and submits the request to the httpserver controller through Ajax. After receiving the request, the httpserver controller parses the specific path and parameters of the request, and finds that it is the request of the integrated development environment controller. Therefore, after receiving the request data, the integrated development environment controller transfers the request. The integrated development environment controller calls the specified function according to the request path, and passes the request parameters to the function. The function calls the corresponding model. Here is the integrated development Development environment model. After the model receives the specific data, it calls the corresponding module for processing, and reads the processing result and returns it to the online integrated development environment controller. The controller receives the returned result of the model. The results are organized into a specified json data format and fed back to the online integrated development environment page. After receiving the results, the script parses the results in json format and reads the corresponding fields to the corresponding area for visual display.

2.3 Design of Authority Management Based on Unified Authority Management

It can be seen from the overall requirements of the platform that there is an intersection of users among different modules in the platform. At the same time, considering the future expansion of the platform, the authority management of user identity should at least meet the principle of global allocation. Therefore, in the authority management of the platform, the authority management is designed based on the idea of unified authority management.

The authority management design of the platform refers to role-based access control (Role Based Access Control, RBAC) programme, Design according to the actual situation. In the design of rights management, the relationship between users, user groups, roles, and permissions is shown in the following figure (Fig. 3).

In practical application platform, roles and user groups are usually one-to-one relationship. In this case, user groups can be regarded as roles.

The authority management of the teaching platform is relatively fixed, as long as the maintenance of the teaching platform and users with access rights can. However, the definition of the authority of functions and resources is quite variable, depending on the different business logic of the teaching platform, and the implementation method may also be different depending on the design of the teaching platform. If the authority of functions and resources is also entrusted to the unified user management, the unified user management must be modified with the addition of each new user, which will inevitably affect the stability of the unified user management. At the same time, the design of teaching platform is difficult to adapt to the authority of unified user management and maintenance functions and resources.

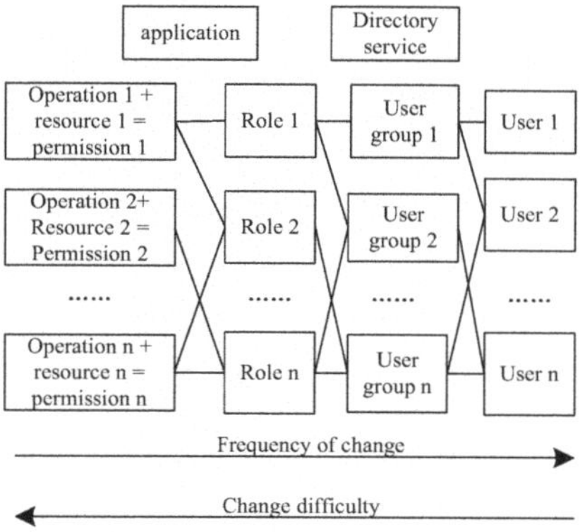

Fig. 3. Permission relationship

Therefore, functions and resource permissions and assignments between roles, roles and user groups are maintained by the application itself, while application access permissions and user group assignments are maintained by directory service management. The role permissions in the platform are divided into student roles, teacher roles, and administrator roles. The comparison of roles and permissions is shown in the following table (Table 1).

Table 1. Role permission cross reference table.

Authority	Root	Resource library				
		A1	A2	A3	A4	A5
Library	√	√	√	√	√	√
browsing	√	√	√	√	√	√
Upload	√		√			√
Download	√	√				√
Review	√			√		√
Maintain	√				√	√
Classification	√					√

In the table, A1 indicates the user, A2 indicates the uploader, A3 indicates the reviewer, A4 indicates the maintainer, and A5 indicates the administrator.

The authority management design based on unified authority management idea is shown in Fig. 4.

Through the above content to complete the design of authority management in the teaching platform of industrial robot visual programming. According to the above content, there are many users with different permissions, so the transmission bandwidth is allocated reasonably to ensure the normal operation of the platform.

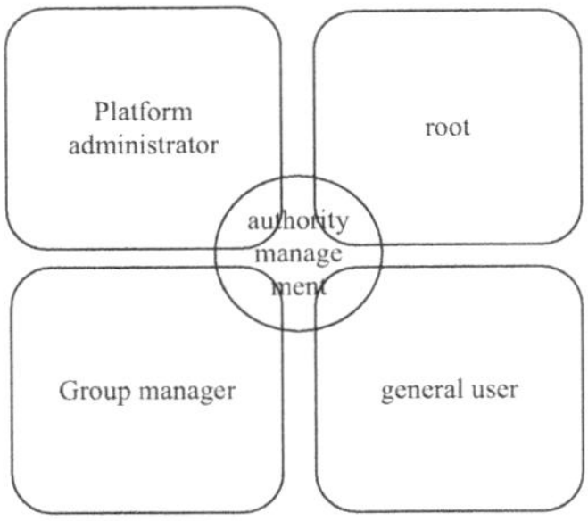

Fig. 4. Authority management design based on unified authority management idea

2.4 Allocate Remote Transmission Bandwidth

In order to ensure the quality of teaching, determine the priority of transmission rate, allocate the network bandwidth resources to the appropriate users.

Set Z_{ic} represents the n-th local user group in network s, The users of the local user group are registered users. For the terminals that users access the system, the transmission priority is determined by the decision factors of different teaching tasks. A matrix of $u \times u$ is formed by comparing the priority decision factors

$$U = \begin{bmatrix} a_{11} & a_{12} & \cdots & a_{1u} \\ a_{21} & a_{22} & \cdots & a_{2u} \\ \cdots & \cdots & \cdots & \cdots \\ a_{u1} & a_{u} & \cdots & a_{uu} \end{bmatrix} \tag{1}$$

Formula: a if Represents different decision factors. The weight vector of each decision factor is $\lambda = [\lambda_1, \lambda_2, \cdots, \lambda_m]$, Is the eigenvector corresponding to the maximum eigenvalue of matrix U, According to this vector, the weighted value of decision factors can be obtained。Each decision-making factor in the platform is compared with each other according to the degree of influence on the teaching task, and the weighted value of the decision-making factor is obtained. According to the weighted value, the transmission rate priority is judged, and the priority decision rules are formed. Based on this, the network bandwidth resources are allocated to different user terminals.

The optimal bandwidth allocation matrix is:

$$X = \frac{Z_{ic}(r, v)}{s(r, v)} \tag{2}$$

In the formula: r represents the user terminal, v represents the network transmission rate, and $s(r, v)$ represents the spectral efficiency of the c th bandwidth resource in the network s to the user terminal z of the teaching service.

Due to the limited bandwidth resources and platform resource capacity constraints, the optimal broadband allocation matrix is constrained by certain conditions. The constraints of the bandwidth allocation matrix are:

$$X_{\min} \leq \sum_{c=1}^{C} \sum_{i=1}^{I} X \leq X_{\max} \quad (3)$$

In the formula: $X_{\min}$ and $X_{\max}$ represent the actual maximum and minimum bandwidth resources of the user terminal supporting the teaching task. The requirements of the actual teaching task are met by the above constraints. So far, the design of visual programming teaching platform for industrial robots based on PBL and multimedia has been completed.

3 Research on the Teaching Platform of Industrial Robot Visual Programming

In the process of experimental research of visual programming teaching platform for industrial robots, the traditional teaching platform is used to measure the load capacity of the platform. A comparative experiment is designed and the actual load capacity of the teaching platform is analyzed according to the experimental results.

3.1 Experimental Environment Configuration

The visual teaching platform of industrial robot based on PBL and multimedia is studied to ensure the smooth and reliable operation of the platform. First, configure java web framework. Java web configuration uses XML file to publish information and generate web.xml file, which is saved under directory inf. The web.xml file configures the necessary information for the program to run, including the initialization of servlet parameters, the corresponding mapping of JSP files, the configuration of security domain parameters, environment variables, etc. Complete the deployment of the descriptor XML file, declare the XML version used, and make new rules for the character encoding of the file.

In addition to configuring the struts development framework, the core function of the struts.xml file is to manage the business controller. Under normal circumstances, the system has a default state. In the Inf directory, the specified struts.xml file is automatically loaded and executed by the Struts2 framework. In this way, the Struts2 framework provides a modular way to manage and configure the above files. Using an open source framework to operate the database, JDBC is lightweightly packaged, making it easier to operate on different platforms in the platform. The relevant content of its configuration file is shown below (Fig. 5).

The figure shows the mapping and connection of the database in the xml file. Through the above configuration, the database and other functions of the industrial robot visual programming teaching platform can be operated.

```
<GlobalNamingResources>
  <Resource name="UserDatabase" auth="Container"
            type="org.apache.catalina.UserDatabase"
            description="User database that can be updated and saved"
            factory="org.apache.catalina.users.MemoryUserDatabaseFactory"
            pathname="conf/tomcat-users.xml" />
</GlobalNamingResources>

<Service name="Catalina">
  <Connector port="8080" protocol="HTTP/1.1"
             connectionTimeout="20000"
             redirectPort="8443" />
  <Connector port="8009" protocol="AJP/1.3" redirectPort="8443" />
  <Engine name="Catalina" defaultHost="localhost">
    <Realm className="org.apache.catalina.realm.LockOutRealm">
      <Realm className="org.apache.catalina.realm.UserDatabaseRealm"
             resourceName="UserDatabase"/>
    </Realm>

    <Host name="localhost"  appBase="webapps"
          unpackWARs="true" autoDeploy="true">
      <Valve className="org.apache.catalina.valves.AccessLogValve" directory="logs"
             prefix="localhost_access_log." suffix=".txt"
             pattern="%h %l %u %t &quot;%r&quot; %s %b" />
    </Host>
  </Engine>
 </Service>
</Server>
```

Fig. 5. Configuration file content

3.2 Platform Load Capacity Test

Based on the above configuration, verify the load capacity of different industrial robot visual programming teaching platforms. Record the experimental results of the traditional Spark-based programming teaching platform as experimental result 1, the experimental results of the teaching mode-based programming teaching platform as the experimental result 2, and the experimental results of the industrial robot visual programming teaching platform based on PBL and multimedia as the experimental results 3. The results of experiments using third-party software statistics are shown below (Fig. 6).

Observe the results in the figure, from the whole of the three experimental results, when the number of virtual online people is the most, the network delay belongs to the normal range, but the highest network speed and the lowest network speed, the experimental results of the three groups are the best. According to the results of Experiment 1, the highest network delay is 209 ms, the highest network speed is 6.37 mb/s and the lowest network speed is 0.63 mb/s when the number of virtual online users is the same; the highest network delay is 424 ms, the highest network speed is 9.04 mb/s and the lowest network speed is 2.97 mb/s in Experiment 2; the highest network delay is 49 mb/s in Experiment 3 ms, the maximum network speed is 10.43 mb/s, and the minimum network speed is 5.11 mb/s.

In conclusion, compared with the other two teaching platforms, the designed teaching platform based on PBL and multimedia for visual programming of industrial robots has the lowest network delay and high network speed, which shows that the load capacity of the designed teaching platform is significantly better than the traditional teaching platform.

Number	Number of virtual online	Network delay	Internet speed (H)	Internet speed (L)
1	25	23	5.36MB/s	2.54MB/s
2	36	34	6.37MB/s	3.07MB/s
3	494	45	6.36MB/s	3.47MB/s
4	57	78	4.24MB/s	1.55MB/s
5	74	79	3.24MB/s	1.69MB/s
6	83	84	4.69MB/s	2.22MB/s
7	92	67	4.41MB/s	2.13MB/s
8	117	105	4.24MB/s	2.47MB/s
9	146	140	4.50MB/s	2.04MB/s
10	153	117	3.21MB/s	1.52MB/s
11	168	136	3.26MB/s	1.44MB/s
12	177	147	4.01MB/s	2.07MB/s
13	189	125	4.22MB/s	2.06MB/s
14	206	157	3.17MB/s	1.04MB/s
15	224	169	3.06MB/s	1.59MB/s
16	256	201	2.54MB/s	0.97MB/s
17	271	204	2.56MB/s	0.63MB/s
18	289	183	2.59MB/s	0.88MB/s
19	304	179	1.98MB/s	0.74MB/s
20	322	208	2.68MB/s	0.96MB/s
21	358	209	2.93MB/s	1.05MB/s
22	390	186	1.74MB/s	0.86MB/s

(a) Experimental results 1

Number	Number of virtual online	Network delay	Internet speed (H)	Internet speed (L)
1	25	45	8.45MB/s	5.24MB/s
2	36	64	6.21MB/s	4.32MB/s
3	494	54	7.45MB/s	3.64MB/s
4	57	156	6.00MB/s	4.69MB/s
5	74	424	5.44MB/s	3.04MB/s
6	83	87	8.21MB/s	6.22MB/s
7	92	123	7.24MB/s	5.69MB/s
8	117	79	5.45MB/s	2.98MB/s
9	146	45	6.33MB/s	3.54MB/s
10	153	55	7.21MB/s	3.87MB/s
11	168	98	9.04MB/s	6.13MB/s
12	177	64	6.44MB/s	4.25MB/s
13	189	23	7.11MB/s	4.63MB/s
14	206	78	8.00MB/s	5.74MB/s
15	224	166	7.25MB/s	5.41MB/s
16	256	165	6.39MB/s	4.01MB/s
17	271	87	7.45MB/s	3.74MB/s
18	289	31	7.62MB/s	4.65MB/s
19	304	48	7.33MB/s	3.55MB/s
20	322	78	6.57MB/s	3.74MB/s
21	358	154	5.87MB/s	4.21MB/s
22	390	167	6.09MB/s	2.97MB/s

(b) Experimental results 2

Fig. 6. Load capacity test results of different platforms

Number	Number of virtual online	Network delay	Internet speed (H)	Internet speed (L)
1	25	11	9.45MB/s	6.93MB/s
2	36	15	9.50MB/s	5.56MB/s
3	494	9	9.47MB/s	5.79MB/s
4	57	13	8.66MB/s	6.54MB/s
5	74	21	10.43MB/s	7.01MB/s
6	83	7	7.54MB/s	5.32MB/s
7	92	19	9.51MB/s	6.44MB/s
8	117	16	7.21MB/s	5.21MB/s
9	146	21	8.65MB/s	5.32MB/s
10	153	18	8.34MB/s	5,88MB/s
11	168	22	9.55MB/s	6.13MB/s
12	177	24	8.99MB/s	6.10MB/s
13	189	25	7.57MB/s	6.51MB/s
14	206	19	7.43MB/s	5.06MB/s
15	224	31	8.59MB/s	6.07MB/s
16	256	27	7.61MB/s	5.08MB/s
17	271	44	8.61MB/s	6.19MB/s
18	289	49	7.62MB/s	5.11MB/s
19	304	37	8.66MB/s	6.01MB/s
20	322	39	9.64MB/s	6.26MB/s
21	358	28	8.11MB/s	6.13MB/s
22	390	47	7.23MB/s	5.14MB/s

(c) **Experimental result 3**

Fig. 6. *(continued)*

4 Concluding Remarks

Visual programming teaching platform, as a form of modern teaching technology, has changed traditional teaching concepts, combined with modern technology, promoted the development of teaching to information technology, and implemented standardized and efficient teaching tasks. Design a visual programming teaching platform for industrial robots based on PBL and multimedia, and design a comparative experiment for the problems existing in traditional teaching platforms. The experimental results prove that the visual teaching platform for industrial robots based on PBL and multimedia can effectively solve the traditional teaching platform In the existing problems, its load capacity has been significantly improved.

References

1. Xi, Z.J., Wang, C., Zheng, B.: Reform and practice of PBL teaching method in pathogenic biology and immunology. Chin. J. Immunol. **35**(17), 2147–2149 + 2155 (2019)
2. Zhu, Y.M., Yang, L.P.: Application and discussion of problem based learning in the course of epidemiological experiment. Mod. Prev. Med. **46**(11), 2108–2112 (2019)
3. Zhang, C.Y., Wu, Q.F., Jiang, J.H., et al.: Design and implementation of double angle sensors of industrial robot measurement system based on STM32. Mach. Tool Hydraul. **47**(11), 24–28 (2019)

4. Li, N., Zhang, S.Y.: Teaching and training platform for virtual equipment of replenishment based on Web3D. J. Syst. Simul. **31**(06), 1136–1141 (2019)
5. Wu, J.L., Shang, S.S.: Factors affecting the use of MOOCs based on tacit knowledge and explicit knowledge learning. J. Manage. Sci. China **22**(03), 21–39 (2019)
6. Zheng, H.Y., Zhou, Y.P., Huang, Y.: Application of digital human platform in flipped class model for the teaching of human anatomy. Chin. J. Anat. **42**(01), 93–94 (2019)
7. Zhang, L., Zhang, R.Y., Ma, L., et al.: Effectiveness of learning with mobile "100-day Training" APP among general practitioners in Beijing: an empirical study. Chin. Gen. Pract. **22**(19), 2374–2379 (2019)
8. Li, H.Y., Ye, D.P., Qiu, R.B., et al.: Construction and exploration of mobile robot cooperative experimental platform in "Mechatronics" course. Mod. Electron. Tech. **42**(15), 150–153 + 156 (2019)
9. Sha, Y., Li, Q.P., Li, Y.: Development and design in computer simulation experiment teaching of fluid mechanics. J. Exp. Mech. **33**(04), 655–664 (2018)
10. Lin, X.H., Lin, D.H., Zhong, L.: An empirical study on the teaching path of meta literacy in the blended teaching model. Libr. Inf. Serv. **62**(23), 65–71 (2018)

Construction of Network Course System of Construction Machinery Specialty Based on Cloud Class

Xu You-jun(✉)

College of Rail Transit, Nanjing Vocational Institute of Transport Technology, Nanjing 211188, China
xuyoujun788522@163.com

Abstract. At present, the learning module of online courses for engineering machinery majors is chaotic and data storage is not timely, which leads to the defect of low knowledge conversion rate in online courses. Aiming at this problem, a new network course system for engineering machinery specialty based on cloud class is designed. Based on modular curriculum structure, level of course phase steps and coordinated network curriculum development process design process, and on this basis, from the perspective of learners, design a cloud platform network curriculum content, making learning modules, design of the real-time database storage system, strengthen network curriculum knowledge conversion, finally realizes the operation of the network curriculum system, major in engineering or mechanism. The experimental results show that: compared with the traditional three kinds of network course system for engineering machinery, the network course system for engineering machinery designed in this paper has greatly improved the knowledge conversion rate, which fully shows that the network course system for engineering machinery has better application performance.

Keywords: Cloud class · Construction machinery · Network · Courses

1 Introduction

In the modern society of informationization, great changes are taking place in every aspect. Under the background of the development of computer technology, network technology and modern education theory, education is gradually showing the characteristics of digitalization and networking. As an information-based education model, web-based course has become an important aspect in the field of educational technology, and it has gradually become an effective form of lifelong learning. The network course breaks the traditional mode of listening in the classroom in the past, and is more beneficial to the learners to study. It not only provides abundant learning resources, but also enables the learners to get rid of the limitation of time and place, and can arrange the study autonomously according to time in the study. On the other hand, from the teacher's point of view, the environment of the network course can provide the teachers with a free

S. Liu et al. (Eds.): eLEOT 2020, LNICST 339, pp. 88–98, 2020.
https://doi.org/10.1007/978-3-030-63952-5_8

and up-to-date teaching platform. The network course system can also help the teachers to track the students' learning progress and degree of mastery in the teaching activities, and provide corresponding technical force support for the teachers. Through this system, the teachers can monitor the whole process of the students' learning to make the best response [1].

Engineering Machinery is an applied subject that studies and solves all the theoretical and practical problems in the development, design, manufacture, installation, application and repair of various machines. This major prepares students to master the basic knowledge and application of mechanical design, manufacturing, electromechanical engineering and automation. It prepares students to engage in the research, design, manufacturing, control and programming of various machinery, electromechanical products and systems, equipment and devices, the development of numerical control equipment, computer aided programming, the design, manufacture, development and application research of advanced technical products and systems such as industrial robots and precision electromechanical devices, intelligent machinery, micromachinery and power machinery, as well as senior engineers and technicians engaged in technical management in scientific research institutes, enterprises, and advanced technology companies. The educational results of engineering machinery professional courses play a vital role in national development [2].

According to the existing research results, there are three widely used systems: Moodle based network course system, Cloud based network course system and UCD based network course system. The above three systems have the defect of low knowledge conversion rate. Therefore, this paper puts forward the construction of engineering machinery specialty network course system based on cloud class. Cloud class is a new teaching mode. Cloud class refers to the teaching form that teachers prepare lessons, classroom teacher-student interaction, assignment and other steps are concentrated on the cloud service platform. Cloud classes as the basis for the construction of engineering machinery professional network course system, for the construction machinery professional training to provide more powerful support.

2 Network Course System for Engineering Machinery Specialty

2.1 Network Course Process Design

Process refers to a series of actions which are purposeful, repetitive and stylized, and which rationalize, transparent and consensus tasks in a series of forms. Cloud class is a new teaching mode. Therefore, the first step is to use the design process of cloud class to replace the single course design process of teachers in traditional one-off course design. After summing up, the design of network course flow of engineering machinery specialty is divided into three steps, which are modular course organization, hierarchical course stage and collaborative course development [3].

Among them, modular curriculum organization refers to the course development process based on the characteristics of cloud class, which is divided into curriculum planning period, curriculum production period and curriculum operation period. Each module is listed in the work of the module tasks, as well as the completion of the task required to do the course preparation, so that teachers can more clearly understand the process of curriculum production, as shown below (Fig. 1).

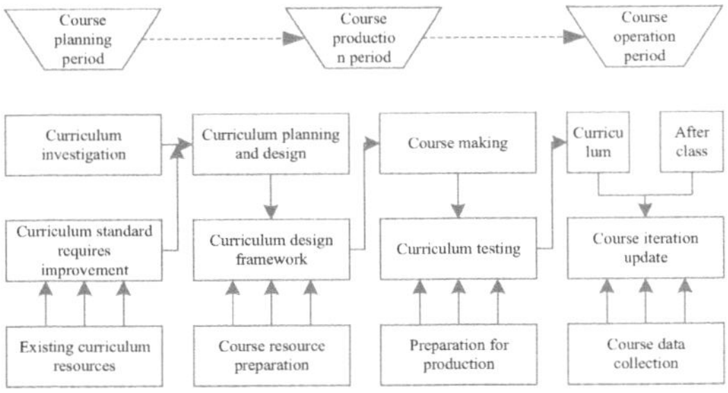

Fig. 1. Organizational Structure of Modular Courses

After the modular design of the organizational structure of the web-based courses, the specific steps of each module need to be further clarified. Therefore, the development design of each stage of the course needs to be broken down into multiple steps and the tasks required for the course development need to be understood more clearly [4].

Based on the "Five in One" theory, the schematic diagram of the "Five in One" theory is shown in the following figure.

As shown in Fig. 2, the five design elements of people, action, purpose, scene and media fully embody the ideological connotation of the theory of "Five in One". Applying the viewpoint of "Five Elements of Design" to Network Course Planning, this paper points out that the five elements of learning crowd, learning scene, learning content, learning aim and learning form should be defined. Students majoring in construction machinery need to be involved in the determination of these five points. Students majoring in construction machinery need to propose their expected learning contents, learning scenes, learning forms and learning purposes.

Based on the learner's curriculum expectation and curriculum indicators, the final curriculum design framework is established, including curriculum content design framework and user experience framework. The curriculum content framework includes the curriculum chapter catalogue, the curriculum innovation spot, the curriculum heavy difficulty analysis, the curriculum examination standard four points, the user experience framework includes the curriculum experience system, the curriculum interaction system, the curriculum feedback system three points, as shown in the following figure (Fig. 3).

The collaborative curriculum development process needs to be implemented in various steps. For example, when the user groups of the courses are investigated, the characteristics of the major learning groups will be displayed according to the collected data, and then the user portrait will be made. When the volunteers recruited for the courses are subsequently to participate in the curriculum content design and course experiment, the major learning groups will be recruited according to the user portrait of the initial major learning groups; according to the learning objectives and learning methods of the pre-curriculum design, the learning methods will be determined based on the

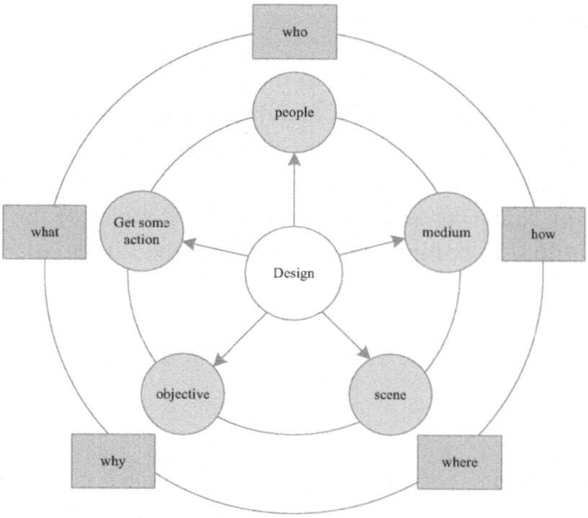

Fig. 2. Schematic diagram of "Five in One" theory

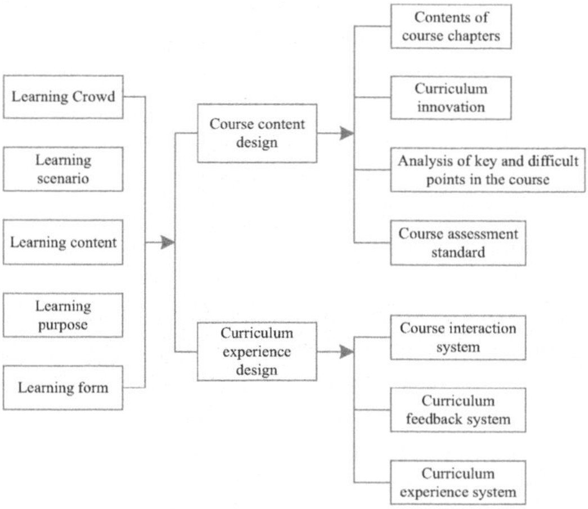

Fig. 3. Level of Course Stage Steps

platform for the course opening and the design of the courses, and the investigation on the platform for the course opening and the teaching methods of the same type of the courses in the pre-curriculum design and feedback system; in the course experience design and feedback system, various teaching services will be provided according to the network platform, which will greatly help the design of the course content and services in the future. Therefore, in the process of curriculum design, establishing the relational structure of the curriculum, we can find the real needs of students, and then update the curriculum content [5].

2.2 Network Course Content Design

From the angle of the learner, the content of the network course of engineering machinery specialty needs to add the learner's goal demand and content demand to the existing teaching index and course content. Content design is divided into three steps, respectively, 1) to determine the learning population; 2) to obtain the content of user needs; 3) integration of teaching materials and user needs. The content of the three steps and the tools or methods required to complete them are described in detail below [6].

Determining the study crowd only needs to locate the university in the construction machinery specialized student, the step is simpler, does not do excessively elaborates.

Methods for obtaining user course content requirements are shown in the following table (Table 1).

Table 1. Method of acquiring user course content requirements

Method	Brief introduction	Access way
Diary research	By recording the user's behaviors and ideas in daily life, this paper summarizes the user's background, lifestyle, interests, habits and other characteristics	Notes, email, platform message board, social media, etc
survey by question naire	Through the design of relevant issues about the research content, users can receive quantitative or qualitative data collection methods	Questionnaire distribution and recovery
User interviews	User interview can intuitively and deeply understand the needs of learners for course content	Direct conversation for information
Card sorting	Participants were invited to write down their understanding of the content on the cards printed with the relevant links or objects of the product, and organize and classify the cards	Card issuance and recovery
QFD method	QFD method can transform user requirements into design requirements, calculate key design requirements and optimize resource allocation	Card analysis

Integrating the content of textbook and the content of users' needs, we first select the real needs of most of the users' feedback, and then select the content needs of the network course syllabus for the specialty of construction machinery again, then add these user needs into the course design plan, integrate the course content and user needs, and design a testable prototype of the course. Then the feasibility of the course prototype is tested and the learners are invited to experiment to verify whether it meets their real needs [7]. Finally, according to the results of the test on the course iterative design, the design of a sound engineering machinery professional network courses.

2.3 Learning Module Design

According to the teaching demand of engineering machinery major, the learning module of web-based learning course is divided into seven modules: teaching item, teaching design, exercise question 1, exercise question 2, assignment, interactive evaluation and learning experience. According to the engineering machinery specialized teaching information design carries on the overall contact surface the design work, its concrete content including the character, the color, the contact surface [8].

In order to make the teaching content more vivid and vivid, the author joins the module of teachers' teaching video and tries to increase the diversity of the learning content. Cloud classes can be directly through the upload control to add video modules, and through the PHP code settings can be uploaded locally to control the video size of about 1 GB, which greatly relaxed the teachers upload video space restrictions. The educational effect of video is more intuitive and deeper for students, so this function is particularly important.

In addition, the interactive evaluation sub-module is also crucial. Interactive evaluation includes two kinds, one is the mutual evaluation between students, the other is the teacher evaluation, cloud class evaluation function, voting function is very effective. One of the motives of continuous learning is to arouse students' enthusiasm for learning by evaluating the learning results. The evaluation indicators within the evaluation function are not invariable, on the contrary, corresponding adjustments may be made according to the needs of the actual situation, and the evaluation results shall be reflected and counted immediately, so as to enable teachers to control the situation of students and obtain first-hand learning feedback in the shortest time. The evaluation covers a wide range of fields, including teachers, students and students. The evaluation covers a wide range [9].

The teaching evaluation system is shown in the table below (Table 2).

Table 2. Teaching Evaluation System

Essential factor	Achievement		Weight
	Yes	No	
Essential factor 1	–	–	1
Essential factor 2	–	–	1
Essential factor 3	–	–	1
Essential factor 4	–	–	2

2.4 Database Design

Database is the key module of the network course system of engineering machinery specialty. Its main function is to store and save the task information, course information and course content information.

The task information is shown in the following table (Tables 3, 4, and 5).

Table 3. Task information

Field name	Data type	Length	Key
Task ID	Unique identifier type	–	Primary key
Task category	Character	10	no
Task title	Character	50	no
Course ID	Character	10	Foreign key
Node ID	Character	10	Foreign key
Release time	Time type	–	no
Deadline	Time type	–	no
Task content	Character	2000	no
Task score weight	Character	2	no
Associated task ID	Character	10	Foreign
Associated topic ID	Character	10	Foreign

Table 4. Course Information

Field name	Data type	Length	Key
Course ID	Unique identifier type	–	Primary key
Course category	Character	10	no
Course title	Character	50	no
Teacher ID	Character	6	Foreign key
Assistant ID	Character	60	Foreign key
Release time	Date type	–	no
Opening hours	Date type	–	no
End time	Date type	–	no
Course introduction	Character	2000	no
Home page recommendation or not	Boolean type	–	no
Course status	Boolean type	–	no
credit	Character	2	no
Key word	Character	50	no

Table 5. Course Content Information

Field name	Data type	Length	Key
Content ID	Unique identifier type	–	Primary key
Task ID	Character	10	Foreign key
Content category	Character	10	no
Content headings	Character	50	no
Content information	The binary type	–	no
Node ID	Character	10	Foreign key
Release time	Time type	–	no
Effective time	Time type	–	no
Number of visits	Character	10	no
Whether to associate scores	Boolean type	–	no
Task score weight	Character	3	no

Through the above process, the construction and operation of the network course system of construction machinery specialty is completed, which provides a new form for the training of construction machinery professionals [10].

Through the above process, the construction and operation of the network course system for construction machinery speciality have been completed, providing a new form for the training of construction machinery speciality.

3 System Testing and Effectiveness Analysis

3.1 System Performance Testing

The system performance test mainly carries on the comprehensive examination diagnosis to the construction machinery specialized network curriculum system based on the cloud class class class, the test goal is as follows:

One is to find out and correct the system problems as far as possible, find and solve the system loopholes. Enable the system to run effectively for a long time to prevent the occurrence of predictable security problems;

Second, check whether each functional module meets the basic requirements for ensuring the smooth operation of the system, whether the functional realization is complete, and put forward opinions on modifying and adding new functions according to the test;

Third, whether the system's performance meets the initial requirements, whether the basic user experience to meet the requirements;

Fourth, the requirements of data integrity and consistency, correctness of form verification, link accessibility, cloud class setting and normal interaction of interface.

The login test table is shown below (Table 6).

Table 6. Login Test Sheet

Function	Test point	Test result
Sign in	Registered account, correct password	Successful login
	Registered account, wrong password	Display error
	Log in with an unregistered account	Display error
Cancellation	Interface prompted to return after background management logout	yes
	Only partially refresh the login module after learning the relevant page to log out	yes
Other	Whether the user successfully logs in to the corresponding interface	yes
	Use back and refresh after successful login. Do you want to keep login	yes
	Whether keyboard control login is supported	yes
	Use verification code for login	nothing

Cloud class interface test, the test home page is shown below (Fig. 4).

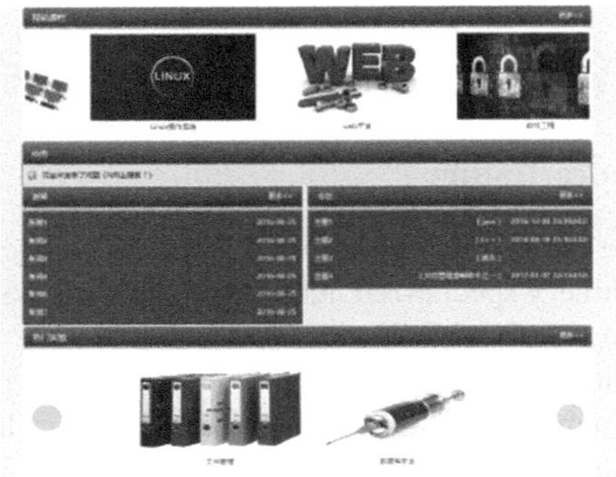

Fig. 4. Schematic diagram of the test main page

Through the test results, we can see that the network course system of construction machinery specialty is feasible and can be carried out smoothly.

3.2 Selection of Experimental Indicators

Students will be graded for each of the four phases of the course. In each stage of the performance scoring, teachers will be each student's work were four indicators of scoring, scoring standards for the full 10 points, the lowest 0 points, 1–3 points for the poor, 4–6 points for good, 7–10 points for each stage of the student performance data statistical analysis.

Knowledge conversion rate refers to the degree of effectiveness of online courses. The formula is

$$\zeta = \frac{\sum_{i=1}^{4} t_i}{n} * \delta \tag{1}$$

Among them,ζ represents knowledge conversion;t_i represents the scoring value for each stage;δ indicate the score t test results.

3.3 Analysis of Experimental Results

The performance of the system is demonstrated by the conversion rate of knowledge, which is compared with the existing Moodle-based, Cloud based and UCD based Engineering Machinery Specialty Network Course.

The knowledge conversion ratio obtained from the experiment is shown in the following table.

As shown in Table 7, the knowledge transfer rate of the design system is much higher than that of the existing three systems, with a maximum of 92%.

Table 7. Comparison of Knowledge Conversion/%

	System based on cloud class	Moodle based system	System based on cloud platform	UCD based system
10	89	65	45	46
20	80	61	43	44
30	87	59	40	51
40	86	55	49	48
50	90	66	48	52
60	91	67	48	60
70	91	68	52	54
80	92	60	51	51
90	90	77	56	42
100	89	54	49	44

According to the experimental results, compared with the existing three systems, the designed system greatly improves the knowledge conversion rate, and has better performance.

4 Closing Remarks

This paper puts forward a new network course system for engineering machinery specialty aiming at the common defects of traditional network course learning. Into cloud class class technology, based on the modular curriculum structure, level of course phase steps and co-ordinated network curriculum development process design process, and on this basis, the design of a cloud platform network curriculum content, making learning modules, strengthen network curriculum knowledge conversion, real-time database system is designed, finally realizes the operation of the network curriculum system, major in engineering or mechanism. The experiment verifies that the system designed in this paper has greatly improved the knowledge conversion rate and has better teaching effect. However, due to the small amount of experimental data, the experimental conclusions still need to be verified. Therefore, further optimization of the design system is needed in future studies.

Fund Project. Research Project on the Modern Education Technology of Jiangsu Province (Project No.: 2019-R-74828).

References

1. Sorrentino, F.S., Matteini, S., Bonifazzi, C., et al.: Diabetic retinopathy and endothelin system: microangiopathy versus endothelial dysfunction. Eye (Lond). **32**(7), 1157–1163 (2018)
2. Alcantara, J., Nazarenko, A.L., Ohm, J., et al.: The use of the patient reported outcomes measurement information system and the RAND VSQ9 to measure the quality of life and visit-specific satisfaction of pregnant patients under chiropractic care utilizing the webster technique. J. Altern. Complement. Med. **24**(1), 90–98 (2018)
3. Rachel, B., Will, W., Susan, R.: T63 towards a comprehensive semantic memory netliminary results using magnetoencephalography (MEG) in schizotypy. Schizophr. Bull. **44**(suppl_1), S138–S139 (2018)
4. Frederico, N.L., Eduardo, S.H., Humberto, A.J.: A blended learning method applied in data communication and computer networks subject. IEEE Latin Am. Trans. **16**(1), 163–171 (2018)
5. Mu, D., Wang, G., Fan, Y., et al.: Study on course keeping of POD propulsion unmanned surface vessel. J. Harbin Eng. Univ. **39**(2), 274–281 (2018)
6. Zhang, X.S., et al.: Antibiotic-induced acceleration of type 1 diabetes alters maturation of innate intestinal immunity. Elife **7**(e37816), 1–37 (2018)
7. Wang, R., Jiang, B., Liu, J.: Fault estimation and accommodation for a class of nonlinear system based on neural network observer. Trans. Nanjing Univ. Aeronaut. Astronaut. **35**(2), 318–325 (2018)
8. Mangalathu, S., Heo, G., Jeon, J.S.: Artificial neural network based multi-dimensional fragility development of skewed concrete bridge classes. Eng. Struct. **162**(1), 166–176 (2018)
9. Sheroug, A.A., Zeinab, A.M., Banazier, A.A.: Brain tumor classification using principal component analysis and artificial neural network. J. Clin. Eng. **44**(2), 70–75 (2019)
10. Cimellaro, G.P., Marasco, S., Noori, A.Z., Mahin, S.A.: A first order evaluation of the capacity of a healthcare network under emergency. Earthq. Eng. Eng. Vibr. **18**(3), 663–677 (2019). https://doi.org/10.1007/s11803-019-0528-3

Research on Innovation and Entrepreneurship Education Model of Higher Vocational Colleges Based on Internet Perspective

You-jun Xu(✉)

College of Rail Transit, Nanjing Vocational Institute of Transport Technology, Nanjing 211188, China
xuyoujun788522@163.com

Abstract. Under the Internet environment, higher vocational students will face more opportunities and challenges, and the Internet as a big platform will bring more information resources integration and funding sources, which is an important feature of the Internet environment to the era of innovation and entrepreneurship, especially the government policy support and social environment to encourage entrepreneurship and innovation to provide more help for higher vocational college students' innovation and entrepreneurship. Innovation and entrepreneurship education is an important direction of China's vocational education reform and development. This paper expounds the influence of Internet on innovation and entrepreneurship education, probes into the problems existing in the current innovation and entrepreneurship education mode, and advances some reform ideas and ways. Based on the practice of innovation and entrepreneurship education mode reform in a vocational and technical college, this paper introduces the curriculum system of innovation and entrepreneurship education, the cooperation of innovation and entrepreneurship training and the innovation and entrepreneurship competition of students, and puts forward some suggestions on further improving the quality of talent training in innovation and entrepreneurship education.

Keywords: Internet + · Higher vocational colleges · Innovation and entrepreneurship · Education model

1 Introduction

Compared with the undergraduate vocational college students, vocational college students have no advantages in their own quality, innovation and entrepreneurship ability, campus platform and access to funds [1]. Although there are many opportunities for innovation and entrepreneurship of higher vocational students in the current Internet environment, it is also necessary to face various challenges. How to effectively use the Internet innovation and entrepreneurship dividends and overcome various difficulties to achieve their own transformation and growth is a topic worthy of study [2]. For higher vocational colleges, the Internet should be effectively integrated with education,

S. Liu et al. (Eds.): eLEOT 2020, LNICST 339, pp. 99–112, 2020.
https://doi.org/10.1007/978-3-030-63952-5_9

with the help of the Internet to reform the innovation and entrepreneurship education model, combined with the characteristics of vocational students to cultivate innovative and entrepreneurial talents to adapt to the development of the Internet age. However, from a practical point of view, the current situation of innovation and entrepreneurship education in higher vocational colleges is not objective, there are still some problems. Therefore, it is pointed out in the paper that innovation and entrepreneurship education in higher vocational colleges should be reformed according to the actual needs of students and the social needs. In the social context of Internet plus, higher vocational colleges should also combine the characteristics of the times and social background to implement innovation and entrepreneurship education reform. Therefore, based on the Internet the background of innovation and entrepreneurship education mode in higher vocational colleges to explore.

2 Innovation and Entrepreneurship Education Model in Higher Vocational Colleges

2.1 Investigation on the Teaching of Innovation and Entrepreneurship

At present, the concept of innovation and entrepreneurship has been deeply rooted in the hearts of the people, so most of the higher vocational colleges are actively promoting innovation and entrepreneurship education. In the training of talents in higher vocational colleges, it is necessary to set up the relevant teaching mode according to the goal of talents training and the orientation of talents, but some of the higher vocational colleges do not set up the course of innovation and entrepreneurship according to the goal of talents training of their own, the orientation of the course of innovation and entrepreneurship is vague, which leads to less class hours of the course of innovation and entrepreneurship, and the lack of effective practical education system. In the process of teaching and practice, teachers explain more, less interaction between teachers and students. More case education and less experience of substitution. More lectures, less participation in practice; Popularization of education, less personalized training.

In addition, in the process of innovation and entrepreneurship education, the development of innovation and entrepreneurship education is slower because of the downward trend of economic development in recent years and the low success rate of students in higher vocational colleges [3]. The curriculum system of innovation and entrepreneurship education in some schools is not based on the students' actual majors, and is not closely related to professional courses. Colleges and universities are the main body of innovation and entrepreneurship education and the most suitable place for innovation and entrepreneurship education. Innovation and entrepreneurship education runs through the actual project operation and helps students in higher vocational colleges to complete innovation and entrepreneurship practice with innovation and entrepreneurship plans. Many innovation and entrepreneurship innovation centers in colleges and universities have become a kind of display, lack of actual innovation function, and can not carry out actual innovation and entrepreneurship guidance from each link of innovation and entrepreneurship education. In the actual curriculum system design, there is little interaction between the professional construction planning, talent training program and innovation and entrepreneurship in colleges and universities, and there is no good pattern of innovation and entrepreneurship, the design of innovation and entrepreneurship curriculum system is relatively random, and there is no prominent school characteristics and students' professional characteristics.

The main task of innovation and entrepreneurship education is completed in colleges and universities, but the education platform and resources depend on the government, society and enterprises. At present, many colleges and universities do not attach importance to the development of innovation and entrepreneurship education for higher vocational colleges, especially higher vocational colleges. Innovation and entrepreneurship education in higher vocational colleges On the one hand, the curriculum system for Innovation and entrepreneurship education is relatively undeveloped and lacks the cultivation of necessary skills and qualities for Innovation and entrepreneurship under the Internet environment; on the other hand, Innovation and entrepreneurship education focuses on task-oriented and input-based education, does not give innovation and entrepreneurship practice opportunities, and lacks heuristic Innovation and entrepreneurship education [4]. Therefore, compared with the innovation and entrepreneurship education system of other countries, there are the following problems in China's innovation and entrepreneurship education system: Firstly, there is no innovation and entrepreneurship education system throughout the whole process, and foreign institutions have carried out the relevant education since primary and secondary schools, and the government and society continue to provide innovation and entrepreneurship training after leaving school. However, there is no sustainable mechanism for domestic innovation and entrepreneurship education, and college education is not perfect. Second, there is no mature innovation and entrepreneurship education system, the current higher vocational education has not combined innovation and entrepreneurship needs to establish a comprehensive operation, marketing, investment and financing curriculum system, there is no perfect teacher allocation. Third, innovation and entrepreneurship education lacks practicality.

With the development of innovation and entrepreneurship education in our country, its curriculum, teaching methods and teaching process are gradually changing, but it is still in the traditional teaching mode. Lecturing in class, lack of innovation in theoretical knowledge and lack of emphasis on innovation in practical links lead to the lack of students' interest in learning and practical ability, thus affecting its effectiveness [5]. Along with the rapid development of information technology, the application of network in all walks of life is more and more extensive, which brings opportunities and challenges to the development of education. Especially, the implementation of educational reform and the innovation of traditional educational and teaching mode are also important and urgent affairs. However, at present, the innovation of innovation and entrepreneurship education is not enough to meet the needs of economic and social development, the needs of development of innovation and entrepreneurship education, and the needs of training innovative talents. All of these need to be treated as a key point in the future research, and the innovation of innovation and entrepreneurship education needs to be strengthened [6].

Innovation and entrepreneurship education is a brand-new educational concept based on innovation education, innovation and entrepreneurship education, quality education, vocational education and other educational concepts. Its aim is to create new vocational and work-post teaching practice, so as to enable college graduates to carry out self-employment, flexible employment, independent innovation and entrepreneurship education reform practice. Innovation and entrepreneurship education is an educational activity aiming at cultivating students' innovation and entrepreneurship spirit, innovation and entrepreneurship ability and innovation and entrepreneurship quality. In a word, innovation and entrepreneurship education meets the requirements of knowledge and skills on the basis of innovation education, while innovation education becomes more concrete and real.

2.2 Optimization of Innovation and Entrepreneurship Curriculum System

Based on the above problems, further innovate and optimize the innovation and entrepreneurship education in higher vocational colleges, coordinate and pool the innovation and entrepreneurship curriculum resources to form a joint force to serve the all-round development of students, which is the purpose of innovation and entrepreneurship education. Innovation and entrepreneurship education, as the bridge and link between all parties, forms a network teaching relationship structure with which the whole society supports the innovation and entrepreneurship of higher vocational college students. In order to turn the discipline of innovation and entrepreneurship education into a systematic project, it is necessary to comprehensively consider various social and psychological factors that affect and restrict innovation and entrepreneurship education and grasp the complex relationship between innovation and entrepreneurship education and external factors such as government policies, economic development, social progress, scientific and technological innovation and cultural evolution. Based on this, the structural relationship of innovation and entrepreneurship education is analyzed. The specific structural relationship of innovation and entrepreneurship education is shown as follows:

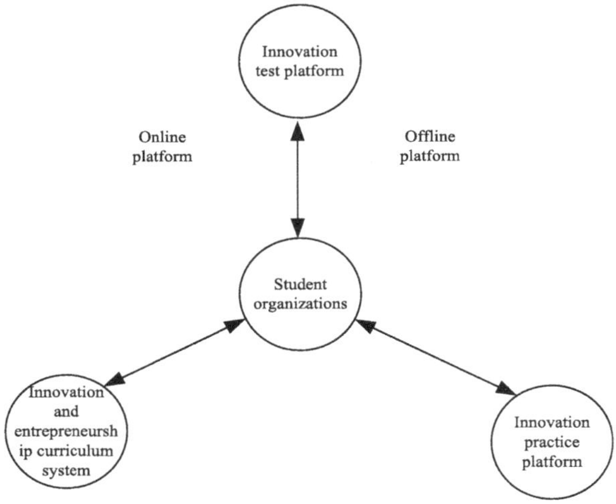

Fig. 1. Structure of innovative entrepreneurship education

As is shown in the figure, the open nature of innovation and entrepreneurship education has put forward new and higher requirements for discipline development orientation, teachers' quality requirements and teaching method reform, requiring us to attach great importance to the integrated characteristics of innovation and entrepreneurship education [7]. Innovation and entrepreneurship education is by no means the result of a simple addition of management courses such as marketing, finance, operations management, human resources, and quality control methods. It requires that this knowledge be structured around the life cycle of an enterprise into a system that integrates independent and decentralized functional courses in a new way based on the innovation and entrepreneurship process model, thus helping students to develop a comprehensive and profound understanding of the chaotic and unpredictable innovation and entrepreneurship process (Fig. 1).

For innovation and entrepreneurship education in higher vocational colleges, "Internet Plus" has greatly expanded the ideas and space of innovation and entrepreneurship education, and promoted its rapid development from another angle. According to the relevant data provided by the Innovation and Entrepreneurship Education Forum of National Higher Vocational Colleges, it can be seen that the innovation and entrepreneurship education of most higher vocational colleges in our country is mainly based on the guidance of innovation and entrepreneurship thinking mode, theoretical policy analysis, guidance for t innovation and entrepreneurship work process, etc., in addition, some collegeses directly rely on the traditional innovation and entrepreneurship education, and do not highlight the content of "Internet Plus" and innovation with the times. In order to solve the above problems, this paper collects and analyzes the influencing factors in the innovation and entrepreneurship teaching process, judges the influence degree and influence relationship of different factors, and further draws a graph, and sets up a Timons model based on the matching and balance of the ree core elements o business opportunity-driven, team-driven and resource-driven [8]. The central problem solved by the innovation and entrepreneurship teaching process model is the balance of the whole body. The details are as follows:

According to the above figure, we shall further establish six curriculum systems with the credit system as the medium, namely, the three-innovation elective curriculum system, the minor curriculum system, the certification curriculum system, the national vocational qualification training curriculum system, the skills training curriculum system, and the postgraduate training curriculum system; we shall, by focusing on the general core curriculum system, set up three modules of general innovation and entrepreneurship courses such as the public compulsory courses for innovation and entrepreneurship, the limited selection of the public compulsory courses for innovation and entrepreneurship, and the public compulsory courses for general knowledge, and set up the professional compulsory courses for innovation and entrepreneurship such as the professional compulsory courses for innovation and entrepreneurship and the professional compulsory courses for reading. Innovation and entrepreneurship curriculum is based on the content of innovation and entrepreneurship education, the evaluation of education is also in accordance with its direction [9] (Fig. 2).

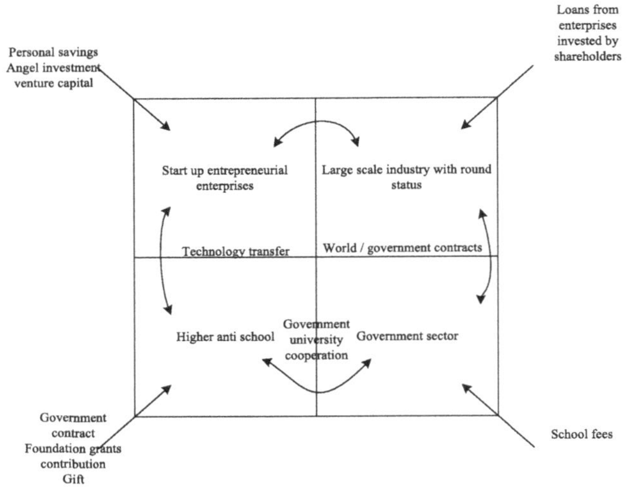

Fig. 2. Timmons model for innovative entrepreneurship teaching

The content and goal of innovation and entrepreneurship education are determined by the ability of students in higher vocational colleges. At the same time, the requirements of innovation and entrepreneurship for students in higher vocational colleges also determine the talent training and development model, innovation and entrepreneurship education discipline system and teaching resources development, innovation and entrepreneurship education teaching methods and training model [10]. Each major offers elective courses corresponding to the professional field, such as project research and development training courses, thesis study courses, professional innovation and entrepreneurship practice courses, etc. Courses offered include: Global Trends and China Opportunities, Technology and Design. The contents of the specific curriculum system are as follows:

Table 1. Construction of curriculum system

Modular		Curriculum
Creation,innovationandEntrepreneurship	Innovativeeducationmodule	Electivecourses27courses
		ShaftMinor2501
		Skilltraining,suchasSYBtraining101
	Employmenteducationhasgreatpotential	Internationalcertification71course
		Postgraduatetrainingcourse
		Seconddegreeconstruction
	Theteachingofcertificate	7coursesofvocationalqualificationcertificate
		2coursesofindustryqualificationcertificate
		Levelcertificate

In the above table, courses related to innovation and entrepreneurship policy opportunities. Policy opportunities refer to new industries, markets and opportunities arising from changes in government laws, regulations and policies. Innovators and entrepreneurs discover new opportunities for innovation and entrepreneurship by learning relevant knowledge. Courses offered include: Fundamentals of Economics, Legal Fundamentals, Current Affairs and Policy. Courses related to technological opportunities for innovation and entrepreneurship. Technological opportunity refers to the innovation and entrepreneurial opportunity brought about by technological changes, which mainly comes from the potential market opportunities brought by new technological breakthroughs and applications of new technologies. And timely investigation and judgment of the emergence of new technologies, new product development and application, technology upgrades may bring new business opportunities (Table 1).

2.3 Innovation and Entrepreneurship Education Model Optimization

Since the innovation and entrepreneurship education in our country is just at the initial stage, although the research on innovation and entrepreneurship education has aroused great attention of scholars. But how to integrate the innovation and entrepreneurship education into the current higher education system, how to cultivate the innovation and entrepreneurship education ecosystem in colleges and universities, there is no extensible paradigm or regulation in theory or in practice. Therefore, it is necessary to constantly absorb external nutrition and resources, and form close contact with external supporting factors, so as to help the internal subjects of the innovation and entrepreneurship ecosystem of the Mass Innovation Space to continuously interact and communicate with each other, share resources and services, and jointly build the innovation and entrepreneurship teaching circle in the Mass Innovation Space. To provide guiding opinions for innovative and start-up students to evaluate the feasibility, market analysis and prospect forecast of innovative and start-up projects; to provide technical services for innovative and start-up enterprises, and guide the development of new products and technical research; and to guide investors to invest in innovative and start-up enterprises through market channels, so as to help improve the profitability and management level of innovative and start-up students.

In the process of innovation and entrepreneurship education, we shall take the "Internet Plus" strategy as the guiding ideology, take our own specialties as the orientation, take learning and enhancing vocational skills as the means, and take the cultivation of innovation and entrepreneurship spirit and ability as the goal, so that innovation thinking and innovation and entrepreneurship ideas can be rooted in students' learning outlook and outlook on life, deeply integrate into students' learning and life, and establish correct employment outlook and employment outlook for students. According to the students' own characteristics and development goals, we should teach students according to their aptitude, guide them to combine the Internet plus with their majors, and plan their own career, especially their academic career in school. Firmly establish students' innovation and entrepreneurship awareness, so that students have a clear professional orientation. Construction of the corresponding innovation and entrepreneurship model framework, as follows (Fig. 3).

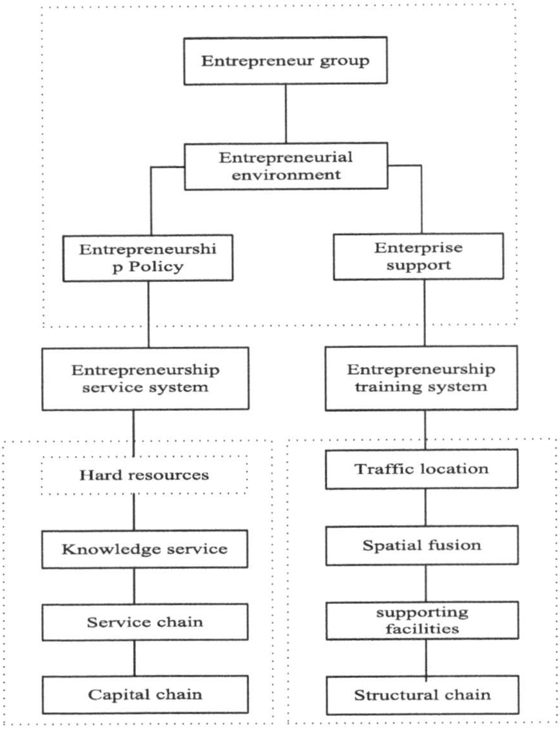

Fig. 3. Innovative entrepreneurship model

In view of the above innovation and entrepreneurship model framework to optimize the meaning and steps of innovation and entrepreneurship teaching system, we can give some examples from the following points.

(1) The "Internet Plus" innovation and entrepreneurship ecosystem is composed of many elements. For example, Maker Space, Maker, University, Government, Innovation and Entrepreneurship Mentor and so on, each factor has its role orientation, together with the ecosystem construction process.
(2) The relationship between the elements of the "Internet plus" innovation and entrepreneurship ecosystem is a mutual-benefit symbiotic relationship. Although each element in the system has different positioning, but also has its own characteristics, but in the crowd space, each element will exchange values, a resources, so as to become a mutual-benefit symbiosis.
(3) The development process of the innovation and entrepreneurship ecosystem based on the "Internet Plus" is a dynamic and balanced process. The elements that stand out from the competition in the innovation and entrepreneurship ecosystem will be more adaptable to the environment than the elements that are eliminated, and the system can also better achieve development and achieve a balanced state.

In addition, due to the imperceptible change of the original form of vocational skill appraisal and examination by Internet technology, the paperless and intelligent vocational skill appraisal and examination have emerged as the times require, greatly improving the work efficiency of vocational skill appraisal, eliminating the artificial factors in the appraisal link, controlling the overall operation cost investment, and ensuring the fairness, impartiality and objectivity of vocational skill appraisal. At the same time, in order to ensure the safety of appraisal and examination, the quality of appraisal and examination can be improved greatly. For example, taking DCS simulation for example, it can simulate the specific operating environment, and give the simulation system to evaluate the appraisal process, which is helpful to ensure the impartiality of the appraisal.

In addition, the introduction of AR technology and VR technology for the realization of virtualization skills identification has a significant value. In addition, we shall give full play to the role of Internet technology, continuously and progressively carry out the appraisal of vocational skills in a vertical manner, combine the preliminary training and practice links of skill appraisal with the "Internet Plus", develop more operable teaching resources, and embed them in the teaching system and daily teaching period in a real sense. Frati perspeca the resources database s by building vocational education online schools and other methods. From the static perspecti, The collegie-ledi innovation and entrepreneurship education ecosystem includes microcosmic, meso-ascopi macroscopic and oth hierarchical structures, and different hierarchical structures include several constituent empoents with different connotations, characteristics and functions. Further, the innovation and entrepreneurship curriculum structure elements are displayed as follows (Fig. 4).

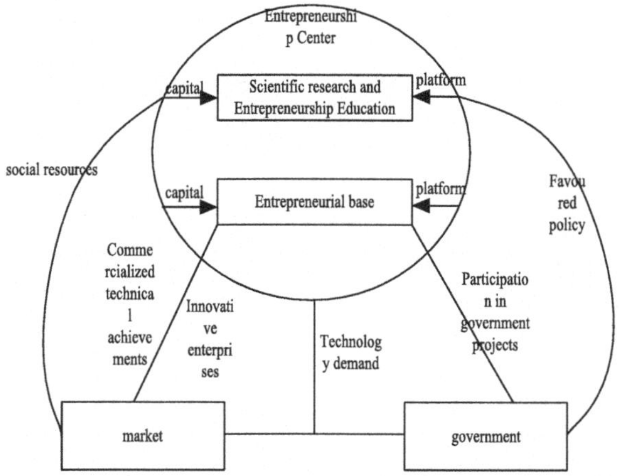

Fig. 4. Elements of innovative entrepreneurship curriculum

Because innovation and entrepreneurship is a social behavior with high environmental sensitivity, successful innovation and entrepreneurship requires a well-structured and functional innovation and entrepreneurship ecosystem. Innovation and entrepreneurship education is a systematic project, which needs systematic support from many factors.

Strengthening its construction is just like creating a benign cycle ecosystem. The innovation and entrepreneurship education in domestic colleges and universities started late. Compared with foreign colleges and universities, there is a certain gap in the development of education philosophy, education mode, education environment and system guarantee. The ecosystem of innovation and entrepreneurship education in colleges and universities has not been fully formed. The in-depth development of innovation and entrepreneurship education still depends on the top-down and internal-external optimization reform. Based on this, combining the current situation and trend of innovation and entrepreneurship education in our country, this paper deeply analyzes the construction process of internal integration and external integration, and completes the construction and operation of the ideal model of the innovation and entrepreneurship education ecosystem dominated by colleges and universities under the premise of following the education law. The specific normative model for innovation and entrepreneurship teaching is structured as follows (Fig. 5):

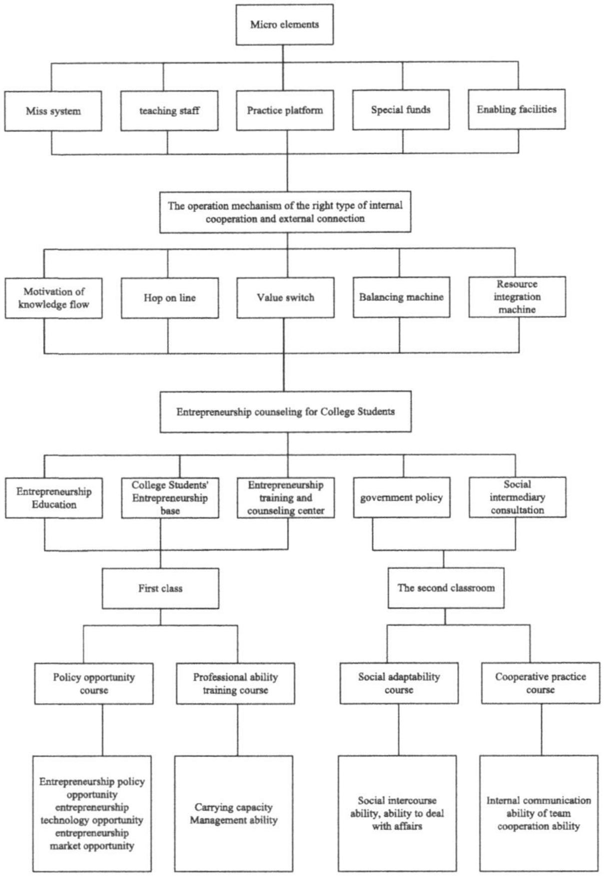

Fig. 5. Normative model of innovation and entrepreneurship teaching

Scientific and reasonable curriculum system is the foundation of innovation and entrepreneurship education. The design of innovation and entrepreneurship education curriculum system should be integrated into the process of talent training. First of all, the curriculum system is divided into general curriculum platform, professional curriculum platform, innovation and entrepreneurship curriculum platform. On the basis of completing the general courses and professional courses, the curriculum system of innovation and entrepreneurship education is constructed as shown in the figure (Fig. 6).

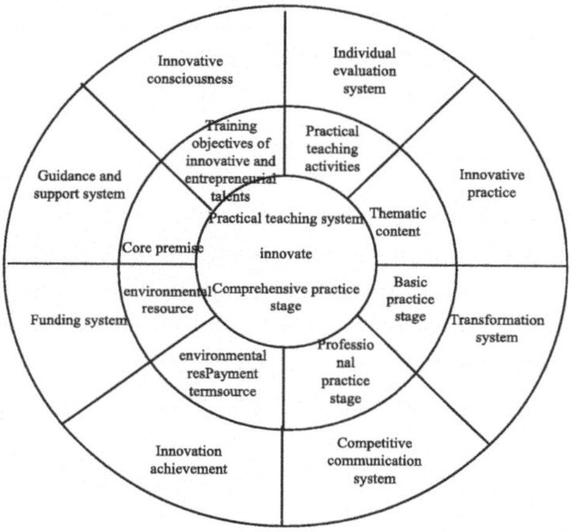

Fig. 6. Innovative entrepreneurship teaching rules

Design teaching link between the first classroom and the second classroom, the design concept must conform to the law of innovation and entrepreneurship education, so that students have enough time and space to absorb and digest the knowledge learned, and practical activities to apply. The complete curriculum system is divided into basic experimental teaching, creative experimental teaching, sociological practical teaching, cooperative practical teaching.

3 Analysis of Experimental Results

In order to verify the practical application effect of the mode of innovation and entrepreneurship education in higher vocational colleges based on the Internet + perspective, an empirical study was conducted.Through questionnaire survey and interview, the degree of satisfaction and love of teachers and students on innovation and entrepreneurship teaching in higher vocational colleges was investigated, and the specific contents of the questionnaire survey were shown as follows:

Table 2. Questionnaire content settings

Problem	Content%	Identity
What do you think of entrepreneurship?	18	Teacher
In order to make money	16	Student
To start a business or company	16	parent
Accumulate working experience	34	Government official
Just start a business	7	others
Develop some cutting-edge science and technology projects	3	–
A way to become a talent Do not understand	6	–

Based on the data in the above table, this paper further analyzes the satisfaction degree of innovation and entrepreneurship education model in higher vocational colleges from the perspective of Internet. The attitudes of the students, experts, teachers, the government and parents towards the traditional teaching methods and the teaching methods put forward in this paper are summarized, compared and recorded respectively. The specific results of the survey are shown as follows (Fig. 7) (Table 2):

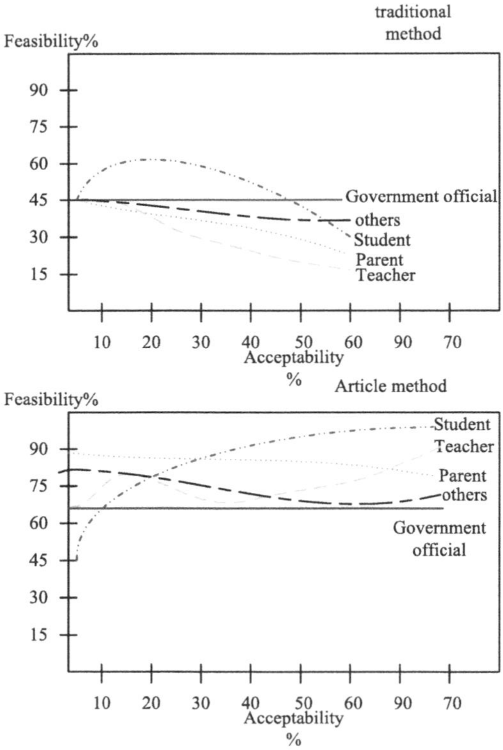

Fig. 7. Survey results

As can be seen from the above chart, compared with the traditional teaching mode, the overall survey satisfaction and practicability of the innovation and entrepreneurship education model proposed in this paper are relatively high, and the support of the relevant people is also significantly improved, which fully meets the research requirements.

4 Conclusion

The discipline construction of innovation and entrepreneurship education is a systematic project.Due to the rapid development of innovation and entrepreneurship education in colleges and universities in China, it objectively determines the integrity, openness and epochal characteristics of innovation and entrepreneurship education in colleges and universities.To strengthen the construction of the platform and the cultivation of talents, it is necessary to optimize the educational model, improve the teaching methods, and clarify the disciplinary boundaries and main fields.

Fund Project. Research Project on Philosophy and Social Sciences of the Universities in Jiangsu Province (Project No.: 2019SJA0615).

Fund Project: Research Project on the Transportation Vocational Education in 2019 Funded by National Transportation Vocational Education Teaching Steering Committee (Project No.: 2019B03).

Fund Project: Research Project on Higher Vocational Education Funded by Nanjing Vocational Institute of Transportation Technology (Project No.: 19JY111).

References

1. Wu, Q., Zhang, P.: E-Learning user acceptance model in business schools based on UTAUT in the background of internet plus. J. Shanghai Jiaotong Univ. **52**(2), 233–241 (2018)
2. Bernard, L.H., Tamara, G.B., Mary, H.P., et al.: The prevention of lower urinary tract symptoms (PLUS) research consortium: a transdisciplinary approach toward promoting bladder health and preventing lower urinary tract symptoms in women across the life course. J. Womens Health **27**(3), 283–289 (2018)
3. Oo, P.P., Sahaym, A., Juasrikul, S., Lee, S.-Y.: The interplay of entrepreneurship education and national cultures in entrepreneurial activity: a social cognitive perspective. J. Int. Entrepreneurship **16**(3), 398–420 (2018). https://doi.org/10.1007/s10843-018-0229-4
4. Ebru, O.K., Pinar, K.D.: Investigation of entrepreneurship trends and general competency levels of university students studying at faculty of sports sciences. J. Educ. Training Stud. **6**(4), 212 (2018)
5. Robert, A.R.: A critical analysis of the development of the US research university and emergence of the neoliberal entrepreneurial model. Entrepreneurship Educ. **25**(1), 1–15 (2018)
6. Rui, H., Wang, Y., Peng, B., et al.: Marta Peris-Ortiz, Jaime Alonso Gómez, José M. Merigó-Lindahl, Carlos Rueda-Armengot (eds.): entrepreneurial universities: exploring the academic and innovative dimensions of entrepreneurship in higher education. High. Educ. **76**(1), 183–186 (2018)
7. Andrea, M.P., Andy, A.P., Nathan, S.B.: Management training in global health education: a health innovation fellowship training program to bring healthcare to low-income communities in central america. Global Health Action **11**(1), 1408359 (2018)

8. Chikaishi, Y., Uramoto, H., Tanaka, F.: Construction and practice about the education of students' professional quality system in higher vocational colleges. J. South. Vocat. Educ. **31**(12), 4451–4456 (2011)
9. Bogoch, E.R., Elliot-Gibson, V., Wang, R.Y., et al.: On situation and policy of construction of party conducts and incorruption administration in higher vocational college **27**(1), 604–618 (2012)
10. Shervin, A.: Life expectancy gain due to employment status depends on race, gender, education, and their intersections. J. Racial Ethn. Health Disparities **5**(2), 1–12 (2018)

Effect Analysis of Physical Education Course Based on Artificial Intelligence

Tian Xiong(✉)

Physical Education Department of Shaanxi, University of Traditional Chinese Medicine, Xianyang 712046, China
xiongtian0078910@outlook.com

Abstract. The traditional physical education curriculum teaching stage effect is unable to make the analysis comprehensively to the curriculum each stage factor, therefore proposes based on the artificial intelligence sports curriculum teaching stage effect analysis. Through the collection of PE course teaching stage effect data, judge each stage effect entity relation, calculate each stage effect analysis credibility, complete the teaching stage effect measurement. Simulation experiments are designed to compare the effectiveness of the analysis method based on artificial intelligence and the traditional analysis method in the teaching stage of physical education.

Keywords: Artificial intelligence · Physical education · Teaching · Effect analysis

1 Introduction

The evaluation of physical education is an important part of physical education, which is the feedback to the evaluation of the quality of physical education and the effect of physical education, and plays a positive and important role in improving the quality of physical education [1]. At present, the evaluation of students is mainly based on the judgment of the development and changes of students' morality, intelligence and physique, and the process of giving guidance to the development of students' morality, intelligence and physique. And the reasonable and correct evaluation of students is not only the main problem faced by the effect evaluation of the course teaching stage, but also the problem that must be solved by the effect evaluation of the course teaching stage [2]. Therefore, this paper puts forward the effect analysis of physical education teaching stage based on artificial intelligence and constructs the evaluation method of artificial intelligence.

At present, the evaluation index method of physical education has become the baton of physical education. The actual teaching content of the physical education department is mainly determined by the indexes in the evaluation method, that is, the teaching content depends on the indexes. And the greater the weight of sports evaluation index is, the higher the degree of attention will be. Scientific and reasonable evaluation index

S. Liu et al. (Eds.): eLEOT 2020, LNICST 339, pp. 113–123, 2020.
https://doi.org/10.1007/978-3-030-63952-5_10

method of physical education quality can adjust teaching behavior, so as to obtain better evaluation results [3]. In this way, the scientific and reasonable evaluation index method will guide the teaching of track and field teachers and students' learning gradually to the scientific standardization, in the objective will inevitably promote the improvement of the teaching quality of physical education curriculum. The theory of artificial intelligence is consistent with the general direction of cultivating innovative consciousness and spirit in physical education in China. Literature [4] has built a smart sports classroom based on "wechat public platform" and wearable devices applied to heart rate monitoring. The main research conclusion: the intelligent teaching mode includes three parts: pre class "prophet", in class "perception" and after class "exploration". It realizes three functions: pre class multimedia micro course electronic textbook preview, in class interactive teaching and after class micro course sports guidance. It aims to improve the teaching efficiency and quality of physical education classroom, and scientifically evaluate the achievement effect of physical education classroom goal, to realize the real integration of physical education in and out of class. Literature [5] studies the practice of college physical education curriculum reform. The results show that the effective strategies and key links of curriculum construction and management of community activities are to include community activities in physical education scores and credits; The establishment of extracurricular sports activity guidance center, the construction of scientific system and standard system, the implementation of community tutor system and the construction of evaluation index and system of sports community provide organization, system, technology and incentive guarantee for the effective implementation of community activity curricular. The implementation of community activity curricular in cultivating students' Sports interest, improving sports skills, forming exercise habits and promoting The comprehensive ability has obvious effect. However, due to the nature of extracurricular teaching and overall teaching, the application of the above methods is not applicable to the teaching of physical education, and the research on the specific application of artificial intelligence in physical education is blank, therefore, the method of evaluating the effect of artificial intelligence in the teaching stage of physical education has certain guiding significance.

2 Effect Analysis of Physical Education Teaching Stage of Artificial Intelligence

2.1 Data Collection of the Effect of the Teaching Stage

The advantage of the method of effect analysis in the teaching stage of physical education course of artificial intelligence lies in its strong background data support. Therefore, in the method design, especially in the information management method, the design of data collection is very important and needs to be carefully processed and realized [5]. In the teaching stage effect evaluation method, involves many kinds of data operation processing.

The data collection of the effect analysis method in this teaching stage includes many entities, such as user entity, student entity, user category entity, indicator detail entity, evaluation form entity and so on [6].

For the effect of teaching stage, it mainly refers to the user objects that need service in this method [7]. The numbering attribute is used to indicate the effect of different teaching stages, and is the primary key of the whole column. Other attributes in the method are listed in Fig. 1:

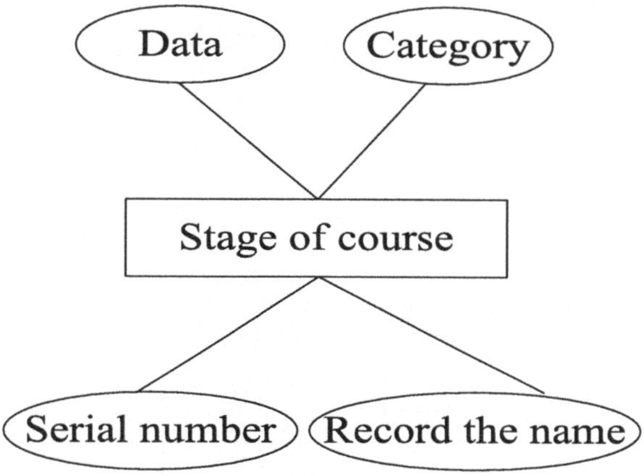

Fig. 1. Attributes of teaching stage

Since this method is mainly used to evaluate the effect of teaching stage and involves a large number of operations related to the effect data of teaching stage, the effect of teaching stage is designed separately to provide the efficiency of the method. Among them, the primary key that distinguishes the effect data of different teaching stages is the number [8].

Course categories are used to classify different course categories and to label users with different identities. The primary key of the entity is the numbering attribute.

Indicator detail entity the indicator detail entity is used to store each evaluation indicator and related information in the method, where the primary key is the indicator number.

The evaluation table entities are numbered for the primary key of the evaluation table, and other attributes are listed in the figure below (Fig. 2).

The relation between entities mainly indicates the relation between different entities in this method. In the method of effect analysis in the teaching stage, there is a many-to-many relationship between users and evaluation forms. There are multiple users, and evaluation of different students can generate multiple evaluation forms. There is a many-to-many relationship between students and archives. Each student has his own archives. There is also a many-to-many relationship between the user and the student files. Different users can view the file information of multiple students. Similar relationships exist between other entities. The relationship between entities of the effect analysis method in the teaching stage is shown in Fig. 3.

Each table in the data collection is designed to reflect the interrelationship between the tables in the entire data collection. This paper mainly describes the administrator

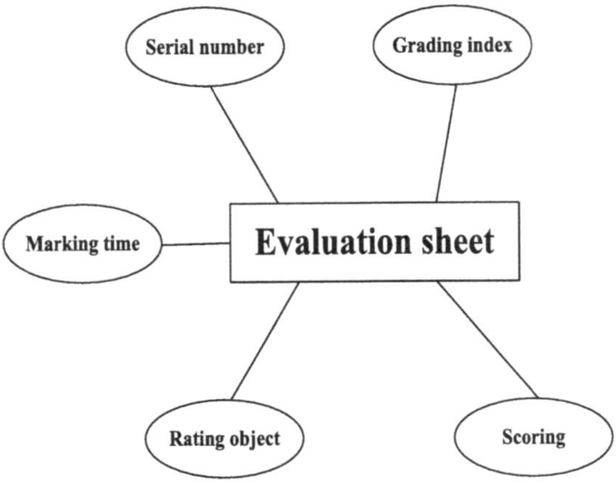

Fig. 2. Evaluation represents intent

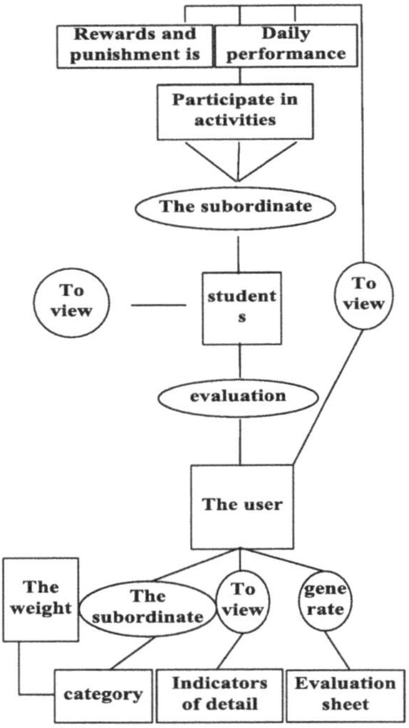

Fig. 3. Effect analysis of entity relation in teaching stage

table, user table, student table, indicator list, evaluation table and weight table of the teaching stage effect analysis method in detail.

The administrator has the authority to manage and modify the entire method, so its information must be stored in the entire method. When the administrator logs in the method, the login information will be compared with the administrator information stored in the background of the method. Only after it is completely correct can it enter the evaluation method and conduct corresponding operations. The specific information is shown in Table 1:

Table 1. Course management data

The field names	Meaning	Can the field type be null	Can the field type be null
Id	Management number	Int	A primary key
Name	The login name	Varchar	Null
Password	Password	Varchar	Null
Endtime	Last login time	Datetime	Null

The course information sheet mainly stores the information of the course, which is used for the comparison and management of the user's identity information. The content of the course information sheet is as follows (Table 2):

Table 2. Information table of course stage

The field names	Meaning	Can the field type be null	Can the field type be null
u_id	Serial number	Int	主键
L_name	Login name	Varchar	Null
L_pwd	Password	Varchar	Null
u_name	The name	Varchar	Null
t_id	Category	Int	Null
startDate	Time	Dateime	Null
endDate	Last session time	Dateime	Null
CardNum	Identity number	Varchar	Null
Birthday	The date of	Varchar	Null
Mobeilphone	Number	Int	Null

Student tables are used to store and represent information about students and themselves in methods. As for the operation of the student table, it can directly affect the records of the students, and then affect the assessment of students' academic performance and the authority in the method, so it needs to be carefully designed. The list of students is as follows (Table 3):

Table 3. Learning information of students in the course stage

The field name means whether the field type can be null	The field name means whether the field type can be null	The field name means whether the field type can be null	The field name means whether the field type can be null
stu_id	Serial number	Int	A primary key
stu_num	Student id	Varchar	Null
stu_pwd	The name	Varchar	Null
sex	gender	Int	Null
professional	professional	Varchar	Null
class	The class	Varchar	Null
grade	grade	Varchar	Null
department	Is don't	Varchar	Null

The evaluation form mainly stores the contents and information of the corresponding evaluation questionnaire (Table 4).

Table 4. Evaluation form

The field names	Meaning	Can the field type be null	Can the field type be null
G_id	Serial number	Int	A primary key
a_id	Index class number	Varchar	Null
G_u_id	Rating object	Varchar	Null
Gd_u_id	Rated object	Int	Null
G_Date	Marking time	Varchar	Null

2.2 Calculate the Effect Credibility of the Teaching Stage

Reliability refers to the reliability of the results, which is used to reflect the size of the random error in education measurement. The higher the reliability index, the more reliable the test results. The test with high reliability can provide teachers with reliable information, and indicate that teachers' evaluation of students is objective and reliable, and also makes students' understanding of themselves highly consistent with the actual situation, thus contributing to the improvement of teaching and learning methods.

There are many methods to calculate reliability, such as retest reliability, homogeneity reliability and grader reliability. The most commonly used of these is the homogeneity reliability, also known as the internal consistency coefficient, which refers to the degree to which an exam measures the same content. The calculation methods of reliability include halving method, coulomb method, and kolkstedt formula, etc. This method USES kolkstedt formula to find the reliability, see formula (1):

$$R = \alpha \frac{\mathrm{k}}{\mathrm{k}-1}(1 - \frac{\sum_{\mathrm{i}-1}^{\mathrm{n}} S_{\mathrm{i}}^2}{\mathrm{s}^2}) \tag{1}$$

Where, R is the reliability of an evaluation, and α is the evaluation reliability coefficient; k is the total number of course stages; $\mathrm{s}_{\mathrm{i}}^2$ is the score variance of each evaluation object; s^2 is the variance of the total score.

The value of the reliability coefficient a ranges from 0 to 1. The closer to 1, the more real the score. The evaluation criteria for the value of reliability coefficient are shown in Table 5:

Table 5. Reliability coefficient value criteria

Reliability coefficient	Evaluation standard
0 ~ 0.6	Low credibility
0.6 ~ 0.8	Moderate credibility
0.8 ~ 1	High reliability

From formula (1), it can be seen that increasing the number of exam questions, controlling the difficulty of the questions between 0.4 and 0.7, taking various means to improve the differentiation of the test questions, and making the grading standards as objectively as possible can improve the effect reliability of the teaching stage of the course [9].

2.3 Effect Measurement and Analysis in the Teaching Stage

In general, the effect measurement in the teaching stage of a course is to induce certain reactions of students through examinations or tests, and then to evaluate these reactions through quantitative or qualitative descriptions, which are the results of the effect measurement in the teaching stage of a course [10].

Classical Test Theory (CTT) was developed from the early 20th century to the 1950s. It is an operational statistical analysis method for questions and tests. The theoretical basis of classical test theory is true fraction theory. The so-called true score, that is, the expected value of the real score of the test, is expressed by (2):

$$T = E(X) \tag{2}$$

Where, X is the real score in the test, is the mathematical expectation, E is the real score. Due to the existence of measurement error, the true score T cannot be measured directly. The measured score is the actual score obtained in a test, which includes two parts: effective score and measurement error. The measurement error is composed of method error and random error. Therefore, the relationship between the measured score (X), effective score (V), random error (E) and method error (I) can be expressed as follows:

$$X = V + E + I \tag{3}$$

In formula (3), the effective fraction V and the method error I usually appear stably. We call the sum of the two as the true fraction, from which formula (4) can be obtained:

$$T = V + I \tag{4}$$

Random error E is caused by accidental factors, individual and the size of the random error of plus or minus no obvious regularity, thus causing the observed score will fluctuate within a certain scope, but on the whole consistent with the statistical law, therefore, the classical measurement theory is through the method of measurement by some accidental factors, the process of estimate of the true score is obtained.

Reliability and validity are used as two indexes to measure the overall quality of the test paper, and difficulty and differentiation are used as two local indexes to measure the quality of the test paper. The analysis of test scores is also divided into question analysis, unit analysis and overall analysis.

3 Simulation Experiment

3.1 Experimental Preparation

In order to verify the effectiveness of the method of physical education teaching stage effect analysis based on artificial intelligence, a simulation experiment is designed. Under the same experimental conditions, the traditional artificial physical education teaching stage effect analysis method is compared with the artificial intelligence-based physical education teaching stage effect analysis method.

In the process of experiment, the traditional artificial physical education teaching stage effect analysis method adopts the method of artificial analysis, through the method of artificial statistics and data analysis, the teaching effect of each stage course is analyzed.

In the physical education curriculum teaching stage effect of artificial intelligence analysis method, the browser server architecture is adopted, with the help of a browser to access can be realized access to relevant methods, B/S structure is mainly using the Web browser technology, and integrated with a variety of scripting languages, such as JavaScript, VBScript, Perk Python, PHP, etc., as well as the ActiveX technology, achieve strong functional requirements, and don't have to be like the original complex special-purpose software must be used, which greatly saves development costs. The B/S method architecture can meet the requirements of simplifying terminal node load, saving cost and ensuring the flexibility of the method.

Computer: Windows 2000/XP/2003, installed IE6.0 or above, installed Windows MediaPlayer 10.0, installed sound card, and equipped with speakers or headphones. Administrator client: Windows 2000/XP/2003, installation method management client, install Office 2003, install Windows Media Player 10.0, install sound card, and equipped with speakers or headphones.

Web Server: Windows 2003 Server operation method.

Collect data Server: Windows 2003 Server operation method, install SQL Server 2008 to collect data.

Web and data collection server hardware: 2 Xeon MP E7320 processors, 8 GB DDRII memory, 584 GB SAS disk and gigabit Ethernet card.

Network environment: Intranet on campus.

Method to open the Internet Information Services (IIS, Internet Information Services), in Windows Server 2003 is the default is not installed IIS 6, need to install another. After installing IIS 6, you also need to turn on support for ASP. It is used to support the operation of the effect analysis method of physical education teaching stage based on artificial intelligence.

In the process of the experiment, two methods were used to analyze the same experimental object, and the experimental data were analyzed on the data of physical education courses of each grade in a certain school. The data analysis of the course stage is divided into three categories, namely, the theoretical knowledge of physical education, the practical courses of physical education and the application of process assessment. The course stages are divided into different categories according to the course categories, including (1) pre-class preparation; (2) group activities; (3) exhibition of works; (4) self-evaluation; (5) mutual evaluation; (6) teacher evaluation; (7) feedback and improvement. The results of the two methods were compared.

3.2 Analysis of Experimental Results

In the experiment, the effects of the two groups of methods were analyzed, as shown in Fig. 4:

The traditional analysis method of the effect of artificial physical education teaching stage, when analyzing the effect of the same object in the course stage, is difficult to evaluate objectively, and the judgment will change with the differences of the collective. The traditional analysis method adopts manual data analysis, which is difficult, time-consuming, heavy workload and subjective error. There is a lack of quantitative analysis, so there are fewer analysis and evaluation indexes in the test results, and the analysis degree is shallow, the lowest analysis result is only 30%.

Comparatively speaking, the artificial intelligence method of the effect analysis in the stage of physical education teaching determines a standard beyond the set of evaluation objects, and compares the evaluation object with the objective standard, so as to make an objective judgment on the evaluation object. Because this method selects multiple fields as the benchmark in the evaluation object set, and then compares each evaluation object with the benchmark, the evaluation result is not limited by the overall level. Comparing the past and present of the evaluated person, or comparing several aspects of the evaluated person, can better reflect individual differences. The viewpoint of presupposition evaluation is divided into several items and evaluated separately. According to certain evaluation objectives and requirements, the situation of the evaluation object is described in detail, and an appropriate evaluation is made, which can describe the objective facts in detail, with high reliability.

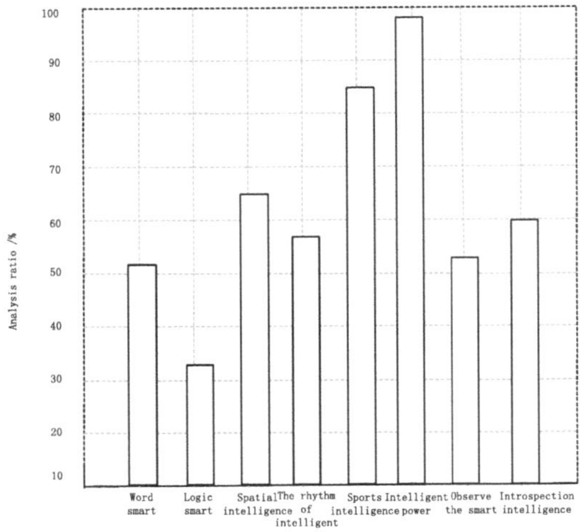

(a) traditional manual analysis methods

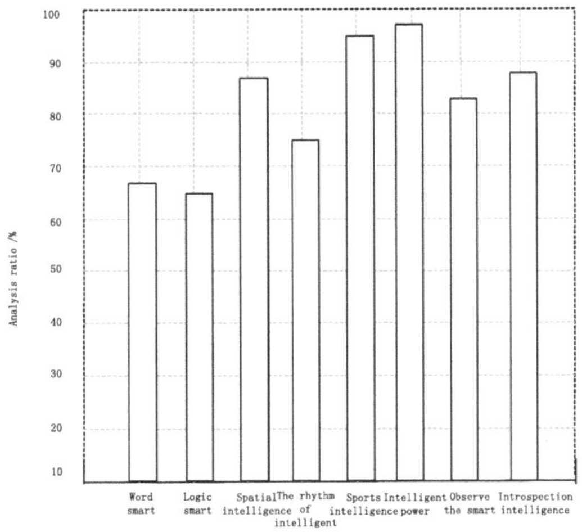

(b) artificial intelligence analysis method

Fig. 4. Comparison of analysis effects between two groups of methods

After the analysis, it can be seen that the artificial intelligence method can better analyze the effect of the teaching stage of the physical education course and clarify the future development direction of the course.

4 Conclusion

The beginning of the application of the effect analysis of artificial intelligence in the teaching stage of physical education is not the end of the research. Meanwhile, there are certain deficiencies and defects in other aspects, which will be left for further improvement in the follow-up research.

With a rational view of today's educational dynamics, it can be predicted that the future education will achieve two integration, namely, the integration of education concept and artificial intelligence theory, and the integration of technical means and information technology. It is believed that with the gradual deepening of the teaching practice research guided by the artificial intelligence theory, it will inject new vitality into China's education reform and produce positive and far-reaching influence. Although computer assisted instruction already common in China, but in theory, and technology development compared with developed countries still have many unsatisfactory place, courseware how the more reasonable and more fully integrated together with the process of chemistry teaching, how to merge with all kinds of audio-visual media more naturally, and above all kinds of the frontier problems of the application of information technology in the field of teaching, will be the general education workers in the future work to learn, explore and practice direction. Teachers should set up modern educational concepts, accelerate the pace of research on the integration of information technology, artificial intelligence theory and curriculum, so that students can fully develop artificial intelligence, so that each student can succeed in their own fields of advantage.

Looking back in the century, what we are doing is to find out the successes and shortcomings in every step we have taken in the past, so as to provide direction and guidance for the future development. What we hope is that more schools can integrate artificial intelligence teaching and courseware technology into the quality education and information teaching reform of schools, so that more children can benefit from it.

References

1. Liu, Q., et al.: Classroom teaching behavior analysis method basde on artificial intelligence and its application. China Educ. Technol. (09), 13–21 (2019)
2. Liu, J., Liu, W.: Effectiveness of sexuality education curriculum in primary schools based on sexual health knowledge and gender stereotypes. Chin. J. Sch. Health **40**(03), 350–354 (2019)
3. Zhou, J., Chai, J.: The impact of website marketing information on MOOC's revenue—based on Heckman two-stage model. Soft Sci. **32**(09), 98–102 (2018)
4. Dou, L., Chen, H., Qian, C.: Study on the values and models of "smart physical education classroom" in colleges and universities. Sports Cult. Guide (11), 136–140+146 (2018)
5. Zhu, W., Deng, Y., Jiang, Z.: Construction and practice of the curriculumization of students' sports club activities. J. Guangzhou Sport Univ. **38**(02), 124–128 (2018)
6. Xiao, J., Li, H.: The theoretical basis and practical effect of junior high school physical education "administrative class + option" teaching. J. Phys. Educ. **25**(01), 110–112 (2018)
7. Bo, H., Li, H., Zhang, H.: Exploration on the construction of platform of production management experiment micro-lectures for application-oriented talents. Res. Explor. Lab. **37**(08), 191–196 (2018)
8. Tian, H., Wang, Y., Han, Y.: ESP teaching and its effects for English majors at sport colleges. J. Beijing Sport Univ. **41**(06), 76–83 (2018)
9. Yin, R., et al.: The deep integration of artificial intelligence and subject teaching creating intelligent curriculum. Educ. Res. **24**(06), 70–80 (2018)
10. Liu, X., Chen, L., Wang, L., Feng, M.: A study on construction of core literacy for information technology curriculum in wisdom age. China Educ. Technol. (10), 55–61 (2018)

Construction of Dual System Teaching System for Automobile Detection and Maintenance Under 1+X Certificate System

Hai-jing Zhou[1(✉)] and Shao-feng Han[2]

[1] Chongqing Vocational Institute of Tourism, Qianjiang 409099, China
zhouhaijing554@yeah.net

[2] Vocational Education Center of Qianjiang Chongqing, Qianjiang 409099, China

Abstract. Facing the urgent demand of "zero-distance" applied talents in automobile maintenance manufacturing industry, it is imperative to reform the current teaching system, teaching contents and teaching methods. Therefore, this paper proposes a dual system teaching system for automobile detection and maintenance under the 1 + X certificate system. This paper analyzes the connotation and function of "1 + X certificate system", and probes into the "dual system" in Germany, including its meaning and enlightenment to China's vocational education. Under the background of 1 + X certificate system, combined with the "dual system" in Germany, the dual-system teaching system of automobile detection and maintenance was established to strengthen the professional ability training of professional teachers with "X" certificates. Finally, the benefits of the dual-system teaching system of automobile testing and maintenance specialty are analyzed. The results show that: after the implementation of the dual-system teaching system under the 1 + X certificate system, the performance of the experimental class is significantly improved compared with that of the ordinary class, which fully demonstrates the improvement of teaching quality and proves the advantages of the implementation of the teaching system under the 1 + X certificate system.

Keywords: 1 + X certificate system · Automobile inspection and maintenance · Dual system · Teaching system

1 Introduction

The rapid development of vehicles and the continuous progress of The Times have expanded the scale of the automobile market. From 2009 to 2018, China's automobile production and sales volume has been the world's largest for ten consecutive years. In this context, the automobile aftermarket will be an important link affecting the rapid development of the automobile industry [1]. With the explosive growth of the number of automobiles and the continuous innovation of science and technology, the demand for high-skilled automobile maintenance service personnel in automobile aftermarket is increasing day by day. Therefore, how to train a group of high-skilled automobile

S. Liu et al. (Eds.): eLEOT 2020, LNICST 339, pp. 124–136, 2020.
https://doi.org/10.1007/978-3-030-63952-5_11

maintenance service personnel to meet the needs of industrial enterprises has become the development goal of secondary vocational colleges. Secondary vocational schools as a car repairs the important source of skilled personnel, the secondary vocational school vehicle maintenance and repair of professional personnel training quality put forward the challenge, however, secondary vocational school talent training quality guarantee is the most key factors of "high quality and match the industry enterprise needs" the construction of curriculum system, it is also a secondary vocational school curriculum system reform is facing an important problem [2].

In view of the above problems, China introduced the "dual system" cultivation model. As the core of vocational education in Germany, it is a vocational education system in which enterprises and vocational colleges cooperate with each other to train highly skilled talents under the protection of national laws [3]. In the "dual system" vocational education, students are the main body of the teaching activities, the curriculum is based on vocational activities, the theory is combined with practice, and the cultivation of students' practical ability is highlighted. Generally, students in vocational colleges receive theoretical knowledge education on campus and practical education in enterprises. Through the coordination of teaching content and practical training content between vocational colleges and enterprises, students can make full preparations for employment. However, the real introduction of German "dual system" work process-oriented curriculum development is still in the exploratory stage. To this end, the State Council on implementation plan notice issued by the national vocational education reform is put forward, in vocational colleges, the applied undergraduate colleges and universities start degree certificate + a number of professional skill levels, namely the "1 + X" pilot certificate system, encourage students to obtain qualifications at the same time, actively obtain more professional skill level certificate, in order to improve employment and entrepreneurial skills. This paper takes this as the background, takes the implementation of "1 + X" certificate system as the guidance, and constructs the dual-system teaching system of automobile detection and maintenance specialty under the "1 + X" certificate system. The research includes four aspects: 1 + X certificate system analysis;Analysis of "dual system" in Germany; Under the background of 1 + X certificate system, combined with the "dual system" in Germany, the dual-system teaching system of automobile detection and maintenance was constructed. The results show that: after the implementation of the dual-system teaching system under the 1 + X certificate system, the performance of the experimental class is better than that of the ordinary class, which proves the effectiveness of the system constructed in this paper.

2 Research on Dual System Teaching System of Automobile Detection and Maintenance Specialty Based on "1 + X"

In recent years, the automobile industry has developed rapidly, and automobile technology is changing with each passing day. The demand for high-quality professionals in the automotive repair industry is increasing and the requirements are becoming stricter. The country has listed automotive maintenance technical talents as one of those in short supply. As the main training for ground vehicle maintenance personnel, secondary vocational schools must improve the quality of personnel training in order to meet the needs of society. A scientific and reasonable curriculum system is one of the most important guarantees for the cultivation of high-quality talents. The maintenance course system has a constantly improving and perfect position in the realization of high-quality personnel training [4]. Therefore, it is imperative. Therefore, under the guidance of the 1 + X certificate system, combined with the German "dual system", a dual-track teaching system for automotive inspection and maintenance majors was studied.

2.1 1 + X Certificate System Analysis

Vocational education is a type of education that is different from ordinary education, and it needs to have corresponding institutional arrangements to reflect the "cross-boundary" characteristics of vocational education, which are the combination of educational demand and industrial demand, the cooperation of school education and enterprise education, and the unification of individual development and vocational development. The "crossover" feature to the vocational education need to reflect the personalization, socialization degree certificate and the level of industry, enterprise and the professional comprehensive vocational ability level degree of several kinds of join each other professional skill level certificate and accommodation, we focus on the "1 + X" certification system, is the modern vocational education system framework about personnel training mode, evaluation model of a system design.

1 + X certificate system. In short, "1" is the diploma, which refers to the diploma obtained by the learner after completing the learning tasks of a certain educational stage in the school or other educational institutions that implement the education of diploma within the schooling system. "X" is the certificate of several vocational skill levels. "1 + X certificate system", is that students in the academic certificate at the same time, obtain a variety of vocational skill level certificate. It is this "X" that is most concerned in and out of vocational education. When implementing the "1 + X certificate system", it is undoubtedly necessary to deal with the relationship between "1" of academic certificate and "X" of vocational skill level certificate. "1" is the foundation and "X" is the supplement, reinforcement and expansion of "1". The degree certificate and the vocational skill level certificate are not two parallel certificate systems, but two kinds of certificates of mutual connection and mutual integration. The cohesion and integration of documents and documents is the essence of "1 + X certificate system", which is mainly reflected in the following five aspects as shown in Table 1.

"1 + X certificate system" is a basic system in the construction of national vocational education system, and also a major institutional innovation in the construction of vocational education development model with Chinese characteristics. The implementation of the "1 + X certificate system" will certainly push the reform of vocational colleges further. Its specific functions are mainly reflected in the following four aspects, as shown in Table 2.

Table 1. The essence of "1 + X certificate system"

Serial number	Essence embodiment
1	Vocational skill level standards and professional teaching standards of all levels of vocational education are mutually connected
2	The training content of "X" certificate and the curriculum content of professional personnel training program are integrated with each other
3	The training process of "X" certificate and the teaching process of academic education are organized and implemented simultaneously
4	The vocational skill assessment of "X" certificate and the curriculum examination of academic education are arranged as a whole, and the examination and evaluation are carried out simultaneously
5	Academic certificate and vocational skill level certificate reflect the mutual conversion of learning achievements

Table 2. Specific implementation of "1 + X certificate system"

Serial number	Specific role
1	It is conducive to further improving the vocational education and training system, will effectively promote vocational colleges to adhere to both academic education and training, deepen the reform of talent training mode and evaluation mode, and better serve the economic and social development
2	It is conducive to stimulating the endogenous power of social forces to participate in vocational education, fully mobilizing the enthusiasm of social forces to hold vocational education, promoting the integration of industry and education, the continuous enrichment and improvement of school enterprise cooperative education mechanism, and forming a diversified pattern of vocational education
3	It is beneficial for colleges and universities to integrate new technology, new technology, new norms and new requirements into the talent training process in time. It will also force colleges and universities to actively adapt to the new trend of science and technology development and the new demand of the employment market, continuously deepen the "three education" reform, and improve the ability of vocational education to adapt to the needs of economic and social development
4	"1 + X certificate system" realizes the development of vocational skill level standards, teaching materials and learning resources, and the implementation of assessment and certification by third-party institutions. The separation of teaching and testing is conducive to the objective evaluation of talents and the scientific evaluation of the quality of vocational colleges

2.2 Analysis of "Dual System" in Germany

Dual system is originated from a German vocational training model, the so-called dual, refers to the vocational training requires that the training personnel must go through two places of training, one refers to the vocational school, its main function is to teach professional knowledge related to the occupation; Another yuan is enterprises or public institutions and other off-campus training places, its main function is to let students in enterprises to receive professional training in vocational skills. Dual system is a school-running system jointly built by the university and the enterprise, that is, the enterprise and the school jointly undertake the task of training talents, according to the requirements of the enterprise on talent organization teaching and post training. This model has been widely applied in German enterprises and has been adopted by many Chinese enterprises in recent years [5].In recent years, China's vocational education can get the following enlightenment:

(1) Compared with school vocational education, dual vocational education pays more attention to the cultivation of practical skills and guarantees them. This makes the vocational education to train the practical operation personnel in the first line of production truly become the welcome education of the enterprise. Although China now attaches great importance to the training of students' practical operation skills, the training mode of school system objectively makes students far away from the front line of production, and the centralized arrangement of production practice is not conducive to the timely combination of theory and practice.
(2) Under the dual vocational education system, because students study in a specific working environment, students and enterprises have more opportunities to communicate, greatly reducing the risk of unemployment after training. This is of certain reference significance to the problem of employment of counterparts which has been difficult to solve for many years in China [6].
(3) Compared with the current teaching content of vocational education which emphasizes the system theory, the dual vocational education which takes the job requirement as the training target is more popular among enterprises. It should be an important part of the reform of vocational education in our country to set up a teaching program and a teaching content system to meet the requirements of workers' technical grade assessment standards.
(4) Because of the unparalleled advantages of cross-enterprise training centers in other forms, they are increasingly used in the former east Germany as a remedy for the deficiencies of training institutions. For China, it is difficult for many small and medium-sized enterprises to independently hold vocational education centers, so it is a very important way to develop vocational education to organize enterprises to jointly hold or cross-enterprise training centers hosted by the industry [7].

2.3 Construction of Dual System Teaching System for Automobile Detection and Maintenance

Under the background of certificate system of 1 + X, draw lessons from the German "dual system" curriculum development experience, to create a suitable for our province higher vocational colleges "learning field" curriculum development model, to explore a set of relatively complete courses in the major of higher vocational vehicle inspection and maintenance of a complete set of development methods, provide theoretical guidance for our province higher vocational education curriculum construction and demonstration.

(1) Guiding ideology for the construction of teaching system
The construction of the teaching system should reflect the characteristics of higher vocational colleges and the concept of keeping pace with The Times. It should be close to the reality of the development of talents needs of enterprises. The construction of the teaching system should cooperate with industrial enterprises, determine the core competence of vocational posts and job groups according to the vocational post setting of automobile maintenance service enterprises, and integrate the learning of job knowledge, vocational quality training and vocational ability training with the requirements of vocational post knowledge and ability and accomplishment [8]. In setting up the teaching system, we should implement the concept of "ability-oriented, learning-oriented", highlight the status of practical training courses of technology and skills, and break the traditional disciplinary teaching system.
(2) Design of teaching system framework
The general idea of the framework design of the dual-system teaching system for automobile detection and maintenance major under the 1 + X certificate system is as follows: firstly, analyze the typical tasks of this major, analyze the occupational ability objectives, summarize the action areas according to the work process, and then design the corresponding learning areas. Curriculum standards shall be jointly formulated by full-time teachers of the school, experts from the professional guidance committee and experts from enterprises. Based on the requirements of post task and career core ability, determine the teaching items of professional courses; Taking the project as the teaching carrier, the corresponding work situation is created and the work task is designed [9]. The integrated teaching mode of "teaching and doing" is adopted to enable students to master the knowledge and skills required by jobs and improve their core professional competitiveness, as shown in Fig. 1.
(3) Teaching system
When designing the teaching system, according to the principle of large platform, small module and orientation, the curriculum is divided into five modules: public and basic course module, professional group platform course module, professional core platform course module, professional direction platform course module and career development ability platform course module. Many main courses have been reorganized or integrated with obvious features and good effects, which integrate theory teaching with practice teaching and increase the practicability of the courses. The skill modules of this major are subdivided and correspondingly connected with the core courses of this major, so as to build a modular teaching system, formulate professional teaching standards and reform of talent cultivation model [10] (Fig. 2).
(4) Implementation guarantee of the teaching system
Secondary and higher vocational colleges not only link up the school level, but also deepen, extend and develop the curriculum. The specific courses to be offered, the semester to be offered, the class hours, the course objectives, etc., all require the

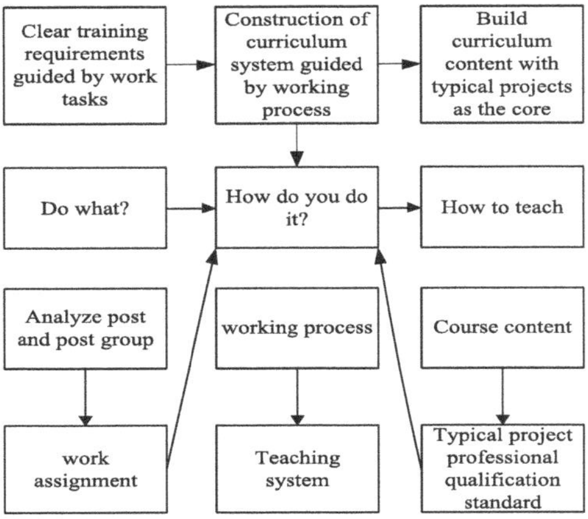

Fig. 1. Teaching system framework

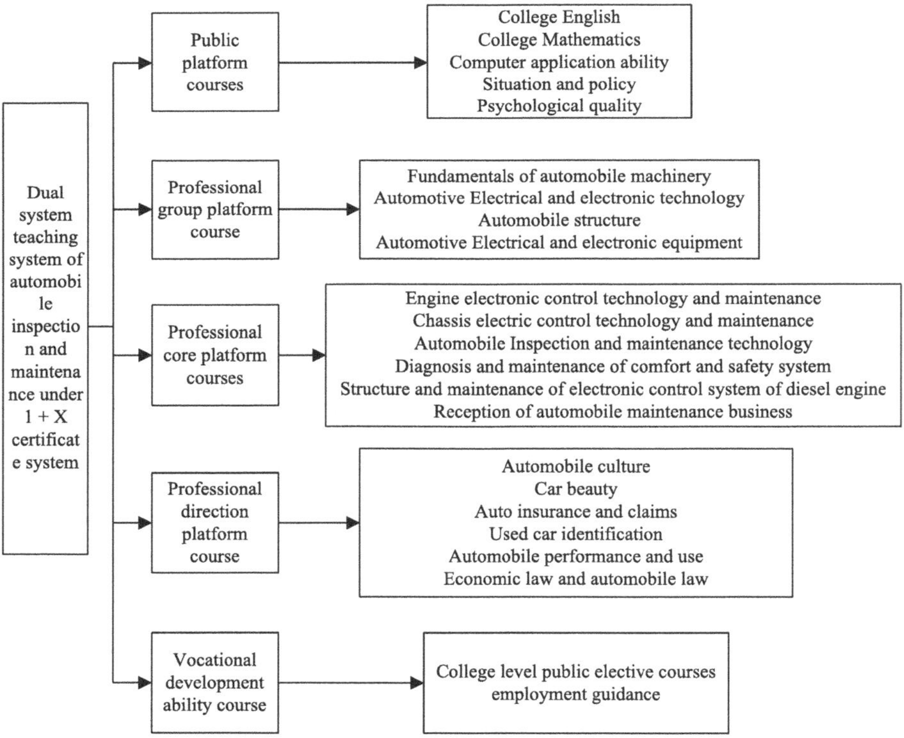

Fig. 2. Dual teaching system

professional leaders and backbone teachers in middle and higher vocational colleges to communicate with each other from time to time and participate in the research and study. The same course can be based on the unified curriculum standards, and the training of secondary vocational colleges and higher vocational colleges in different stages can be distinguished objective, so as to form a complete system of organic connection between high and middle vocational colleges.

At present, the automobile detection maintenance profession chooses the national plan teaching material more. Planning textbooks have applicability, but lack of regional characteristics, especially due to the planning textbook publishing cycle is long, the update is slow, many knowledge points are lagging behind, can not keep up with the requirements of The Times. Therefore, according to local industry characteristics and the needs of the enterprises, in accordance with the "overall planning, promotion" in vocational train of thought, play to the role of the teaching steering committee, between the two sides to jointly develop training materials and training projects, the construction of teaching resource, rich teaching resources, broaden the students learning path, establish the platform of students' autonomous learning.

The construction of the bridging curriculum system of high and middle vocational colleges under the "1 + X" certificate system needs to build a teaching team that can accurately grasp the advanced vocational education concepts, conduct in-depth research on the level standards of professional skills, have profound theoretical foundation and excellent practical skills, and can do a good job in teaching overall design to meet the training needs of "X" certificate. Firstly, the study and training of "1 + X" certificate related system for professional leaders should be strengthened, and the teaching team should be led to conduct the decomposition and research of vocational qualification standards, so as to facilitate the development and design of courses. Secondly, the training of professional backbone teachers should be strengthened, and the teaching implementation ability of backbone teachers should be improved through vocational skill standard training and enterprise production exercise. In addition, through the introduction of industrial enterprises technical ability, skill masters and other ways, optimize the teacher structure, comprehensive improvement of the professional skills of the teaching team.

"1 + X" certificate system in higher vocational curriculum effective connection can't depart from the support of relevant policies and education of education funds investment, such as vehicle inspection maintenance specialty of secondary vocational education, higher vocational education two phase of the cultivation of students' vocational ability, cannot leave the training rooms and self-contained campus off-campus practice base of sharing between colleges, it must be based on the sufficient funds investment and on the basis of the vocational education policy in place. Only by implementing the vocational education policy and increasing financial support, can we ensure the orderly connection of secondary and higher vocational training and promote the successful establishment of the overpass of secondary and higher vocational talent training.

3 Benefit Analysis of Dual-Element Teaching System

In order to verify the effectiveness of the dual system of auto inspection and maintenance under the 1 + X certificate system constructed in this paper, the pre-test situation of the experimental class and the ordinary class is first analyzed, and then the staged test situation is compared to obtain the curriculum system reform After the innovation of the teaching model, the achievement of the experimental class is improved, and the validity of the dual system teaching system is completed.

(1) Comparative measurement analysis of experimental class and ordinary class
Before the implementation of the dual-system teaching system for automobile detection and maintenance under the 1 + X certificate system, the students of the teaching system under the 1 + X certificate system were tested for their learning and vocational ability. The evaluation table is shown in Table 3. The main contents include professional knowledge, professional skills, practical ability, professional quality and professional attitude. The distribution of test results of the two classes is shown in Table 4. There are 42 students in the experimental class, and the average score of the whole class is 75.2 points. The total number of regular class is 41, and the average score of the whole class is 76.1. For the scores of the two classes of examinees, the author used SPSS statistical analysis software to analyze the results. As shown in Table 5, in the LEVENE test project, Sig > was 0.05, that is, the variance difference was not significant. In the mean value equation t-test, Sig(on both sides) is > 0.05, indicating that the mean value has no significant correlation. That is to say, the knowledge level and occupational ability of the experimental class and the ordinary class are similar, with no obvious difference.

Table 3. Evaluation of students' learning and vocational ability before implementation

Project	Index	
Name		
Major		
Course title		
Assessment time		
Evaluating indicator	• Excellent (8–10 points) • Good (6–8 points) • General (4–6 points) • Poor (0–4 points)	
Development of professional quality (key ability)	• Cultural accomplishment • Professional quality and professional attitude	
Mastery of theoretical knowledge (professional ability)	• Process evaluation • Summative evaluation	
Operation skills (professional ability)	• Process evaluation • Summative evaluation	
Analysis and evaluation of students' learning situation and professional ability		

Table 4. Summary of test results of the two classes

Project	Experimental class	Regular class
Total number	42	41
90–100 points	3	4
80–90 points	11	9
70–79 points	17	19
60–69	8	7
Below 60 points	3	2
Average	75.2	76.1

Table 5. Comparison results of experimental class and normal pre-test test

Project	Experimental class	Regular class
Total number	42	41
Average X	75.2	76.1
Level test of variance equation, sig	>0.05	>0.05
Standard error Z	2.251	2.247
Mean equation t test, sig (bilateral)	>0.05	>0.05

(2) Comparative analysis of staged tests between experimental classes and regular classes
The experimental class was taught in a three - month work-process-oriented integrated course, while the regular class was taught according to the traditional teaching mode. Then, the knowledge and professional ability of the two classes are tested, and the results are shown in Table 6 below. The average value of the experimental class was 73.2 s, and the Sig value was > 0.05. The average of the regular class was 71.18 points, and the Sig value was also > 0.05. It shows that there is

Table 6. Comparison between experimental class and regular class staged experiment

Project	Experimental class	Regular class
Total number	42	41
Average X	73.25	71.18
Level test of variance equation, sig	>0.05	>0.05
Standard error Z	1.875	2.035
Mean equation t test, sig (bilateral)	>0.05	>0.05

no significant correlation between the learning knowledge and the comprehensive vocational ability of the two classes, and the overall level of the two classes is the same. The causes of this phenomenon may be selected class for final year students, they have already accustomed to the traditional curriculum model, thinking habit already cured, such as teaching system for the purpose of this article may be time to adjust to, 1 + X certificate system oriented curriculum system after implementation of the advantage of also can't so fast.

(3) Comparative analysis of experimental class and ordinary class
According to Tables 6 and 7, the average score of the experimental class under the teaching system of 1 + X certificate system is as high as 78.59 points, while that of the ordinary class is only 71.21 points. SigG0.05 indicated significant variance difference and mean difference. That is to say, there is a significant difference in test scores between the two classes. After the implementation of the teaching system under the 1 + X certificate system, the performance of the experimental class improved significantly and the quality of teaching was improved, which fully demonstrates the advantages of the teaching system under the 1 + X certificate system.

Table 7. Comparison and summary statistics of experimental class and ordinary class

Project	Experimental class	Regular class
Total number	42	41
Average X	78.59	71.21
Level test of variance equation, sig	0.034<0 05	0.041<0 05
Standard error Z	2.364	2.102
Mean equation t test, sig (bilateral)	0.016<0 05	0.022<0 05

To sum up, after the reform of the existing curriculum system and the innovation of the teaching model, the results of the experimental class are integrated the improvement of the volume is obvious, which indicates the applicability of the dual-system teaching system of automobile detection and maintenance under the 1 + X certificate system to a certain extent. Students' work in the study, learn on the job "of the course teaching and activities, improve their professional knowledge and skills at the same time, the construction of professional cognition and professional accomplishment, form a future professional ability and the key ability of the corresponding work, so as to improve the quality of personnel training of secondary vocational school, in line with the industry enterprise demand for high quality talents.

4 Conclusion

To sum up, the training goal of higher vocational education is to train highly skilled talents who are needed in production, construction and management, etc., and the training of skills requires a scientific and reasonable practical teaching system. The core of this system is the content system, which contains three layers of basic skills, professional skills and technical application times. In addition, practice teachers, practice resources and practice materials are the important guarantee of practice teaching system. In order to ensure that this system can be truly implemented, there needs to be a sound supervision system. This paper constructs the system of 1 + X certificate under vehicle inspection maintenance professional teaching system, dual system under the system, vehicle inspection maintenance professional student's beginning ability has been greatly improved, and the comprehensive quality enhanced markedly, and the dual system of vocational colleges theory to guide the students in at the same time, also let the students receive professional training in vocational skills in enterprises. The satisfaction of both enterprises and students has been greatly improved.

5 Fund Projects

(1) 2019 research project of college level teaching reform of Chongqing Tourism Vocational College, key project, project name: research and practice of automobile inspection and maintenance technology construction based on 1 + X certificate system, Project No.: yjg2019002.
(2) 2019 college level teaching achievement cultivation project of Chongqing Tourism Vocational College, project name: Exploration and practice of "post rotation" practical teaching based on work station under 1 + X certificate system, Project No.: yjcg2019006.

References

1. Rong, Z., Broadstock, D.C., Peng, Y.: Initial submarket positioning and firm survival: evidence from the British automobile industry. Small Bus. Econ. **51**(4), 965–993 (2018)
2. Keeley, K.A.: Equipment safety: maintenance and inspection. What the oral surgeon needs to know. **29**(2), 209–221 (2017)
3. Gessler, M.: The lack of collaboration between companies and schools in the German dual apprenticeship system. Hist. Background Recent Data **4**(2), 164–195 (2017)
4. Worringen, U., Meng, K., Bitzer, E.-M., et al.: Development and current status of the health education curriculum of the German pension insurance. Die Rehabil. **56**(4), 232–239 (2017)
5. Nestler, T., Huber, J., Laury, A.M., et al.: Thromboprophylaxis and the route of administration of chemotherapy in testicular cancer patients in German-speaking countries. World J. Urol. **36**(6), 913–920 (2018). https://doi.org/10.1007/s00345-018-2222-x
6. Kostev, K., Jacob, L.: Association between depression and persistence with oral antihyperglycemic drugs in type 2 diabetes mellitus patients in Germany. Psychiatry Res. **261**(2), 90–93 (2017)

7. Gassenmaier, M., Eigentler, T.K., Keim, U., et al.: Serial or parallel metastasis of cutaneous melanoma? A study of the german central malignant melanoma registry. J. Invest. Dermatol. **137**(12), 2570–2577 (2017)
8. Wang, Y., Zhang, S., Fu, J.: A study on the optimization design of the training program of curriculum system for cross-border e-commerce talents in higher vocational colleges based on the CIPP model. Revista de la Facultad de Ingenieria **32**(8), 589–596 (2017)
9. Raina, S., Kumar, R., Kumar, D., et al.: Game change in Indian health care system through reforms in medical education curriculum focusing on primary care - recommendations of a joint working group. J. Fam. Med. Prim. Care **7**(3), 489–494 (2018)
10. Al Amin, Md., Greenwood, J.: The examination system in Bangladesh and its impact: on curriculum, students, teachers and society. Lang. Test. Asia **8**(1), 4–15 (2018)

The Construction of the Remote Interactive Platform of the Practical Training Teaching in the Employment Domain of Colleges and Universities Under the 1 + X Certificate System

Hai-jing Zhou(✉) and Shou-liang He

Chongqing Vocational Institute of Tourism, Qianjiang 409099, China
zhouhaijing554@yeah.net

Abstract. In view of the problems of poor interaction and non-reservation in the existing college employment training teaching platform, which leads to the decline of students' interest in learning, therefore, under the influence of the 1 + X certificate system, a new college employment work domain training teaching remote interaction platform is constructed. The platform takes the 1 + X certificate system as the goal, establishes the appointment mechanism of training teaching, designs the long-distance interactive mode of training teaching platform by setting the way of video and audio playing in the platform, and realizes the construction of the long-distance interactive platform of training teaching in the field of employment in colleges and universities. The experimental results show that the long-distance interactive platform for training teaching is highly interactive. Students can improve the performance of training teaching through using the platform, and the application effect is better.

Keywords: 1 + X certificate system · University employment domain · Practical teaching · Remote interactive platform

1 Introduction

In order to improve the employment rate and expand the employment direction of college students, many colleges and universities have constructed practical teaching platform. By setting up a training teaching resource management platform, the training content will be uploaded to a page, so that students can query at any time in their spare time, and learn training related courses [1]. Some scholars have proposed the construction of training platform based on distance education, which uses face recognition to realize the process control of distance education. Take the knowledge block as the construction unit, take the professional skill promotion as the goal, reconstruct the distance education teaching resources [2]. Some scholars also put forward the framework of network-based

S. Liu et al. (Eds.): eLEOT 2020, LNICST 339, pp. 137–147, 2020.
https://doi.org/10.1007/978-3-030-63952-5_12

modular interactive hybrid laboratory, and discussed the efficiency of practical teaching platform [3].

In order to further improve the training platform and improve the test results of students. Therefore, based on the 1 + X certificate system, a new long-distance interactive platform for practical teaching in the field of employment in Colleges and universities is constructed. The platform has appointment module, and the audio and video playing mode is more flexible, and the interaction between students and teachers is better. It can enhance students' interest in learning, provide more reliable teaching support for graduates' employment.

2 Appointment Mechanism of Establishing Practical Teaching Platform Under 1 + X Certificate System

According to the implementation plan of national vocational education reform, the state will launch the pilot project of "diploma+several vocational skill level certificates" in vocational colleges and application-oriented undergraduate schools, i.e. 1 + X certificate system. It is used to encourage students to actively take multiple vocational skill level certificates while learning textbook knowledge and theory. Therefore, taking the 1 + X certificate system as the construction goal, the platform reservation mechanism is established. The purpose of the platform is to let students interact with teachers face to face actively by appointment, and to strengthen the learning of practical training content in the field of employment. The platform is linked with teaching activities to realize the automatic practical teaching in the field of employment in colleges and universities.

With the development of cloud technology, students can easily access cloud services, storage resources, computing resources, software and hardware resources through terminal devices. The reservation platform consists of user service platform, teaching reservation platform, authorization platform and control service platform. The structure is shown in Fig. 1:

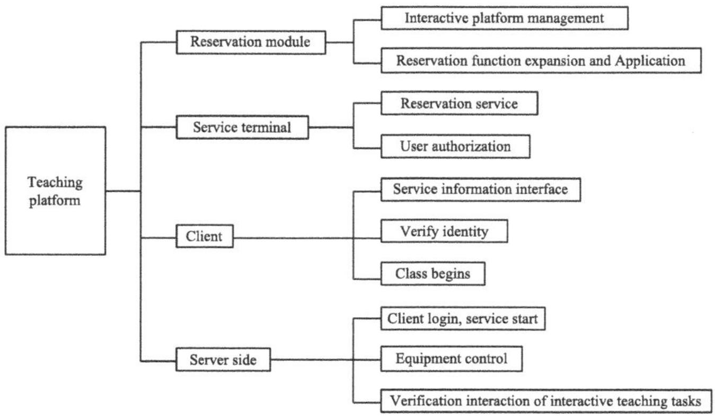

Fig. 1. Reservation module of remote interaction platform for practical teaching

According to Fig. 1, the use of page display can reflect the advantages of the reservation platform and emphasize the concept of time. At the same time, it can inform people through various media in time, with simple and practical functions. Formula (1) is the reservation algorithm set according to the reservation mechanism:

$$\sigma = \frac{\Delta k}{q} = \frac{\varphi \omega_i - s}{q} \tag{1}$$

In formula (1): σ represents the reservation control parameter; Δk represents the reservation usage; q represents the average reservation item; φ represents the total amount of reservation after temporary increase; ω_i represents the weight; s represents the asynchronous reservation data. Set the reservation mode of the platform according to the above algorithm.

For teaching activity reservation, you can make a corresponding reservation activity plan through the visual calendar presentation, and reserve teaching activities through the corresponding arrangement of the timetable. Select an interactive classroom, interact with participants, make an appointment to start the corresponding classroom equipment at the same time, and inform people of the appointment information through SMS and email in time. The calendar management module displays the calendar information, the daily booking activity record is displayed in the log, the day, week and month functions are reserved, and the schedule can be synchronized to realize the automatic call; the booking information entry of the booking module, the entry personnel can be selected, and the time and notification media can be selected; the equipment management module notifies the equipment to start according to the time, and controls the terminal and relevant through the start-up equipment Start of equipment in activity room.

The user management module adjusts the appointments reasonably, supports multiple teachers to participate in interactive [4] simultaneously, and the communication module adopts multiple classrooms or multiple display terminals. The classroom reminds the reservation classroom reminder, calls the appointment information through the intelligent terminal, and compares the time of the call before the start of the activity and the start of the activity, so as to remind the teacher to enter the activity in time. The reservation mode can select the schedule synchronization mode, adapt to the fixed reservation mode of the schedule, and realize the automatic reservation activity; regularly synchronize the schedule information, and achieve the intelligent interactive teaching remote mode; open the remote interaction through the public network, Cross School interactive mode interactive screen; customize the interactive reservation playing mode through the interactive screen, and automatically save the recording and broadcasting resources.

According to the above content, the appointment mechanism of the training teaching platform is established to ensure that under the guidance of the 1 + X certificate system, students can improve their employment competitiveness and increase the professional skills to obtain various certificates through the appointment of employment training teaching content.

3 Interactive Mechanism of Establishing Practical Teaching Platform Under 1 + X Certificate System

Video and audio are the most important media in the network learning platform. Only by establishing a real-time, clear and stable video and audio system, can we ensure the information exchange between teachers and students in the network environment [5]. The user interface of e-learning platform consists of four parts: user information control, audio and video display, information sharing and text exchange, as shown in Fig. 2:

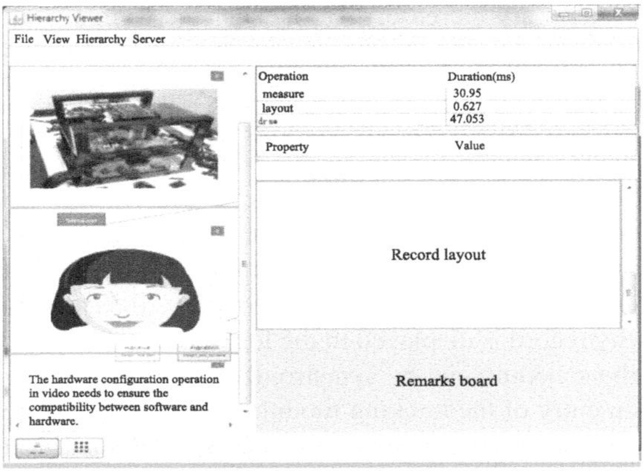

Fig. 2. User interface of e-learning platform

According to the user interface in Fig. 2, the user information control area displays the current classroom name, the names of online teachers and students, member status and other information, so as to realize the functions of role assignment and authority control; the audio and video display area mainly displays the video windows of current online teachers and students, as well as the voice volume fluctuation of speakers; the information sharing area mainly displays Teachers and students share teaching information to achieve the function of whiteboard writing in the teaching process, while the text exchange area realizes the function of text exchange between teachers and students, students and students. Audio and video are important modules for interaction between teachers and students, which are realized by streaming media technology [6]. The following two modules are designed.

3.1 Audio Module Design

(1) Audio on demand function

According to the control center, the server transmits the directory and files of the audio files that can be on-demand to the terminal, and the terminal requests the files on demand from the server. The server is responsible for delivering the directory content to the terminal, so that the terminal can select the files that it wants to play on demand. After the terminal determines the selected file, the server transmits the content of the file to the terminal in the mode of "request transfer" for the terminal to play freely. The whole process improves two main steps: the transmission of directory and the transmission and reception of audio data stream. The processing mode of the directory is shown in Fig. 3.

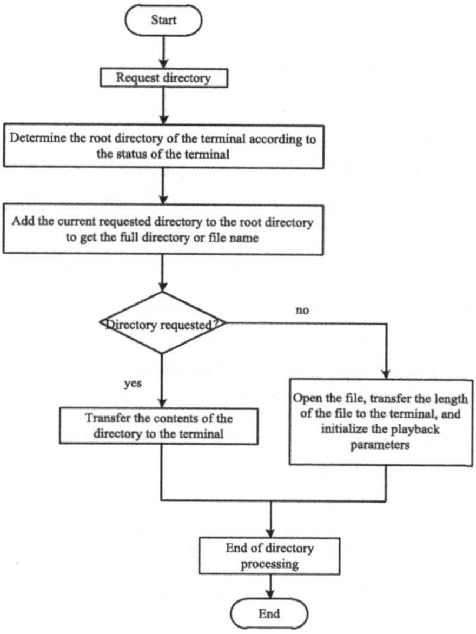

Fig. 3. Directory processing flow

In order to make the audio stream play continuously in real time, the system adopts the "preprocessing double buffer queue mechanism". Because the speed of network receiving stream is much faster than that of stream playing, if we play by the way of "receiving, playing, receiving and playing", there must be a gap, which shows that there is an intermittent pause in playing. The way to solve this problem is to adopt the mechanism of pre receive double buffer queue, whose main idea is "receive and send at the same time, double buffer is used alternately".

Suppose that the two buffer queues are W_1 and W_2 respectively. After the receiving thread is started, the data will be received into W_1 queue. When W_1 is full, on the one hand, the data will continue to be received and placed into W_2 queue, on the other hand, the data in W_1 buffer will be played. Because the receiving process is far faster than the playing process, when W_2 receives the full data, it is likely that W_1's data hasn't played out, so the receiving thread will be suspended; when W_1's data plays out, it will turn to W_2's data, then resume the receiving thread, and put the received data in W_1 buffer queue, and when W_1 is full, it will be suspended until y plays out. To control this alternate process, the following formula can be used to obtain the control parameters:

$$\begin{cases} W_1 = \mu_1 \sin \beta tn \cdot x \\ W_2 = \mu_2 \sin \beta tn \cdot x \\ g(w) = m\lambda - b_i \end{cases} \tag{2}$$

In formula (2), μ_1 and μ_2 respectively represent the constraints of two queues; β represents the buffered data; t represents the buffering time; n represents the load completed amount of playing content; x represents the control parameters of necessary conditions; $g(w)$ represents the identification function for the alternation of two queues; m represents the identification parameters; λ represents the progress indicators of two queues; b_i represents the alternation offset of the ith stage. According to the above control process alternation, the playback thread is guaranteed to execute all the time, so as to make the playback real-time and smooth.

(2) Voice live broadcast design

Voice live broadcast is mainly to collect voice data from microphone through sound card, and then broadcast it through network, so that students can hear the teacher's voice [7]. This function is the basis of the whole system, the quality of voice directly determines the success of the whole system. Voice live broadcast is implemented by windows low-level audio functions, because they can operate on each voice data block. Low level audio services include querying audio devices, turning device drivers on and off, allocating and preparing audio data blocks, managing audio data blocks, applying MMTIME structures, and handling errors. The reason why low-level audio functions can operate on each sound data block is attributed to the message mapping of windows, which will send relevant messages after collecting and playing a data block. The important messages and trigger conditions involved in playing sound are shown in Fig. 4 below.

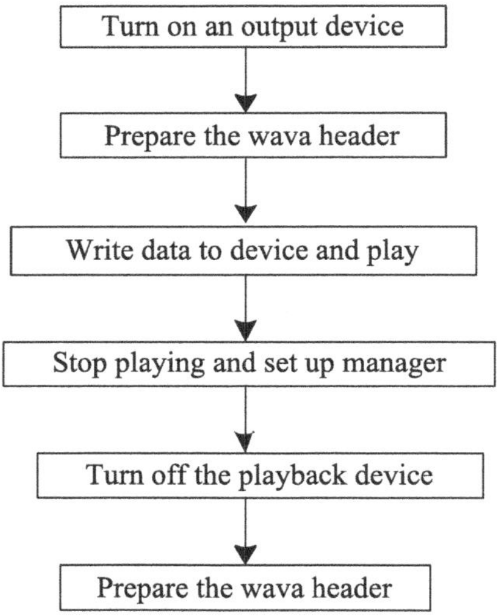

Fig. 4. Voice live broadcast process

The audio and video module also has a function. On the teacher's computer, it can record and broadcast the content. The teacher has the right to record the content in the classroom, and then play it to the students selectively at a certain time.

3.2 Video Design

(1) VOD design
Users can choose to watch video courses according to their own wishes, which fundamentally changes the shortcomings of passive watching teaching content, does not need to comply with the traditional schedule, and fully realizes the initiative of users to obtain information [8]. After the request acceptance, the server prepares the accessible course types in the storage subsystem and displays the course on demand list on the user screen. After the user selects the teaching category, the server takes the course content from the storage subroutine and synthesizes one video data stream, which is transmitted to the client through the network.

(2) Live video design
The live video uses a video camera to collect video in real time and send it to the students through the network, so that students can see the head and shoulders of teachers, just like sitting in a real classroom [9]. Moreover, it has a great auxiliary effect on teaching, especially when teaching practical manual courses, students can see the teacher's design actions through live video, which plays a very important role in training students' actual operation [10]. At the same time, the video and audio are shared, and the synchronization of video and audio is realized by FMS.

4 Design the Remote Interactive Mode of Practical Teaching Platform

Through the design of teaching audio and video broadcast mode, the distance interaction mode of training teaching platform is designed. Figure 5 is the structure diagram of the interaction mode of the platform.

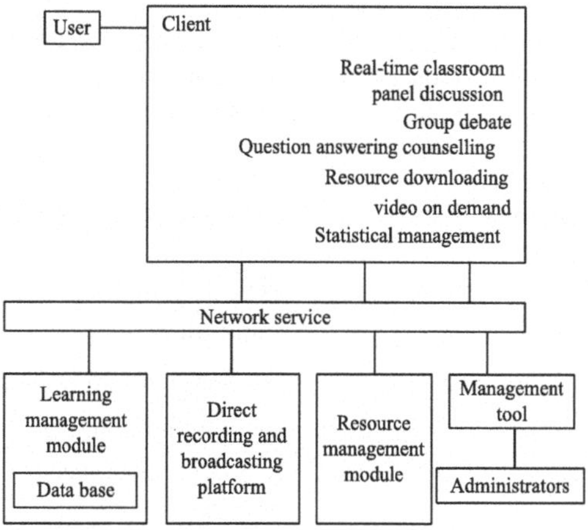

Fig. 5. Structure diagram of remote interaction mode of practical teaching platform

Based on the existing teaching resource management system and the simple learning management system, the remote interactive platform shown in this paper realizes the functions of real-time classroom, group discussion, group debate, question answering guidance, resource download, video on demand and management on the client side in the way of network service. In order to deal with the problems in a unified way, the types and categories of training teaching resources are integrated. The types of resources provided are text, audio and video. Each type of resource should control the size, format and category settings of the uploaded resources, so as to facilitate the management of resources. The resource management function will provide user upload (teacher user) and resource download (student user). Table 1 is the standard design table of shared resources upload.

Table 1. Upload standard of shared resources

Resource type	Format	Size restriction	Remarks
Text	.xps	<10 m	Office document printing format
Audio frequency	wina	<10 m	Time less than hours, bit rate < 320 kbs
Video	Mp4 wmv	<15 m	Resolving power 640*480 No longer than 30 min

In order to control the smooth operation of the interactive program of the remote interactive platform for practical teaching, the evaluation index of the platform is set, and the calculation equation of the interactive index is as follows:

$$\gamma = \sum_{i=2}^{n} \varphi_i - f\max \tag{3}$$

In formula (3): γ represents the interaction index; $f_{\max}$ represents the maximum interaction deviation; φ_i represents the ith interaction result; n represents the number of iterations. The data in Table 2 is the evaluation elements and index system.

Table 2. Evaluation elements and index system

First level index	Two level index	Three level index
Learning behavior	Online record	Online duration and login frequency
	Question answering	Number of questions and answers
	Participate in discussion	Discussion frequency
Learning process	Learning plan	Number of completed plans of the course webpage visited
	Learning tasks	Whether the course webpage you browse has completed the established learning task and learning goal
	Learning log	Records of students in the course of learning

According to the above parameters, the interaction index is set up. Through the improved remote interaction mode of the training teaching platform, the construction of the remote interaction platform of the training teaching in the employment domain of colleges and Universities under the 1 + X certificate system is realized.

5 Experimental Results and Analysis

In this paper, a comparative experiment is proposed to compare the distance interaction platform of high-efficiency employment work area training teaching with the training platform (traditional platform) based on configuration and multimedia software. Analyze the differences between the two platforms. In the experiment, the proposed construction method was used as the experimental group and the traditional platform as the control

Table 3. Basic information of test objects

Name code	Examination results	
	Written examination	Practical training
01	94.5	84.5
02	92.5	80.5
03	92	80.5
04	96.5	88
05	94	84
06	90.5	78.5
07	91	79
08	92.5	79.5
09	98.5	89.5
010	97.5	84.5
011	95	85.5
012	95	83.5
013	95	80
014	97	82
015	96.5	90.5
016	96.5	90
017	94	91.5
018	94.5	86.5
019	92.5	87
020	93	89.5

group. In a university with a large number of specialties, 20 students with different specialties are randomly selected as the experimental test objects, and the basic information of the experimental objects is shown in Table 3.

According to Table 3, students' performance in culture class is normal and above the excellent level, but the training test results are not ideal. Most of the students are 90 points away from the excellent file, which is a certain distance away. The results of the two training platforms were compared. Figure 6 shows the comparison results of this experiment.

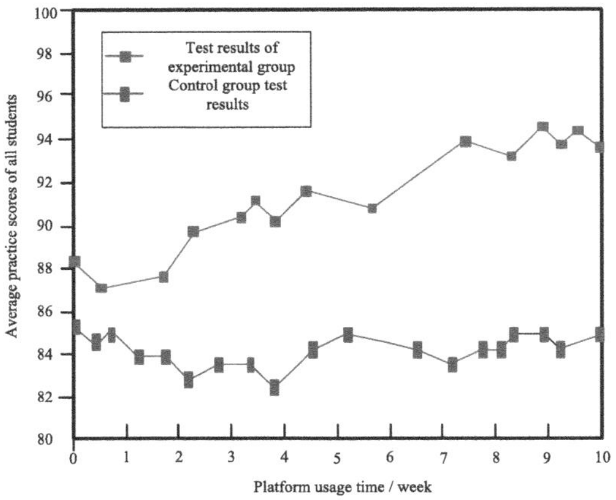

Fig. 6. Comparison of students' performance after learning in different systems

According to the experimental results in Fig. 6, taking 10 weeks as the experimental test cycle, there are great differences between the two training teaching platforms, which are embodied in the students' scores. According to the curve trend, the design of the remote interactive training teaching platform, due to its superior video and audio display, teacher-student interaction, as well as the function of appointment, deepens students' interest in learning, makes students increase the enthusiasm of self-help training, so improves the training test results. The traditional training teaching platform, because of its weak function, can not meet the students' understanding of the training content, and there is no online interaction, which reduces the enthusiasm of students, leading to the training performance has been below the excellent level. Based on the above experimental results, it can be seen that this platform can improve the practical training level of students and enhance their employment competitiveness.

6 Conclusion

Under the condition of considering the 1 + X certificate system, the platform designed in this paper can enhance the video and audio teaching effect of the platform, and set up the program and interactive mode that can be reserved. At the same time of improving the enthusiasm of students, we should strengthen the training ability of students, so as to provide guarantee for the graduates' employment choice in the future. But this design is designed for students and teachers. In the future, other hardware facilities can be optimized to further improve the real-time feedback of the platform.

7 Fund Projects

(1) 2019 research project of college level teaching reform of Chongqing Tourism Vocational College, key project, project name: research and practice of automobile inspection and maintenance technology construction based on 1 + X certificate system, Project No: yjg2019002.

(2) 2019 college level teaching achievement cultivation project of Chongqing Tourism Vocational College, project name: Exploration and practice of "post rotation" practical teaching based on work station under 1 + X certificate system, Project No: yjcg2019006.

References

1. Tian, K.Y., Shang, F.F., Tian, Y.Y., et al.: Apprenticeship system of American NCCAOM Certification of acupuncture and oriental medicine. Zhongguo Zhen Jiu=Chin. Acupunct. Moxibustion **39**(4), 429–432 (2019)
2. Wu, L.D., Huang, W.Q., Xiao, L.W.: Construction of teaching and training platform of distance vocational education based on VR. J. Ningbo Radio TV University **16**(2), 96–101 (2018)
3. Lei, Z., Zhou, H., Hu, W., et al.: Modular web-based interactive hybrid laboratory framework for research and education. IEEE Access **17**(6), 20152–20163 (2018)
4. Cheshire, M.H., Strickland, H.P.: Distance learning teaching strategies in registered nurse to baccalaureate nurse programs: advancing cultural competence of registered nurses in providing end-of-life care. Teach. Learn. Nurs. **13**(3), 153–155 (2018)
5. Achilleos, A.P., Mettouris, C., Yeratziotis, A., et al.: SciChallenge: a social media aware platform for contest-based STEM education and motivation of young students. IEEE Trans. Learn. Technol. **12**(1), 98–111 (2018)
6. Li, G., Wang, F.: Research on art innovation teaching platform based on data mining algorithm. Cluster Comput. **22**(6), 13867–13872 (2019)
7. Rodríguez-Prieto, A., Camacho, A.M., Merayo, D., et al.: An educational software to reinforce the comprehensive learning of materials selection. Comput. Appl. Eng. Educ. **26**(1), 125–140 (2018)
8. Fan, Y., Zhang, J., Yu, H., et al.: Research on digital and analog electronic experiment teaching course management based on UltraLab network experiment platform. Int. J. Plant Eng. Manage. **32**(4), 206–215 (2018)
9. Bai, Y., Huang, F., Wang, Q., et al.: Development of practical teaching model based on intelligent comprehensive nursing practice platform. Stud. Health Technol. Inform. **250**(5), 240 (2018)
10. Ranga, J.S.: Multipurpose use of explain everything iPad app for teaching chemistry courses. J. Chem. Educ. **95**(5), 895–898 (2018)

Education Reform of Construction Specialty in the Context of Upgrading of Intelligent Construction Industry

Wei-wei Zhu and Man-li Tian(✉)

School of Road Bridge and Architecture, Chongqing Vocational College of Transportation, Chongqing 402247, China
szshuishi13@163.com, ixneux@163.com

Abstract. Traditional architectural education in Colleges and universities pays more attention to theoretical knowledge, and the correlation between professional courses and engineering practice is low. Therefore, the paper puts forward the education reform of construction specialty under the background of intelligent construction industry upgrading. First of all, combining the teaching characteristics of architecture specialty and the related contents of the intelligent buildings involved in the teaching of universities, it sums up from different aspects; integrates the concept of intelligent architecture into architecture education, adds new knowledge points in all grades of architectural majors, and cuts down old knowledge points, and finally, regulates the teaching methods of teachers, and collates the framework of the reform curriculum system, so as to complete this task. Under the background of the upgrading of intelligent construction industry, the education reform and design of construction specialty was carried out. The research results show that the scores of students on the degree of relevance between the reformed professional courses and engineering practice are relatively high. Therefore, it can be proved that the reform on the education of Architectural Specialty in the context of upgrading the intelligent construction industry plays a certain role in improving the degree of relevance between the architectural courses and engineering practice.

Keywords: Smart building · Education reform · Knowledge system · Teaching method

1 Introduction

Human society has successively experienced the Stone Age, Agricultural Age, and Industrial Age. The development process has always been accompanied by the progress of technology and civilization. The history of human development is not only the history of civilization progress, but also the history of continuous evolution of human tools. The development of buildings is the same. From earthen pits and cave dwellings to brick buildings and reinforced concrete high-rise buildings, the functions and quality are also

S. Liu et al. (Eds.): eLEOT 2020, LNICST 339, pp. 148–158, 2020.
https://doi.org/10.1007/978-3-030-63952-5_13

more perfect, including the development of intelligent buildings and intelligent buildings with networked, integrated security and fire protection. As a result, living environments are becoming safer, more comfortable and more convenient. With the increase of population and technological progress, the negative impact of construction is also increasing [1]. Land occupation, green space reduction, energy consumption increase, environmental damage and other issues are urgent to be solved. Architectural scientists around the world are also constantly exploring the development direction of future architecture. At present, the construction industry is also a labor-intensive industry. In order to better cultivate more managerial and compound building technical talents, the Ministry of education and the Ministry of housing and urban rural development jointly pointed out that the education concept oriented by employment should establish the comprehensive quality standard and ability standard: vigorously implement the construction orientation, the combination of work and learning, and highlight the cultivation of practical ability [2].

The traditional education of architectural majors in colleges and universities pays more attention to theoretical knowledge, and the correlation between professional courses and engineering practice is low. To this end, the reform of the education of architectural professionals in the context of the upgrading of the intelligent building industry is proposed. First of all, comb the relevant knowledge system of intelligent buildings, summarize the domestic and foreign intelligent building evaluation systems, combine the teaching characteristics of architectural majors, and the related content of intelligent buildings involved in teaching in different universities. Aspects are summarized; in architecture education, we should integrate the concept of intelligent architecture, add new knowledge points and delete old knowledge points in all grades of architectural majors, finally adjust the teaching methods of teachers, and sort out the framework of the reform curriculum system, thus completing the design reform of Architectural Education in the context of smart building industry upgrading.

2 The Reform of Architectural Education Under the Background of the Upgrade of Smart Construction Industry

The research on the theory of intelligent architecture has gradually attracted people's attention to the problems existing in the way of architectural education. For a long time, the strict division of different courses in architectural education has resulted in the separation of design, technology and theory, making the final design results pay more attention to art forms and ignore the technical elements and design intent of Architecture [3]. This thesis is based on the study and data collation of the development background of domestic and foreign architectural education, the theory of intelligent architectural education at home and abroad, the relevant contents of intelligent architectural education of various colleges and universities at home and abroad, and socially relevant scholars and architects. The second chapter summarizes the current curriculum adjustments and teaching reforms adopted by universities at home and abroad for the reform of smart building education, and analyzes them in a classified manner. It selects a suitable reform method that achieves good teaching results. The integration of smart building concepts into the education of architecture professionals provides good practice teaching methods.

At present, foreign architecture colleges begin to pay attention to the integration of design, technology and theory, integrate the theory and technical knowledge of intelligent building into the design, change the traditional architectural education mode, and explore the new mode of Architectural Education for the needs of social development. Aiming at the reform of architectural education, the following technical routes are designed: (Fig. 1)

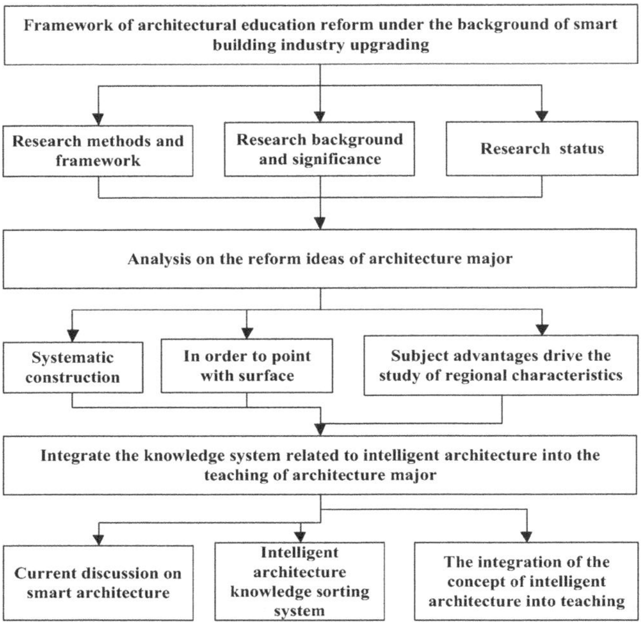

Fig. 1. Technical roadmap for education reform

According to the above route, the reform of Architectural Education in China is designed.

2.1 Review the Knowledge System of Smart Buildings

Through the understanding of the relevant theories and practices of smart building and the summary analysis of the evaluation system of smart building in various countries [4], we have a whole understanding of the relevant contents of smart building. See the following table for the contents of domestic and foreign smart building evaluation system (Table 1):

We can understand that the assessment contents of smart buildings in different countries are basically the same, but different countries have different emphases on the specific contents of the assessment items. In general, the assessment contents generally include: site planning and land use, health and comfort of indoor environment, energy utilization, utilization and transportation of materials and resources (including water resources),

Table 1. Contents of smart building assessment systems in various countries

Name	Evaluation index	Range of application
England BREEAM	Management, health and comfort – indoor and outdoor environments, energy, transportation, water, raw materials, land use, regional ecology, pollution	Office buildings, residential buildings, retail buildings, campus buildings
The United StatesLEED	Site conditions, efficient use of water resources, energy and atmosphere, materials and resources, indoor environmental quality	New building, commercial interior decoration, residential, community planning and development
JapanCASBEE	Indoor and outdoor environment, service environment, energy and materials, building environment	New construction, existing construction, renovation and operation, temporary construction
Other countriesGBTool	Resource consumption, environmental load, environmental equipment quality, cost, operation management	Office buildings, congregations, school buildings

and later operation management [5]. Different countries have set up different versions of targeted evaluation systems for different types of intelligent buildings.

Combining the teaching characteristics of architecture majors and the relevant contents of smart buildings involved in teaching in universities, the intellectual architecture knowledge system is sorted out from four parts: the basic theory part of smart architecture, the ontology part of smart building specialty, the technical discipline part of smart building, and Part of smart building practice method system [6]. Intelligent architecture involves a wide range of related technical disciplines, from materials to structures, from structures to equipment and so on. It includes the basic knowledge of physical control of building environment (architectural acoustics, optics, thermology), intelligent building materials (new materials, local materials), intelligent building structure, intelligent building structure, intelligent building equipment (water, heating, electricity, power supply), as well as the expanded knowledge of building energy saving technology, intelligent building technology, intelligent building construction technology, intelligent building operation management, etc. The smart building practice methods mainly include: research and design of smart building actual projects (focus on the practical issues of smart building design, design cooperation and communication ability training, data collection and smart building technology application ability), smart building construction site learning, and building performance evaluation (understand the index items in the smart building evaluation standards from practice), maintenance and operation management of built smart buildings, etc. The practice of intelligent building can not only stay in the practical design part, but also in the design, construction, operation and demolition of intelligent building, experience the whole process of the whole life cycle, better understand and feel what is intelligent building.

2.2 The Integration of the Concept of Intelligent Architecture into the Education of Architecture

In the future, the intelligent building is not a single building, but a building cluster, even the building ecology. The change of data quantity and data type of intelligent building will be beyond imagination. In the big data environment, it is not only necessary to create real-time data, but also need to process the data in real-time flow, and feed back the data analysis results to the user in real time [7]. Perform deep and complex analysis through data analysis, data mining, machine learning and other technologies to mine the potential value of data. The traditional data storage and processing technology can no longer meet the new requirements. Therefore, data collection, storage, mining analysis, processing and use will be realized through cloud computing and big data technologies. Data is maximized through sharing and cross-reuse. Cross professional or even cross industry data platform is the development trend of data processing in the future, which will play a huge role in the value-added of the construction industry.

In the course system, the architecture education integrating the concept of intelligent architecture still adheres to the teaching system with architecture design as the main axis and technology, theory and practice as the auxiliary courses. The learning of architecture professional knowledge is a step-by-step process. The cultivation of the concept of intelligent architecture also follows the principle of step-by-step, from the understanding and understanding of intelligent architecture to the learning and design of intelligent architecture technology, as well as the application of intelligent architecture analysis tools, and finally the practical learning and knowledge expansion of intelligent architecture. In the architecture professional knowledge system, based on the learning characteristics and professional education methods of students, a systematic and comprehensive intelligent building knowledge system is gradually integrated into the architecture teaching system, and the original architecture teaching system is improved, focusing on architecture and landscape. Multi-disciplinary studies in planning, technology, etc., expand the knowledge on the basis of learning basic knowledge, and encourage special research and comprehensive use [8].

On the basis of the original architectural design course, adjust the architectural design course, expand the knowledge of intelligent architectural design in the design course, increase the knowledge lectures and design task requirements related to intelligent architecture, and add related design topics, such as intelligent architectural design, ecological architectural design, solar architectural design, and old architecture design According to the teaching resources, choose the appropriate design topics to train the students in the design of intelligent buildings, focus on the cultivation of students' design awareness of intelligent buildings, and establish the concept of sustainable development. See the following table for the knowledge points of intelligent architecture design in the architecture design course integrated with the concept of Intelligent Architecture (Table 2):

In recent years, under the guidance of relevant national policies, the construction of smart city has been developed rapidly and comprehensively, and smart building will be the specific application and important component of smart city, which plays an important

Table 2. Smart building design knowledge points that need to be added in each grade

Grade	Need to add knowledge
Grade1	Understand the basic concept of intelligent architecture and set up a correct view of the built environment
Grade2	Master the rational use of main and passive design measures in smart architecture design, and understand the tools of smart architecture function analysis and environment analysis
Grade3	Master the design principles, strategies and concepts of smart architecture, design the indoor and outdoor environment of smart architecture, and test the "wisdom" of smart architecture. And further improve and adjust the design of smart buildings
Grade4	Pay attention to sustainable development issues in urban design and residential planning and design, understand the performance analysis of smart buildings, expand the understanding of smart buildings, sustainable development, ecological buildings and other design
Grade5	The related contents of smart architecture are applied comprehensively

role in human life and work. Facing the future development of smart city, we should also develop a smart complex based on the urban Internet of things and cloud architecture. The development of smart cities requires smarter buildings and the implementation of smart buildings and their Internet technologies.

With the progress of science and technology, people began to pay more and more attention to the close relationship between architecture and environment [9]. The changes and progress of architectural research also affect architectural education. The content and mode of architectural education can not be changed, and the knowledge system of architecture should be adjusted and expanded with the development. At the Third International Conference on intelligent building, intelligent building and building energy conservation, it was mentioned that "from the perspective of building development", its historical change has gone through five stages: the first stage is the practical building stage; the second stage is the art building stage; the third stage is the functional building stage; the fourth stage is the stage of space architecture (China is still at this stage); the fifth stage is the stage of intelligent architecture, also known as ecological architecture The stage of study. The integration of the concept of intelligent architecture into the education of architecture in this article is a preliminary exploration of China's approach to the stage of intelligent architecture. In the previous, through a comprehensive and systematic review of the knowledge system of intelligent architecture, the knowledge points of intelligent architecture I have a clearer understanding, but for the education of architecture major, it is mainly architectural design. Considering the learning ability and understanding ability of students, the relevant knowledge of smart architecture cannot be added to the education of architecture profession in disorder. It needs to be screened and considered to select relevant content that is suitable and consistent with the characteristics of architectural education. Cheng content and arrangements, the wisdom of building-related knowledge into the education of architecture in the form of both integration.

The specialized technical courses of architecture are mainly composed of a series of courses, such as building structure, building physical environment control, building material and structure, building safety, etc. To integrate the concept of intelligent architecture into the knowledge system of architecture professional technology courses, we need to adjust the content of technology courses, as shown in the following table (Table 3):

Table 3. Knowledge points to be deleted

Course	Textbook	Knowledge points to be deleted
Building structure	《Type selection of building structure》 《Architectural mechanics》	In-depth calculations of building structures
Physical environment control	《Building energy efficiency》 《Environmental control science》	Repetition of knowledge between courses
Building materials and construction	《Building materials》 《Architectural construction》	Construction equipment in the professional too strong knowledge points
Building safety	《Construction of disaster prevention》 《Building intelligence》	Explanation of materials and structures that have been rejected

The above table lists the technical knowledge points to be understood, including deleting outdated and complicated technical knowledge, integrating similar courses and adding optional courses. On the one hand, the adjustment of teaching content is the renewal of teaching materials, on the other hand, the teachers control the course content, and the renewal of teaching materials takes a relatively longer time, which requires teachers to impart new knowledge to students in time according to the current latest development, regardless of the teaching materials themselves.

2.3 Adjust Teaching Methods

How to integrate the knowledge of intelligent building design into the architectural design course requires further thinking and exploration. According to the methods adopted by the current domestic and foreign colleges and universities of architecture that have been collated and analyzed in Chapter 2, after discussion and research, several suitable and reference teaching methods are summarized. Based on the above discussion, a curriculum system framework can be established, as shown below (Fig. 2):

It mainly includes: 1. According to the different knowledge points of intelligent building design that need to be integrated into different grades, appropriate design tasks are added in the design task book. Meanwhile, in the process of design, a series of lectures (involving architectural design principles, intelligent building design knowledge,

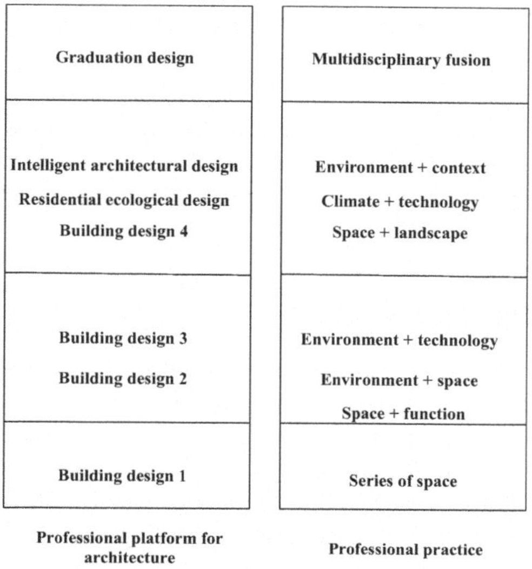

Fig. 2. Framework of the reform curriculum system

building technology, etc.), special lectures, actual visit and learning (refer to View a certain type of building, intelligent building, etc.), discussion and communication between teachers and students; 2. Design course mode is diversified, breaking the traditional teaching mode of two same class hours in a semester, and changing to "one long and one short" or "one long and many short"; 3. Introduce architectural design competition, practical projects, etc. into the senior design class, and the topic of Architectural Design Competition closely around today's society The students can understand the hot issues and take the competition as the design task in the classroom, which not only helps them better understand the hot issues of the society, but also exercises their creativity and social responsibility; 4. Advanced design courses offer a variety of optional design topics, including smart building design topics, historical cities and building protection topics, certain types of architectural design topics, regional architecture topics, etc.; 5. Breaking design courses and technical courses 3. The clear boundaries between theoretical courses, the three achieve the integration of the course content, the time schedules are interconnected, and the teachers and students communicate with each other [10].

In the new teaching pilot, the auxiliary role of technology, theory, practice, etc. is more clear and targeted, avoiding the phenomenon that students have no use after learning the previous courses. The relevant courses of intelligent building technology are closely followed by the design courses, so as to achieve the effect of learning for use. At the same time, the courses offered by thermal energy, civil engineering and other colleges and universities are integrated with those offered by the school of urban planning and architecture to avoid repetition and achieve the effect of refinement and practicality. So far, we have completed the education reform and design of construction specialty in the context of upgrading the intelligent construction industry.

3 Investigation on Students' Learning After the Reform of Architectural Education

In order to verify the effectiveness of the education reform of construction specialty in the context of the upgrading of intelligent construction industry, a questionnaire survey is designed and the results of the survey are analyzed, which is helpful to further understand the actual situation after the reform.

3.1 Pre Research Preparation

The purpose of this survey is to examine the relationship between the reformed curriculum of construction majors and engineering practice, which can be expressed in terms of the degree of fit between the curriculum and engineering practice. The relationship between the curriculum and engineering practice can be divided into two parts: specific and general. At the general level, students are directly asked about the degree of relevance between architecture courses and engineering practice; at the specific level, students are asked whether the content ratio of theoretical courses and practical courses is balanced, if not, which category is too much or too little. The correlation formula is:

$$r_{xy} = \frac{\sum_{i=1}^{n} (x_i - \overline{x})(y_i - \overline{y})}{\sqrt{\sum_{i=1}^{n} (x_i - \overline{x})^2 \sum_{i=1}^{n} (y_i - \overline{y})^2}} \tag{1}$$

In the formula: r_{xy} represents the correlation coefficient between the course and engineering practice, $\overline{x}$ and $\overline{y}$ are the average values of the course score and the engineering practice scores x and y, x_i and y_i are the weighted values of the course score and the engineering practice. What is the effect of the implementation of the education reform in architecture, students have the most say. This study surveyed 630 four-graduate students from 6 research universities in China, and recovered 536 valid samples with an effective recovery rate of 85.08%.

3.2 Research Results and Analysis

The percentage and frequency distribution of customs clearance degree can be summarized from the obtained questionnaire (Table 4):

The scores of 6 schools for the degree of relevance between the reformed architectural courses and engineering practice are shown in the table below (Table 5):

The above table shows that the average value of the six universities is 4.18, which shows that the scores of students on the degree of relevance between the professional courses and engineering practice after the reform are relatively high, slightly higher than the "high" degree.

Table 4. Relevance distribution of architectural courses and engineering practice

Correlation	Percentage	Frequency
Very low	2%	8
Lower	5%	25
General	11%	60
Higher	44%	236
Most high	38%	206
Aggregate	100%	536

Table 5. Relevance scores of architectural courses and engineering practice

School	Mean value	N	Standard deviation
A	4.53	108	0.612
B	4.48	69	0.752
C	4.25	79	0.881
D	4.04	82	0.761
E	3.89	112	0.721
F	3.87	86	0.756
mean value	4.18	536	0.747

4 Concluding Remarks

This article analyzes the reform of the education of architectural majors in the context of the upgrade of the intelligent construction industry, introduces the concept of intelligent architecture into the education of architectural majors, adds knowledge points of emerging technologies and deletes old knowledge points to adjust the teaching methods of teachers, and completes the intelligent construction industry Reform design of architectural education under the background of upgrading. Therefore, it can be proved that the reform of the construction professional education in the context of the upgrading of the smart construction industry has improved the relevance of the construction curriculum and engineering practice.

References

1. Ju, Q.: Improvement and innovation of professional teaching environment construction in practical application of architecture. North. Archit. **3**(06), 69–71 (2018)
2. Zhou, Q., Yang, X.: The policy attributes and professional education of urban planning. Planners **34**(11), 149–153 (2018)

3. Zhang, Y.: Construction and practice of the curriculum system of architectural interior design specialty double talents under the vision of "Precision Supply". J. Wuhan Polytechnic, **18**(05), 69–74 (2019)
4. Wang, X.: Research on the "Post Guide" talent cultivation mode under the perspective of supply-side reform. Liaoning Higher Vocational Tech. Inst. J. **20**(06), 14–15, 19 (2018)
5. Li, H.: Research on construction and countermeasures of high-level traditional architectural specialty group driven by the "Double High-level Construction Plan". Chongqing Archit. **18**(11), 10–13 (2019)
6. Li, Y., Huang, G., Yan, J., et al.: High efficient green smart building integration solution. Heat. Ventilat. Air Condition. **49**(10), 123–128 (2019)
7. Xiang, H., Shen, J., Jia, K.: Development trend of smart buildings and relationship with smart cities. Intell. Build. City Inf. (11), 44–47 (2019)
8. Shen, Q., Zhu, Y., Li, X., et al.: Review of data standards on intelligent building operation and maintenance. China Stand. (15), 77–81 (2019)
9. Xu, X., Wu, Z., Fu, B.: Key technologies for driving innovative application of intelligent building. Build. Electr. **38**(10), 57–61 (2019)
10. Du, M.: Design of smart architecture and city operation and maintenance software based on BIM+Multi-agent enhancing learning. J. Inf. Tech. Civil Eng. Archit. **10**(06), 1–9 (2018)

Design of Traditional Teaching Method of Micro-teaching Based on Blended Learning

Fang-yan Yang(✉)

College of Sports and Health, Changsha Medical University, Changsha 410219, China
xuenxuen152@163.com

Abstract. The traditional teaching method of traditional micro-teaching method for students is inferior in academic performance. Therefore, a traditional teaching method of micro-teaching method based on blended learning is designed for this purpose. First set the teaching goals of traditional exercises and micro-teaching, then set the evaluation standards for the teaching effects of traditional exercises and micro-teaching, and finally achieve hybrid-based teaching by constructing a curriculum knowledge point system, choosing an online learning platform, and being familiar with the teaching strategies of online learning Design of Traditional Teaching Method of Traditional Micro-learning of Gongfa. The experiment shows that the students' performance of the traditional micro class teaching mode based on hybrid learning is higher than that of the traditional teaching mode, which improves the students' satisfaction and has practical application significance.

Keywords: Blended learning · Traditional exercises · Micro-lecture teaching · Network · Model

1 Introduction

With the development of information technology and network communication, the development of online education such as MOOCs and micro-classes has been promoted, and a wave of education reform has been set off in China. Blended teaching has changed and reshaped traditional classrooms tremendously. Under this model, the roles of teachers and students, the teaching process (including the relationship between the classroom and after class), and the teaching medium will all change dramatically. In fact, the process of entering the college English curriculum field of mixed teaching mode is always accompanied by voices of doubt. The focus of the question is whether the traditional exercises focusing on skill training are compatible with the mixed teaching model. There are a lot of discussions on this issue. Many scholars have proved their adaptability from different perspectives, and some scholars have expressed different views. Through teaching practice, I hope to join in the discussion of this problem and explore the traditional micro teaching mode. After the traditional micro class teaching mode, students' learning effect is poor and their satisfaction is low. Therefore, this paper designs a traditional micro class teaching mode based on hybrid learning. According to the goal of traditional

S. Liu et al. (Eds.): eLEOT 2020, LNICST 339, pp. 159–170, 2020.
https://doi.org/10.1007/978-3-030-63952-5_14

micro course teaching, the teaching effect is evaluated, and the design of traditional micro course teaching mode based on hybrid learning is completed by constructing the course knowledge point system, selecting the network learning platform and being familiar with the implementation strategy of network learning platform teaching.

The mixed teaching mode emphasizes the cooperation of online and offline teaching activities, involving more teaching links than traditional teaching. As far as teachers are concerned, the main links of online teaching include micro video design and recording, test question design and correction, network platform discussion design, etc. Line teaching links include classroom teaching design and implementation, after-school consolidation and expansion of the design and correction of homework. Therefore, in addition to adaptability, the other purpose is to summarize the operating experience of online and offline teaching links, grasp the key points and difficulties of curriculum design, and explore the effectiveness of hybrid teaching mode based on micro courses.

2 The Design of Traditional Micro Course Teaching Mode Based on Hybrid Learning

2.1 The Establishment of the Teaching Objectives of Traditional Micro Courses

Before making teaching objectives, the paper analyzes the form of micro course, which is a high-efficiency micro course with 8–10 min of time and knowledge points as the unit. Its intuitive image is very suitable for the characteristics of short concentration time of vocational students, which is very helpful to stimulate students' interest in learning and improve their ability of independent learning. "Task driven, spiral promotion three-stage" hybrid teaching mode refers to task-driven learning in the three stages before, during and after class. Learning strategies can be a mixture of independent inquiry, collaborative learning, competitive learning, group discussion and other learning strategies based on any available media. The task difficulty of each stage should have a certain gradient. Gradients should conform to the theory of "Recent Development Zone" and the learning law of higher vocational students. Through three stages of learning and training, students can realize the spiral improvement of skills and transform knowledge learning into application practice. The whole teaching design and implementation is mainly guided by the constructivism learning theory and carried out under the dual main teaching mode, giving full play to the leading role of students and teachers, realizing multiple knowledge internalization, guiding and helping students to independently complete the construction of knowledge meaning. Therefore, in teaching objectives, teaching preparation plays an important role. The process of teaching preparation is shown in the following figure (Fig. 1):

On this basis, analyzing the characteristics of students, students of traditional exercises generally have a poor knowledge base, a low level of interest in learning, and a weak ability to learn independently, but Oita students have a strong curiosity and agile thinking. Students already have the relevant knowledge base of the leading courses such as "Computer Fundamentals" [2] and "Computer Network Fundamentals", but the basic level is poor. In the early stage of the study of network equipment configuration, they may have resistance or encounter difficulties. Based on this, this research is based on

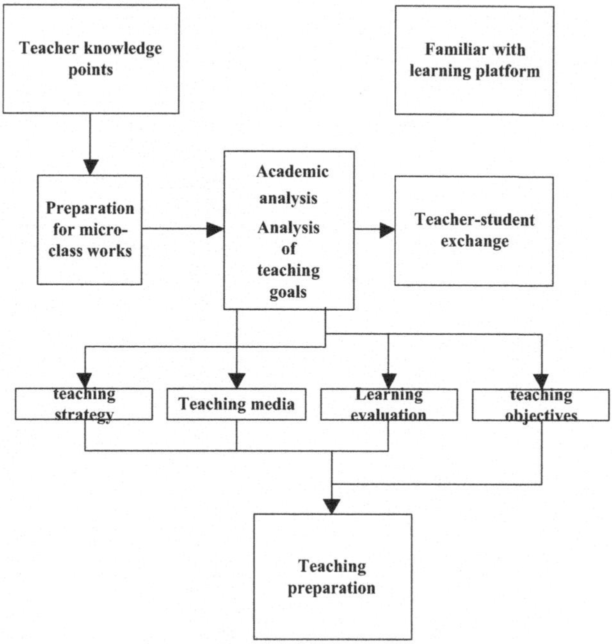

Fig. 1. Teaching preparation process

an online learning platform, using a combination of constructivist learning theory, dual-master teaching modes and other advanced teaching theories, problem-based teaching, project teaching, and pedestal teaching strategies, using multimedia classrooms [3], the Internet Teaching media and methods such as laboratories and simulation software explain profound theories in a simple way, pay attention to the accumulation effect, slowly cultivate interest, and strive to visualize abstract content, simplify complex content, and stimulate and maintain appropriate learning motivation. Through the above analysis, the following goals were formulated (Table 1):

2.2 The Determination of the Evaluation Index of the Micro Course Teaching of Students' Traditional Skills

The condition factors of the teaching mode are various, which have certain influence on the evaluation index. The specific influence contents are as follows (Fig. 2):

Such as teachers, students, technology, environment, time, space, etc. First of all, under the new teaching mode of Internet + teaching, teachers' teaching methods, authority roles, and teacher-student communication methods are all challenged. In the role of teachers, they have changed from traditional "constructors and decision makers" to new types of "constructors and decision makers". "Collaborators, guides, helpers", in teaching activities, the place of teaching activities changed from classroom to online + offline [4], the teaching method changed from indoctrination to interactive research, reflecting the subject status of students, teachers must adapt Changes in teaching methods,

Table 1. Teaching objectives of traditional micro courses

Serial number	Target dimension	Set forth
1	Knowledge and skills	Emphasize the acquisition of basic knowledge and basic skills, and focus on developing students' ability to acquire and use information
2	Process and method	Constructing knowledge through learning methods such as autonomous learning, cooperative learning, and inquiry learning
3	Emotional attitudes and values	Emotional attitudes and values are the ultimate purpose of teaching

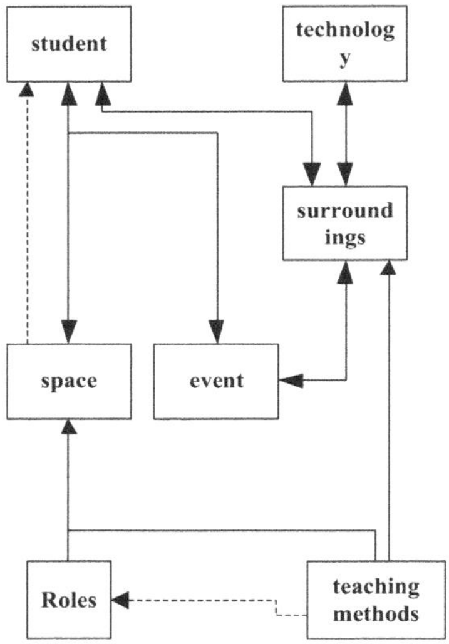

Fig. 2. Conditions of teaching mode

while further improving professional skills. Secondly, the implementation of the mixed teaching mode places higher requirements on the online platform, because the platform education is almost different from the traditional classroom teaching, and the degree of humanization of the teaching platform [5], operability, and interactivity are extremely great Affects the effectiveness of teaching. Humanization of the online system. Thirdly, we will formulate sound management methods for online education organizations, and form an efficient, coordinated, orderly and open education management mechanism.

Teaching evaluation should also follow certain developmental principles. The ultimate purpose of evaluation is to promote the development of learners, from the evaluation of students' knowledge system and skills to promote the comprehensive development of learning work attitude, scientific research innovation awareness, practical ability, core literacy and other aspects. The process of evaluation is the process of improvement and development, not only limited to examination results and homework results, which is the final evaluation result. Teaching evaluation system should be changed to soft index evaluation, such as learners' information retrieval ability, personalized autonomous learning, core literacy formation, etc., because these factors can not be presented to the evaluators in the form of scores, therefore, in the evaluation process, it is still necessary to conduct process evaluation for learners at any time, and combine learners' learning achievements to conduct a comprehensive system for learners Evaluation. The mixed teaching quality evaluation system is shown in the table below (Table 2):

Table 2. Hybrid teaching quality evaluation system

First-level indicators	Secondary indicators	Tertiary indicators
Pre-class preparation	Emotional performance of pre-class learning	Learning to be proactive
	Behavioral performance before class	Resource utilization platform usage
Face-to-face class	Effectiveness of pre-class learning	Basic test scores
	Class participation	Whether thinking is active
	Classroom learning effect	Actively participate in discussions
Reflection after class	Learning after class	Homework completion Summarizing reflection Resulting evaluation Overall learning results Cognitive factors Final grade
Overall learning results	Cognitive factors	Task completion information literacy
	Emotional realization	Content value judgment

2.3 The Implementation Strategy of Traditional Micro Course Teaching

Operating procedures refer to the various processes of teaching activities and the specific methods of different stages. Any teaching mode will have relatively fixed operating procedures, but it is not an absolute solidification [6], which concretely reflects the organization and guidance of teaching content and teaching methods in the teaching process. And the mixed application of methods, the transmission and guidance of teaching emotional value. The operation process of mixed teaching in Internet plus environment is mainly focused on three parts: online learning, classroom learning and offline summarization [7]. Online learning (based on online teaching platform): teachers organize teaching materials-distribute tasks-learners complete tasks-ask questions. Classroom learning: student problem feedback—group interaction—teachers explaining difficult issues—problem solving—arrange assignments. Offline summary: strengthening blind spots [8]-knowledge combing-homework completion-homework (work) display. The pre-school auxiliary phase process is as follows (Fig. 3 and Table 3):

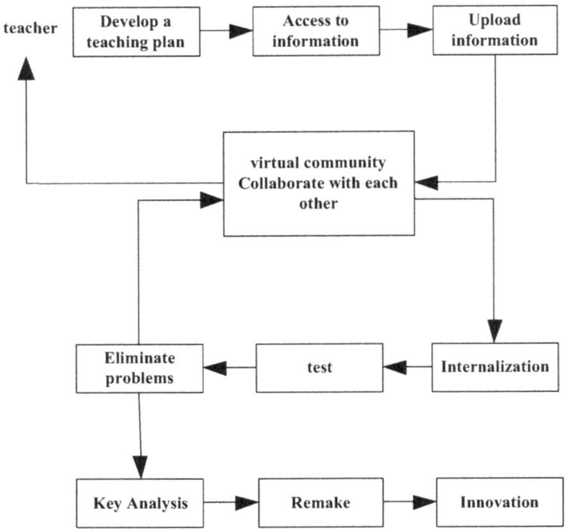

Fig. 3. Flow chart of the auxiliary stage before class

Table 3. Division of teaching content

Serial number	Refine project	Elaborate
1	Dividing the course content into units	Chapter content is divided into multiple small units
2	Refine the content of the unit into specific knowledge points	After dividing the course content into multiple teaching units, the unit content is further refined into specific knowledge points
3	Identify the types of knowledge points	Abstraction is divided into four categories: factual knowledge, conceptual knowledge, procedural knowledge and metacognitive knowledge

The specific operation procedures are as follows:

(1) Build the knowledge point system of the course [9], build the knowledge point system structure of the course, provide the fulcrum for the preparation of micro course works and the design of task projects, and divide the teaching content, as shown in the following table:
(2) Select an online learning platform, prepare course teaching resources, use the digital teaching platform currently used by the college as a learning platform, and use WeChat and other instant communication tools, rain classes, etc. as auxiliary tools.

Teachers collect, transform or transform Production of micro-lecture works, design of pre-class learning tasks (projects), preparation of network simulation software, teaching cases and other learning materials. And mix teaching content, the specific content is as follows:

Finally, the teacher uploads learning materials such as course basic information, simulation software, and micro-lecture works to the learning platform (Table 4).

(1) Be familiar with the online learning platform, understand the basic information of the course. After the teacher issues the registration notice to the students, the students register and log in to the platform, be familiar with the platform function and learning environment, and understand the basic information of the course. At this time, teachers should communicate with students fully before class, further understand students' learning needs and personality characteristics, and make necessary modifications and updates to teaching resources;
(2) Teaching implementation, students analyze learning tasks and projects, watch micro-lecture videos (including teacher demonstration videos) with questions; use Packet network simulation software to simulate exercises "network static routing configuration with two routers" project and verify connectivity Have online and offline discussions with your classmates and complete the collaboration. You can also ask the teacher for help online; then summarize the gains and raise any existing difficulties or difficulties. Teachers use scattered time to answer questions in time, and further clarify the key points and difficulties of classroom teaching according to students' pre class learning. Based on this, they choose classroom teaching strategies and design classroom training programs. The teacher leads the students to analyze the learning tasks and present the confusion encountered by the students before the class; watch the micro-lecture video with the students, pause at the confusion, the teacher gives detailed explanations and highlights, and resolves the confusion encountered during the pre-class study; classroom training project "including four routers with static routing configuration"; students carry out project training (independent exploration [10], collaborative exploration, group discussion); teachers and students who have completed tasks provide individual guidance; display works after participating in tasks and participate in Evaluation, teacher comments, revealing errors, affirming results; students reflecting, correcting errors, teacher summary. The flowchart of the face-to-face teaching phase is as follows:

According to the situation of classroom training, the teacher designs the after-school training projects which promote the transfer of knowledge (skills) (Fig. 4).

3 Example Analysis

3.1 Content of Case Analysis

In order to verify the effectiveness of the traditional micro class teaching mode based on hybrid learning, experiments were carried out, and the traditional teaching mode was compared with the designed teaching mode. A school of selected location was selected as

Table 4. Mixed content

Serial number	Mixed content	Method
1	Textbook and courseware resources	Mixed model of teaching resources
2	Teaching environment	Online environment, face-to-face environment
3	learning method	Autonomous learning and collaborative learning
4	Evaluation method	Diagnostic evaluation, process evaluation, summative evaluation

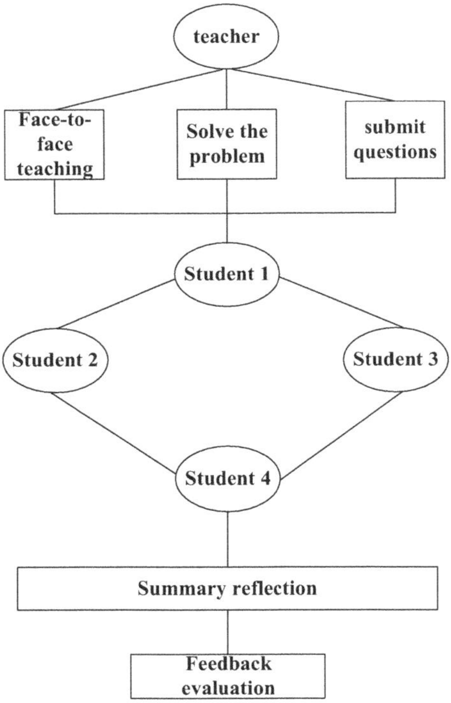

Fig. 4. Extreme process of face-to-face teaching

the experimental object. 20 students were randomly selected and divided into 2 groups. One group applied the design mode and the other group used the traditional accounting practice teaching mode of "Internet plus". Compared with the scores of the two models, the 20 students scored the following results (Table 5):

This case analysis involves a lot of data, so an experimental platform is established, as shown in the following figure (Fig. 5):

Table 5. Results of last examination

Student	Professional knowledge	Practical results
1	56	56
2	66	47
3	70	58
4	85	69
5	68	95
6	69	86
7	78	76
8	98	64
9	57	84
10	48	76
11	56	81
12	89	73
13	56	72
14	63	84
15	58	82
16	86	83
17	78	85
18	54	82
19	89	75
20	96	71

3.2 Discussion of Experimental Results

The comparison results of the traditional method and this method are shown in the following table (Table 6):

It can be seen from the analysis of the above table that the students who applied the traditional micro course teaching mode based on hybrid learning have significantly improved their professional knowledge and practice scores. However, the students who use the traditional learning mode have no significant improvement in professional knowledge and practice. This is because the designed learning mode uses the mixed learning mode, which improves the students' learning performance. Therefore, the above experiments can prove that the designed learning mode can improve the students' learning performance, and has practical application significance.

In order to further verify the effectiveness of this teaching mode, according to the students' reaction in the classroom and the proficiency of practical operation, the paper compares and analyzes the students' satisfaction of the traditional teaching method of

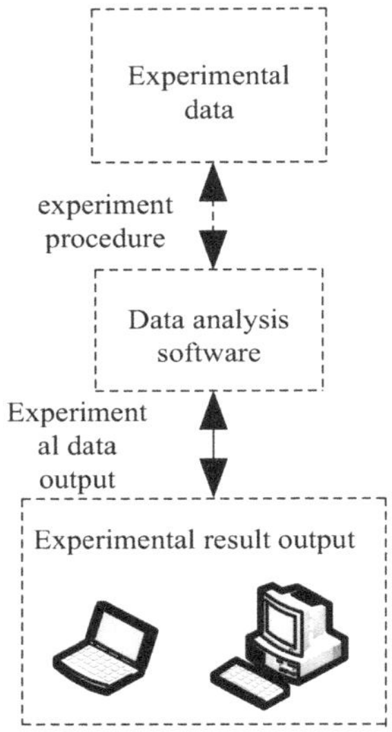

Fig. 5. Experimental platform

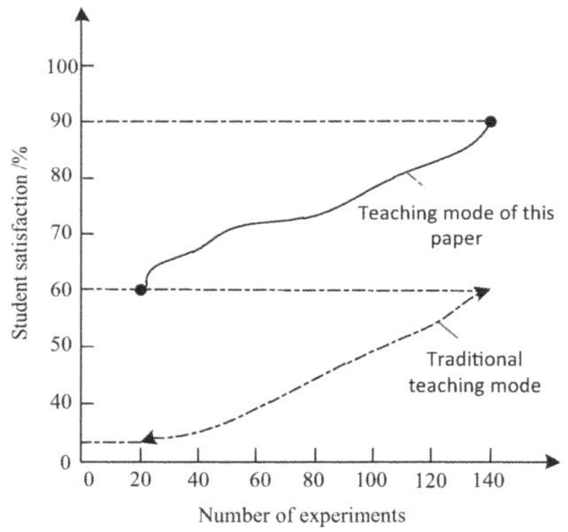

Fig. 6. Comparative analysis of students' satisfaction

micro teaching based on blended learning and the accounting practice teaching mode of Higher Vocational Colleges under the background of "Internet plus".

According to Fig. 6, the student satisfaction of the traditional micro class teaching mode based on hybrid learning designed in this paper is up to 90%, while the student satisfaction of the accounting practice teaching mode in Higher Vocational Colleges under the background of traditional "Internet" is up to 60%, which shows that the traditional micro class teaching mode based on hybrid learning designed in this paper is popular with students.

The test results of the teaching mode designed in this paper are compared with those of the past without the teaching mode. The comparison results are shown in Table 7.

Table 6. Comparison of academic performance

The professional knowledge of the design mode	Practical results of this design pattern	Traditional mode expertise	Traditional model practice results
70	70	58	60
78	90	70	50
75	93	60	75
90	94	65	88
80	95	59	84
95	98	89	88
90	96	79	89
80	97	58	87
95	86	90	80
98	97	96	76

Table 7. Comparison of test results

Student	Before application	After application
1	62	85
2	65	86
3	72	90
4	83	95
5	56	87
6	72	86
7	78	93
8	80	96
9	82	98
10	65	94

According to Table 7, we can see that the learning scores of the application of this teaching mode are all above 85 points, which is higher than the test scores of the application of this teaching mode in the past.

4 Concluding Remarks

The research on the construction of mixed teaching mode in colleges and universities has been a relatively hot topic in recent years. Whether it is the reform and improvement of the teaching system or the comprehensive development of teachers and learners, it is of great significance. The validity of the learning model designed this time is proved by example analysis, but there are still some shortcomings. Based on the "Internet+" background, mixed teaching should have different implementation modes for different disciplines, curriculum characteristics, students' cognitive stages and levels. The specific implementation of mixed teaching refinement varies from school to school, and from student to different. Further thinking is needed on the implementation of blended teaching for specific courses. The hybrid teaching model constructed in this thesis is based on the research of the current era background. With the further changes of the times and the further updating of teaching ideas and educational concepts, subsequent research and development will be carried out. The co evolution of human and technology promotes the further reform of teaching mode, and the exploration of mixed teaching mode will not be the terminal. At this stage, the college mixed teaching mode is only applied in a small number of subject courses. With the development and development of teaching concepts and modern technology, exploring mixed teaching modes with disciplinary characteristics will become a hot spot.

5 Fund Projects

Research on the Application of Blended Learning in Traditional Gongfa Teaching.
Xiangjiao Tong [2019] No. 291-1009.
Hunan Province's Higher Education Teaching Reform Project 2019.

References

1. Li, X.H.: On the construction of accounting practice teaching system of higher vocational colleges under the background of "Internet+". Vocat. Tech. Educ. **38**(14), 41–44 (2017)
2. Liu, X.J., Tian, C.Y., Gao, S.Z., Yang, Y.X., Yu, X.R., Wang, L.: Construction of practical teaching system oriented towards applied talents cultivation—taking Dalian Oceanic University for example. J. Shenyang Agric. Univ. (Soc. Sci. Ed.) **21**(1), 81–85 (2019)
3. Wang, W.Y., Wang, H.X., Chen, H.: Constructing a school-based, individualized college English curriculum. Foreign Lang. China **15**(4), 18–26 (2018)
4. Ke, J., Hu, Y., Lin, X.: Research on evaluation and optimizing countermeasures of university network teaching information ecosystem. Mod. Inf. **39**(7), 27–36 (2019)
5. Xu, X.Y.: Quality standard of undergraduate teaching in universities: concept definition and system construction. Tsinghua J. Educ. **39**(3), 58–66 (2018)
6. Zhang, W.N.: The structure and order of the cognitive tools of blended learning. Tsinghua J. Educ. **39**(1), 54–61 (2018)
7. Hu, C., Zhang, R., Wang, Z.Y.: Interactive behavior analysis in blended collaborative learning of college physics. Coll. Phys. **37**(3), 48–54 (2018)
8. Yang, L., Fan, S., Song, Z.S.: Exploratory study on information literacy instruction of blackboard with SPOC pattern. Libr. Inf. Serv. **63**(3), 90–97 (2019)
9. Wang, X.C., Li, F.Z., Wang, Z.W., Liu, X.F.: Problems and countermeasures of stem project learning classroom management in primary school. Chin. J. Med. Educ. Res. **18**(11), 1155–1159 (2019)
10. Wei, L.X., et al.: Exploration of the teaching model of acupuncture in the foreign fair. Zhongguo Zhen Jiu **36**(9), 991–994 (2016)

Personalized Recommendation Technology of Network Teaching Resources Based on Ant Colony Algorithm

Hai-long Liu[1] and Lei-lei Jiang[2](✉)

[1] Computer and Information Engineering, Inner Mongolia Chemical Vocational College, Hohhot 010010, China

[2] Anhui Radio and TV University, Hefei 230022, China

hjk18709@sina.com

Abstract. In order to solve the problem of low recall rate in traditional network teaching resources personalized recommendation technology, an ant colony algorithm-based network teaching resources personalized recommendation technology was designed. By describing the user's online teaching resource interest, the user's online teaching resource interest is acquired, and the ant colony algorithm is used to dynamically adjust the user's online teaching resource interest to obtain information that the user is interested in, that is, the user's personalized characteristics, and to generate a synthesis User interest models, including individual user models, group user interest models, and integrated user interest models, build a personalized recommendation model for online teaching resources, including the application layer, business logic layer, and data layer, to achieve personalized recommendation for online teaching resources. In order to prove the high recall rate of the personalized recommendation technology of network teaching resources based on ant colony algorithm, the traditional personalized recommendation technology of network teaching resources was compared with this technology. The experimental results show that the recall rate of this technique is higher than that of the traditional personalized recommendation technique.

Keywords: Ant colony algorithm · Network teaching resources · Personalized recommendation of resources

1 Introduction

At present, online teaching has become an important way to cultivate talents and promote the development of scientific research and education. However, the network is only the carrier of information transmission, the acquisition and sharing of teaching resources is the purpose of people using the network. In order to make the network and information technology truly serve for teaching and realize the optimization of teaching process and teaching resources, it is necessary to have abundant teaching resources to support [1]. The prerequisite for the development of online teaching is to build a complete and

S. Liu et al. (Eds.): eLEOT 2020, LNICST 339, pp. 171–180, 2020.
https://doi.org/10.1007/978-3-030-63952-5_15

substantial system of online teaching resources. The construction of teaching resource base is the core content of educational informatization. In the development of online teaching, countries all over the world have realized that the sharing of teaching resources and the interoperability of systems are decisive to the practicability and economy of online education. At present, the teaching resource database system is mainly used for the management of teaching resources such as materials, courseware, integrated parts, online supplementary materials and teaching plans that have been developed and made, and for the uploading of teaching resources, searching of teaching resources and downloading of teaching resources [2]. It mainly focuses on "objects" and fails to reflect the idea of "people-oriented". In particular, the existing teaching resources are not personalized and intelligent, which makes it difficult to manage and inconvenient to use teaching resources. Due to the individual differences in users' learning starting point, learning style, learning desire and learning pace, there is a general contradiction between massive teaching resources and users' personalized needs. Because of the existence of this contradiction, on the one hand, caused a huge waste of teaching resources, on the other hand, for users to find and use the teaching resources caused great difficulties [3]. All these problems hinder the play of teaching resources in teaching, resulting in a great waste of teaching resources.

In the teaching resource database system to add personalized services, so that the user network teaching resources personalized recommendation will fundamentally solve this contradiction. The essence of personalized recommendation is to respect users, study their habits and interests, and provide better services for users to choose the teaching resources they need. Based on this, a personalized recommendation technology of network teaching resources based on ant colony algorithm is designed.

2 A Personalized Recommendation Technology of Network Teaching Resources Based on Ant Colony Algorithm Is Designed

2.1 User Interest Extraction and Adjustment

Firstly, the user's interest in network teaching resources is described, then the user's interest in network teaching resources is acquired, and finally the user's interest in network teaching resources is dynamically adjusted based on ant colony algorithm [4]. Interest to the user's network teaching resources is described first need to grasp the user's interest, user's interests is the user's personalized features, it is determined by the human individual characteristics in its demand for teaching resources of the combination of characteristic information, and is determined by the particular user demand for the teaching resources of relations and produce a series of useful information for the individual. After the teaching resource is characterized by keywords, the user's interest in a teaching resource can be equated with his interest in the teaching resource keywords. If users have a great interest in a teaching resource, they will spend their energy to acquire it. As the basic way for Web users to acquire teaching resources is to browse, the user's previous browsing of teaching resources contains the user's personalized characteristics. The more times the user visits the teaching resources and the closer the recent access time is, the more interested the user is in the teaching resources. That is, the intensity of interest should include the number of visits and the last visit date, the two actual interest indicators [5].

Then, there are two ways to acquire users' interest in network teaching resources and obtain personalized information reflecting users' information: The first method is to record the user's access characteristics by the teaching resource library system into a log file, and then summarize the user's interest model by analyzing the log file or the log file generated by the browser. The second way is for users to provide their own personalized feature information by filling in the form. The second method is used to collect the initial personalized characteristics of users, and the first method is used to timely track the personalized characteristics of registered users. The basic information base of users is used to save the static information of users. A user personality library is used to store the dynamic information of the user, that is, the user personalized access characteristics. The formal definition of their structure is as follows:

Definition l: user static information *US*, Namely, the basic information base of users, which is a database:

$$US = \{UID, NAME, SPECIALIZED, GRADE\} \tag{1}$$

Where, *UID* represents the user number; When the user registers, the system automatically generates; *NAME* represents the description of *US*, that is, the user name; *SPECIALIZED* represents the constraint of *US*, the user's specialty; *GRADE* represents the constraint of *US*, the user's grade [6].

Definition 2: user dynamic information *UD*, that is, the database of user personality characteristics is a database:

$$UD = \left\{ \begin{array}{l} UID, KEY\_WORD, COUNT, \\ LAST\_DATE, UNITE\_INDEX \end{array} \right\} \tag{2}$$

Where, *UID* represents the user number; When the user registers, the system automatically generates; *KEY_WORD* represents key words; *COUNT* represents the cumulative visits of users to keyword *KEY_WORD*; *LAST_DATE* represents the last access date for saving the user to keyword *KEY_WORD*; *UNITE_INDEX* is a distribution function of *KEY_WORD* to [0, 1], Indicates the degree of user interest in *KEY_WORD*. Is the comprehensive interest index of users on keyword *KEY_WORD*, which is obtained according to *COUNT* and *LAST_DATE*. While *KEY_WORD* belongs to *KEYS*, as shown in formula (3):

$$KEY\_WORD \in KEYS \tag{3}$$

Where, *KEYS* represents the keyword set.

User personality traits in the library all the words from the users are most interested in teaching resources of keywords selected, weights of each entry in the library reflects the word and the relevance of the user interests, because in a specific time, the user's interest is relatively stable, the user's interest is approximated by a finite number of keywords can express. When the user is successfully registered, the teaching resource database system will ask the user to fill in a demand information form for teaching resources, the demand information is the initial characteristics of the user's interest, and will establish a user personality characteristics database for the user to record these initial characteristics of interest [7].

Finally, based on ant colony algorithm, the user's interest in network teaching resources is dynamically adjusted, and the user's browsing and related feedback on teaching resources are timely adjusted and updated. That is, extract all keyword names, cumulative visits and recent access dates of teaching resources of interest to users, and add the user's personality library according to the following algorithm:

Algorithm: adjustment of the user's personality feature library: according to the user's browsing of teaching resources or related feedback, the corresponding keyword *key* is added to the user's personality feature library.

Input: teaching resource keyword *key*, current date *D*, user personality library *UD*.
Output: a library of user characteristics.
Methods
if the user's personality characteristics database capacity is full {the response ratio of each keyword is calculated systematically S_i; Eliminate the keywords corresponding to the maximum value;}
else
{add a record:
$KEY\_WORD =$ user keyword k;
$LAST\_DATE =$ current date D:
$COUNT = 1$;}
Calculate the comprehensive interest index *UNITE_INDEX* of keyword *key*.

In the adjustment algorithm of user personality characteristic library, response ratio is defined as:

$$S_i = \frac{D_t - D_i}{C_i} \tag{4}$$

Where, S_i represents the response ratio of each keyword; D_t represents the current date; D_i represents the most recent visit date of the keyword; C_i represents the cumulative visit times of the keyword. The algorithm flow of personalized recommendation technology for network teaching resources based on ant colony algorithm is shown in Fig. 1.

As can be seen from Fig. 1, it can be seen that: if the keyword's recent access time is the same, the access frequency is less to be eliminated; If the keyword access times are the same, the most recent access time far from the current time is eliminated. This adjustment strategy considers the time and times of users' interest, which is a better method.

2.2 Building a User Model

Personalized service of teaching resources is not a pointer to a user, but to provide the information that the user really needs, that is, the problem of accurate filtering. A user model is a representation of a user's information needs or interests. There are two steps to get a user model. First, the information that the user is interested in, that is, the

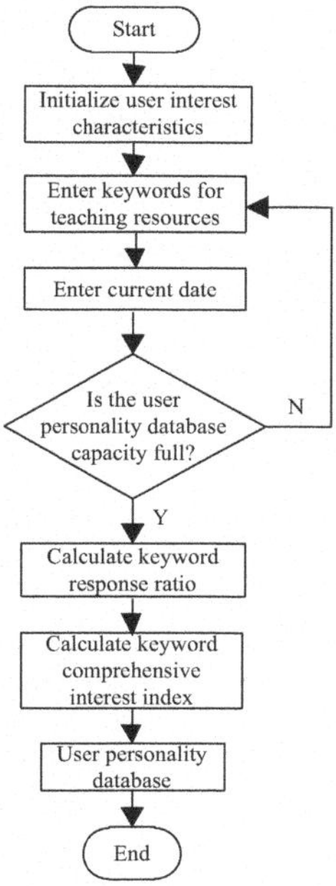

Fig. 1. Algorithm flow of personalized recommendation technology for network teaching resources based on ant colony algorithm

personalized characteristics of the user, and then the user model is constructed according to these characteristics. Design a library of user characteristics for each user to obtain and track the user's personalized access characteristics; Individual user model was adopted to realize individual filtering, group user model to realize collaborative filtering, and comprehensive user model to realize comprehensive filtering.

Firstly, the individual user model is constructed, which is the description of individual user's personalized interest in teaching resources. The vector space model is used to represent the user's interest, which is regarded as a vector of multi-dimensional space, and is closer to the user's demand than the keyword matching. Therefore, a keyword-based user model U can represent the user vector by a pair (character item, weight) according to the traditional vector representation [8].

Then build the group user interest model, the group user interest, can have a more important effect on the individual user interest. Therefore, the group user interest model is generated according to the individual user interest clustering, and the comprehensive user model is formed through the individual's inheritance of the group user interest, so as to realize the conceptual expansion of the process of teaching resource filtering, and the user model has the ability of keyword expansion and self-adaptation [9]. First, the 20 users whose interest is closest to that of the individual user are found, and these 20 users and the designated user jointly form a group. The first 100 keywords of the group's common interest are extracted, and the group user model centered on the designated individual user is obtained. Compared with the individual user model of the specified user, the group user model contains a broader range of interests, which can effectively extend the interest characteristics of the specified user.

From the previously generated individual user interest vector and group user interest vector, 100 keywords with high comprehensive interest index and corresponding comprehensive interest index are selected to construct the comprehensive user interest vector *I* (if there is repetition, remove one item with small comprehensive interest index). Then this comprehensive user interest vector not only reflects the individual user's personalized interest characteristics, but also contains the group interest characteristics of multiple users with similar interests. The steps for generating a comprehensive user interest model are shown in Table 1.

Table 1. Steps for generating a comprehensive user interest modelserial number

	Step	Content
1	Create individual user interest vector	According to the individual filtering technology, the first 100 high weight keywords in the user's personality database are selected to create the individual user's interest vector *U*
2	Select users to form user groups	According to the collaborative filtering technology, multiple users closest to the specified user's interests are selected to form a user group
3	Build group user interest vector	According to the interest characteristics of the user group, the first 100 keywords with the largest comprehensive interest index value are selected to construct the group user interest vector *G*
4	Building a comprehensive user interest vector	From the individual user interest vector and group user interest vector generated previously, 100 keywords with high comprehensive interest index and corresponding comprehensive interest index are selected to build the comprehensive user interest vector *I* (if there is repetition, remove the one with small comprehensive interest index)

2.3 To Achieve Personalized Recommendation of Network Teaching Resources

The construction of personalized recommendation model of network teaching resources includes application layer, business logic layer and data layer. Through the construction of network teaching resources personalized recommendation model to achieve personalized recommendation of network teaching resources. Of application layer is the view layer of the model, to provide users with services, the main features are: resources construction and sharing of learning resources (including upload and download, update and delete uploaded a resource, resource information search and preview), user management functions, including user registration, users' personal information preview, update, and delete), grade management functions (including learning resources for grading and evaluation in words).

Data layer is deposited personalized recommendation model all the data needed for the network teaching resources information, mainly including user basic information, learning resource information, various recommended number display Settings information, user history grading and evaluation information, etc., these data are from the model of interactive activities [10].

The business logic layer is the recommendation algorithm part of the model, which is also the difficulty and key part of the model. It is responsible for recommending learning resources that meet learners' interests and preferences and their own needs. The work of this layer includes the construction of user project rating matrix, the calculation of similarity between projects, the generation of pseudo-rating matrix, the calculation of similarity between users, the assessment of resource prediction and the generation of recommendation list.

The input part of the personalized recommendation model of network teaching resources includes the basic information of users and the score information of resources, and the output part is the personalized recommendation list of learning resources, which is presented to the target users in the form of a list. The recommendation based on the user's basic attributes and the recommendation of ATCF shall go through three steps of data processing, recommendation algorithm calculation, and prediction resource score to generate the recommendation data set, as shown in Table 2.

3 Experimental Research and Analysis

3.1 Comparative Experimental Study

Five categories with relatively uniform sample distribution and obvious category characteristics were selected, including computer science and technology, literature, mathematics, history, sports and so on. Among them, 60 articles in each category, a total of 300 texts, were used as experimental data. The configuration required for program operation in the experiment is shown in Table 3.

The personalized recommendation experiment of network teaching resources was carried out by using experimental data. In order to ensure the comparability of the experimental data, the traditional network teaching resource personalized recommendation technology is compared with the ant colony algorithm-based network teaching resource personalized recommendation technology designed in this paper. The traditional network teaching resource personalized recommendation technology includes the network teaching resource personalized recommendation technology based on the coordination and filtering technology and the network teaching resource personalized recommendation technology based on the personalized service model. Compare the recall rate of each technology. Recall rate refers to whether the number of relevant resources recommended to users can cover all qualified resource records. It is generally used to describe the ability of personalized recommendation of relevant resources.

Table 2. Recommended steps

Serial number	Step	Content
1	Data processing	It is mainly responsible for preprocessing and calculating the data information in the system to provide a data basis for personalized recommendation technology
2	Recommended algorithm calculation	The recommendation algorithm is a key part of the entire recommendation model. Adopt user basic attribute recommendation technology, repeat the calculation according to the similarity formula, find out the most similar K users among the target users, and establish similar user data sets
3	Generate recommendation data set	The recommendation result uses the target user's similar user set to obtain the target user's predicted score for unscored items. and according to the score level to get the final top-N resources for recommendation, so as to realize the recommendation of the target user

Table 3. Configuration required for program operation in the experiment

Serial number	To configure	Content
1	Hardware configuration	CPU: Intel Pentium 4-m 2. 00 GHz, memory: 1 GB, hard disk: 80 g
2	Software configuration	Operating system: Windows XP, database system: SQL Server 2005, client: IE6. 0 or above

3.2 Research and Analysis of Experimental Results

The experimental results of recall comparison between the traditional personalized recommendation technology of network teaching resources and the personalized recommendation technology of network teaching resources based on ant colony algorithm are shown in Fig. 2.

According to the comparison experiment results of recall in Fig. 2, the recall rate of personalized recommendation technology of network teaching resources based on ant colony algorithm is higher than that of personalized recommendation technology based on coordination filtering technology and personalized service model.

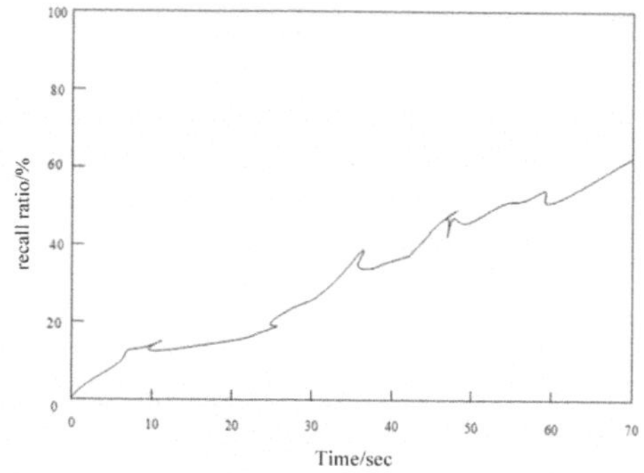

(a)Recommendation technology based on coordination filtering technology

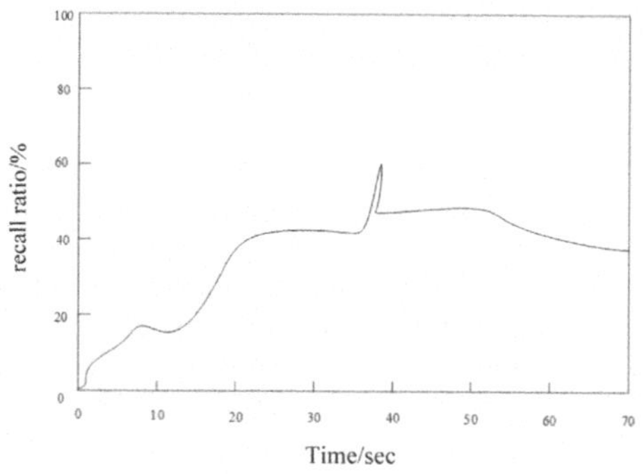

(b)Recommendation technology based on personalized service model

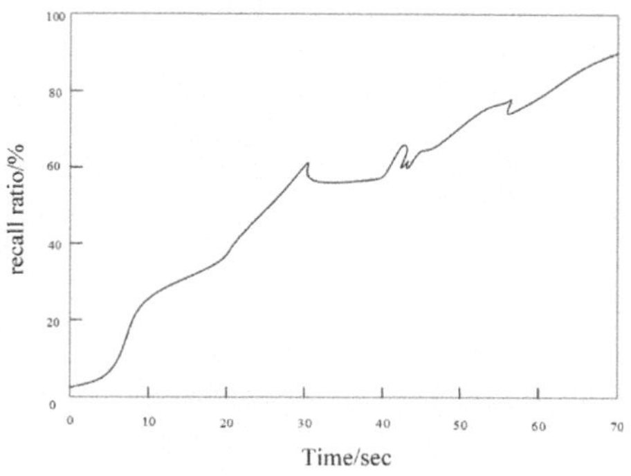

（c） Recommendation model based on ant colony algorithm

Fig. 2. comparison of recall results

4 Conclusion

The personalized recommendation technology of network teaching resources based on ant colony algorithm can solve the problems of users' difficulty in finding the needed teaching resources and low utilization rate of teaching resources to some extent, and realize personalized active recommendation.

References

1. Watt, A., Gråstén, A.: A motivational model of physical education and links to enjoyment, knowledge, performance. Total Phys. Act. Body Mass Index. J. Sports Sci. Med. **16**(3), 318–327 (2017)
2. Goldenberg, A., Smadar, C.C., Goyer, J.P., et al.: Testing the impact and durability of group malleability intervention in the context of the Israeli-Palestinian conflict. Proc. Natl. Acad. Sci. USA **115**(4), 696–701 (2018)
3. de Medeiros Engelmann, P., et al.: Environmental monitoring of water resources around a municipal landfill of the Rio Grande do Sul state, Brazil. Environ. Sci. Pollut. Res. Int. **24**(26), 1–14 (2017)
4. Afonso, A., Gutiérrez, A.J., Lozano, G., et al.: Metals in Diplodus sargus cadenati and Sparisoma cretense—a risk assessment for consumers. Environ. Sci. Pollut. Res. Int. **25**(3), 2630–2642 (2018)
5. Jeong, J.Y.: Effects of short-term presalting and salt level on the development of pink color in cooked chicken breasts. Korean J. Food Sci. Ani. Res. **37**(1), 98–104 (2017)
6. Zhang, J., Xing, H., Lu, Y.: Translating molecular detections into a simple temperature test using a target-responsive smart thermometer. Chem. Sci. **9**(16), 3906–3910 (2018)
7. Moon, G.S., Narbad, A.: Monitoring of bioluminescent lactobacillus plantarum in a complex food matrix. Korean J. Food Sci. Ani. Res. **37**(1), 147–152 (2017)
8. Park, S.-J., Jung, J.-H., Choi, S.-W., et al.: Association between egg consumption and metabolic disease. Korean J. Food Sci. Ani. Res. **38**(2), 209–223 (2018)
9. Pouraboli, B., Abedi, H.A., Abbaszadeh, A., et al.: Self-care in patient with major thalassemia: a grounded theory. J Caring Sci. **6**(2), 127–139 (2017)
10. Fatihah, S.N., Muhd-Farouk, H., Amin-Safwan, A., et al.: Histological characteristics on the testes of mud spiny lobster, panulirus polyphagus (Herbst 1793). Pak. J. Biol. Sci. **20**(7), 365–371 (2017)

Dynamic Adjustment Mechanism of Intelligent Classroom Learning Resources in Universities Based on Network Teaching Platform

Lei-lei Jiang[1], Rong Xu[1](✉), and Hai-long Liu[2]

[1] Anhui Radio and TV University, Hefei 230022, China
ljhs87109@sina.com
[2] Department of Computer and Information Engineering, Inner Mongolia Vocational College of Chemical Engineering, Hohhot 010010, China

Abstract. The resource adjustment mechanism currently used lacks reliable path selection process design steps, resulting in long adjustment time and low efficiency. Based on this, this paper puts forward a dynamic adjustment mechanism of university intelligent classroom learning resources based on the network teaching platform. According to the framework of network teaching platform, the function of network teaching resource platform is analyzed. Under the constraints of online learning resource capacity, this paper studies the dynamic adjustment principle of learning resources based on the network teaching platform. This paper uses genetic algorithm to solve the objective function, completes the time required to dispatch the subtask hall, designs a dynamic adjustment reliable path, and completes the dynamic adjustment of University intelligent classroom learning resources. The experimental results show that the braking dynamic adjustment effect of the machine is good.

Keywords: Network teaching platform · Intelligent classroom in universities · Learning resources · Dynamic adjustment

1 Introduction

Many colleges and universities have built excellent course websites, opened online courses and established a teaching resource pool. It achieves the display and sharing of high-quality teaching resources, expands the space-time environment of teaching and learning, and promotes the improvement of educational and teaching levels [1]. In the era of network teaching characterized by advocating personalized services, focusing on interaction and using collective wisdom [2]. The construction of teaching resources platform is also moving towards the direction of focusing on "personalized resource services, enhancing shared value, and promoting knowledge services" [3]. Network learning space and wisdom education begin to enter the public horizon, and have received the support and attention of many educators [4]. The introduction of network teaching technology and knowledge management technology into the construction of smart classes

S. Liu et al. (Eds.): eLEOT 2020, LNICST 339, pp. 181–192, 2020.
https://doi.org/10.1007/978-3-030-63952-5_16

in Colleges and universities will help to speed up the creation, sharing and update of resources, facilitate the acquisition, generation and innovation of learning resources, and thus enhance the application value of teaching resources platform [5].

In order to integrate the web-based learning space with education and teaching, it is necessary to use the web-based learning space flexibly to promote the dynamic adjustment of learning resources so as to make students more interested in learning. The existing resource adjustment mechanism has the problems of long adjustment time and low efficiency. This paper puts forward a dynamic adjustment mechanism of University intelligent classroom learning resources based on the network teaching platform. The time required to schedule subtask halls, design dynamic adjustments of reliable paths, and dynamically adjust resources. And then improve the efficiency of the adjustment mechanism.

2 Intelligent Classroom Analysis in Universities Based on Network Teaching Platform

The core of intelligence education is to cultivate students' creative thinking ability and problem solving ability, and intelligent classroom is the core of intelligence education. Intelligent class is a teaching mode that makes use of the network teaching platform, pays attention to the interaction between teachers and students, and achieves personalized learning.

Based on the network teaching platform is built to effectively support classroom teaching, guided by school-based courses, teachers combine traditional teaching and information-based teaching concepts. Allocate digital teaching resources in network space, organize learning activities such as exercises, assignments, tests, collaboration, discussion, etc. To effectively supplement the classroom teaching, teachers arrange the learning process according to the teaching plan, students complete the learning tasks in a specified term according to the teachers' teaching progress, and launch online and offline integrated teaching [6].

The hardware system relies on the campus network platform and considers the capacity, reliability and scalability requirements of the platform. Using disk array and RAID architecture, high-speed data transmission and fault tolerance are achieved, and efficient and safe storage of resources is guaranteed [7]. At the same time, in order to ensure uninterrupted application access requirements of the platform, a dual-host architecture is used to configure applications and services in a master-slave manner to ensure the continuity of applications and services. Based on the framework of web-based teaching platform, as shown in Fig. 1.

The network teaching resource platform should be based on the professional teaching resource database to realize the functions of resource management, user management, excellent course management, network teaching, personalized portal, etc. the specific functional framework is shown in Fig. 2.

The professional teaching resource database is the material foundation of the network teaching resource platform. In order to facilitate the management, use and retrieval, the resources are first classified according to the specialty, and each specialty can establish its own curriculum system and professional sub database. The professional sub database

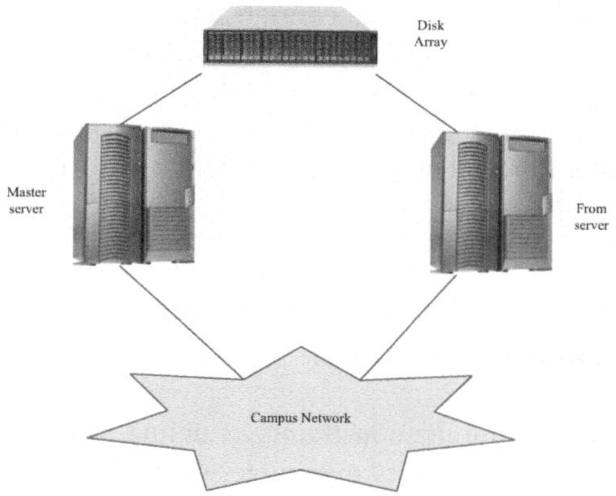

Fig. 1. Framework of network-based teaching platform

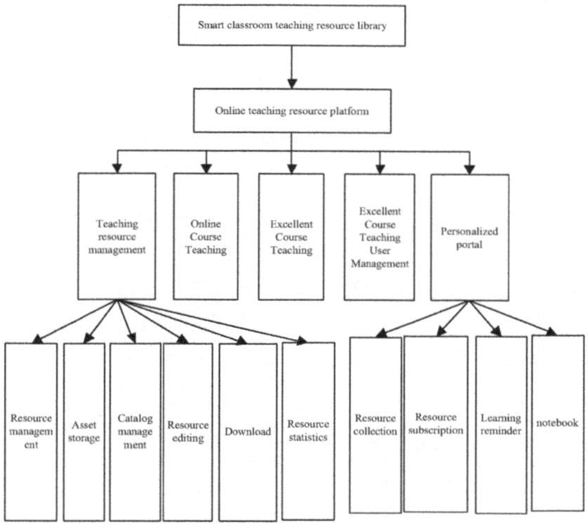

Fig. 2. Functional framework of network teaching resource platform

includes curriculum standard database, courseware database, project case database, test question database, industry resource database and material database, etc. when the resources are put into storage, you can choose the resource institute Major sub library and related courses [8].

The management of teaching resource base is one of the key functions of network teaching resource platform. It has the functions of resource type management, resource warehousing, resource outbound, resource audit, resource browsing and retrieval, resource download, resource evaluation and use statistics, etc. Smart classroom learning is the core application of the network teaching resource platform, and the value of resources mainly embodies the knowledge growth and skill improvement obtained by users through resources. Therefore, the network teaching resource platform should support the implementation of intelligent classroom learning through the network, and be able to realize a variety of elements of course teaching in a virtual way, including class management, class grouping, video teaching, classroom interaction, online question answering, assignment arrangement, assignment marking, learning process monitoring, online examination, etc. [9].

3 Dynamic Adjustment Principle of Learning Resources Based on Network Teaching Platform

Under the condition of meeting the constraints of online learning resource capability, the online learning resource user utility maximizes the resource allocation in the online teaching platform. The demand function of online learning users is obtained. Based on this function, the dynamic adjustment model of distributed online learning resources is constructed. The specific process is as follows.

All resource allocation sets that meet the constraints of online learning resource capability, that is:

$$S=\{s|0 \leq \mathrm{s}_i \leq n_j, \sum_{i=1}^{m} \mathrm{s}_i \leq n_j \tag{1}$$

In formula (1), s_i is the ith personalized use vector of online learning resources, n_j is the resource attribute vector, m is the dimension of online learning resources, and s is the relevant function of all resource scheduling.

By using formula (2), the resource allocation scheme for maximizing the total utility of learning resource users is given, that is:

$$\max: \sum_{i=1}^{\mathrm{m}} R_{\mathrm{i}} s_i \cdot \sum_{i=1}^{\mathrm{m}} M s_i' \leq I \tag{2}$$

In formula (2), M is the total amount of data waiting to be sent for resource scheduling; s_i' is the priority of online learning resource scheduling; R_{i} is the task size of online learning resource scheduling; I is a constant.

The utility function method of network teaching platform is introduced to establish the user demand function of online learning [10]. Assuming that Q is the quality of service required by online resource scheduling and W is the reserved cost for completing the learning resource scheduling task, the utility function of online learning resource scheduling is as follows:

$$R(Q, W) = \mathrm{t}I\mathrm{n}(U) + I\mathrm{n}(W) \tag{3}$$

In formula (3), $I\mathrm{n}(U)$ is the scheduling value of completion U; $I\mathrm{n}(W)$ is the priority sequence of resource scheduling; t is the scheduling time.

Under the network teaching platform, there is a balance point between supply and demand of resources. The equilibrium state of competition is that marginal substitution rate equals to learning resources.

$$\frac{\lambda R/\lambda Q}{\lambda R/\lambda W} = \frac{\mathrm{t}W}{(1-t)Q} = P \tag{4}$$

In formula (4), λR is the dynamic change parameter of each online learning resource, λQ is the resource scheduling status information, and λW is the online learning resource scheduling task.

Under the given equilibrium state, each online learning resource user can maximize their own interests on the online teaching platform, and use formula (5) to express the obtained online learning user demand function:

$$F = \max\left(\frac{(1-P)}{(1-t)P}, \frac{F'}{P}\right) \tag{5}$$

In formula (5), F' is the sum of the demands of multiple scheduling service agents, and P is the personalized supply and demand equilibrium price of learning resources under the network teaching platform.

Based on the user demand function of online learning, the principle of dynamic adjustment of learning resources based on online teaching platform is studied.

4 The Realization of the Dynamic Adjustment Mechanism of Learning Resources in the Intelligent Classroom of Colleges and Universities

The genetic algorithm is used to solve the objective function, and the sub task resource scheduling time cost is used to constrain the fitness function, so as to adjust the fitness function value to complete the dynamic adjustment of online learning resources.

The specific process is as follows: according to the resource usage, the sub tasks in the online learning resource scheduling task set are classified. The classification results are coded to generate multiple sets of resource scheduling sub task sequences. Genetic algorithm is used to decode the sub task sequence of resource scheduling, and formula (6) is used to give the chromosome decoding process:

$$\begin{cases} G_1 : \{\mathrm{k}_2, \mathrm{k}_3, \mathrm{k}_4, \mathrm{k}_5, \mathrm{k}_6\} \\ G_2 : \{\mathrm{k}_1, \mathrm{k}_2, \mathrm{k}_3, \mathrm{k}_4, \mathrm{k}_5, \mathrm{k}_6, \mathrm{k}_7, \mathrm{k}_8, \mathrm{k}_9\} \\ G_3 : \{\mathrm{k}_5, \mathrm{k}_6, \mathrm{k}_7, \mathrm{k}_8\} \end{cases} \tag{6}$$

In formula (6): $\mathrm{k}_2, \mathrm{k}_3, \mathrm{k}_4, \mathrm{k}_5, \mathrm{k}_6$ is the number of resource scheduling sub task; $\mathrm{k}_1, \mathrm{k}_2, \mathrm{k}_3$ is the number of resource in each chromosome.

The decoding result of formula (6) is used to further calculate the time needed to complete the office column of the scheduling sub task. Take the maximum value of the calculation result, and the completion time of the private subtask in the resource scheduling task is as follows:

$$Qt(i) = \sum_{j=1}^{m} t(\mathrm{i,j})(G1 + G2 + G3)j \quad (7)$$

In formula (7): m is the number of subtasks assigned to each learning resource, $t(\mathrm{i,j})$ is the time required for the execution of the jth subtask assigned to the online learning resource scheduling resource.

Combined with the obtained $Qt(\mathrm{i})$ and F, the cost of resources needed to complete all online learning resource scheduling subtasks is calculated, that is:

$$Y(\mathrm{i}) = \sum_{j=1}^{m} Qt(\mathrm{i}) \times X(\mathrm{i}) \quad (8)$$

In formula (8): $X(\mathrm{i})$ is the cost of online learning resource scheduling task per unit time of each learning resource.

In the dynamic adjustment mechanism of online learning resources, the completion time and resource cost of all subtasks of online learning resource scheduling should be considered simultaneously. By using genetic algorithm, the maximum time Mt and the maximum cost C constraints of all online learning resource scheduling subtasks are obtained as follows:

$$\begin{cases} Mt = \mathrm{t_{min}} + n \times (\mathrm{tmax} - \mathrm{t_{min}}) \\ C = Y(\mathrm{i})_{\mathrm{min}} + m \times (Y(\mathrm{i})_{\mathrm{max}} - Y(\mathrm{i})_{\mathrm{min}}) \end{cases} \quad (9)$$

In the process of dynamic adjustment of learning resources, it is necessary to consider the execution time and the fitness function of execution cost required by all subtasks to complete the scheduling task. The fitness function is given by formula (10):

$$\mathrm{h}(i) = \frac{1}{t(i)} \times \mu \quad (10)$$

In formula (10): μ is the load factor of balancing resource scheduling task. The larger the load factor is, the higher the utilization rate of online learning resources is.

In the fitness function considering the time constraint of dynamic adjustment of learning resources, the higher the utilization rate of scheduling resources is, the shorter the time required for all subtasks of dynamic adjustment of online learning resources to complete. Considering the adaptive function of cost constraint of dynamic adjustment of online learning resources, the lower the cost of resource scheduling and the larger the adaptive value of all subtasks of dynamic adjustment of online learning resources. Therefore, it can shorten the dynamic adjustment time of information resources by closely connecting the start resources to the end resources. Design dynamic adjustment of reliable path, and Fig. 3 shows the selection process of reliable path.

It can be seen from Fig. 3 that the reliable adjustment path is designed based on the determination of the network teaching platform, in which the absolute reliable path model can select the shortest path in the network scene. The relatively reliable path

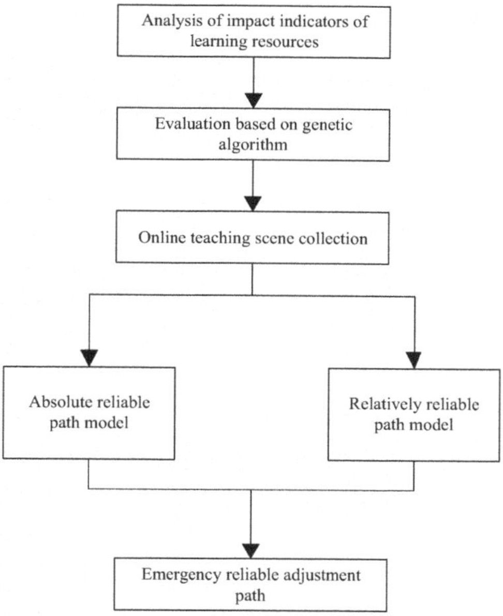

Fig. 3. Reliable path selection process

can select the optimal path related to the scene in the network scene, that is, select the shortest path related to the scene in a scene.

According to the characteristics of network teaching platform, the time factor is regarded as the goal of dynamic adjustment of learning resources in University smart classroom, and the shortest path is chosen as the alternative path to realize the dynamic adjustment of learning resources in University smart classroom.

5 Experimental Results and Analysis

In order to verify the comprehensive effectiveness of the dynamic adjustment mechanism of learning resources in University smart classroom based on network teaching platform, a simulation experiment is needed. The experimental simulation software is Matlab2013, and the simulation platform is Cloudsim.

5.1 Evaluation Index of Learning Resource Base

In order to ensure the accuracy of implementation effect analysis, an effective resource evaluation mechanism must be established. The evaluation index system of learning resource base is shown in Table 1.

5.2 Experiment Preparation and Treatment

After obtaining data according to SPSS Clemntine data mining tool, it is necessary to carefully check the data quality. For the case of too many missing values, you can

Table 1. Evaluation index of learning resource base

First level index	Second level index	Third level index
Knowledge management	Knowledge renewal and integration	Interchain
		Knowledge innovation
	Appearance of tacit knowledge	Collaborative teaching and learning
	Intellectualization	Distributed storage and acquisition
		Data mining
		Repository sharing
Resource usage effect	Teaching organization	Teaching organization
	Teaching implementation	Teaching of teachers
		Autonomous Learning
	Teaching management	Task management
		Member management
	Teaching evaluation	Self-evaluation
		Curriculum testing
	Survey feedback	Teaching evaluation
		Special survey
	Individualization	Personalized panel
	Use value	Resource access statistics

choose to delete them. At the same time, you can create fields that do not need the effective package before the data query restriction to delete. You can repeatedly extract and transform the data for many times to obtain the precise fields and formats required by the experiment to meet the correct data source. Read the data into Clemntine and send the processed data to the relevant location.

5.3 Experimental Environment and Parameter Setting

The experimental data is selected from the enterprise information database of an economic company from October 31, 2018 to December 31, 2018, including 500 service records of 500 users. In this experiment, set the service cycle as 30 days, select 70% of the service time as the training set time and 30% of the service time as the test time.

The experimental parameters are:

(1) Experimental equipment processor: Intel(R)Core^{TM}i5 – 4590CPU@3.30 GHz
(2) Server memory: 64 GB
(3) Operating System type: Windows 8, 32-bit.

5.4 Experiment and Analysis

In order to verify the advantages of the resource adjustment mechanism studied, the methods of literature [4] and literature [5] were used as the experimental control group, and the black box test was carried out in the above experimental environment. The content of application black box test is shown in Table 2.

Table 2. Content of black box test

No	Test content
1	Registration module test
2	Export student registration information
3	Using system without login
4	Courses setting for up to 30 min

The content of black box test is as follows:

50 students were selected for the test, with 45 correct information and 5 error information.

(1) The error message is ID card number error;
(2) Using JavaScript functions, submit the form for judgment.

After the actual user requirements, the three system test results are shown in Table 3.

Table 3. System test results

Function point	Mechanism of reference [4]	Mechanism of Reference [4]	Research mechanism
Page setup	Pass	Not Pass	Pass
Add message information	Pass	Pass	Pass
Students register online	Pass	Not Pass	Pass
Student learning survey	Not Pass	Not Pass	Pass
Browse the course video	Not Pass	Not Pass	Pass
Browse online help	Not Pass	Not Pass	Pass
System background settings	Pass	Pass	Pass
Manage message information	Not Pass	Not Pass	Pass
Manage enrollment information	Not Pass	Pass	Pass
Management evaluation information	Pass	Not Pass	Pass

The test results show that most of the traditional mechanism test results are failed, and the mechanism is not stable; the dynamic mechanism test results are all passed, and the mechanism is relatively stable.

(1) Adjust time
In order to further verify the performance of the mechanism in adjusting time, a comparative experiment was carried out. Test three mechanisms to adjust the adjustment time of the same target resources, and the comparison results of time adjustment time are shown in Fig. 4.

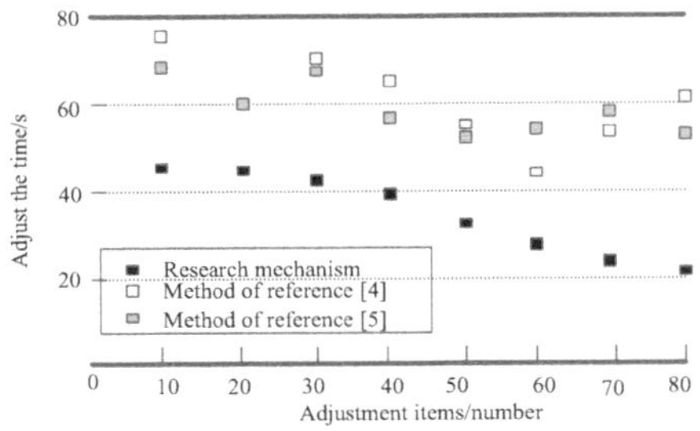

Fig. 4. Comparison results of adjustment time of three mechanisms

It can be seen from Fig. 4 that in the test process, the adjustment time of the two traditional methods is higher than 40 s, and the adjustment time is unstable; the average adjustment time of the studied method is lower than 40 s, and it gradually decreases with the increase of adjustment items. The adjustment time of the mechanism studied is significantly longer than that of the traditional method.

(2) Adjust efficiency
Under the premise of keeping the adjustment time consistent and the adjustment items consistent, compare and analyze the adjustment efficiency of the three mechanisms, and the results are shown in Fig. 5.

It can be seen from Fig. 5 that the adjustment efficiency of the two traditional mechanisms decreases with the increase of test time, with a minimum of 5%; while the resource adjustment efficiency of the mechanism studied is better, with a maximum of 99%. The reason for this result is that the mechanism designed the reliable path selection process, which is helpful to improve the efficiency of resource adjustment.

To sum up, the adjustment time of the dynamic adjustment mechanism of learning resources in university smart classroom based on the network teaching platform is shorter and the adjustment efficiency is higher.

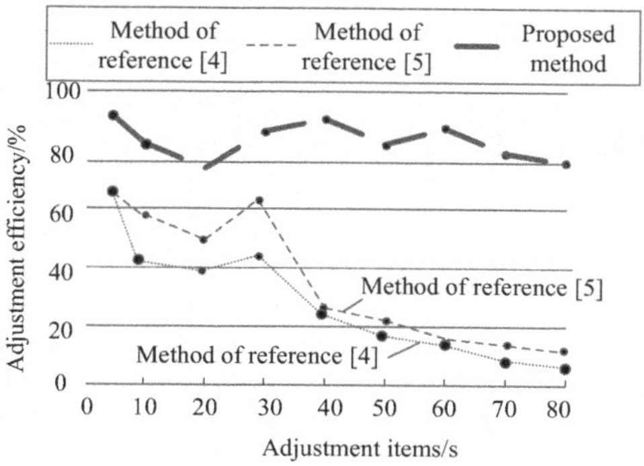

Fig. 5. Comparison results of adjustment efficiency of three mechanisms

6 Conclusion

In view of the problems of long adjustment time and low efficiency in the adjustment mechanism of learning resources, this paper proposes a dynamic adjustment mechanism of learning resources in University intelligent classroom based on the network teaching platform. According to the framework of the network teaching platform, under the condition of meeting the capacity constraints of online learning resources, genetic algorithm is used to solve the objective function, and a reliable path of dynamic adjustment is designed for the intelligent classroom. The innovation of teaching mode provides guarantee.

Fund Project. Anhui Quality Engineering Project No.: 2017zhkt123.

References

1. Klašnja-Milićević, A., Ivanović, M., Vesin, B., et al.: Enhancing e-learning systems with personalized recommendation based on collaborative tagging techniques. Appl. Intell. **1**, 1–17 (2017)
2. Li, G., Wang, F.: Research on art innovation teaching platform based on data mining algorithm. Cluster Comput. **22**(6), 13867–13872 (2019)
3. Moshovos, A., Albericio, J., Judd, P., et al.: Value-based deep-learning acceleration. IEEE Micro **38**(1), 41–55 (2018)
4. Yin, C., Yamada, M., Oi, M., et al.: Exploring the relationships between reading behavior patterns and learning outcomes based on log data from e-books: a human factor approach. Int. J. Hum. Comput. Inter. **1**, 1–10 (2018)
5. Merayo, N., Ruíz, I., Debrán, J., et al.: AIM-Mobile Learning Platform to enhance the teaching-learning process using smartphones. Comput. Appl. Eng. Educ. **26**(5), 1753–1768 (2018)
6. Remington, T.L., Bleske, B.E., Bartholomew, T., et al.: Qualitative analysis of student perceptions comparing team-based learning and traditional lecture in a pharmacotherapeutics course. Am. J. Pharmaceutical Educ. **81**(3), 55 (2017)
7. Chatterjee, N., Paul, S., Chattopadhyay, S.: Task mapping and scheduling for network-on-chip based multi-core platform with transient faults. J. Syst. Architect. **83**(2), 34–56 (2018)

8. Tang, J., Yuan, X.: The construction and application of digital resources in rural primary school english teaching and learning. Soc. Network. **7**(2), 89–96 (2018)
9. Huali, X.: The Enlightenment of the Teaching Method of SIOP to bilingual teaching in colleges and universities in china under the background of creating "world-class universities and disciplines-double first rate". J. High. Educ. **4**, 5–15 (2018)
10. Duncum, P.: Responding to big data in the art education classroom: affordances and problematics. Int. J. Art Des. Educ. **37**(2), 325–332 (2018)

Design of APP Learning Platform for Oil Storage Tank Mechanical Cleaning Technology Course Based on Mobile Terminal

Jun-ru Wang(✉)

Chongqing Vocational College of Transportation, Chongqing 402247, China
xjenxuejn@163.com

Abstract. In view of the high level of network flow consumption existing in the traditional app learning platform of tank mechanical cleaning technology course, the app learning platform of tank mechanical cleaning technology course based on mobile terminal is designed. This paper analyzes the actual needs of different users for the learning platform, completes the database design of the learning platform according to the database design principles, references the W5100 expansion board, realizes the command receiving function based on the mobile terminal, and adds the learning navigation service in the learning platform to help users learn the mechanical cleaning technology of the oil tank, so far the design of the learning platform is completed. The test results show that: compared with the traditional learning platform, the designed app learning platform based on mobile terminal mechanical cleaning technology course has lower network flow consumption level, and the learning platform is more suitable for promotion and use.

Keywords: Mobile terminal · Oil tank · Mechanical cleaning · Learning platform

1 Introduction

With the rapid development of China's economy and society, the demand and consumption of refined oil have increased dramatically. The buried oil tank at the gas station is used as a container for refined oil. The cleanliness of the tank is the key to ensuring the quality of the oil, so it needs to be cleaned regularly or irregularly. With the promulgation and implementation of the new "Environmental Protection Law" and the increasing emphasis on safety issues, it is urgent to promote mechanical cleaning technology to replace the traditional manual oil tank cleaning method [1]. China's current research on mechanical cleaning technology for buried oil tanks at gas stations is still in its infancy.

In recent years, with the rapid development of Internet communication technology, computer software and hardware technology, especially the development of mobile communication technology in the telecommunication industry, it has greatly promoted the application and popularization of mobile smart phones [2]. With the advent of Android, people's living habits have changed from computers to mobile phones. Because of its

S. Liu et al. (Eds.): eLEOT 2020, LNICST 339, pp. 193–203, 2020.
https://doi.org/10.1007/978-3-030-63952-5_17

open-source nature, Android operating system has undergone various evolutions, which has pushed the software development of smart phones based on Android operating system to a new climax, bringing great changes to our life and learning [3–5]. It can be imagined that in the era of smartphone popularization, the development of Internet and communication technology will change our education mode and bring unprecedented new atmosphere to the education field [6]. Therefore, we have the responsibility to promote the in-depth development of China's education sector, as well as to speed up the process of information-based reform in the field of education, especially to change and improve the educators' own deeper understanding and understanding of information-based education.

The reform of information technology is gradually changing the way of learning. In this era of relatively developed materials, smartphones have been widely popularized, and more and more people have become the most active consumer groups of mobile terminals. Therefore, people have mastered mobile terminals. The ability to learn. In order to better improve the learning efficiency of oil tank mechanical cleaning technology, improve the ability of users to learn autonomously, and allow users to gain more knowledge autonomously in free space, it is necessary to develop a set of oil tank machinery based on mobile terminals Cleaning technology course APP learning platform.

All kinds of apps used by mobile terminals need to rely on the network provided by operators, which requires users to spend a certain amount of money to obtain network traffic [7]. In the past, the app learning platform, a technology course, required a large amount of network traffic, which led to a large amount of user consumption, which was not conducive to the study of tank mechanical cleaning technology. In order to solve this problem, an app learning platform based on mobile terminal is designed to solve the problems in the traditional learning platform.

2 Design of APP Learning Platform for Oil Storage Tank Mechanical Cleaning Technology Course Based on Mobile Terminal

2.1 Database Design

The Oracle database is a database system that has accumulated many leading technologies and leads the industry in cluster technology, high availability, business intelligence, security, and system management [8]. Oracle 10g, 11g, and Real Application Clusters cluster technologies provide nearly unlimited scalability and overall availability.

Oracle Database 11g can run on cluster server or single server of windows, Linux and UNIX. It provides comprehensive functions for related transaction processing, business intelligence and content management, with industry-leading performance, scalability, security and reliability [9]. Its architecture is as follows (Fig. 1).

Utilize Oracle to provide Oracle Real Application Cluster cloud technology to build an Oracle database cloud based on a mobile terminal learning platform to solve the needs of the platform in preventing single point of failure, load balancing, dynamic expansion, and continuous availability [10]. Oracle Database Cloud uses virtualization technology to allow a single database to be accessed by multiple Oracle programs simultaneously.

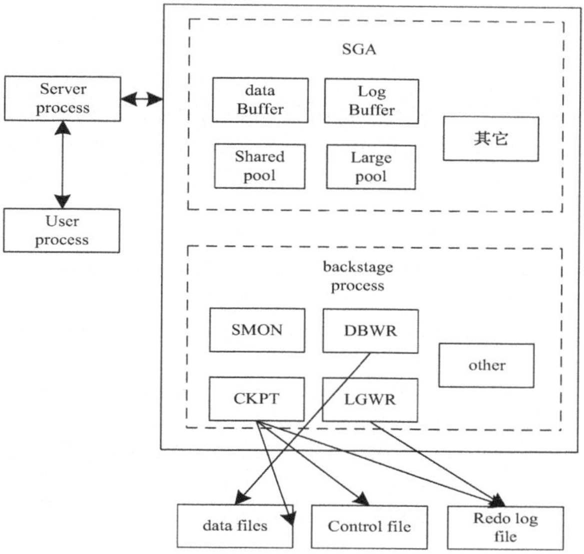

Fig. 1. Oracle database architecture

If one server crashes, transactions can be redirected to other surviving servers in the shortest downtime.

In this database, according to the design principles of database tables and the actual needs of users, database tables are designed.

The design principles are as follows:

(1) Naming convention: The names of libraries, tables, and domain names used in database design must be named in accordance with uniform rules, and these names must be explained in order to allow design, maintenance, or query More convenient.
(2) Index specification: a database index is a well-structured index used in the storage engine to quickly find records. It can greatly improve the performance of the database, especially as the amount of data in the table increases, the impact of the index on performance becomes more and more important. Index specification requirements: each table must have a primary key and best exist on the primary key, create index for possible field of the where the query, if there are multiple fields in a where clause should be created joint index, a unique index to the only fields in a table, long for the table of the text field and create FullText indexing requirements like matching field.
(3) Fixed data format definition: the user number uses the field name uniformly, and the data type is int. for the storage of time, the int type is used uniformly, and the 10 bit second time stamp is stored, except for special requirements.
(4) Foreign key specifications: Effective and standardized foreign keys ensure a high degree of consistency and integrity of the data. The main purpose of setting a foreign key is to control the data stored in the foreign key table. To associate two tables,

the foreign key can only reference the values of columns in the foreign table or use null values.

According to the analysis of the actual needs of the app learning platform for the mechanical cleaning technology course of oil storage tank, it is determined that the learning platform consists of five entities: students, teachers, courses, comments and notes

(1) a student can watch more than one course, and a course can be watched by more than one student.
(2) a course can only be uploaded by one teacher, but one teacher can upload multiple courses.
(3) a student may comment on the same course for many times, and the teacher may reply to a comment for many times.
(4) one comment corresponds to one student or one teacher and is related to only one course.
(5) one note can only be initiated by one student.

An entity-attribute diagram is designed for the platform, as shown in Fig. 2.

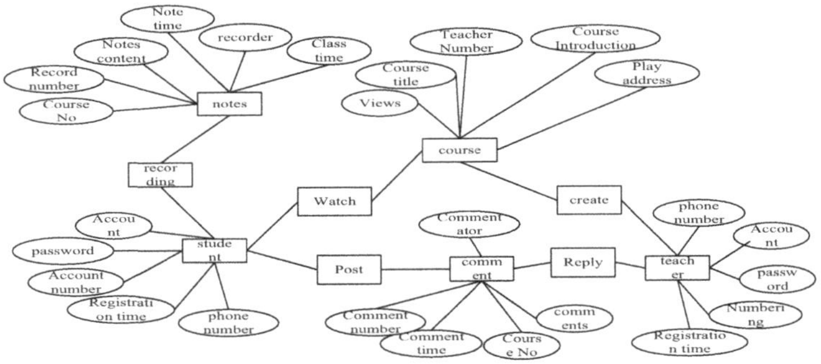

Fig. 2. Entity contact diagram

The attributes of the corresponding entities are as follows:

Combined with the contents of Fig. 2 and Table 1, complete the design of database in the app learning platform.

2.2 Design of Instruction Receiving Function Based on Mobile Terminal

In the design of the APP development platform for the oil tank mechanical cleaning technology course, the Arduino board is used as the basic electronic open platform. The Arduino board is a small microprocessor board with USB. It is connected to the IDE development environment on the computer via USB. Program changes in the IDE can be downloaded directly to the Arduino board via the USB cable. Various sensors

Table 1. Entity attribute data type and length table

Entity	Attribute	Data type and length	Key
Student users	User ID	4-byte integer	Unique primary key
	Account name	50-length string	
	Password	100-length string	
	Registration time	4-byte integer, 10-bit time stamp	
	Phone number	50-length string	
Storage tank mechanical cleaning technology course	Course No	4-byte integer	Primary key
	Course title	250 length string	
	Course title	250 length string	Foreign key
	Views	Course Video Traffic	4-byte integer
	Course Introduction	Long text	
	Playback address (URL address)	250 length string	
Teacher user	User ID	4-byte integer	Primary key, unique
	Account name	50-length string	
	Account password	100-length string	
	Registration time	10-bit timestamp	
	Phone number	50-length string	
Notes	Note number	4-byte integer	Primary key
	Student User Number	4-byte integer	Foreign key
	Course No	4-byte integer	Foreign key
	Note time	10-bit timestamp	
	Course play time	4-byte integer	
	Notes content	Long text	
Comment	Comment number	4-byte integer	
	Course No	4-byte integer	
	Comment time	10-bit timestamp	
	Comments	Long text	

are connected to external equipment and connected to external electronic devices and devices through connectors.

However, the Arduino development board can not receive the remote instructions directly. In order to receive the control instructions sent by the remote Android phone, the remote instructions must be received through the network connection through the network expansion board.

Arduino can be connected to the Internet through the Arduino Ethernet class library. The use of Arduino Ethernet class library requires corresponding hardware support. The DFRduino Ethernet W 5100 expansion board is used in the design of the learning platform. It is an expansion board with a built-in WizNet W5100 TCP/IP microprocessor. This board is connected to the Arduino board through a long pin header. The Ethernet library installed by default in Arduino IDE can make this expansion board connect to the Internet and communicate with other network devices. This expansion board supports the connection of 4 sockets at the same time. Arduino can communicate with W5100 and SD card through SPI port (using ICSP head). This is the number 11, 12, 13 on the Duemilanove/Uno and the 50, 51, 52 on the Mega. These ports cannot be used as general input and output. On Mega, hardware SS port 53 cannot be used for W5100 and SD card, but it must be used for output port, otherwise the SPI interface cannot work. Expansion board working voltage: W5100 expansion board, as shown in Fig. 3:

Fig. 3. Structure of W5100 DFRduino Ethernet W5100 expanding board

W5100 is the key to realize the Ethernet function of Arduino network expansion board. The application scope is mainly various embedded systems with low cost, high performance and high integration. Supports TCP/IP and other common network protocols, and supports full-duplex/half-duplex mode for automatic response. Its structure is shown in Fig. 4.

Through the application of W5100 expansion board and the setting of related ports, the instruction reception is realized on the mobile terminal.

2.3 Functional Design of Navigation Services for Technical Courses

The mechanical cleaning technology of oil storage tank is a course with high requirements for technical level. The design of learning navigation service function can guide

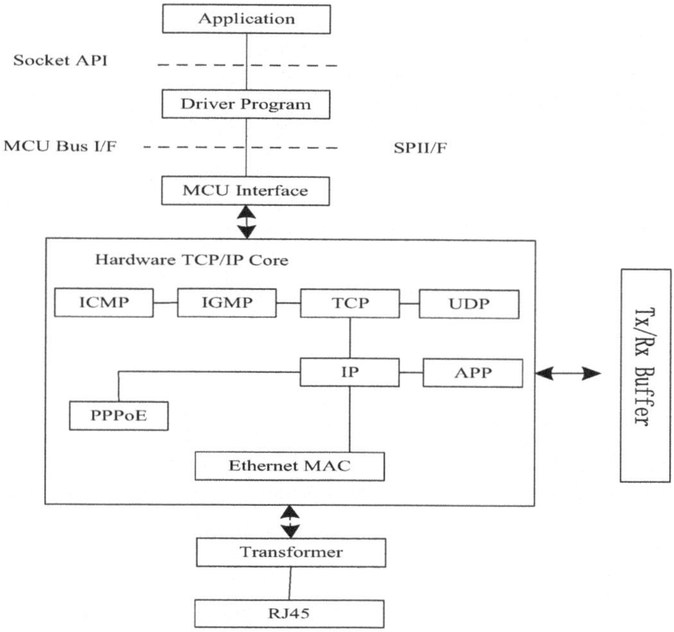

Fig. 4. Structure of W5100

students and help them to learn the course. In order to realize the five blessings of the automatic navigation of the learning platform, the learning objectives and teaching methods are combined to establish a learning activity relationship diagram, as shown in Fig. 5. Then according to different learning objectives to find different learning paths.

For the design of learning navigation service, it can be regarded as a scheduling problem with several constraints, so it can be generalized as constraint satisfaction. Firstly, a set of basic variables and constraints are defined according to the general constraint satisfaction planning problem, and then the constraints are further improved according to the characteristics of the learning platform to make it conform to the characteristics of the autonomous learning process. The constraints are as follows:

$$K(x) + Span(x) = J(x) \tag{1}$$

$$\begin{cases} J(x_0) \le K(x_i), i \in \{1, 2, \ldots, n\} \\ J\left(x_j\right) \le K(x_n), j \in \{0, 1, \ldots, n-1\} \end{cases} \tag{2}$$

In the formula: $K(x)$ represents the moment when learning activity x begins, $Span(x)$ represents the duration of learning activity x, $J(x)$ represents the moment when learning activity ends, and i, j, n represents a constant. For synchronization constraints, if the set of tasks that need to be performed simultaneously between multiple learners $r_i, r_{i+1}, \ldots, r_{i+n}$ is $\{x(r_i), x(r_{i+1}), \ldots, x(r_{i+n})\}$, Then there are:

$$\begin{cases} K(x(r_i)) = K(x(r_{i+1})) = \ldots = K(x(r_{i+n})) \\ J(x(r_i)) = J(x(r_{i+1})) = \ldots = J(x(r_{i+n})) \end{cases} \tag{3}$$

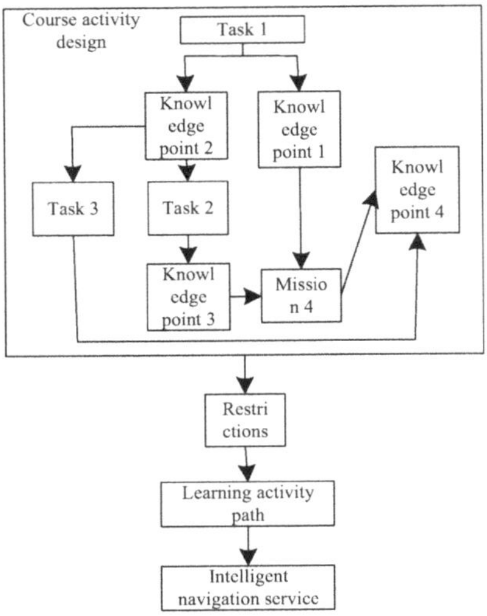

Fig. 5. Learning activity relationship

Through the above process, a scheduling problem is transformed into a general problem model, a more accurate model is established for the scheduling planning in the learning platform, and a learning navigation service for the storage platform mechanical cleaning technology course learning platform is better provided.

3 Testing Research on APP Learning Platform for Storage Tank Mechanical Cleaning Technology Course

For the test and research of the learning platform of mechanical cleaning technology of oil tank based on mobile terminal, taking the level of network flow consumption as the standard, using the traditional learning platform of mechanical cleaning technology of oil tank as the reference, a comparative test is designed, and the advantages and disadvantages of the learning platform are analyzed according to the results.

3.1 Network Traffic Collection

First, we create WiFi hotspot on the computer. The intelligent computer connects to the WiFi, runs the app learning platform purposefully, and uses Wireshark to monitor the wireless network card that generates WiFi to collect data packet traffic. In order to ensure the effectiveness of the collected flow, we should collect enough data package flow for the learning app of the mechanical cleaning technology course of oil storage tank, and ensure that the flow should be as pure as possible, that is, there is no other flow unrelated to the learning platform of app (the learning platform has certain fault tolerance, even if it is introduced Some impurity traffic will also be blocked) to ensure that all network behaviors of the app are covered and belong to its own network behaviors. Figure 6 is the flow diagram of the collected app learning platform.

No.	Protocol	source address	target address	Source port
1321	HTTP	192.168.9.30	192.168.9.255	137
1322	TCP	192.168.9.30	234.123.12.1	20141
1323	TCP	192.168.9.20	192.168.9.255	137
1324	HTTP	192.168.9.111	255.255.255.255	54443
1325	HTTP	192.168.9.213	224.0.0.252	57272
1326	HTTP	192.168.9.213	192.168.9.255	137
1327	TCP	192.168.9.210	224.0.0.252	60979
1328	HTTP	192.168.9.210	224.0.0.252	57317
1329	HTTP	192.168.9.112	239.255.255.250	1900
1330	TCP	192.168.9.210	192.168.9.255	137
1331	HTTP	192.168.9.58	61.160.224.11	10058
1332	HTTP	192.168.9.22	239.255.255.250	54033
1333	TCP	192.168.9.190	255.255.255.255	3601
1334	HTTP	192.168.9.117	227.88.88.89	6677
1335	HTTP	192.168.9.119	239.255.255.250	49502
1336	TCP	192.168.9.118	224.0.0.253	

Fig. 6. Schematic diagram of learning platform traffic

In addition to collecting traffic for learning, we also need to collect traffic for verification and mixed traffic. When collecting the traffic for verification, you only need to ensure that the collected traffic is as pure as possible, and you do not need to run the target app multiple times. Use the third-party software to count the changes of different app learning platform traffic.

3.2 Test Results and Analysis of Network Traffic

Use the traditional communication protocol-based course APP learning platform test to obtain the test result 1, use the traditional ZigBee technology-based learning platform to obtain the test result 2, and use the designed mobile terminal-based learning platform test to obtain the test result 3. The specific results are shown below (Fig. 7).

Observe the results in the graph. Test result 1 shows that the traffic has a large change in the test time. Most of the time is between 1000–1500 KB/s. There are the lowest peak and the highest peak. Analysis shows that there is a peak of 1800 KB/s between 90–120 min; Test result 2 shows that during the test time, the network traffic is mostly between 500–1500 KB/s, and the network traffic is at a high level during 0–50 min Test result 3 shows that the network traffic level is low during the test time, and the overall trend is decreasing, and it is always within 1000 KB/s.

To sum up, the designed mobile terminal based mechanical cleaning technology course app learning platform network traffic level is lower than the traditional learning platform, the learning platform is better than the traditional learning platform.

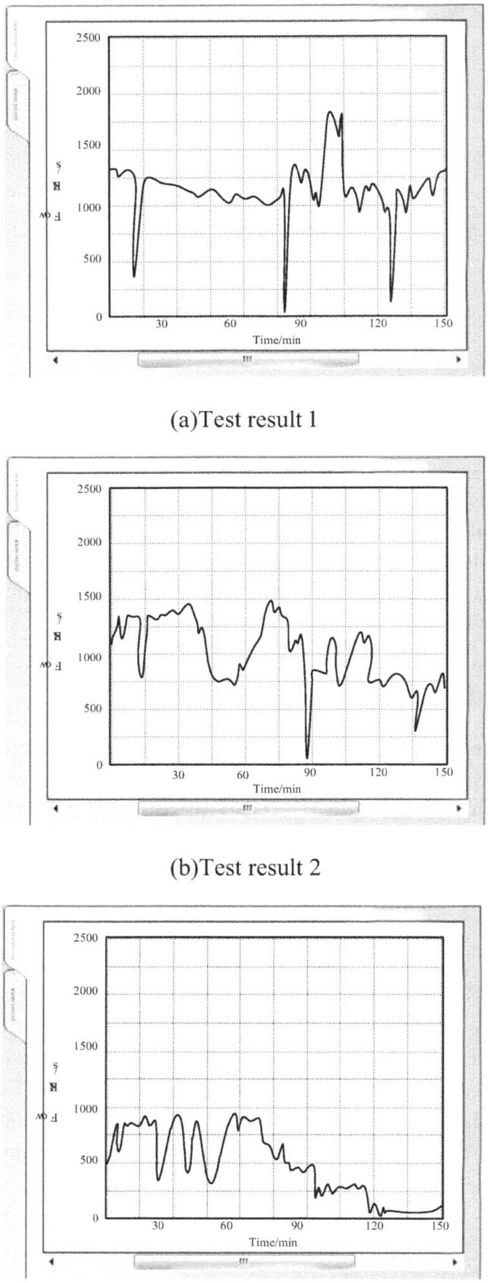

(a)Test result 1

(b)Test result 2

(c)Test result 3

Fig. 7. Network traffic test results of different learning platforms

4 Conclusion

In this era of information explosion, people have to accept a lot of information at all times. The fast working rhythm makes people have to use fragmented time to study. The curriculum APP learning platform has emerged to meet the development of the times. The app learning platform of tank mechanical cleaning technology course based on mobile terminal is designed to enable users of related specialties to receive new knowledge anytime and anywhere, and meet the learning needs of users' fragmentation. This research has a broad application prospect.

References

1. Zhang, L., Zhang R.Y., Ma, L., et al.: Effectiveness of learning with mobile "100-day training" APP among general practitioners in Beijing: an empirical study. Chinese General Practice **22**(19), 2374–2379 (2019)
2. Xu, Y.K., et al.: Research on the combined waterjet and mechanical pipe cleaning technology. Fluid Mach. **47**(5), 7–12 (2019)
3. Zhang, H., Sun, Z.L., Gao, H.X., et al.: Investigation on influencing factors of health literacy and analysis on health education demand based on mobile terminal among college students. Chongqing Med. **47**(15), 2055–2060 (2018)
4. Guo, W.: APP development method of scientific journals based on cloud platforms: taking Changbaishan academic activity as an example. Chin. J. Sci. Techn. Periodicals **29**(5), 485–490 (2018)
5. Zhao, W.J., Xie, S.M.: The relationship among perceived value, satisfaction and behavioral intention of college students' mobile reading: taking the superstar mobile reading APP platform as an example. Libr. Inf. Serv. **63**(3), 98–107 (2019)
6. He, Z., Wang, J.: Exploration on the "teaching-learning-practicing" teaching model in blood transfusion test technology course of a vocational medical college. Chin. J. Blood Transfus. **32**(1), 84–86 (2019)
7. Wu, J.L., Shang, S.H.: Factors affecting the use of MOOCs based on tacit knowledge and explicit knowledge learning. J. Manag. Sci. China **22**(3), 21–39 (2019)
8. Li, J., Zheng, Z.Y., Zhang, D.Z. et al.: Research on real-time BDS/GPS single-frequency PPP technology for Android mobile terminal. Sci. Surv. Mapp. **44**(3), 149–153 (2019)
9. Zhao, Y.N., Cheng, Z.X., Jing, R.T.: Interface design and evolving mechanism of platform organization. J. Manag. Sci. **32**(3), 3–15 (2019)
10. Liu, Y., Zeng, X.L., Hu, X., et al.: Construction and teaching practice of the open online courses of principles of chemical engineering. Chin. J. Chem. Educ. **39**(24), 7–14 (2018)

Innovation and Entrepreneurship Education System of New Engineering Talents Based on Knowledge Base

Yan Wang[1(✉)], Fang Sonh[2], and Hai-hong Bian[3]

[1] School of Information and Control,
Shenyang Institute of Technology, Shenyang 113122, China
hp20190808@163.com
[2] Shanghai Kuanrui Information Technology Co., Ltd., Shanghai 118300, China
[3] Nanjing Institute of Technology, Nanjing 210000, China

Abstract. Due to the poor performance of the traditional innovation and entrepreneurship education system for new engineering talents, the online examination system for innovation and entrepreneurship education and training for new engineering talents is optimized based on the knowledge base. Microsoft asp.net is used as the development tool and SQL server is selected As the database platform of the system, 2005 designed and implemented an intelligent test paper online examination system, and discussed the design and implementation process of typical modules. Furthermore, the traditional genetic algorithm is improved, and the mutation operator and hybrid operator in the genetic algorithm are optimized. Finally, the black box test method is used to test the performance of the system, and the effectiveness of the application of the system is verified.

Keywords: Knowledge base · New engineering talents · Innovation and entrepreneurship education · Online examination

1 Introduction

With the continuous reform and development of China's education system, innovation and entrepreneurship education has become an important part of China's education system and an indispensable part of China's future diversified education system development. In recent years, with the rapid expansion of the scale and quantity of many domestic educational institutions, extensive and centralized innovation and entrepreneurship examination has become a problem faced by many educational institutions [1]. The organization and management of innovation and entrepreneurship education examination is very heavy because of the learning level, the diversification of learning mode and the complexity of students. In addition, the innovation and entrepreneurship examination is a centralized organization mode in a short time, which brings heavy work burden to the organization and personnel of innovation and entrepreneurship examination.

S. Liu et al. (Eds.): eLEOT 2020, LNICST 339, pp. 204–216, 2020.
https://doi.org/10.1007/978-3-030-63952-5_18

The traditional mode of examination management has become more and more unable to meet the current management needs. It is more and more urgent to carry out online examination information and networking needs [2]. With the rapid development of educational informatization in China, the innovation and entrepreneurship online examination mode has been widely used as a new assessment method and examination method in the actual teaching examination, and gradually evolved into a hot field of research and application in the current education industry informatization construction [3]. Based on the above reasons, this paper starts from the actual needs of innovation and entrepreneurship examination management, aiming at the current situation of innovation and entrepreneurship examination in China, analyzes the problems and shortcomings of the current innovation and entrepreneurship examination mode, and demonstrates the significance and goal of the construction of the examination teaching system.

Through in-depth analysis and exploration, this paper designs a solution of online examination system of innovation and Entrepreneurship Based on knowledge base, and on this basis, studies the online examination system of innovation and entrepreneurship. First of all, it analyzes the feasibility of online examination system construction, and makes a detailed demand analysis of innovation and entrepreneurship online examination system [4]. Using a variety of software development technologies, on the basis of clarifying the system design objectives, this paper analyzes and designs the functional modules, system modeling, system architecture, system input and output, system security and system database of the innovation and entrepreneurship online examination system, and then constructs a multi-layer architecture innovation and entrepreneurship online examination system. On the basis of the system design, using the object-oriented software engineering design mode, the program of the system is developed, and finally an online innovation and entrepreneurship examination system with perfect functions is developed and realized.

2 Education and Training Online Examination System

2.1 System Hardware Configuration

The background of the innovation and entrepreneurship education examination system is the operation interface for system administrators, teachers, marking personnel, etc., and the management of system paper formation, marking, etc. is carried out in the background [5]. In terms of design, the innovation and entrepreneurship education examination system adopts the standard engineering design mode, and uses the standard engineering design theory to design the functional framework of the system. The system can be divided into modules with independent functions to enhance the scalability of innovation and entrepreneurship education examination system.

In order to discuss the design of the system, this paper draws the functional modules of the system by using the structural diagram of the functional modules. The online examination system of innovation and entrepreneurship education is divided into two parts. In the functional design, the back-end is mainly designed into four functional blocks: system user management, examinee performance management, innovation and entrepreneurship education examination management, and innovation and entrepreneurship education examination management New entrepreneurship education question bank management function block [5]. The function module structure of innovation and entrepreneurship education online examination system is shown in Fig. 1.

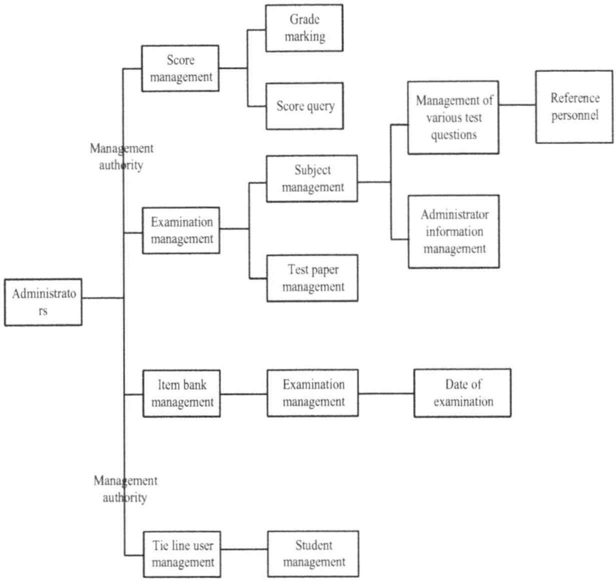

Fig. 1. Function module structure of online examination system for innovation and Entrepreneurship Education

The front desk of innovation and entrepreneurship education online examinee system is mainly designed for examinee services, as shown in the figure. Administrators manage users in the background, and examinees register through the registration function provided by the system, and the front desk of the system is designed with the registration function. For the registration of the system, it is found in the preliminary research that there are roughly three requirements as follows:

(1) Some schools or educational institutions need candidates to register successfully according to one or two of ID card, student number, registration number, etc., that is, before candidates register, they need to verify and control the authenticity of the examination through the above-mentioned unique ID information to ensure the validity of candidates' identity.
(2) Some schools or educational institutions do not need to provide registration function, but use the unique ID information such as student number to assign password to the corresponding exam in advance, and the examinee can directly log in to the exam system for examination after getting the password.
(3) Some schools or educational institutions need to control the entrance of examinees according to the examination permit before examinees enter the examination room of the examination system. After qualified examinees enter the corresponding seats,

they can enter the examination permit number to effectively avoid the trouble caused by examinee registration [6].

Even if the registration function is not designed in the innovation and entrepreneurship education examination system, the network system of the remote online innovation and entrepreneurship education examination also needs the registration function to control the security and browsing authority of the system.

The online examination system of innovation and entrepreneurship education based on the knowledge base mode adopts the application mode based on the multi-layer system architecture, and uses the multi-layer system structure based on the B/S architecture mode and the knowledge base environment to achieve [7]. Multi tier architecture can effectively separate the performance layer, general business logic layer, core business logic layer and data layer, so as to ensure the scalability of innovation and entrepreneurship education online examination system.

The system layered architecture design is conducive to reducing the difficulty of development, making the program developers have their own responsibilities, clear division of labor, and multiplying the collaborative efficiency of system program development [8]. At the same time, the use of layered design is conducive to reducing the coupling degree of the system, and because users can only access the database through the data access layer, reducing the entry point of data operation, many security risks of the system are shielded. The designed system architecture is shown in Fig. 2.

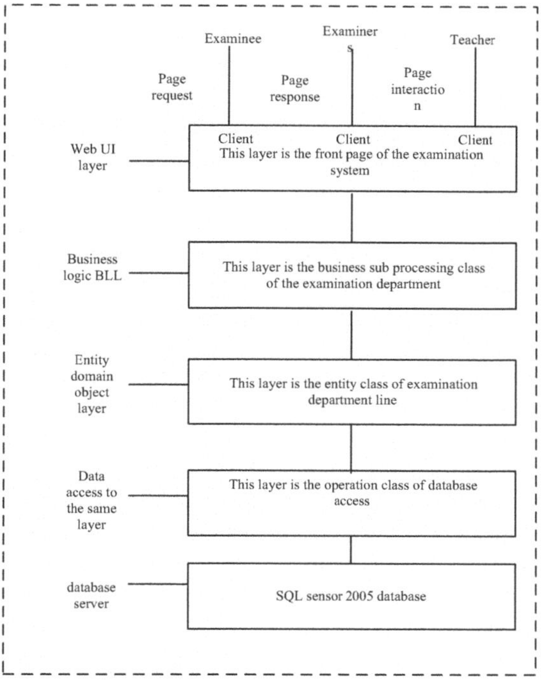

Fig. 2. Hierarchy of innovation and entrepreneurship education examination system

As can be seen from the figure, the online innovation and entrepreneurship education examination system is designed as a four-tier system architecture, with each layer calling each other and progressing layer by layer, and finally realizing the operation of the database. The system's knowledge base UI layer provides a knowledge base service interface for examinees, examiners and teachers, so that users can realize information interaction in the knowledge base environment only through the front-end client [9]. Such a design effectively guarantees that the online examination system can carry out information interaction based on remote places, and effectively meets the management business of innovation and entrepreneurship education online examination based on the knowledge base environment [10]. This module is the core of the system. Its basic functions include three parts: intelligent test paper, artificial test paper and borrowing historical test paper. Among them, the manual test paper formation method is to customize and output the test paper according to the basic needs of the operators, so as to meet the basic needs of the test paper makers; Genetic algorithm is a computational model simulating the natural selection and genetic mechanism of Darwinian biological evolution. It is a method to search the optimal solution by simulating the natural evolution. Genetic algorithm starts from a population which represents the potential solution set of the problem, and a population consists of a certain number of individuals encoded by genes. Intelligent test paper generation mainly adopts the strategy based on genetic algorithm to set the basic constraints according to the basic needs of users, and then uses the strategy based on genetic algorithm to automatically extract questions from the test database, and finally generates and outputs the test papers that meet the requirements.

2.2 System Software Optimization

With the continuous development of intelligent technology, the basic steps of the commonly used algorithm for generating test papers are as follows: firstly, the system matches the knowledge distribution, question type distribution, cognitive classification distribution, difficulty distribution, discrimination distribution, time distribution and score distribution of the test papers according to the overall requirements of the test papers entered by the users, and forms the parameter table for generating test papers, and then selects topics from the test paper database according to the parameter table. This method does not consider the mutual restriction among various parameters, such as knowledge distribution, question type distribution, difficulty distribution, etc. Therefore, the test questions that can not meet all the attributes are often found in the question bank during test paper formation, so they have to be replaced by the test questions with approximate attribution, which will eventually reduce the index of test paper formation. In view of this problem, the relevant topic selection methods are studied.

In the process of system users registering personal information, the main participants in the process are students. Only when students register personal information and pass the system verification can they participate in the system process of online examination system, such as students' online examination, query results, edit personal information, etc. [11]. When students register, they need to fill in some personal information, and the password also needs at least six digits. If the input information does not meet the requirements, the system will display a prompt message, and then return to the registration page and re-enter the information that meets the requirements. After the user registers correctly, the corresponding personal information is stored in the background database of the examination system, and the ID number obtained by the student is displayed in a fixed position on the page. The time sequence diagram of the student's personal information registration is drawn by the business process of the system. The class involved in the time sequence diagram of the student's registration is the student class. From the overall point of view of the online examination system, the student information registration is In the first part, only after the student registration information is verified by the system, can the system be used normally for online examination. The system administrator can manage the student information through the high authority information management function, and can arrange the required examination questions for different candidates. The user registration module management sequence diagram is shown in Fig. 3.

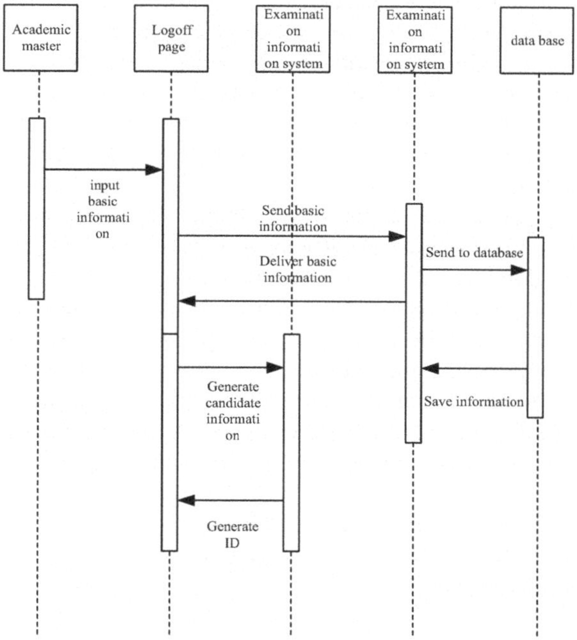

Fig. 3. Management sequence diagram of user registration module

Further scene description based on the above figure:

Step 1: students enter the registration page;
Step 2: input the name, student number, email, password and other information, and send the information to the system database;
Step 3: the system verifies whether the input information format and other aspects meet the requirements;
Step 4: return basic information;

Step 5: insert the user information into the corresponding table in the database without the user information;
Step 6: send the information to the database for saving;
Step 7: display the user's ID number in a fixed position on the page and prompt for successful registration.

Based on the above steps, the system is further optimized. The online examination system uses two input pages to complete the input of various types of questions. After logging in to the system, the teacher user clicks the corresponding question entry link to enter the page of adding test questions. In the page, select the name of the set questions, set the number of the test questions and other information, enter the content of the test stem and the correct answer, and then click the add button to enter it into the test question database [12]. The specific process of adding new questions is mainly to connect the test database, bind the test data and update, add and delete the data. The main controls in the new test question page are list controls and text box controls. Through these controls, information such as the subject, question number and question type of the question can be input. These controls are bound with the corresponding table fields in the test question database. After the teacher edits all the contents of the test question, click the Add button to submit all the information of the test question to the background database The test questions are added [13].

Taking the single choice questions as an example, this paper introduces the implementation process of adding and modifying test questions, and the state chart and sequence chart of adding or editing test questions. In this module, the core to effectively complete intelligent test paper formation is the basic requirements of test paper users, mainly including the following aspects: the proportion of knowledge points; the difficulty of knowledge points; the number of test questions. The essence of this problem is a problem solving problem with multiple constrained objectives [14]. In order to solve this problem effectively, three basic test paper forming processes are set up and implemented. The basic basis of the three processes are as follows:

(1) Based on the percentage of knowledge points;
(2) According to the distribution of knowledge points in questions;
(3) Randomly group papers.

Users can choose according to the actual situation. The management module of the question bank completes the management function of the related question database of the test paper system. Firstly, the system assigns permissions to users. The database for teachers with permissions to edit test questions mainly includes the entry, modification, query and deletion of test questions. The typical input flow of question bank is shown in Fig. 4.

The basic idea of coding method based on the real number matrix is as follows: take each test question in the test question bank as the analysis object, when the test question is coded independently in real number, when the test question has n attribute values, its eigenvector is $n + 1$ dimension, and each dimension corresponds to each parameter of the paper formation problem, such as the number of knowledge points, difficulty, question type, etc. The mapping method is as follows: the test paper corresponds to a

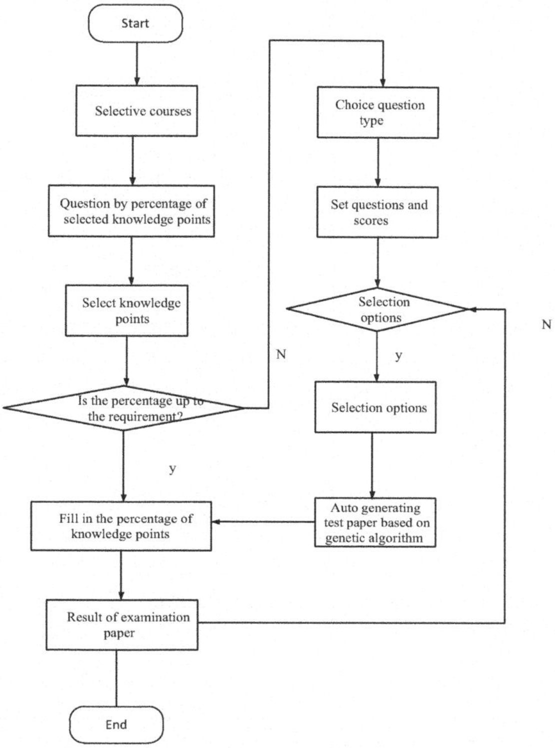

Fig. 4. Edit the sequence of test questions

matrix chromosome, in which the test questions correspond to matrix vectors, and the test attributes are the gene positions in the chromosome. If the number of test questions is n and the attribute of test questions is m, the problem of generating test papers in this test question bank can be described as a matrix of $(n + 1) * (m + 1)$. Each column of the matrix represents each attribute value of the test question. The matrix model of test paper coding is optimized as follows.

$$a =_i \begin{Bmatrix} a_0, & a_1, & a_2, & \ldots, a_n \\ a_{10}, & a_{11}, & a_2, & \ldots, a_{1n} \\ \ldots & & & \\ a_{m0}, & a_{m1}, & a_{m2}, & \ldots, a_{mn} \end{Bmatrix} \begin{matrix} \ldots\ldots \text{Evaluation value of test paper} \\ \text{Question A1n} \\ \ldots \\ \text{Question } A_{m0} \end{matrix} \quad (1)$$

In order to effectively design the fitness function for the problem of generating test papers, this paper proposes the fitness function based on the linear scale transformation. The basic idea can be described as follows: the corresponding mark attribute is weighted to intercept, and combined as the objective function to calculate the overall fitness value. The weight allocation method of target attribute is: wi = 1. In this paper, we use the piecewise function to design the scalar function, and its definition is shown in formula 2.

EI is the attribute value of each target, and M is the error range.

$$f = \begin{cases} \left| \frac{a_i - n}{e_n} - \frac{m}{e_n + a_i} \right| \leq m_i \\ 1, \frac{a_i - 1}{e_n} \gg m_i \end{cases} \tag{2}$$

According to the weight distribution of the objective attribute, the objective function of the whole paper can be expressed as:

$$g_{\min} = \sum \log w_i f / \ln z(a_i + 1) \tag{3}$$

In order to effectively maintain the diversity of population in the actual calculation process, this paper introduces the exponential proportion transformation method into the transformation of fitness function, that is, the fitness function is transformed into the objective function by formula 3.

$$k = \frac{\prod (a_i + 1)^m}{\sum \Delta \ \sin 4\pi * g_{\min}} - f \tag{4}$$

2.3 The Realization of Innovation and Entrepreneurship Education Training Online Examination

The overall structure of online examination system is divided into the following modules: examinee login module, online examination module, question bank management module, examination system maintenance module. Next, the class diagram of the system is designed, and then the specific implementation of these functional modules in the system is introduced in detail. An abstraction and summary of a group of objects with similar attributes, behaviors and structures is summarized and abstracted from the external characteristics of multiple objects. A class has two special components: methods and attributes. Methods are the operations that can be performed by the objects instantiated by a class. Attributes are the states of the objects instantiated by a class. According to the needs analysis, a system can be drawn Class diagram. In order to fully guarantee the security of online examination system of innovation and entrepreneurship education, users need to log in and verify their identity before entering the system. The way of

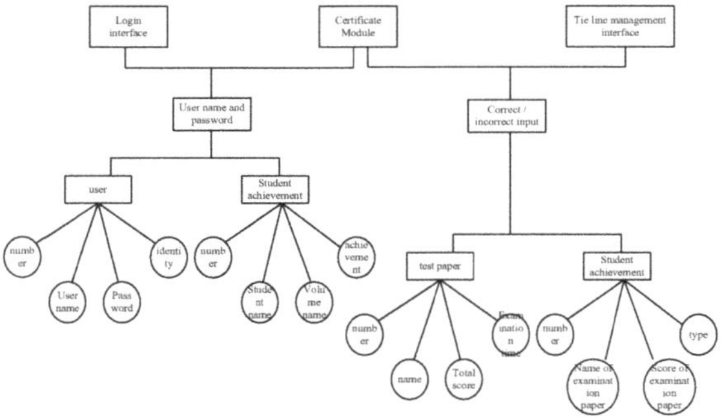

Fig. 5. Test training system control module

verification is mainly through user name and password. If the user name does not match the password, you cannot enter the system. The specific control implementation process is shown in Fig. 5.

It can be seen from the examinee examination interface that the online examination system based on knowledge base has replaced the traditional paper and pen examination mode. In order to facilitate the examinee to grasp the examination time, the system provides a timer. When the test time is 15 min away, the system will automatically pop up a prompt dialog box. When the test time is over, the system will automatically close the interface of the test, effectively preventing the unfairness brought by the examinee after the test. As shown in Fig. 6 is the flow chart of the examinee's program.

Based on the above steps, we can effectively optimize the online examination system of innovation and entrepreneurship education and training for new engineering talents.

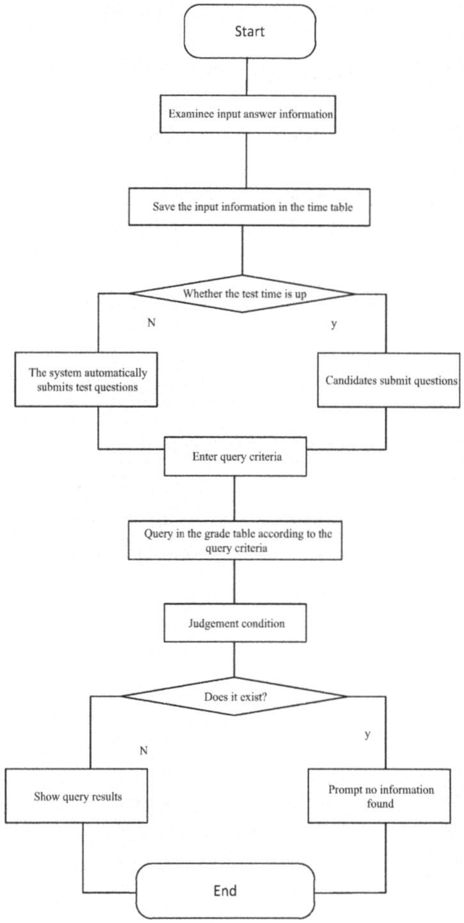

Fig. 6. Optimization of education examination and training process

3 Analysis of Test Results

Further optimize the operation effect of the online examination system for innovation and entrepreneurship education and training of new engineering talents. The test platform of the system mainly tests the business logic and function of the system, which is limited to the complexity of software and performance. Therefore, the paper carries out unconventional simple performance test, and does not elaborate the performance test of the system specifically. The following will discuss the system test from the business logic function test. The system test platform is divided into hardware platform and software platform, specifically as follows:

3.1 Experimental Environment

Hardware platform for system test:

CPU package: dual core Intel Pentium t24102000 MHz (15 × 133)

A main board: ThinkPad R73

System memory: DDR3 SDRAM, 2016 MB

Hard disk: 5400t 320 G

Display card: NVIDIA Quadra NVS 140 M (256 MB)

Display: Samsung b632

Software environment for system testing:

Operating system: Microsoft Windows Vista Ultimate (Table 1).

Table 1. Experimental parameters

Number	Test content	Duration
1	User login test (database connection)	2 h
2	Score information addition test	90 min
3	Score list display and modification test	2 h
4	Test category information initialization test	2 h
5	Test category list display and modification test	90 min
6	Add test questions	90 min
7	Marking test	90 min

3.2 Test Results

Based on the above experimental environment, the actual application effect of the current entrepreneurship education and training examination system is analyzed and tested, and the results are recorded by comparing the fake case side, as follows (Fig. 7):

Based on the analysis of the above test results, it is not difficult to find that the test results show that each functional module of the online examination system of innovation and entrepreneurship education operates normally and achieves the expected design goals.

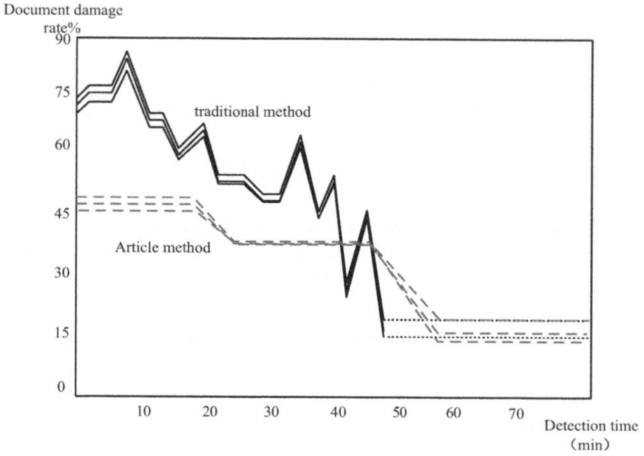

Fig. 7. Comparison test results

4 Concluding Remarks

With the continuous development of computer technology, the integration of computer and other fields is also in-depth. Among them, the computer-aided teaching system produced by the combination of computer and teaching has been continuously concerned and developed. Through comparative research, it is found that in the computer intelligent test paper and online examination system, the more widely used is the random test paper algorithm, which has been used in the test paper generation It has strong randomness, poor control ability to various indexes such as the difficulty and ease of the test paper, low stability of the test paper, and is not suitable for the needs of users. With the deepening of the research on intelligent test paper system, people have initially seen the combination of artificial intelligence algorithm such as genetic algorithm and test paper problem, and applied it to intelligent test paper strategy, and achieved a series of research results. Based on the theory of knowledge base, this paper focuses on improving the test speed and test quality of intelligent test paper generating system. The online examination system of innovation and entrepreneurship education and training for new engineering talents is studied. This study has a wide range of application prospects, but due to the large amount of data, the phenomenon of computer crash will appear, resulting in the system running effect not reaching the expectation, so in the future research, a large capacity CAI system will be designed.

5 Fund Projects

Shenyang Institute Of Technology school level key teaching reform project. Project No.: XJJG2019020, project name: exploration on the cultivation of innovative and entrepreneurial ability of new engineering talents. Project leader Wang Yan.

References

1. Al Amin, Md., Greenwood, J.: The examination system in Bangladesh and its impact: on curriculum, students, teachers and society. Lang. Test. Asia **8**(1), 4 (2018)
2. Kolhar, M., Alameen, A., Gharsseldien, Z.M.: An online lab examination management system (OLEMS) to avoid malpractice. Sci. Eng. Ethics **24**(4), 1367–1369 (2017). https://doi.org/10.1007/s11948-017-9889-z
3. Langton, D., Ahmed, I., Avery, P., et al.: Investigation of taper failure in a contemporary metal-on-metal hip arthroplasty system through examination of unused and explanted prostheses. JBJS **99**(5), 427 (2017)
4. Bagyura, Z., Kolossváry, M., Merkely, B., et al.: Computer tomography examination of the coronary system - National Plaque Registry and Database, Hungary. Orv. Hetil. **158**(3), 106 (2017)
5. Liu, P.-L.: Re-examination of the cable capacitance in the key distribution system using resistors and noise sources. Fluct. Noise Lett. **16**(3), 1750025 (2017)
6. Almaiah, M.A., Alismaiel, O.A.: Examination of factors influencing the use of mobile learning system: an empirical study. Educ. Inf. Technol. **24**(1), 885–909 (2018). https://doi.org/10.1007/s10639-018-9810-7
7. Greenberg, J.R., Sinclair, S., Janssen, C.A., et al.: An electronic screening system for oral health examination and collection of critical data in a nonclinical setting: validation trial. Compend. Contin. Educ. Dent. (Jamesburg, NJ: 1995) **39**(5), 318 (2018)
8. Wei, L.H., Thurusamy, R.: An examination of the effects of task technology fit and hospital information system satisfaction in public hospital Malaysia: a structural model. Adv. Sci. Lett. **24**(2), 1479–1483 (2018)
9. Stewart, S.L., Hamza, C.A.: The Child and Youth Mental Health Assessment (ChYMH): an examination of the psychometric properties of an integrated assessment developed for clinically referred children and youth. BMC Health Serv. Res. **17**(1), 82 (2017). https://doi.org/10.1186/s12913-016-1970-9
10. Harrison, M.E., Clarkin, C., Rohde, K., et al.: Treat me but don't judge me: a qualitative examination of health care experiences of pregnant and parenting youth. J. Pediatr. Adolesc. Gynecol. **30**(2), 209–214 (2017)
11. Schein, M.: The first supper: the role of the digestive system in mental life and the evolution of eating disorders. Br. J. Psychother. **35**(3), 431–447 (2019)
12. Kamel, R., Abbas, H., El-Naa, M.: Composite carbohydrate interpenetrating polyelectrolyte nano-complexes (IPNC) as a controlled oral delivery system of citalopram HCl for pediatric use: in-vitro/in-vivo evaluation and histopathological examination. Drug Deliv. Transl. Res. **8**(3), 657–669 (2018). https://doi.org/10.1007/s13346-018-0506-8
13. Bruno, A., Lapsley, I.: The emergence of an accounting practice: the fabrication of a government accrual accounting system. Account. Audit. Account. J. **31**(4), 1045–1066 (2018)
14. Williams, W.M., Yore, M.M., Whitt-Glover, M.C.: Estimating physical activity trends among blacks in the United States through examination of four national surveys. Aims Public Health **5**(2), 144–157 (2018)

Design of Embedded Course Teaching System Based on Cognitive Computing

Hai-hong Bian[1](✉), Yi-qun Zhong[1], and Yan Wang[2]

[1] Nanjing Institute of Technology, Nanjing 210000, China
xiexung233@163.com
[2] School of Information and Control,
Shenyang Institute of Technology, Shenyang 113122, China

Abstract. The traditional embedded curriculum teaching system is not comprehensive, which leads to poor learning performance of students. Therefore, an embedded curriculum teaching system based on cognitive computing is designed. The design of the system mainly includes two aspects: hardware and system software. The hardware part of the system includes three parts: controller, memory and microprocessor. The software part of the system focuses on the design of database, the detailed division of teaching content, students' situation, curriculum situation, etc., and the setting of evaluation standards, the evaluation of students' learning situation, so as to complete the embedded system based on cognitive computing. The design of course teaching system. Experiments show that the design of the embedded curriculum teaching system based on cognitive computing has higher scores than the traditional system, and has practical significance.

Keywords: Cognitive computing · Embedded · Teaching system · Controller · Evaluation index

1 Introduction

With the rapid development of information technology and the wide application of computers in various fields, all majors in Colleges and universities have established close ties with computers. Cultivating and training students' professional comprehensive ability in computer labs has become an indispensable part of undergraduate teaching in Colleges and universities. Therefore, the construction of computer labs has become an important work in Colleges and universities. But so far, there are still many problems in the construction and management of university computer laboratory. How to make full use of the development results of new technology and build a more efficient use of teaching system is worthy of our deep research.

Cognitive computing represents a new computing paradigm that encompasses a vast array of technological innovations in information analysis, natural language processing, and machine learning that can help policymakers uncover extraordinary insights from vast amounts of unstructured data. Cognitive systems are capable of interacting with

S. Liu et al. (Eds.): eLEOT 2020, LNICST 339, pp. 217–229, 2020.
https://doi.org/10.1007/978-3-030-63952-5_19

humans in a more natural way; they specialize in capturing a vast amount of different types of data and extrapolating from that information; and learning from their own interactions with data and people. One goal of cognitive computing is to enable computer systems to learn, think, and make the right decisions, just like the human brain. Human brain and computer have their own advantages. Cognitive computing system can be a good assistant tool to solve some problems that human brain is not good at solving. Therefore, it is applied to the design of embedded course teaching system to solve the problem of poor school effect after traditional system learning. Experimental results show that the embedded course teaching system based on cognitive computing has higher performance than the traditional system, which proves the effectiveness of the system.

2 Framework of Embedded Course Teaching System Based on Cognitive Computing

The embedded curriculum teaching system based on cognitive computing mainly includes: laboratory management, curriculum management, teaching evaluation and various experimental environments (such as virtual machine, virtual desktop [1], virtual laboratory, Bi set environment, training environment, etc.). The specific embedded curriculum teaching system based on cognitive computing is shown in Fig. 1.

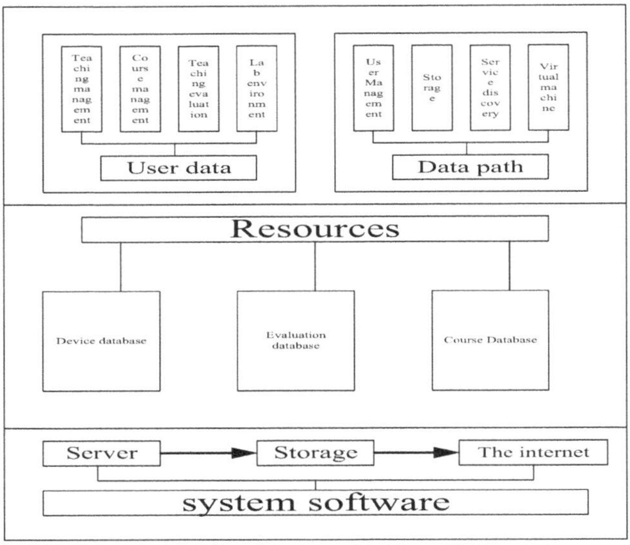

Fig. 1. Framework of embedded course teaching system based on cognitive computing

Laboratory management service mainly completes the unified monitoring and management of experimental equipment (including physical equipment virtual equipment and cloud platform) and laboratory, the arrangement of experimental courses, the generation and management of experimental environment, etc. Curriculum management service is the core service of practical teaching operation [2]. Teachers develop practical courses here, such as experiment content design, experiment environment setting, etc.; curriculum development can be completed by multiple teachers in collaboration. Students choose the practical courses they study here, view the experimental contents, and submit experimental materials (such as experimental reports, procedures, documents, etc.), while teachers review these materials here. For each experiment, students and teachers can also exchange messages. Teaching evaluation service through the analysis and mining of all kinds of data recorded in the process of practical teaching operation, in different levels of teaching classes, teaching courses and even individual students to objectively evaluate the quality of Teaching [3]. All kinds of experimental environments are generated by laboratory management services, where students carry out specific experimental operations. The experimental environment can also be regarded as cloud service, which is generated before class and terminated after class.

3 Hardware Design of Embedded Course Teaching System Based on Cognitive Computing

3.1 Controller Design

The structure of the controller is shown in Fig. 2.

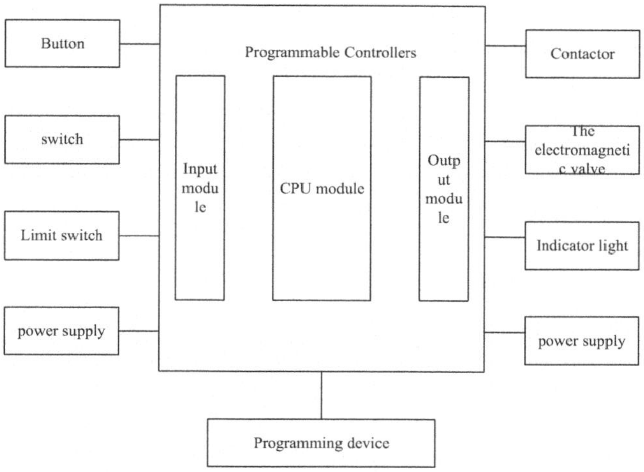

Fig. 2. Controller structure

The controller has a control speed of a high-speed integrated chip and a maximum capacity of 16, which supports the full working mode. The CPU is mainly composed of microprocessor and memory, which is used to run user program, monitor input/output interface status, make logical judgment and data processing, that is, read input variables [4], complete various operations specified by user instructions, send the results to the output end, respond to the requests of external devices (such as programmers, computers, printers, etc.) and carry out various internal operations Judgement and so on. There are two types of internal memory of PLC, one is the system program memory, which mainly stores the system management and monitoring program and the program for compiling and processing the user program. The system program has been fixed by the manufacturer and cannot be changed by the user; the other is the user program and data memory, which mainly stores the application program prepared by the user and various temporary data and intermediate results.

The I/O module is the eye, ear, hand and foot of the system, and is the bridge between the external site and the CPU module. The input module is used to receive and collect input signals. There are two types of input signals: switching input signals from buttons, selector switches, digital dial switches, limit switches, proximity switches, photoelectric switches, pressure relays, etc. And analog input signals of continuous changes provided by potentiometers, thermocouples, tachogenerators, and various transducers. Programmable controllers generally use 220 V AC power. The DC stabilized power supply inside the programmable controller provides DC voltage for the components in each module.

3.2 Memory Design

The memory is 4 KB FLASH memory, programmable and erasable, and fast. It can be programmed using a common programmer, or it can be programmed online. When the 4 KB flash memory in AT89S51 chip is not enough, the user can extend the program memory out of chip, up to 64 KB. The data memory space is divided into two parts: on-chip and off-chip. The AT89S51 microcontroller has 128B of RAM inside it (the enhanced 52 sub-series is 256B), which is used for storing readable/writable data. When the on-chip RAM of AT89S51 is not enough, the system can be extended to 64 KB RAM outside the chip. How much RAM to extend depends on the actual needs of the system. The special function registers are actually the control registers and status registers of each functional unit in the AT89S51 chip.

3.3 Microprocessor Design

Using ARM920T as a bridge between the system and the host computer, ARM920T has the following main features: processor has a high performance RISC architecture; a large number of internal registers make it very efficient, making it an ideal choice for real-time control equipment. On-chip Flash is programmable online. On-chip resources include 2 32-bit timers, 1 A/D input interface, 18 multi-function I/O interfaces, 1 CPLD, 1 64M SDRAM, 1 4M Flash, 1 64M Nand Flash controller; and interrupt controller and system manager.

The processor uses chip S3C2410, S3C2410 with excellent kernel performance, rich external interface and low power. In the system we used two kinds of memory, a SDRAM, a Flash, SDRAM has the advantage of running fast, but can not save data after a power cut. So the system is mainly used to run the operating system, applications and various types of data caching [5]. Flash memory runs slower than SDRAM. But you can save data after a power failure. A general purpose Flash (SST39VF1601) with a capacity of 2 MB is selected in the design of the system, which is mainly used for solidifying the startup code and control application program and saving some system data. A/D conversion, A/D conversion circuit using MAXIM's MAX197, MAX197 using successive approximation technology to achieve fast conversion and low power consumption.

4 Software Implementation of Embedded Course Teaching System Based on Cognitive Computing

4.1 Content Selection of Teaching System Database

Database design is a crucial part of the whole system. The quality of the structure design is directly related to the performance of the whole teaching system. In the database design, the basic idea is to take the three main functional modules of the system as the main line, first design the necessary data tables for each module, then consider the

Table 1. Basic information in the database

Category	Name	Field name
Student	log-in name	Id
	Name	Name
	password	Password
	gender	Sex
	Department	Department
	mailbox	E-mail
Teacher	log-in name	Id
	Name	Name
	password	Password
	mailbox	E-mail
Administrator	log-in name	Id
	Name	Name
	password	Password
Course information	Course number	Id
	Course title	Name
	credit	Mark
	Course type	Dep
Voicemail	Message number	Id
	teacher	Ltea-name
	student	Lstu-name
	content	Lcontent

functional expansion to design the corresponding extended data tables [6], and finally consider the possible links between the tables, set up the corresponding primary keys and indexes. The basic information table in the database is shown in Table 1.

Firstly, the content of the course should be rich, and different levels of students' learning can be taken into consideration; secondly, the content should include some new and cutting-edge knowledge about the computer, so that students can learn more about the new knowledge about the computer, and not be limited to the knowledge in the textbook; thirdly, the network link of relevant knowledge should be provided to guide students to discover and explore knowledge by themselves, and in addition, convenient communication tools should be provided to facilitate the free exchange between students and teachers after class. Hybrid teaching aid system can run through the pre-class [7], online classroom teaching, after-class review, question answering, assignment, homework submission and correction, and other teaching links. On the basis of the previous requirements analysis, design various entities that can meet the needs of users, and their relationships. The external views from different users describing the real world are integrated to form a global conceptual model, which can then be converted into a database mode [8]. The contents of each module in the database are shown in Table 2.

Table 2. Database menu

Administrator module	Teacher module	Student module	Interactive module
User management	Delete job	Course study	Adding classes and teachers
Management teacher	Correcting assignments online	Coursework	Elective
Administrator	Enter discussion forum	Online test	Receiving electives
Add and delete users	Query course	Chatroom	Upload files
Registration application review	Operation	Forum	Download file
Announce	Test	Personal data management	Leave a message
Modify announcement	Grade	Information query	View message
Delete announcement	Chatroom	Question bank management	

According to the above process, complete the database content settings.

4.2 Establishment of Teaching Quality Evaluation Methods

After students log in the system and enter the student information feedback module [9], fill in the corresponding teaching content to be fed back according to the learning situation, which can be directly filled in the corresponding teaching chapter of the teacher. In the system login, the user needs to enter the user name and password, and must provide the correct login information to enter the system. The user login process is as follows (Fig. 3).

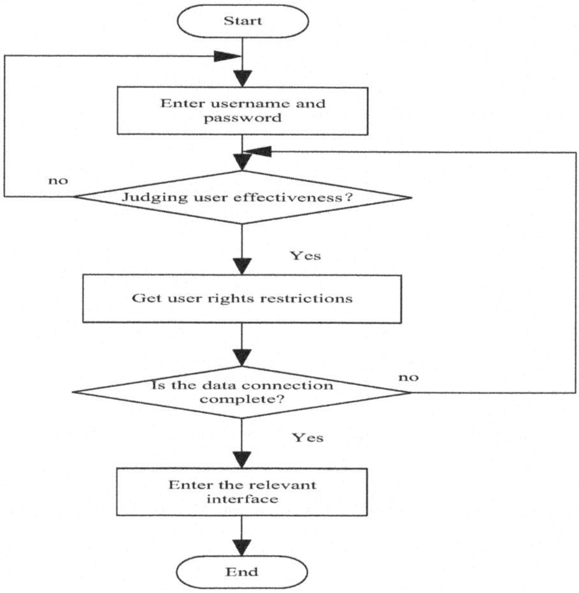

Fig. 3. User login process

Fill in the content including the understanding of the contents of the study, the content has been mastered and can not understand the content, teachers need to provide help such as the answer to the question, the teaching content of some auxiliary learning materials. At the same time, students can grade teachers' classroom instruction or online learning systems, such as teaching methods, content, language organization, etc., usually in the form of feedback sheets. For students to the teacher's score, is the administrator and the school to the teacher's teaching situation, only the system administrator can see. The module of information feedback after class is set as follows: basic information display page, feedback information form filling page, information confirmation upload page [10], etc. The module contains the following messages: system entry message, basic information display, feedback information table fill page, information upload confirmation information page. The sequence diagram of information feedback module after class is shown in Fig. 4.

In order to make the courses interoperable between different platforms, the shared components of different courses can be reused, and the materials for courses can be quickly searched, the construction of the materials for learning resources shall be in line with the norms, and most of the materials for learning resources shall be provided by the content service providers. Schools, teachers and learners may also develop their own. When designing the teaching system for mobile learning, they may provide materials for the design of the experience stage, creation of subject situations, learning process and

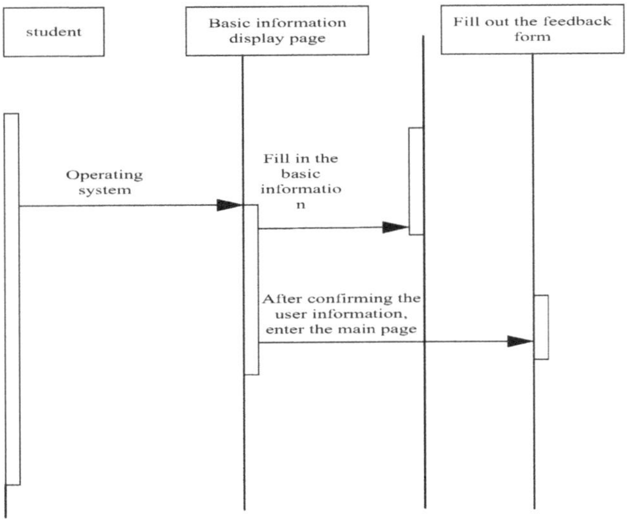

Fig. 4. Information feedback process after class

collaborative creation stage. At the same time, they shall absorb the excellent resources newly generated in these stages into the materials for learning resources, and the supplementary assistance system is divided into the automatic answering system and the manual answering system. When a learner encounters any problem in the process of learning, they may first consider searching for answers in the automatic answering system, and meanwhile may supplement them, or directly transfer them to the manual answering system, and conduct real-time exchanges with the moderator on duty or social experts. When a learner signs a learning contract with a teacher or chooses a learning strategy, they will need the personalized guidance and assistance of the manual answering system. Finally, learners, teachers and social experts will update the design of the whole teaching system at any time by using the convenience of mobile communication terminals to keep close contact with the society.

The purpose of this design system is to improve students' academic performance. Therefore, the teaching quality evaluation method is set. In the evaluation process, the corresponding functional modules need to be found. The functional diagram of this design system is shown in Table 3.

In the evaluation of mobile learning effect, encourage learners to evaluate themselves. Learners can take test questions and submit them to the server for evaluation and feedback, or operate and play in some virtual experimental environment, and the system will automatically analyze the learning effect. At the same time, teachers, social experts and learning partners can be invited to evaluate their performance in group cooperative learning and creation, and ask for their opinions to improve their own learning. Learners can also make self-summary and evaluation according to their own learning situation. Finally, learners can freely choose whether to carry out authoritative certification, which can be graded, and after passing the system, they will get corresponding certificates, and give suggestions on the content of continuing learning. At this time, teachers and social

Table 3. Function diagram of teaching system

Serial number	Classification	Details
1	Course management module	Flexible configuration of course activities
2	Resource module	Electronic documents, sound and video
3	Discussion module	Breaking the control of time and space
4	Chat module	Synchronous communication function
5	Operation module	Layout work
6	Quiz module	Provide online exams and computer auto-grading
7	Voting module	View voting results and everyone's voting situation
8	Questionnaire module	Learning and Thinking Attitude Questionnaire
9	Expansion module	Download the rest of the features

experts play the role of consultants in the evaluation of learning effect. If learners want to pass the authority certification, they will actively strive for others' evaluation of their own learning, if only for learning knowledge, they will also want teachers and experts to give evaluation suggestions. Therefore, in the evaluation of the effect of mobile learning centered on learning, learners should be more free and actively organize their own "evaluation", and teachers, social experts and other evaluators need to think more agile and active.

The grade may be the final test score of the previous semester, or it may be a test score given to the students at the beginning of the semester to set the original level and provide the basic basis for the teachers to give the students homework.

Prior to student learning, learning needs analysis refers to the gap between the present state of the learner's learning and the desired state, that is, the gap between the present state of the learner and the desired state of the learner. Therefore, learning needs analysis is influenced by two factors, namely, the desired state of the learner and the current state of the learner. The latter can be further refined by the analysis of the characteristics of the learner, while the former needs to produce the analysis results in this stage. Therefore, the analysis of the characteristics of learners is shown in Fig. 5.

To evaluate the students' achievements, the first step is to obtain the students' historical achievements. The calculation formula is as follows:

$$H = \int_{i=1}^{w} r * \frac{f}{d \times k} \tag{1}$$

In the formula, H represents the final test result of the previous semester, $\int_{i=1}^{w} r$ represents the student information, d represents the student's current score, k represents the student's learning progress, k represents the difficulty of the test content.

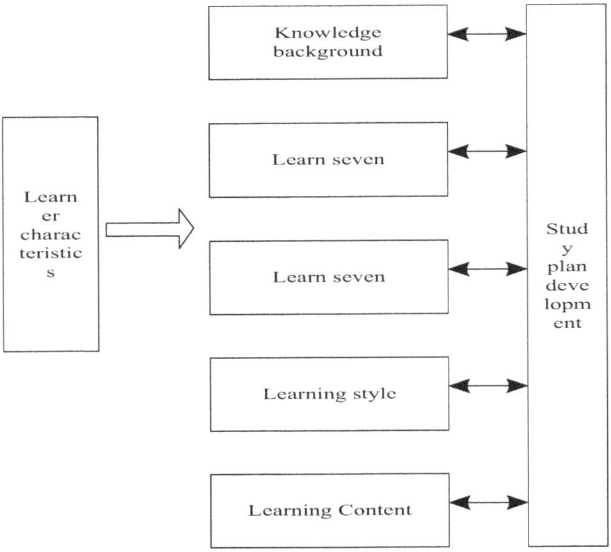

Fig. 5. Contents of learner characteristic analysis

On this basis, the evaluation criteria are set, and the calculation formula is as follows:

$$G = \sum_{I=1} f / \frac{r}{h} \tag{2}$$

In the formula, $\sum_{I=1} f$ represents the evaluation parameters of students' grades, $\frac{r}{h}$ represents the examination information of students, G represents the evaluation parameters of learning situation.

At the same time, the members of the team shall, through the exchange platform, including the exchange with teachers, social experts and peers, abstract and summarize the knowledge learned, carry out collaborative creation by taking the project as a unit, and the team shall prepare the project title, submit the demand analysis and feasibility analysis of the project, outline design, detailed design, organization and division of labor, concrete implementation of works, etc., and may consult teachers or social experts at any time if any problem is encountered in the exploratory creation process, so as to enhance the enthusiasm of the group creation.

According to the evaluation of students' learning ability based on the above calculation, in the process of learning, students give feedback to the teacher-assisted teaching system, classroom teaching, after-class tasks and other contents, and give corresponding evaluation to the teachers' teaching situation, so as to help teachers improve the teaching system or classroom teaching content, teaching methods, thereby improving students' learning performance, and thus complete the design of teaching system.

5 Experimental Demonstration

5.1 Experiment Preparation

In order to further ensure its practical application effect, the simulation experiment is carried out, and the traditional algorithm is used to compare the experimental results in order to enhance the illustration.

In the experiment, 100 students were selected as the subjects, 50 of them applied the designed system, and the other 50 students applied the traditional system. Compared with the two groups, the higher the score was, the more effective the system was.

5.2 Test Environment

The Visual DSP++4.5 integrated development platform is established in the cloud computing environment. The experimental parameters used in the experiment are shown in Table 4.

Table 4. Experimental parameters

Device	Environmental parameters	Description
Processor	Intel (R) Core (TM) 2 Duo	
CPU	2.94 GHz	Maximum running speed
Effective memory	8 GB	
Initial sampling Frequency	0.8 Hz	Maintained during commissioning
Termination frequency	0.15 Hz	$f_1 \leq f_2$
Bit rate	0.59 Bps/s	
Client computer	80 GB	
Operating system	Windows XP	

In order to prevent the phenomenon of illegal copying in the process of experiment, and then search for the answers from the Internet or the question bank and prevent the leakage of examination questions, the function of anti-copying is added to the webpage code; in addition, a score table containing examination information is established, the relevant information is saved in the table at the beginning of the examination, and the examination status of the examinee is marked. The examinee's examination status will be changed when the examination paper is submitted or the examination time is reached the end of the examination automatically, so that the examinee cannot modify the examination result and cannot continue the examination even if he has not submitted the examination paper for any reason. At the same time, obtain the course name, test paper code and other information of the examination, and then save these information and student number, class, exam certificate number, exam course and the score of the examination to the examinee score table. The specific experimental test content is shown in Fig. 6.

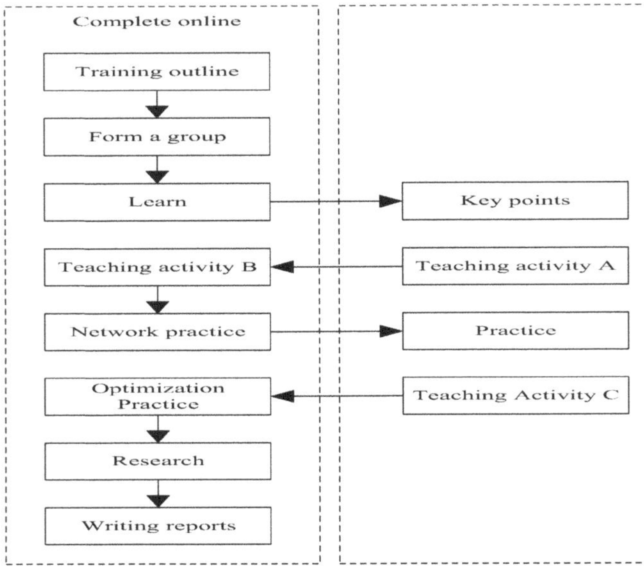

Fig. 6. Experimental test content

The comparison results between the traditional system and this design system are shown in Fig. 7.

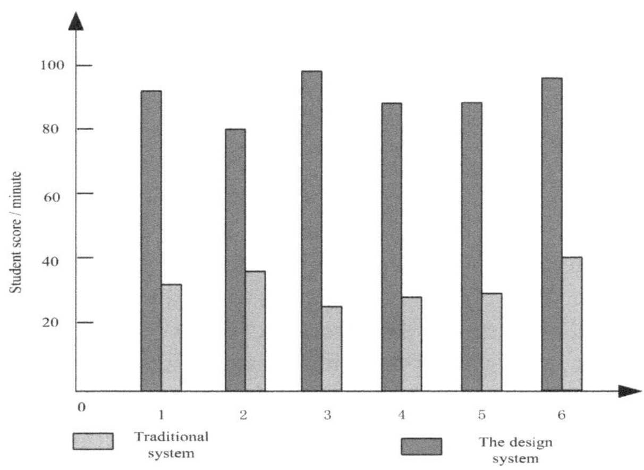

Fig. 7. Experimental comparison

Analysis of the above experimental results shows that the application of the system has a significant improvement in academic performance, and higher academic performance. However, the students' performance after the application of the traditional system is lower than that of the designed system. Therefore, the above experiments can prove the effectiveness of the system, which shows that the system has good application effect and strong practical application significance.

6 Conclusion

CAI system has a wide range of users. It can be researched, developed and applied in various fields. This is of great help to lifelong education and capacity building. Therefore, the system has a broad application prospect. Although some achievements have been made in basic teaching, there is still a long way to go from advanced technology. Therefore, in the next step of learning work, this topic will continue to study, and the computer aided teaching system to modify and improve. From the following several aspects: teaching practice in the future, will be closely integrated information-based classroom teaching and computer assisted teaching online, gradually get rid of the traditional "examination-oriented education" and "cramming" teaching, improve the level of information technology network teaching, improve the network auxiliary teaching system, make the quota restrictions is no longer a bottleneck restricting the development of education, better service for teachers and students. It can be predicted that the application of CAI system will be more extensive.

7 Fund Projects

School-level teaching reform and construction project of Nanjing Institute of Technology in 2019 (NO: JG2019019).

References

1. Dai, X., Wang, T.: RapidIO based communication design and implementation for airborne embedded system. Electron. Opt. Control **24**(12), 95–99 (2017)
2. Gu, X., Zhang, K., Guo, Y., et al.: Design and implementation of ASD children's cognitive education system based on Unity3D. J. Syst. Simul. **31**(5), 893–900 (2019)
3. Chen, J., Wang, Y., Chen, J., et al.: Design and research on intelligent teaching system based on deep learning. Comput. Sci. **46**(06), 550–554 (2019)
4. Pei, S., Cui, F., Xie, X.: Design and implementation of temperature and pressure sensing experiment system based on optical fiber interference. Coll. Phys. **37**(5), 52–56 (2018)
5. Wang, Z., Jiang, Z.: Exploration and practice of research-oriented teaching in the course of solid state physics. Coll. Phys. **36**(10), 57–60 (2017)
6. Wang, Q., Lu, H., Yu, Z., et al.: Cultivation of research consciousness in fine chemicals chemistry teaching. Chin. J. Chem. Educ. **39**(2), 9–12 (2018)
7. Yu, Y., Liu, J., Zhao, Y.: On engineering graphics course teaching integration with model-based definition technology. J. Graph. **40**(4), 816–821 (2019)
8. Pan, X., Jiang, J., Moran, et al.: A comparative study on the "quality matters rubric standards" in the U.S. and the evaluation index system of excellent online open course in China. J. Educ. Sci. Hunan Normal Univ. **18**(3), 105–110 (2019)
9. Zhang, X., Wang, W., Lu, R., et al.: Construction and application of excel-based grade evaluation system for analytical chemistry experiment course. Chin. J. Chem. Educ. **39**(12), 14–18 (2018)
10. Zhang, Z., He, A., Wang, J., et al.: The characteristics of the curriculum system of MOOC in the University of Melbourne and its enlightenment to education in China. Adult Educ. **38**(1), 78–81 (2018)

Research on Online Physical Education Micro Course System Based on Improved Machine Learning

Chang-min Lv[1](✉), Xue-ping Zhang[1], and Jun-peng Ji[2]

[1] Zibo Normal College, Zibo 255100, China
llmn0002@sina.com

[2] The Middle School Affiliated to Zibo Normal College, Zibo 255100, China

Abstract. At present, there are some problems in online physical education micro course system, such as the teaching effect is not ideal and students' performance is low, so it is necessary to design a new online physical education micro course system based on improved machine learning. The hardware of the system consists of three interactive modules: information display unit, information processing unit and terminal interactive unit. The system software is composed of system user module, course management module, independent learning module, database module and online examination module. In the database module, six groups of information parameters, such as administrator information, course information and announcement information, are set. Using the improved machine learning method to design the online examination module. Through the combination of hardware and software, the online physical education micro course system is designed. The comparative experiment shows that the teaching effect of the system is better than that of the traditional system, and the sports performance is improved significantly.

Keywords: Improved machine learning · Online physical education · Teaching micro course system

1 Introduction

Information technology has constantly infiltrated into the field of education. Many educational researches begin to think that in the process of education and teaching, modern information technology based on computer and multimedia and information technology based on network communication need to be applied more comprehensively. The phenomenon of promoting education reform is "education informatization" [1]. Under the condition of educational informationization, the focus of educational field is no longer the only knowledge that is taught to students in books, but also the opportunity to create comprehensive learning for students. Under the guidance of the idea of "health first, people-oriented", physical education in Colleges and universities plays an important role. However, the traditional classroom physical education teaching mode has some

S. Liu et al. (Eds.): eLEOT 2020, LNICST 339, pp. 230–241, 2020.
https://doi.org/10.1007/978-3-030-63952-5_20

limitations, which hinders the all-round development of students' individual personality. With the emergence of network courses, more and more learners can choose their favorite courses to study without going out of their homes. However, there are many existing network courses with various contents and less emphasis [2].

How to make learners quickly position themselves on the Internet according to the content they want to learn, or learn short and concise teaching films and classroom teaching with outstanding emphasis in the classroom is a new development trend. In this case, micro courses should also be applied [3]. However, due to the current online sports teaching micro course system teaching effect is not ideal, resulting in low physical performance of students. Therefore, an online physical education micro course system based on improved machine learning is designed.

2 Design of Online Physical Education Micro Course System Based on Improved Machine Learning

2.1 Design of System Hardware Interaction Module

Because online physical education teachers and students communicate with each other in an all-round way through the network, the design of interaction module is particularly important. The interaction module consists of three parts: information display unit (two interactive electronic whiteboards and two short focus projectors), information processing unit (computer), terminal interaction unit (electronic induction pen and electronic voter) [4]. In this module, the electronic induction pen operates on a double electronic white board. The electronic whiteboard collects the position and movement track information of the electronic induction pen, and transmits the information to the information processing unit (computer) through the data line. At the same time, the electronic voter can also transmit the operation information to the wireless signal receiving device, which then transfers the information to the information processing unit. When the information processing unit receives the information, it will process the information and convert it into the operation of computer programs and internal objects. The calculation results are transmitted to the display interface and the video signal is transmitted to the projector through the line [5]. Finally, the projector transforms the video signal and projects it to the electronic whiteboard for information sharing. The interaction flow of the interaction module is shown in Fig. 1.

The information display unit mainly includes two interactive electronic white boards and two short focus projectors, which is the main part of the whole hardware. The double electronic whiteboard is an electromagnetic induction type whiteboard. The electromagnetic induction coil is embedded in the whiteboard as a stroke sensor to form a stroke receiving device for writing whiteboard. By pressing the tip of the electronic induction pen to contact the surface of the whiteboard, the stroke is captured in the induction area [6]. Short focus projector is a kind of projector that can project about - inch picture in a short distance (generally about one meter). Due to the short projection distance, the projector is installed directly above the interactive electronic whiteboard, which can not only avoid the direct projection of the projector light to the eyes of the speaker, but also

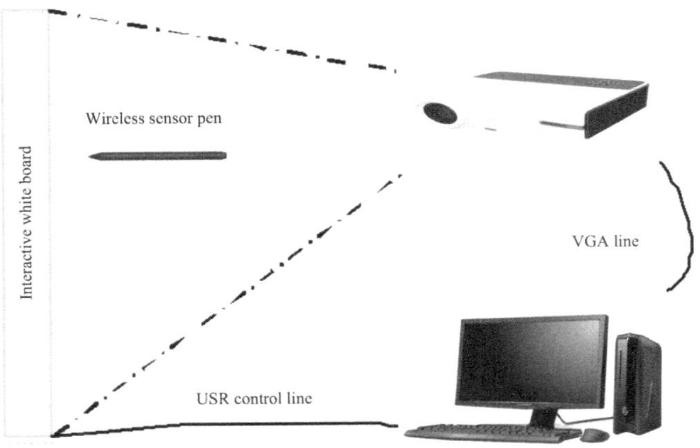

Fig. 1. Interaction flow of interaction module

avoid the shadow of the speaker being transmitted on the screen to block the screen. The combination of double interactive whiteboard and double short focus projector forms a set of interactive system with super information receiving ability and display ability. It can realize double track display, that is, when the left board presents text materials, the right board synchronously displays relevant pictures, animation and video materials. At the same time, it presents a variety of learning resources to provide basic guarantee for the continuity of students' learning process and the efficiency of knowledge coding.

Information processing unit is a computer with interactive "double board" teaching system software, which is an important part of the whole hardware.

Terminal interaction unit refers to electronic sensor and electronic voter. The electronic induction pen is mainly used to operate, write, annotate and draw on the interactive whiteboard interface, so as to indirectly operate the computer (the pen tip is equivalent to the left mouse button, and pressing and holding the red button is equivalent to the right mouse button) And to transfer, modify and adjust learning resources so as to "write everywhere, write at any time", so as to promote the deep interaction between teachers and students and the interactive "double board". The electronic voter is a real-time feedback tool for students to respond to teachers' questions and classroom tests, which is mainly aimed at the problems with options. Through the above two functions, students can immediately convey their own independent thinking or discussion conclusions with other students to teachers. On this basis, teachers summarize and comment on students' views and share them with students, so as to promote the interaction between new and old ideas of students.

3 System Software Design

3.1 Design of System User Module

There are three kinds of users: students, teachers and administrators. Its structure is shown in Fig. 2.

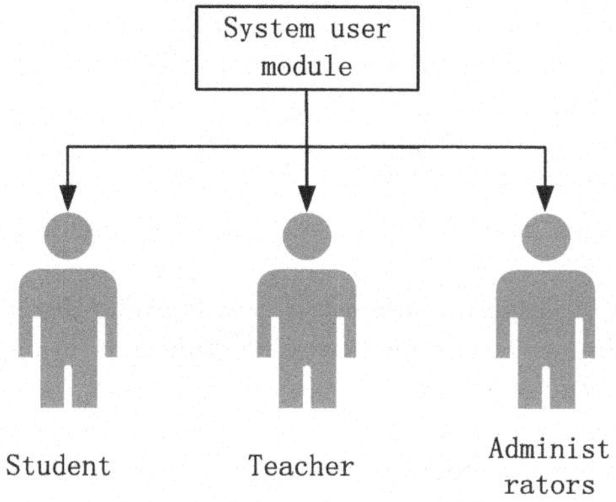

Fig. 2. Composition of user module

Students are the main users of the system, through the system to complete sports knowledge learning [7], after logging in the system, you can view and modify personal data, change password, view course video. You can practice, test, ask questions online and interact with other users. After logging into the system, teachers can view personal data, change password, release learning tasks, upload teaching videos and exercises, manage test questions, answer questions online, evaluate student reports, etc. The administrator is responsible for user information maintenance, class creation, etc.

User login of the system user module: when a user accesses the system through a network address, he/she needs to authenticate, and only legal users can use the system. When logging in, students, teachers and administrators enter user names and passwords, and the system will judge user categories based on user names, passwords and user types. If the matching with the database data is successful, the login is successful; otherwise, the login error will be prompted. After the user logs in to the system, the corresponding function modules are displayed.

User management of system user module: the administrator manages the class, teacher and student users. You can add, modify, and delete students.

3.2 Design of Course Management Module

The curriculum management module is designed and developed for teachers. In this module, teachers manage the PE micro curriculum. The creation of sports micro course is completed by teachers. After the course is created, teachers can view the course information, add chapters for sports micro course, or modify or delete chapters. The teacher is responsible for uploading the video for the corresponding chapters of the sports micro course. The first mock exam is designed for each session, and uploaded to the server in this module for learning and practicing.

3.3 Design of Autonomous Learning Module

Autonomous learning module is designed for students to learn the content and practice of physical micro course online. According to their own needs, students choose PE courses and enter corresponding PE micro courses. The corresponding sports course name, introduction and chapter link will appear in the sports micro course learning interface [8]. Students choose the section they want to study. The videos watched by the students are generally short, with pause and playback functions. After watching the video of each section, students will do the exercises corresponding to the current section on the same page.

In the autonomous learning module, the online learning discussion function can be realized. Online learning discussion is a way of multi-person communication. Teachers and students can participate in the discussion, similar to the public forum. Online discussion can be carried out on a certain topic. You can freely express your opinions and collide with each other's thoughts, which is conducive to in-depth learning and exchange [9]. When students watch the video of each section and do the corresponding exercises, they can discuss the content of this section, and other students and teachers can participate in the reply. Teachers can manage all discussion topics and delete some inappropriate topics or replies. Under the video page, there is a window for learning and discussion. Students can express their opinions by inputting the specific content of the comments. Show the content, author, and time of the discussion in the discussion list.

3.4 Design of Database Module

The database module has created 6 tables, including 'Admin', administrator information table; 'Course', the course information table; 'news', the announcement information table; 'Student', the student information table; 'Teacher', the teacher information table and data information table. The design results of each table are as follows (Tables 1, 2, 3, 4, 5 and 6):

Table 1. Administrator information table

Serial number	Name	Type	Length (character)
1	id	int	4
2	name	nvarchar	50
3	Password	nvarchar	50

Table 2. Course information table

Serial number	Name	Type	Length (character)
1	id	int	4
2	courseID	nvarchar	50
3	courseName	nvarchar	50
4	TeacherId	nvarchar	50
5	teacher	nvarchar	50
6	credithour	nvarchar	50
7	term	nvarchar	50
8	classname	nvarchar	50
9	Address	nvarchar	50
10	BeginTime	nvarchar	50
11	xueyuan	nvarchar	50
12	zhuanye	nvarchar	50
13	zhuanyeid	int	4
14	xueyuanid	int	4

Table 3. Announcement information table

Serial number	Name	Type	Length (character)
1	id	int	4
2	title	nvarchar	50
3	contents	Text	–
4	addtime	nvarchar	8

3.5 Design of Online Examination Module

Design online examination module based on improved machine learning [10]. Using Moodle quiz plug-in, teachers can easily make use of Word template to make Moodle XML test questions in the process of writing test questions library. And set some simple technical parameters for each link of the test. After the examination, the students submit the examination papers and use the improved machine learning to grade the examination questions. The structure of online test module is shown in Fig. 3.

Table 4. Student information table

Serial number	Name	Type	Length (character)
1	id	int	4
2	UserName	nvarchar	50
3	xuehao	nvarchar	50
4	Sex	nvarchar	50
5	chushengriqi	datetime	8
6	Ds	nvarchar	50
7	emal	nvarchar	50
8	pwd	nvarchar	50
9	xueyuanId	Int	4
10	XueyuanName	nvarchar	50
11	zhuanyeId	Int	4
12	ZhuanyeName	nvarchar	50

Table 5. Teacher information table

Serial number	Name	Type	Length (character)
1	id	int	4
2	UserName	nvarchar	50
3	xuehao	nvarchar	50
4	Sex	nvarchar	50
5	chushengriqi	datetime	8
6	Ds	nvarchar	50
7	emal	nvarchar	50
8	pwd	nvarchar	50
9	xueyuanId	Int	4
10	XueyuanName	nvarchar	50
11	zhuanyeId	Int	4
12	ZhuanyeName	nvarchar	50

Table 6. Data information table

Column names	Explain	Type (Length)	Remarks
Id	number	Int (4)	Cannot be empty, primary key
TitleName	Name of data	Varchar (50)	No space allowed
FileDs	Data description	text	No space allowed
FilePath	File address	Varchar (20)	No space allowed
Addtime	Adding time	datetime	No space allowed
FileName	File name	Varchar (50)	No space allowed

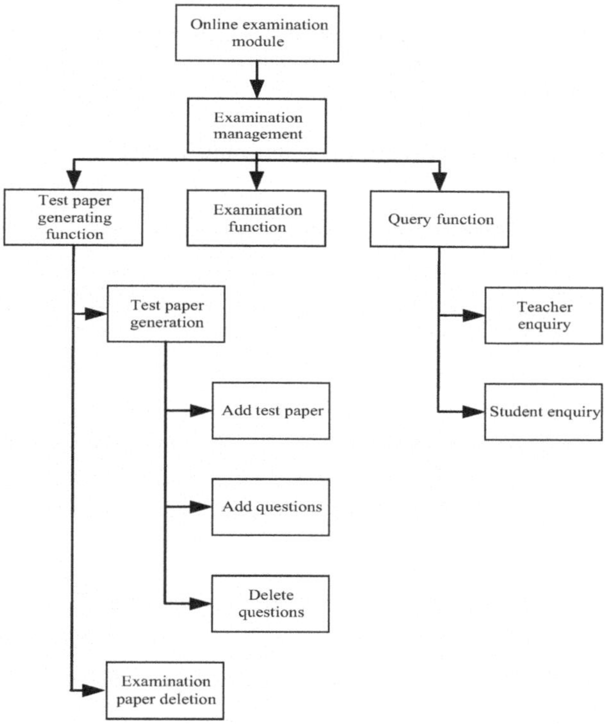

Fig. 3. Construction of online examination module

4 Experimental Results and Analysis

4.1 Experimental Environment

Using the designed online physical education micro course system based on improved machine learning to carry out the experiment. First, the simulation experiment platform of online physical education micro course system is designed, and the hardware structure of the platform is shown in Table 7.

Table 7. Hardware structure of the platform

Serial number	Name	Configuration
1	CPU	Intel Core I3 CPU m 390 @ 2.67 GHz (dual core 4-thread)
2	A main board	HP 1667 (Intel HM55 (ibexpeak-m DH))
3	Memory	2 GB, DDR3
4	Graphics card	Intel HD graphics (ironlake), 256 MB
5	Hard disk	WDC wd5000bevt-60a0rt05400 rpm, 500 GB
6	Monitor	LG Philips LP140WH1-TLC6
7	Network card	Ruiyu semiconductor RTL8101/2/3 family fast Ethernet NIC
8	sound card	Intel 5 Series/34 × 0 chipset PCH - high definition audio device controller

The software structure of the platform is shown in Table 8.

Table 8. Software structure of the platform

Serial number	Name	To configure
1	system platform	WindowsXP
2	Web server	Apache
3	database server	MySQL
4	Database management tools	SQL Manager for MySQL and phpMyAdmin
5	Development tools of web application	Dreamweaver

Other tool software configured for the platform is shown in Table 9.

Table 9. Other tool software configured by the platform

Serial number	Name	To configure
1	Web art and image processing	Adobe Photoshop
2	System diagram drawing tool	Microsoft Office Visio

Based on the simulation platform, an online physical education micro course system based on improved machine learning is deployed for Windows server. Through the installation of IIS components to configure the system server parameters, the core database of the system is built with Windows SQL Server 2008 software to use the system for online physical education.

In order to ensure the contrast of the experimental results, the traditional online physical education micro class system includes the online physical education micro class system based on Web, configuration software and human-computer interaction, and the online physical education micro class system designed in this paper is compared with the online physical education micro class system based on improved machine learning. Compare the teaching effect of each online physical education micro course system. The basis of judging the teaching effect is to use different systems to improve the students' physical performance after online physical education. The higher the promotion rate is, the better the teaching effect is.

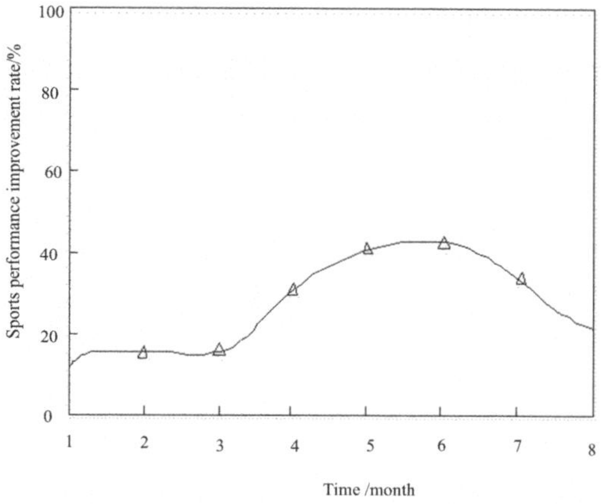

(a) The promotion rate of sports achievement in Web System

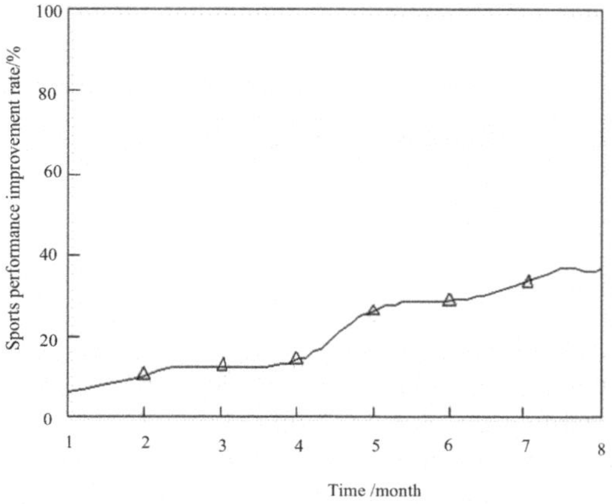

(b) Sports achievement promotion rate of configuration software system

Fig. 4. Experimental results of teaching effect comparison

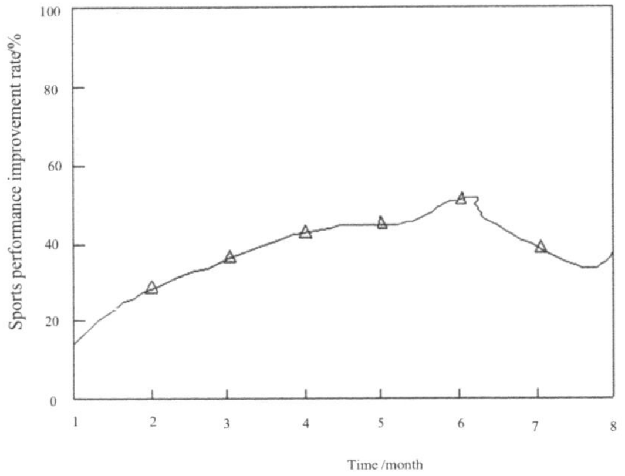

(c) The promotion rate of sports performance in human computer interaction system

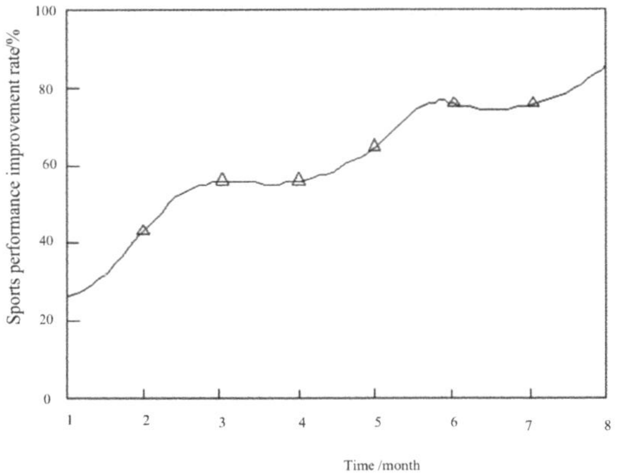

(d) Improving the rate of improvement of physical education achievement of machine learning system

Fig. 4. *(continued)*

4.2 Experimental Analysis

The experimental results of the comparison between the traditional online physical education micro class system and the online physical education micro class system based on improved machine learning are shown in Fig. 4.

According to the experimental results of teaching effect comparison in Fig. 4, the performance improvement rate of web-based teaching system is not higher than 50%. The improvement rate of teaching system based on configuration software is less than 40%. Based on the human-computer interaction teaching system, the improvement rate is less than 58%. Based on the improvement of machine learning, the highest improvement rate of online physical education micro class system is 83%. Its teaching effect is better than the traditional online physical education micro class system, and the improvement of learning performance is obvious.

5 Conclusion

In view of the problem that the teaching effect of online physical education micro course system is not ideal, this paper proposes an online physical education micro course system based on improving machine learning. By improving the system of machine learning design, the online interaction between teachers and students can be realized effectively, the learning effect of students can be detected in time, and the teaching effect can be improved. After verification, the teaching effect of the system is better than the traditional system, which is conducive to the improvement of the online teaching system of micro courses.

References

1. Demir, M.: Using online peer assessment in an Instructional Technology and Material Design course through social media. High. Educ. **75**(3), 399–414 (2018). https://doi.org/10.1007/s10734-017-0146-9
2. Veiga, N., Luzardo, F., Irving, K., et al.: Online pre-laboratory tools for first-year undergraduate chemistry course in Uruguay: student preferences and implications on student performance. Chem. Educ. Res. Pract. **20**(1), 229–245 (2019)
3. Park, H.S., Cheong, Y.F.: Correlates of monotonic response patterns in online ratings of a university course. High. Educ. **76**(1), 101–113 (2018). https://doi.org/10.1007/s10734-017-0199-9
4. Goodfellow, I., McDaniel, P., Papernot, N.: Making machine learning robust against adversarial inputs. Commun. ACM **61**(7), 56–66 (2018)
5. Muggleton, S.H., Schmid, U., Zeller, C., et al.: Ultra-Strong Machine Learning: comprehensibility of programs learned with ILP. Mach. Learn. **107**(7), 1119–1140 (2018). https://doi.org/10.1007/s10994-018-5707-3
6. Nalmpantis, C., Vrakas, D.: Machine learning approaches for non-intrusive load monitoring: from qualitative to quantitative comparation. Artif. Intell. Rev. **52**(1), 217–243 (2019). https://doi.org/10.1007/s10462-018-9613-7
7. Lei, Z., Zhou, H., Hu, W., et al.: Modular web-based interactive hybrid laboratory framework for research and education. IEEE Access **20**(6), 152–163 (2018)
8. Jin, D., Shi, S., Zhang, Y., et al.: A complex event processing framework for an adaptive language learning system. Future Gener. Comput. Syst. **92**(10), 857–867 (2019)
9. Merayo, N., Ruíz, I., Debrán, J., et al.: AIM-Mobile Learning Platform to enhance the teaching-learning process using smartphones. Comput. Appl. Eng. Educ. **26**(5), 1753–1768 (2018)
10. Wei, X., Gu, Q., Luo, Y., et al.: The reform of computer experiment teaching based on O2O model. Comput. Appl. Eng. Educ. **27**(1), 102–111 (2019)

Design of Collaborative Teaching Mode of Online and Offline Based on Supervised Learning Algorithm

Xue-ping Zhang[1(✉)], Fei-fei Qin[2], Ting Zhang[3], and Chang-min Lv[1]

[1] Zibo Normal College, Zibo 255100, China
lknj001500@sina.com
[2] Liangshan Special Education School, Liangshan 272600, China
[3] Liangshan Experimental School, Liangshan 272600, China

Abstract. With the wide application of the Internet plus in the teaching field, the traditional classroom teaching mode is facing severe challenges. The traditional mode restrains students' interest in learning, limits the development of their ability of exploration and innovation, and the MOOC teaching mode with online learning as the core has its inherent defects in the process of teaching implementation, which can not completely replace classroom teaching. Therefore, based on the advantages of traditional classroom teaching and MOOC teaching, combined with a supervised learning algorithm, an online and offline collaborative teaching mode based on supervised learning algorithm is designed. The mode design is divided into four steps: MOOC platform analysis, supervised learning algorithm selection, online and offline collaborative teaching mode design, online and offline collaborative teaching mode implementation. The results show that after the implementation of the online and offline collaborative teaching scheme based on the supervised learning algorithm, the effect is better than before, which proves that the collaborative teaching mode is effective.

Keywords: Supervised learning algorithm · Online and offline · Collaborative teaching model

1 Introduction

The classroom learning community is a kind of teaching mode based on constructivism. Along with our country education reform's advancement, this teaching pattern has carried on the massive practice in the elementary education, and has obtained certain effect. Through investigation, we find that with the deepening of teaching reform in colleges and universities, many teachers are also carrying out the practice of teaching method reform by forming learning communities. At the same time, we also found that there are many problems in the process of implementing the learning community in professional courses, which makes the learning community form without substance [1]. For example, the learning community has been formed, there is a division of labor among the members, but

S. Liu et al. (Eds.): eLEOT 2020, LNICST 339, pp. 242–253, 2020.
https://doi.org/10.1007/978-3-030-63952-5_21

the quality of internal interaction is not high, the enthusiasm of the members is not high, the learning tasks are mainly completed by a small number of members, other members drift away from the team. In the task design, learning task is more about the memory and verification of knowledge, less knowledge construction and innovation. In the situation design lacks the new idea, the member's feeling is only completes the assignment which the teacher assigns, the attraction is insufficient. The lack of information communication between learners and teachers and the lack of guidance leads to the poor quality of task completion. Many learning tasks require members to perform during extra-curricular hours, with the final results reported or reported on, lack of joint interaction with other communities, lack of peer interaction, space-time constraints in which teachers only comment on the final presentation or report on an achievement, and lack of process guidance, leading to diminished significance for improving students' abilities [2]. The evaluation of learning has become a mere formality, focusing on the external forms of evaluation, such as the diversity of evaluation subjects, the process of evaluation and the diversity of evaluation methods. Because of the relative independence of college courses, teachers regard learning community as a means of teaching organization in one course for one semester, but lack continuity in subsequent courses.

In recent years, with the emergence of a large number of "intelligent mobile terminals", "mobile learning" has become a new learning mode, and then "collaborative" teaching mode has become the focus of teaching reform. Therefore, on the basis of discarding the traditional classroom teaching mode and the "Mu-class" teaching mode, this paper proposes an integrated supervised learning algorithm and an online and offline collaborative teaching mode. The model is student-centered, teacher-led, focused on cultivating students' independent learning, aimed at meeting students' individual needs, and centered on strengthening students' theoretical and practical skills in analyzing and solving problems. The contents of teacher-taught courses are divided into three stages, namely, independent learning in front of class, face-to-face teaching in middle class and offline class, and online extended training after class, so as to cultivate students' independent learning ability and inquiry and innovation skills, improve the teaching quality of colleges and universities and realize the co-construction and sharing of excellent teaching resources. [3].

2 Design of Online and Offline Collaborative Teaching Mode

The traditional classroom mainly uses "the teacher classroom instruction" pattern which the subject object opposes carries on the teaching. In teaching activities, teachers play a leading and dominant role and are in a dominant position, while students participate passively in teaching activities and are in an object position. Obviously, the teaching model in the teaching process there are the following 4 drawbacks, as shown in Table 1 below.

In view of the shortcomings of traditional classroom teaching mode, MOOC online learning, a new learning mode of network environment, has been paid close attention to at home and abroad. Especially in 2013, universities have issued MOOC, MOOC learning reports to encourage students to participate in a variety of MOOC platform online learning. But this kind of teaching pattern also has the imperfect place, for example:

Table 1. Four disadvantages of traditional teaching mode

Serial number	Malpractice
1	Students' differences and individual needs are ignored
2	The development of students' exploration and innovation ability is limited
3	The classroom teaching mode is limited by time and place
4	One sided application of information teaching means

The on-line population is huge, the teacher is very difficult to launch the effective interaction, the teacher is unable to take into account each student, the outstanding student is neglected. The traditional classroom teaching mode shortens the distance between teachers and students. Teachers can timely grasp the students' learning dynamics in the process of face-to-face teaching. However, in MOOC learning, teachers can not carry out a comprehensive analysis of the characteristics of all students, the relationship between teachers and students alienated, affecting teaching and learning [4]. Teachers in the course of teaching in addition to the completion of the task of teaching, there are educational functions. In MOOC learning, students can only learn by video, using electronic papers to complete the assessment, a serious lack of campus culture to cultivate sentiment and enlightenment, lack of specific cultural infiltration and spiritual environment. Contemporary college students need to explore the life and understand the society in the process of knowledge learning. MOOC teaching model can do nothing to meet these needs. In addition, students with poor self-awareness and self-control in learning, in the absence of teachers to urge and supervise the situation, the learning effect gradually decreased, MOOC teaching process withdrawal rate soared. Obviously, MOOC teaching mode has subverted the traditional classroom teaching mode and transferred the process of teaching and learning to the online network environment with the help of modern teaching means, but its own disadvantages make it unable to completely replace the classroom teaching mode in a long time.

How to combine the traditional teaching mode with the network teaching mode, select the essence and discard the dross, gather the advantages of the two teaching modes, skillfully combine the online teaching with the offline teaching, and improve the teaching quality of the course has become a hot topic of changing the teaching idea and implementing the reform of the teaching mode. Therefore, based on MOOC and supervised learning algorithm, this paper designs college online and offline collaborative teaching mode in detail.

2.1 MOOC Learning Platform

MOOC, also known as Massive Open and Online Courses, is a "massive open online course". In 2012, with the rise of foreign providers of Coursera, Edx, and Udacity J MOOC courses, the online-learning storm accelerated. "These three platforms are all for higher education, and each has its own learning and management system." What's more, their courses are free. Use a graph to show the course features as shown in Fig. 1 [5]. Moreover, Clayton Christensen, a professor at Harvard Business School, boldly predicts that "half of America's more than 4,000 universities will be closed in the next 15 years, and advanced science and technology will further transform higher education."

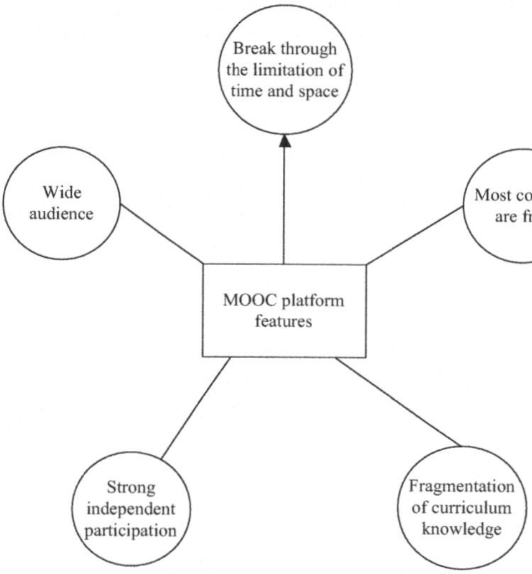

Fig. 1. Characteristics of MOOC courseware platform

In the United States to develop rapidly in France, Britain, Japan, Germany and other countries are also quite rapid. Scholars from all walks of life have different opinions. In fact, we should take an objective attitude to evaluate MOOCS. On the one hand, MOOC has realized the free circulation of high quality teaching resources all over the world, and to some extent, it has satisfied the global students' pursuit of famous teachers. As the Time magazine points out, "MOOC reminds us all that the essence of education is learning. "On the other hand, Mu-class is not omnipotent, the future of education is not all through online platform to solve all the problems, like Taobao has such a powerful function still can not stop the prevalence of physical stores.

2.2 Supervised Learning Algorithm

Machine learning is an interdisciplinary subject to study how to enable computer systems to use data "learning", thus gradually improving the ability to accomplish specific tasks. It is the core of artificial intelligence and promotes the development of artificial intelligence. Supervised learning technology is the most commonly used technique in the field of machine learning, and its purpose is to infer the prediction model through the marked training data. Each sample in the training dataset $D = \{(x_1, y_1), (x_2, y_2), \ldots, (x_m, y_m)\}$ that supervises learning contains conditional attributes (features) x_i and decision attributes (tag or tag) y_i, where conditional attributes are typically vectors while decision attributes are scalars. Suppose $x_i \in X$, $y_i \in Y$, then the purpose of supervised learning is to establish the mapping $f : X \rightarrow Y$ (i.e., model) of the input space X to the output space Y, so that for the new sample x_i of the unknown label, supervised learning predicts its label through the model of training, and the label can be discrete or continuous value [6]. The commonly used supervised learning models are decision tree, random forest, logical regression, support vector machine, neural network and so on. supervise the learning process as shown in Fig. 2 below.

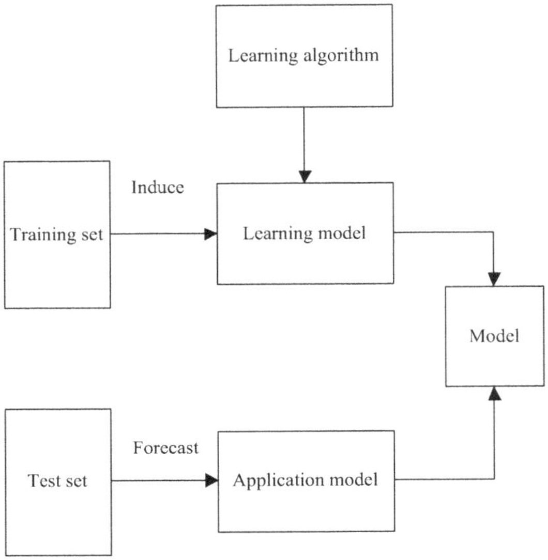

Fig. 2. Supervised learning process

In the research of online and offline collaborative teaching mode of colleges and universities based on supervised learning algorithm, the decision tree algorithm is mainly used. Decision Tree is a simple but widely used classification model that can be represented in a tree structure [7]. Figure 3 shows the decision tree model. There are three types of nodes:

(1) Root node, without inlet edge, with zero or more outlets.
(2) An intermediate node has one or only one inlet edge and two or more outlets.
(3) A leaf node has only one inlet edge and no outlet edge.

2.3 Online and Offline Collaborative Teaching Mode

Online and offline collaborative teaching model, referred to as O2O. There are various editions about the connotation of the "O2O teaching model". On the basis of referring to the views of other scholars, the author sums up the connotation of the "O2O teaching model" as follows: 020 teaching model mainly refers to the teaching model of highly combining online learning and offline face-to-face classroom learning through online MOOC platform (such as Haohao University Online, UOOC Alliance) by using computer information network technology and network media [8]. This collaborative

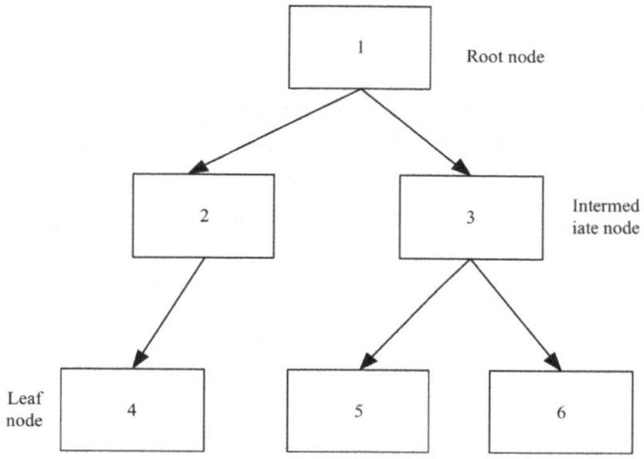

Fig. 3. Decision tree model

teaching mode can not only enable students to participate in face-to-face education in campus classroom, but also enable students to achieve personalized learning goals through online learning. The diagram is shown below in Fig. 4.

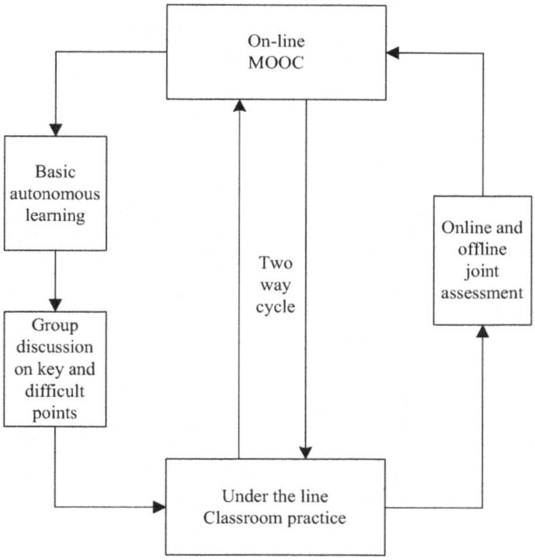

Fig. 4. O2O teaching model

O2O teaching model divides the process of "teaching" and "learning" into three links: the preparation of knowledge before class, answering questions during class and consolidating knowledge after class. In this model, the students become the main body of teaching from the receiver of knowledge, and the teachers play the role of guides and instructors. Therefore, the teacher's leading role in the classroom can be combined with the students' initiative, enthusiasm and creativity in the network teaching, and the classroom efficiency is greatly improved [9]. In addition, the mixed teaching model greatly expands the content of classroom teaching, which can broaden students' horizons and provide more fluent means for the interaction between teachers and students. In a word, this new teaching mode not only changes the arrangement of teaching content and time allocation, but also changes the roles of teachers and students. It can not only integrate teachers and teaching resources effectively, but also arouse students' enthusiasm and inquiry in learning. It is easy to realize individualized learning and has a great promoting effect on improving teaching quality. The specific design is shown in Fig. 5.

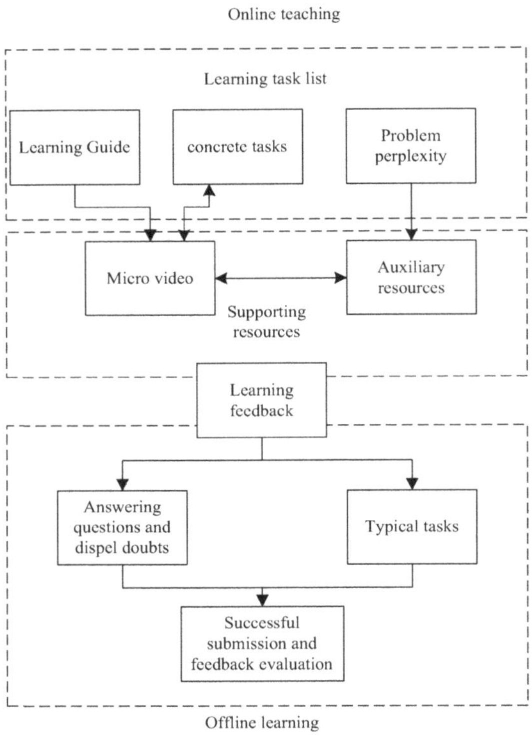

Fig. 5. Design of O2O teaching mode

(1) Preparation of online resources by teachers
The teacher prepares the video recording and uploads it to the Web before the student studies it. Two jobs need to be done:

1) Making digital materials such as teaching videos, PowerPoint or teaching materials, and clarifying the key points of knowledge and key problems. In addition, in the process of playing the video, some exercises are designed to make students have questions and stimulate their enthusiasm.

2) Provide an online learning platform where students can learn online and give feedback via the Internet.

(2) Students study on the mainline
Students are required to complete two tasks on their own initiative during after-school hours:

1) Watching digital materials such as video and PPT, arranging time for independent study and research, and solving problems in video and homework.
2) For the problems that can not be solved by themselves, feedback on the learning platform so that teachers can reasonably arrange the offline learning content and methods.

(3) Offline teacher-student interaction
The aim of classroom activity design is to maximize the teaching effect and promote the mastery of knowledge. Class activities in online and offline mixed mode can be conducted in the following two ways:

1) Teaching of the Basic Knowledge of the Course: According to the feedback from the students' online study, the teacher gives a concentrated explanation in the class to guide the students to master the understanding.
2) The teaching of the course application knowledge expansion part: Firstly, the teacher designs some application problems closely related to the actual content of the course, divides the students into groups, carries on the division of labor and cooperation within the groups, urges the students to better grasp and use the knowledge learned in the course, and trains the students' knowledge transfer and innovation ability.

(4) Teachers' reflection on after-school teaching
The data of assessment and questionnaire of learners are statistically analyzed to evaluate the teaching effect of the new model:

1) Students shall be tested and assessed to evaluate the effect of the mixed online and offline teaching modes.
2) To understand the students' satisfaction and opinions on the mixed online and offline teaching mode through questionnaires.
3) Carry out teaching reflection through the effects and existing problems arising from the implementation of the mixed online and offline teaching mode, and continuously improve and optimize the teaching program in the follow-up practice to further enhance the effect of follow-up teaching [10].

3 Implementation of Online and Offline Collaborative Teaching Mode in Colleges and Universities

3.1 Design of Online and Offline Collaborative Teaching Process

In order to test the effectiveness of the online and offline collaborative teaching mode based on supervised learning algorithm, this paper introduces the process of the implementation of the mode by taking "cam mechanism design" as an example, which is a project in the basic course of mechanical design.

(1) Front-line learning:

Teaching content:

1) Teachers push videos and post tests.
2) Students learn the video independently, complete the test, and create Q&A and difficult communication activities.
3) The teacher monitors the students' learning achievements, and instructs them online.

Teacher activities:

1) Upload and push video: Cam mechanism is widely used in real life and industry. Course Bulletin Questions: How to Design Cam Mechanisms for Practical Use?
2) Upload 4 teaching videos about cam mechanism, release related tests, and answer questions online on Wednesday afternoon.
3) Summarizing and analyzing the students' self-study achievements by using the data of the network platform, summarizing the problems, and condensing the teaching difficulties.

Student activities:

1) Watch the micro video about the cam mechanism pushed by the teacher.
2) Completing the testing activities of corresponding cam mechanism exercises.
3) Discuss problems and difficulties online and carry out interactive communication activities.

(2) Mid-course offline teaching

Teaching content:

1) Focus on teaching difficulties.
2) Task-driven, implement integrated teaching activities of "learning, teaching and doing".
3) Itinerant guidance by teachers and recording of process assessment.
4) Evaluation and summary.

Teacher activities:

1) Comments on students' completion of online learning.
2) Focus on teaching the difficult points: "the displacement line diagram of the follower" and "the principle of inversion method for designing cam contour".
3) Issuance of Project Task Sheet: According to the actual application of cam mechanism, design the cam mechanism with spire type\ roller type direct moving follower. And in the integrated teaching activities of learning and teaching guidance tour, record data process evaluation.

4) Summarizing the exchange and display of the evaluation group, and emphasizing the importance of difficulties.

Student activities:

1) Listen and learn about the design of cam mechanism in the difficult teaching content, and make notes.
2) Accepting the project task list issued by the teacher, and completing the teaching activities such as independent inquiry, group cooperation, exchange and exhibition under the guidance of the teacher.
3) According to the teacher's summary and evaluation, reflect on and consolidate the learning difficulties.

(3) On-line extension after class

Teaching content:

1) Push and expand videos and assign homework after class.
2) Sharing relevant videos and materials on the latest developments.
3) Teaching reflection.

Teacher activities:

1) Teachers will release the video of "Design of Offset Follower Cam Mechanism" on the "Super Star Learner" platform, and release corresponding training tasks.
2) Release the videos and materials on the latest development of the application of the push cam mechanism.
3) Individualized tutoring shall be given to the students with difficulties by using the evaluation of the three stages before, during and after class, and the teaching of the course shall be summarized and reflected.

Student activities:

1) Watch push and expand videos.
2) Accept and complete the development training tasks, upload them to the network platform, and deepen the absorption and internalization of knowledge.
3) Independently reading and watching the latest video materials on relevant cam mechanisms to expand the scope of knowledge.

3.2 Evaluation of the Effectiveness of Teaching Programs

Based on the supervised learning algorithm, the effect of online and offline collaborative teaching is evaluated and graded by using Defield's method. There are four scoring objectives: learner autonomy, time and space limitation, online and offline assessment and personalized needs of students. The assessment process is shown in Fig. 6.

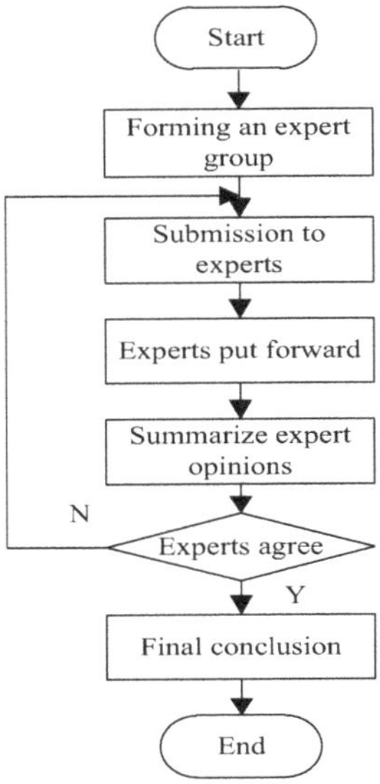

Fig. 6. Defield process

The assessment results are as follows:

(1) Improvement of students' autonomous learning. The online and offline mixed teaching practice has proved that through setting up micro video, conquering difficulties and discussing problems online, students' interest in learning can be aroused, their enthusiasm and initiative can be aroused, and the pre-class learning can be completed on time; and the implementation of teaching activities such as group discussion, team cooperation and achievement demonstration under the guidance of offline classroom teachers can promote students to actively practice, actively explore and innovate and internalize learning motivation. Students' autonomous learning is greatly improved, and the role of students as subjects is really restored.
(2) Break time and space limitations, and realize online teaching at anytime and anyplace. Through the establishment of a learning environment under the Internet, create a network-based sharing high-quality teaching resource database. Teachers may push a batch of micro-videos, PPT, exercise banks and other online resources based on granular knowledge points to enable students to choose the appropriate time and place for online learning according to their individual needs. Online teaching breaks through the limitations of time, space and environment, and makes teaching and learning more flexible.
(3) Pay equal attention to online and offline assessment, and realize the comprehensive assessment of process and results-based teaching quality. Teachers can monitor the learning progress in real time on the network platform, and use big data analysis to master the students' online learning; and in the self-inquiry and group cooperation with "teachers as the leader and students as the main body".

Teachers can have enough time to interact with students in classroom activities such as activity, practice, exchange and display, so as to track and master each learner's learning situation in real-time, and to guide students to solve the existing problems. This kind of teaching activity is helpful for teachers to track students' learning progress and real-time situation, and record it in the process of assessment, so as to achieve a comprehensive teaching quality evaluation of process and result.

(4) Students' individualized needs are met

Through the online teaching of mobile teaching resources pushed by teachers, students can learn according to their own learning habits and rhythm at any time, and in the classroom teaching guided by teachers, students can maximize their main role in teaching activities and give individual learning guidance. This kind of online and offline teaching mode meets the needs of students' differences and personalized needs.

4 Closing Remarks

To sum up, the online and offline collaborative teaching mode based on "Internet +" technology is the mainstream direction of college education and teaching reform and curriculum construction. This can not only give full play to the leading role of teachers, but also fully embody the main role of students' autonomous learning and active practice, and improve the teaching effect and teaching quality.

References

1. Xie, A.J., Tao, Y.W., Luo, S.P., et al.: "Maker Education + SPOC" flipped experiment teaching: determination of trace impurity iron in hydrogen phosphate products as example. Chin. J. Chem. Educ. **39**(14), 44–48 (2018)
2. Deng, J.G., Duan, X.D.: Innovating exploration of online-offline cooperative governance model of information behavior affecting public safety—book review on research on interaction mechanism between paroxysmal public crisis event and network opinion. Libr. Inf. Serv. **62**(15), 145–148 (2018)
3. Yu, Z.H., Xu, N., Wang, Z.Q., et al.: Exploration of the blended teaching in the regional anatomy. J. Anat. **42**(1), 100–102 (2019)
4. Ying, X.Y.: The development trend of adult education in the MOOC era. Adult Educ. **38**(1), 28–30 (2018)
5. Gao, J., Zhao, X.R., Zhou, Y.Q., et al.: Study on the learning evaluation system of MOOC. Coll. Phys. **36**(12), 50–53 (2017)
6. Fu, Y., Shi, W.: Research on sentiment analysis of micro-blog based on enhanced supervised learning. J. Intell. **37**(12), 130–134 (2018)
7. Mo, L.F., Jiang, H.L., Li, X.P.: Review of deep learning-based video prediction. CAAI Trans. Intell. Syst. **13**(1), 85–96 (2018)
8. Ning, Q.: A research on the application of blended learning model of college English follow-up courses. J. Sichuan Int. Stud. Univ. **34**(2), 145–151 (2018)
9. Zhao, H.K., Yang, E.C.: Exploration and practice of blended teaching mode in general course of wonderful world of chemistry. Chin. J. Chem. Educ. **39**(2), 13–17 (2018)
10. Liu, Y., Zeng, X.L., Hu, X., et al.: Construction and teaching practice of the open online courses of principles of chemical engineering. Chin. J. Chem. Educ. **39**(24), 7–14 (2018)

Multi Module Integration Method of Students' Habitual Learning Mode Based on Deep Learning

Zhan-yong Chen[1,2] and Jun Guo[3(✉)]

[1] International Business School of Beijing, Foreign Studies University, Beijing 100089, China
yyg00321@163.com
[2] Zhengzhou Foreign Language School, Affiliated to Beijing Foreign Studies University, Zhengzhou 450121, China
[3] Quanzhou University of Information Engineering College of Software, Quanzhou 362000, China
lcg02650@163.com

Abstract. In order to improve the ability of multi-module integration of students' habitual learning mode and increase the ability of model to deal with more complex situations, a multi-module integration method of students' habitual learning mode is proposed based on deep learning. In order to strengthen and integrate the students' habitual learning mode, construct the data sample processing system, and analyze the influencing factors and mechanisms of College Students' deep learning, on the basis of data analysis, firstly collect the system data, and construct a three-dimensional structure model of deep learning, and carry out confirmatory factor analysis to ensure the reliability and validity of the research structure. The latent variable is introduced to deal with multiple integrated data, so as to realize the research on the multi module integration method of students' habitual learning mode. The experimental results show that compared with the traditional multi module integration method, the multi module integration processing ability of this method is stronger.

Keywords: Deep learning · Students' habitual learning mode · Multi module integration of learning mode · Multi module integration method

1 Introduction

Deep learning is a new research direction in the field of machine learning. In recent years, breakthroughs have been made in speech recognition, computer vision and other applications. The motivation is to build models to simulate the neural connections of human brain. When processing image, sound and text signals, the data features are described through multiple transformation stages, and then the data interpretation is given [1]. Taking image data as an example, the processing of this kind of signal in visual system is edge detection and initial shape, gradually forming more complex visual

S. Liu et al. (Eds.): eLEOT 2020, LNICST 339, pp. 254–270, 2020.
https://doi.org/10.1007/978-3-030-63952-5_22

shape. Similarly, deep learning forms more abstract high-level representation, attribute category or feature by combining low-level features, and finally gives the hierarchical feature representation of data. The reason why deep learning is called "depth" is relative to the "shallow learning" methods such as support vector machine, lifting method and maximum entropy method. In the model learned by deep learning, there are more levels of nonlinear operation [2].

Shallow learning relies on artificial experience to extract sample features, and the single-layer features without hierarchical structure are obtained after network model learning; while deep learning transforms the feature representation of samples in the original space to a new feature space through layer by layer feature transformation of the original signal, so as to automatically learn the hierarchical feature representation, which is more conducive to classification or feature visualization. Therefore, through literature analysis, this paper makes an in-depth understanding of the research on deep learning at home and abroad, analyzes the current situation, trend and shortcomings of deep learning research at home and abroad, and studies the multi-module integration method of students' habitual learning mode.

2 Design of Multi Module Integration Method for Students' Habitual Learning Mode

In recent years, big data and cloud computing have been booming. Big data provides a way to deal with massive data. Cloud computing, through virtualization technology, abstracts entity resources, eliminates the limitations of the original physical configuration, and makes people more efficient use of resources. As we enter the era of artificial intelligence, we can solve the problem of mass data storage and preprocessing by combining them with deep learning. Deep learning technology is to build multilayer neural network model by referring to the multilayer structure of human cerebral cortex, and the training data can continuously obtain more abstract data characteristics in the process of multilayer model training, which is different from general Through machine learning, feature annotation is needed in advance, which makes it possible to solve complex application problems, and has made remarkable achievements in image recognition and speech recognition. A typical neural network structure mainly includes input layer, hidden layer and output layer. The circle in the figure indicates that the neuron refers to a certain operation, and the connection constitutes the connection between different neurons. Each connection is given a weight, and the arrow direction indicates the data flow direction. The training process of the neural network is to input the data representing the original characteristics of the data from the input layer, and pass the data to the output layer through the neuron operation of the hidden layer, according to the junction of the output layer In order to achieve better results, the weights of each neuron connection were adjusted. Neural network prediction is to use the adjusted weights to calculate some input data to get the output results, that is, to complete the prediction. In the training process, the weights between neurons need to be initialized first. After a training, the predicted value will be generated. Our goal is to minimize the difference between the predicted value and the real value, that is, the predicted "loss" is the minimum. This requires reverse weight adjustment. In this training process, the weight will be adjusted to the extent that the loss meets the requirements As a training process, the relationship between input and output is constructed, and then the output results of other inputs can be calculated to achieve the purpose of prediction.

In the complex network model, there are many hidden layers. For the complex problems, we need to make the simple features of the input layer Abstract continuously through the hidden layer to get higher level features and achieve a better representation of the results of the output layer, which is the reason why deep learning can solve the complex problems. The data flow between each layer needs matrix calculation. More layers means massive calculation and a large number of parameters.

The evaluation index of resource scheduling algorithm can be viewed from two aspects: system and user: system perspective:

(1) Optimal time span: indicates the time difference between the start and completion of a series of tasks. The shorter the time difference, the better the performance of the scheduling algorithm and the higher the utilization of resources.
(2) Throughput: the total number of tasks completed by the system in a certain period of time.
(3) Load balancing: load balancing is an important measure of cloud computing system performance. As a scheduling algorithm, it is necessary to realize the load balance of computing nodes, because too much load will unbalance the load of computing nodes, which may cause system downtime; too low load means idle computing node resources. Therefore, a good algorithm should adjust the load, take into account the processing capacity of each node, the resource demand of different tasks, try to achieve full load but not overload.
(4) Fairness: the fairness of the system requires consideration of users, resources and tasks. From the user's point of view, fairness means that users and users are equal to each other, and they can use the resources in the system equally;

From the perspective of resources, fairness means that virtual resources can receive scheduling tasks equally; from the perspective of tasks, fairness means that tasks are equal in the allocation of virtual resources. From the perspective of users:

(1) Waiting time: it refers to the time difference between the submission of a task and the execution of the response in the scheduling process. From the perspective of a single user, each user wants to wait as short as possible to get the response of the computing system faster, and what the administrator can achieve is to make the average waiting time of all users smaller.
(2) Execution time: refers to the time taken by a task from response to completion.

Here's how to solve the specific problems:

(1) According to the different task types, the common network models are investigated.
(2) To design the network model, we need to define the structure of the network and choose the training method. Initialize network

The parameters of the model are usually set by using random numbers or according to historical experience.

(3) Preprocess the data, adopt different strategies to expand the amount of data and transform it into an appropriate structure,

Randomly scramble the training data, and according to the set batch size of each training or the data used

Row mode is used to segment data in batches.

(4) Train the neural network.
(5) Observe the effect of the training process. If the model is not right, adjust the model and go back to the second step. If ginseng

If the number is not correct, adjust the parameters and enter the fourth step.

(6) Keep training many times.

2.1 Construction of Multi Module Data Acquisition Scheme for Students' Habitual Learning Mode

For training data construction, first of all, when reading the corpus, we classify the Q & A pairs from the same document, and filter the unknown words. The thesaurus used is the thesaurus constructed when the sentences are sorted. Turn the question and answer pairs after participle into index sentences. The word vector used in training the model is the word vector trained by Baidu Encyclopedia. The evaluation criteria used in automatic answer extraction are the evaluation criteria of dbqa tasks: MRR and map evaluation criteria. In this paper, activation function is used to get the integrity of data. Because activation function is an important component of deep learning, the input of the model is given, and the activation function transforms it and outputs it. The activation function is to transform the linear input into the nonlinear input, so that the model can be applied to more complex situations, achieve the effect close to the biological neural network, and increase the ability of the model to deal with more complex situations. Firstly, the sigmoid activation function is selected.

The sigmoid activation function can map the output between 0 and 1. The output range is limited and it can be used as the output layer. At the same time, the activation function of sigmoid has a good threshold, and its function curve is continuous, monotonous and easy to derive. However, the activation function of sigmoid also has some disadvantages. In deep learning, as the activation function, it is easy to produce gradient disappearing, resulting in the model can not learn information in the learning process. Another disadvantage of the sigmoid activation function is that it is not zero centered.

Tanh activation function maps the output between -1 and 1. Tanh activation function takes 0 as the center. Compared with sigmoid function, tanh activation function is more suitable for the application of deep learning, and has faster convergence speed compared with sigmoid function. However, Tan activation function still has the disadvantage of the disappearance of sigmoid gradient. Compared with the sigmoid activation function and tanh activation function, the relu activation function is closer to the mechanism of biological neurons. It has sparse activation, relatively wide excitation boundary, better unilateral inhibition, faster convergence speed than the two activation functions, and reduces the problem of gradient disappearance [3].

Set the data storage mode to store the function collection data, and set the data storage diagram as follows (Fig. 1):

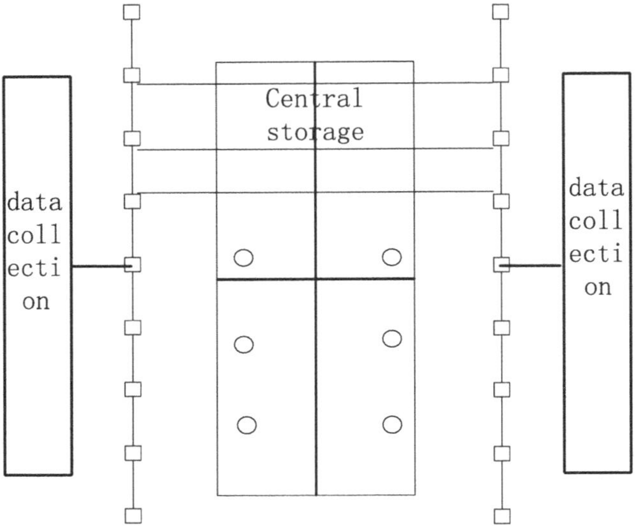

Fig. 1. Data storage diagram

According to the internal processing information, the model is filtered, the system file group is constructed into the same system data file set, and the data is stored in the system, the acquired data is arranged in the order of data information, and the data is arranged in the system to strengthen the operation [4], improve the protection performance of the data itself, and ensure the completion of the data collection process The data sorting process is as shown in Fig. 2

Analyze the data structure, grasp the structure status of the data as a whole, select the data collection space channel according to the structure status of the data, collect the data systematically according to the corresponding channel, filter the data based on the collection, take the system data as the standard [5], filter the data inconsistent with the system requirements, record and store the remaining data, and realize the overall data division Analysis.

Select the appropriate operation position, set the target parameters, track the data systematically, and master the position and flow direction status of the data at all times. Moderately expand the data flow channel to avoid data blocking in the process of data flow. Use linear model to process linear time series data, integrate data processing status, divide data according to different operation types, and store the same kind of data set

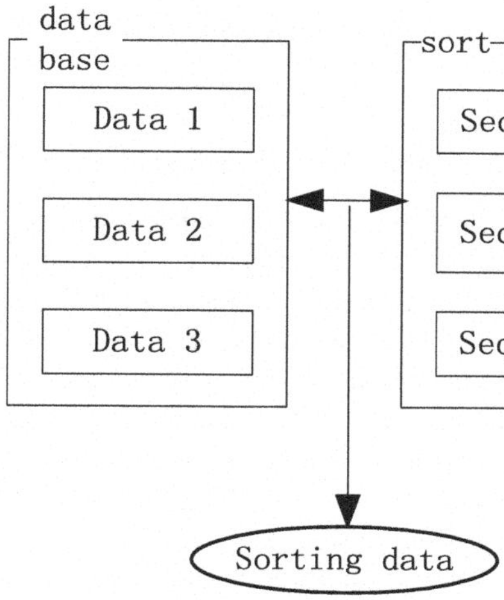

Fig. 2. Data sorting diagram

in the corresponding central system [6]. Predict the data stability, check whether the data storage space is suitable for the data storage state, and set the image for the data prediction process (Fig. 3):

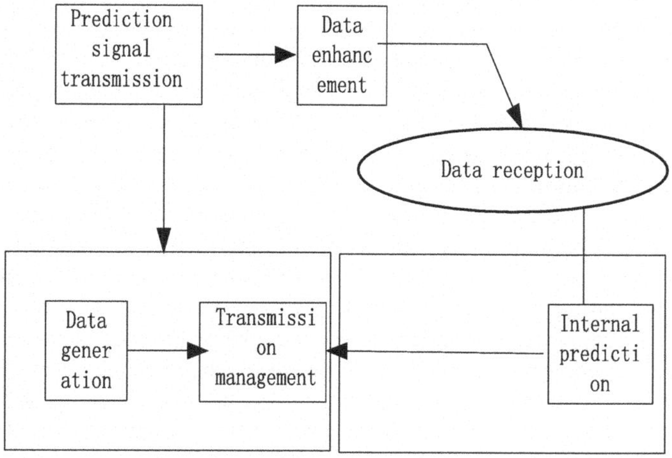

Fig. 3. Data prediction process chart

According to the particularity of data establishment, build the collection model, improve the model construction performance of the system, ensure the normal operation of the system, use machine learning algorithm to classify the collected data, combine the data belonging to the same category, place it in the same data set, analyze the fixed law of data collection, and take data corresponding means to preliminarily collect the data

Filter, filter out the data that meet the system conditions, and realize the initial collection of data.

2.2 Construction of 3D Structure Model for Deep Learning of Data Information

The three-dimensional structure of deep learning includes three parts: high-level learning, reflective learning and integrated learning. High-level learning pays attention to the learners' advanced thinking ability of course perception, including the ability of application, analysis, evaluation and synthesis. Integrated learning emphasizes the dynamic levelness of consciously integrated information, for example, on the basis of mastering relevant materials, to complete a topic Face-to-face analysis; reflective learning focuses on learners' value judgment and finding problems by reviewing their own action measures or ideological results, consciously avoiding the previous problems in the future practice, and developing their own strengths.

Domestic scholars have begun to use the three-dimensional structure of deep learning for relevant research, such as Zhao zongjin of Ocean University of China and others have used the three-dimensional structure to understand the differences of deep learning among different groups of college students, but the discussion on the rationality of the three-dimensional structure has not yet appeared. As the research structure of deep learning is an important foundation of this study, it is necessary to analyze the reliability and validity of deep learning and research structure carefully before exploring the influencing factors [7].

In this paper, the main model design of the system is strengthened, and the second-order model can replace the first-order model, which can make the model more refined and simplified. Therefore, it is necessary to establish the second-order CFA based on the first-order CFA of deep learning 3D structure. First, the latent variables (i.e. the first-order factors) in the first-order CFA should have a moderate correlation (correlation coefficient >0.5) to show that there is consistency between the latent variables, that is, the correlation number among the high-order learning, reflective learning and integrated learning of the first-order factors with the characteristics of the same increase and decrease is 0.6, 0.72, 0.89 respectively, which are greater than 0.5, meeting the requirements. Second, each second-order surface needs at least three first-order surfaces, and the first-order surface has at least two indicators. In the first-order CFA of deep learning three-dimensional structure, there are three first-order surfaces, among which the first-order surface "high-order learning" contains four measurement indicators, the first-order surface "reflective learning" contains five measurement indicators, and the first-order surface "integrated learning" contains four All of the measurement indexes [8] meet the standard. To sum up, the first-order CFA model with three-dimensional depth learning has a good fitting effect, the first-order plane structure is good, and it has the conditions to establish the second-order CFA, assuming h3-1 is tenable.

On the basis of the first-order CFA of the three-dimensional structure of deep learning, remove the correlation of the first-order structure, add the second-order factor deep learning, set the factor load of "integrated learning" as "1", at the same time, add the residual term to the first-order factor high-order learning, reflective learning and integrated learning, decompose the overall operation step by step, and learn from Liu In this paper, we try to apply the attention mechanism in sentences to sentence ordering [9], and propose a sentence ordering model based on the attention mechanism in sentences. Compared with the LSTM feature, the feature extracted by the attention mechanism in sentences can better retain the core information. Compared with the sentence sorting model based on sentence matching, it can better capture the semantic logic relationship between sentences and set the image for the internal data collection process (Fig. 4).

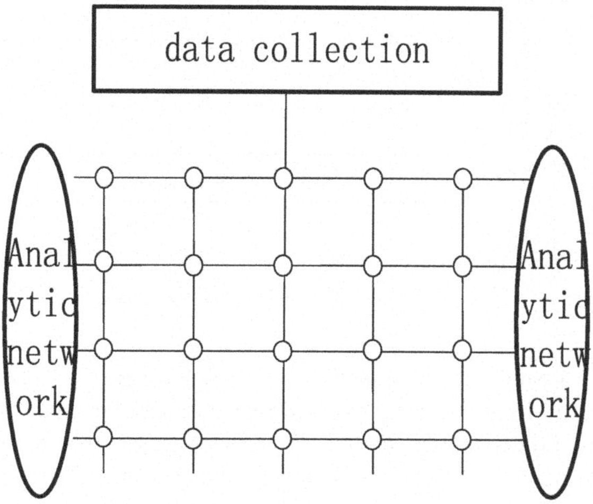

Fig. 4. Studies the data collection diagram

Its basic idea is equivalent to static attention mechanism, which is equivalent to doing static attention calculation for itself, and making two-way LSTM The output is pooled as the final output of the decoding stage, and the output of each node is regarded as the output of the encoding stage. Finally, the feature representation of attention sentences in two sentences is obtained. Then, the feature is multiplied, subtracted and spliced by using the sentence matching method, and finally the feature vector is input into the feedforward neural network. In the sentence sorting based on attention mechanism, the dropout size is set to 0.5, the sentence length input into the model keeps 30 words, the sentence with insufficient length is supplemented with 0, and the sentence with too long length is truncated. The mini batch size is set to 64, and the learning rate is set to 0.3. In each layer of the front and back neural network, batch normalization is added to normalize the data. The length of word vector is 200, the length of bidirectional LSTM hidden layer is 200, and the number of feedforward neural network layers is set to 100. The feature extraction based on static attention mechanism only calculates the hidden layer output and the final output in the decoding stage, and does not update the attention weight distribution dynamically.

Therefore, this paper attempts to introduce the attention mechanism of word alignment into the model. The attention mechanism of word alignment can dynamically update the distribution of attention weight, better capture the relationship between words in sentences, and improve the ability to capture the semantic and logical relationship. Since sentences come from multiple different documents, they can only be solved through the semantic logic relationship between sentences [10], and the monitoring chart of sentence data node is set (Fig. 5):

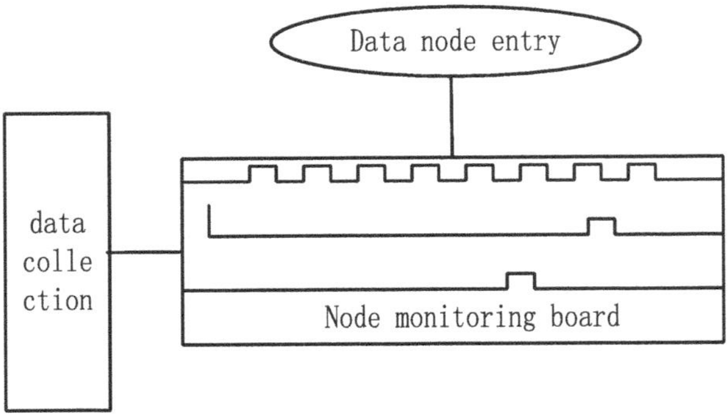

Fig. 5. Data node monitoring diagram

Therefore, in this paper, the main way to solve the sentence order task is by capturing the sentence semantic logic relationship between judgment on whether the associated input to the system of the sentence, namely the relationship between the sentence before and after judgment between sentences is sorting task, semantic logic relationship is an important guarantee of sentence order effect, so can accurately capture the sentence semantic logic relationship between is the important guarantee of model can accurately sort. In order to find the relationship between sentences, this paper attempts to introduce sentence matching into the sentence ordering model to capture the differences between sentences through feature combination and processing, so as to achieve the effect of capturing semantic and logical relations of sentences. Feature vector multiplication is a common feature processing method in deep learning model, which has achieved good results in many problems. Feature vector splicing is one of the most common operations in deep learning. Sentence vector splicing is used in the baseline method. In the deep learning method, the construction of features requires no manual intervention and is automatically trained by word vectors. The general process of feature construction is to use word segmentation tools, such as NLTK and stutter word segmentation, to perform word segmentation of sentences. The sentence after word segmentation is converted into the form of index through word list, and the sentence represented by index is obtained. During model training and model prediction, the sentence represented by index will be transformed into the form of word vector through word vector matrix.

The word segmentation tool used in this paper is stuttering word segmentation, and the two modes of precise word segmentation and new word discovery are tried. The new word discovery model produces a larger vocabulary, and words with the same meaning are classified as new words, so words with the same meaning cannot be learned by the model.

The construction of vocabulary is based on the corpus of xinhua news agency. Firstly, the corpus of xinhua news agency was processed by clause processing. The period, hello, exclamation point as a sentence marker for the clause, and filter the number;

Then, through the precise word segmentation model of stuttering word segmentation, the corpus of xinhua news agency was processed, and the word list and word frequency were counted. Finally, the word list was screened by setting the threshold value. Through experiments, it was found that setting the threshold value to 50 was more reasonable. If the word frequency is less than 50, it will be treated as the unregistered word, and finally a word list of 13w words will be obtained.

When building a vocabulary, filter for special symbols, such as whitespace. In order to prevent the impact of generating word id, the word list was used to filter the corpus of xinhua news agency, filtering out low-frequency words and treating them as unregistered words. The resulting corpus can retain the original vocabulary to the maximum extent and reduce the lexicon at the same time.

The preprocessing of baidu encyclopedia corpus and DBQA corpus is also divided into periods, question marks and exclamation points, and paragraphs with sentences greater than 2 and less than 8 are reserved. The constructed word list is used for filtering, and low-frequency words and unregistered words are treated as unregistered words. The purpose of sentence ordering task is to sort sentences to get semantic coherent text fragments. Since the sentence ordering task is to process the sentences in the sentence set, and these sentences come from different text fragments, they cannot be sorted by their location or time information in the document. To this end, this paper will mine the semantic and logical relationship between sentences to achieve sentence ordering.

In order to build a good data processing environment, this paper carries out structure checking operation. In general, the intermediary effect test, the researchers generally has two kinds of common ideas, one is in the SPSS through the multiple regression analysis to explore the mediation effect, but the problem with this approach is that the analysis of the independent variable, the intermediary variable and the dependent variable is measured variables, and the measured variables are package technology, data the rigour of discounted; One is in the AOMS this study through AMOS21.0 in structural equation model to explore the relationship between variables, variables can be hidden scalar, can also be measured variables, and the mediation effect of inspection is obtained from the Bootstrap, is more powerful in the current statistical method, the correlation analysis of the present study chose the latter, thus completing the data information deep learning the structure of the three dimension structure model.

2.3 Analysis and Integration of Multi-module Data Structure Equation in Students' Habitual Learning Mode

This chapter corresponds to two parts, which adopt different research techniques according to different contents, as follows:

Under the first part, the theoretical framework on college students' learning in all of the students "behavior" and "colleges" factors of confirmatory factor analysis (CFA), has proven its structure, the reliability and validity of these factors can be incorporated into to the structural equation model, the specific research method is to use data analysis software AMOS21.0 confirmatory factor analysis (CFA), through the output ESTIMATE of non-standard results and standardized judgment standard dimensions of each factor; The standardized factor load of the index in the dimension of AMOS21.0 was imported into the software Excel 2007, and the standardized coefficient squared SMC value, standardized residual value as well as the component reliability of the whole dimension and the average variance extraction amount AVE value of each index were calculated by the "convergence validity" operation program (which was programmed in Excel in advance). The convergence effect of the dimension was judged by the model fitness indexes X2, DF, X2/DF, GFI and AGFI in AMOS21.0 to determine whether the dimension could be included in the structural equation model (SEM). The second part, the building up of "student behavior" in AMOS21.0 influence factors to the depth study of structural equation model (SEM) and the school of "condition" influence factors to the depth study of structural equation model (SEM), the output and the model of specific methods is through AMOS21.0 with moderate conditions to modify the model, through the software display of data observed the influence of various factors on the deep learning effectiveness and the correlation between factors. Structural equation model (sem) is a kind of multivariate statistical technique combining factor analysis and path analysis. It is a popular statistical technique in social science research. At the same time, the structural equation model can deal with the relationship of multiple causes and results at the same time, making factor exploration and path analysis more efficient and reliable.

The criterion to judge whether a structural equation model is reasonable is the compliance of model parameter estimation, convergence validity and model fitness index. In students learning investment theory framework, "student behavior" and "colleges" two major categories, discusses the influence of the students for deep learning effectiveness, using data analysis software AMOS21.0, through the establishment of first-order CFA or second-order CFA, judgment of fitting into the structural equation model, reliability and validity of the factors which make reasonable correction in time; For the overlapping and similar fields in different dimensions, by comparing the estimated values of model parameters, convergence validity and model fitness index, the better one can be retained.

First, "the student behavior" category proposed confirmatory factor analysis (CFA) factors include: comprehensive analysis indicators of "cooperative learning", the education process diagnosis index under "course learning behavior", "expanding learning behavior" and "school", learning diagnosis index of "information analysis", "acceptance learning" and "inquiry learning", "cooperative learning" and "cross-cultural learning".

Secondly, the coincidence of measurement indexes between factors and related research hypothesis are set. Under the five indicators of "active cooperation and education process indicators under" course learning behavior "most of the item, therefore, before the confirmatory factor analysis, make two kinds of hypothesis: hypothesis 4-1: dimensions" course learning behavior ", "expanding learning behavior", "school" can be incorporated into the "student behavior" the influence of factors on the depth of college students' learning effectiveness research.

Hypothesis 4–2: the aspects of "active cooperative learning"/"cooperative learning"/ "inquiry learning", "information analysis", "acceptance learning", "cross-cultural learning" and "orientation" can be included in the research on the effect of "student behavior" factors on deep learning of college students. The compliance of the nine factors of the three dimensions covered by the category of "student behavior" in the three aspects of model parameter estimation, convergence validity and model matching index can be roughly divided into three levels: full compliance, basic compliance and non-compliance.

In particular, because the sample size of this study is large, the significance probability P value is not considered in the model analysis.

Category one, full compliance. Reaching the standard completely includes two aspects: "degree of learning" and "active cooperative learning".

"Degree of learning" dimension is up to standard, can be reserved. Specifically, convergence validity: the STD value and SMC value of the four indicators all conform to the standards of 0.6 and 0.36; the CR value is 0.84, which conforms to the ideal value standard of >0.7; the internal consistency of the four indicators under the dimension is relatively high; the AVE value is 0.514, which conforms to the ideal value standard of >0.5. Model fitness: chi-square value/degree of freedom = 2.35, which conforms to the ideal value standard of 0–3; GFI value is 0.997, which conforms to the standard of >0.8; AGFI value is 0.987, which conforms to the standard of >0.9; RMSEA value is 0.028, which conforms to the standard of <0.08; therefore, this dimension is retained. The STD value of sa1c-1 and SMC in the dimension of "active cooperative learning" both met the standards of >0.6 and 0.36, while the CR value and AVE value were 0.81 and 0.47, respectively, meeting the standards of >0.6 and 0.36. Chi square value/degree of freedom = 4.65, conforming to the standard value of 0–5, GFI value is 0.994, conforming to the standard of >0.8, AGFI value is 0.977, conforming to the standard of >0.9, RMSEA value is 0.05, conforming to the standard of <0.08.

The second category, part of the standard.

Part of the standards include "information analysis", "inquiry learning", "cross-cultural learning", "acceptance learning" and "cooperative learning". After index evaluation, "information analysis", "inquiry learning" and "cross-cultural learning" are finally retained, while "acceptance learning" and "cooperative learning" are deleted. First, the correlation analysis of three quasi - preserving dimensions. The STD value of sa4f-1 in the dimension of "information analysis" is 0.43, which does not meet the standard of >0.6, and the SMC value is 0.18, which does not meet the standard of >0.36. The SMC value of the index sa13b-1 in the dimension of "cross-cultural learning" is 0.253, which does not meet the standard of >0.36; the STD value of the index sa13e-1 is 0.39, which does not meet the standard of >0.6; the SMC value is 0.15, which does not meet the standard of >0.36. In addition, the model parameters of the three dimensions are estimated to be up to standard, the reliability of the dimensions in the convergence validity is high, and the internal consistency of the indexes in the dimensions is good.

Secondly, the correlation analysis of three dimensions to be deleted. "Acceptance learning" dimensions in the index, SA4A SA1I - 1-1, SA2A reliability STD value 1 project are: 0.53, 0.32, 0.39, do not accord with standard of >0.6, SMC values were 0.28, 0.10, 0.15, do not accord with standard of >0.36, compose the AVE a value of 0.32, do not accord with standard of >0.36, dimensions in poor reliability, in addition, on the surface of the constitutive model with moderate are up to the standard, but the examination.

Considering that the number of items in the dimension should not be too large, the discussion in this part does not consider "accepting learning". The project reliability STD values of the indicators sa1d-1 and sa1b-1 in the dimension of "cooperative learning" are 0.46 and 0.49, which are not consistent with >0.6.

The SMC value is 0.21, 0.24, which does not meet the standard of >0.36, and the dimension AVE value is 0.34, which does not meet the standard of >0.36, and the dimension reliability is not good. In addition, the model compatibility of the dimension all meets the standard, but considering the repetition of "cooperative learning" and "active cooperative learning", the dimension "cooperative learning" is deleted. The index sa1h-1 in the dimension of "inquiry learning".

The SMC value of However, there are two overlapping items in the second dimension "active learning" of inquiry learning and active cooperative learning, so it is suggested to delete the dimension "inquiry learning".

The third category is completely substandard.

There are two aspects of "course learning behavior" and "extended learning behavior". The STD values of indicators sa11-1 and sa1d-1 in the aspect of "course learning behavior" are 0.44 and 0.40, respectively, which do not meet the standard of >0.6. The SMC values of indicators sa11-1, sa1a-1, sa1b-1 and sa1d-1 are: The AVE value of the dimension was 0.40, which did not meet the standard of >0.36. The convergence validity was poor. The chi-square value/degree of freedom was 8.284, which did not meet the standard of 0-5. "Expand the learning behavior" dimensions of the nine indicators of reliability STD project value and SMC are not meet the criteria of 0,6 and 0.36 >>, the structure of the CR value is 0.48, do not accord with standard of >0.6, AVE a value of 0.11, do not accord with standard of >0.36, dimensions poor reliability, on the surface of the constitutive model with moderate has reached the standards, "further study" compose the convergent validity is poorer, dimensions in the index of the internal consistency is bad, will destroy the final convergence effect of the structural equation model, suggest to delete.

To sum up, after evaluating the reliability and validity of the measurement model from the three aspects of model parameter estimation, convergent validity and model matching index, the four dimensions of "active cooperative learning", "orientation", "information analysis" and "cross-cultural learning" can finally be included in the structural model for subsequent analysis. Therefore, according to the above conclusions, hypothesis A is rejected and hypothesis B is accepted. Based on the above analysis, the hypothesis is further modified as: the aspects of "active cooperative learning", "information analysis", "cross-cultural learning" and "orientation" can be included in the study on the effect of "student behavior" factors on students' deep learning. Thus, the structural equation analysis and integration of the whole data are realized.

3 Comparison Experiment

3.1 Experimental Background

Based on deep learning, the multi-module integration method of students' habitual learning mode can integrate multi-source heterogeneous data, including explicit or implicit user feedback data, user portrait and project content data, and user-generated content. By taking multi-source heterogeneous data as input and adopting an end-to-end mode automatic training prediction model, the deep learning method can effectively integrate multi-source heterogeneous data into the integration system, so as to alleviate the data sparser and single module problem faced by the traditional learning system, and improve the ability of the learning system. Its main advantages are as follows: it can avoid complex artificial feature engineering, especially in the face of unstructured data such as images and videos. The expressive learning ability of deep learning can help extract feature information from unstructured data. It is possible to learn nonlinear multi-level abstract feature representation, and the acquired features are usually dense and low-dimensional, which are not available in traditional shallow learning methods. It can overcome the heterogeneity of different data and learn from users and projects by using various rough raw data as input.

3.2 Experiment Implementation and Parameter Setting

To improve data research result, this paper selected the suitable system to collect means for information retrieval, the signal integrity of the accuracy of the data acquisition, and in the process of collecting secondary data transmission system, the data transmission of accurate, avoid the waste of data resources, to find the contact between data collection, according to the obtained data collect performance data query rules to perfect the system, and enhance the dominant theory of system test operation technology, on the emission signal information delay measurement, data difference, as the basis of data between the data difference factors in monitoring data attributes, Integrate data belonging to the same property, store them in the corresponding data set, set management criteria for system management, achieve good data storage, eliminate the obstacles of data transmission, enhance the reliability of system operation, and set the experimental parameters as shown in Table 1:

Table 1. Experimental parameters

Project	Data
Data structure lookup	Internal structure search
Data language query	Real-time query
Database management	Database management system
Data platform	Deep learning platform
Source lookup	System source lookup
Programming framework	Parallel programming framework
Data rules	Centralized analysis of processing rules
Data management	Resource management system
Data is stored	Internal central memory
Computing framework	Data arithmetic operation
Algorithm analysis	Characteristics analysis
System Settings	Table Settings

3.3 Analysis of Experimental Results

In order to verify the effect of the multi-module integration method of students' habitual learning mode based on deep learning, it is compared with the traditional learning method. The experimental results are shown in Fig. 6:

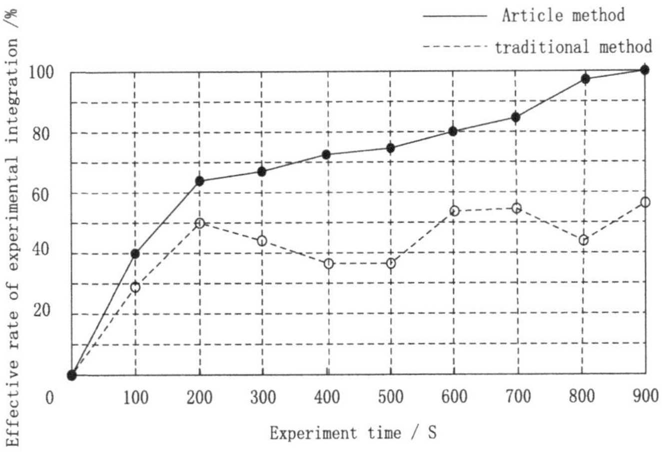

Fig. 6. Comparison of experiments

Comparison Fig. 6 shows that under the same parameters, the experimental integration efficiency of the method in this paper is infinite close to 100%, while the experimental integration efficiency of the traditional method is less than 60%, which shows that the experimental integration efficiency of the method in this paper is high, and the experimental integration efficiency of the traditional method is low, because the data is in the real operation process of research problems, which can not meet the requirements of the system center structure. The method in this paper and The data integration performance in the system is combined to continuously strengthen the data collection management of the system, strengthen the theoretical operation, obtain better comparative data, and integrate efficiently.

4 Conclusion

This paper presents a new more students habit learning model based on the deep learning module integration method, according to the principle of integrating system data collection, data collection and build deep learning three dimension structure model strengthening system operation, select student habit learning mode more integrate module data structure equation and finally realize the study of integral method. Through the comparative analysis of experiments, this paper based on deep learning students habitual learning mode multi-module integration method can improve the integration performance of the system to a higher degree, with better development space.

The number of research publications based on the optimization method of deep learning is increasing exponentially, and deep learning has become an inevitable part of various researches. And deep learning can effectively capture the non-linear and non trivial user project relationship, and can express the data as more complex abstract coding, and can more effectively integrate students' habitual learning information and resources. Therefore, this paper studies students' habitual learning mode, so as to achieve the standardization and deepening of habitual education, and promote the construction of humanistic classroom The construction of the beautiful campus has important practical significance and wide application prospect, which lays the foundation for the healthy growth of students.

Today, Google, Microsoft, Baidu and other well-known high-tech companies with big data are scrambling to invest resources and occupy the technological commanding point of deep learning, precisely because they all see the era of big data, the more complex and powerful depth model can profoundly reveal the responsible and rich information carried in the massive data, and make more accurate prediction of future or unknown events. At the same time of promoting the learning theory and computing theory of deep learning, can we propose a new hierarchical model, which not only has the strong representation ability of the traditional depth model, but also has other advantages, such as easier theoretical analysis. In addition, for specific application problems, how can we design a most suitable depth model to solve the problem? We have seen that there seems to be a common information processing structure such as depth and convolution in both image depth model and language depth model. Even for speech acoustic model, researchers are exploring convolution depth network. Then, a more interesting question is whether there is a general depth model or a modeling language of depth model, which can be used as A unified framework for voice, image, and language? In addition, more research is needed on how to use depth model to represent structured information such as semantics. From the perspective of human evolution, the ability of language is far behind the ability of vision and hearing. In addition to human beings, many animals have a good ability to recognize objects and sounds. Therefore, from this perspective, for neural networks For the structure of collaterals, language is a more difficult task than vision and hearing. To solve this problem successfully is an indispensable step for the realization of artificial intelligence. At present, the parameters of the largest depth model are about 10 billion orders of magnitude, less than one thousandth of human brain. However, due to the limitation of calculation cost, the depth of practical application in products is limited Degree model is much lower than this level. One of the great advantages of depth model is that it is easy to achieve higher accuracy by increasing the model in the case of massive data. Therefore, the development of higher speed hardware suitable for depth model will also be an important direction to improve the recognition rate of depth model.

References

1. Jian-ming, C., Jia-yi, L., Cheng-yong, Y.: Privacy preserving fusion algorithm for data integrity verification in cloud storage. J. Guilin Univ. Technol. **38**(2), 341–347 (2018)
2. Yan, W., Jie, T.: Deep Learning-based personalized paper recommender system. J. Chin. Inf. Process. **32**(4), 114–119 (2018)

3. Zhengping, G., Min, Z.: Fish classification algorithm based on depth learning. Comput. Appl. Softw. **35**(1), 200–205 (2018)
4. Cong, T., Yong-shun, L., Ke-dong, Z., et al.: Object detection method of multi-view SSD based on deep learning. Infrared Laser Eng. **47**(1), 290–298 (2018)
5. Hong-shun, L., Hua, Y., Xiu-jun, G.: Deep learning model for predicting RNA-binding proteins only from primary sequences. J. Comput. Res. Dev. **55**(1), 93–101 (2018)
6. Hai-Hong, E., Wen-Jing, Z.,, Si-Qi, X., et al.: Survey of entity relationship extraction based on deep learning. J. Softw. **30**(6), 1793–1818 (2019)
7. Haojun, L., Zheng, Z., Haidong, G., et al.: Personalized learning resource recommendation from the perspective of deep learning. Mod. Distance Educ. Res. **31**(4), 94–103 (2019)
8. Li-na, Z.: Personal information privacy protection in the informatization construction of university personnel files in the era of big data. Arhives Shanxi **238**(2), 70–72 (2018)
9. Dan-yang, W., Hai-qun, M.: Research on the influencing factors of personal data storage security and privacy protection under network environment. Libr. Theory Pract. **12**(1), 89–95 (2018)
10. Ming, W., Bo, Z., Mao-Nian, W., et al.: A preliminary study of a deep learning-assisted diagnostic system with an artificial intelligence for detection of diabetic retinopathy. Int. Eye Sci. **18**(3), 568–571 (2018)

Curriculum Quality System Model of Entrepreneurship and Innovation Education in Vocational Colleges Across the Straits Based on Internet+

Jun Guo[1(✉)] and Zhan-yong Chen[2,3]

[1] Quanzhou University of Information Engineering College of Software, Quanzhou 362000, China
lcg02650@163.com
[2] International Business School of Beijing, Foreign Studies University, Beijing 100089, China
[3] Zhengzhou Foreign Language School, Affiliated to Beijing Foreign Studies University, Zhengzhou 450121, China

Abstract. With the rapid development of the Internet in the information age, entrepreneurship and innovation education courses have had a huge impact on the traditional teaching model of higher education. In order to improve the quality of entrepreneurship and innovation education in vocational colleges, an internet+ -based model for the quality system of entrepreneurship and innovation education in cross-strait vocational colleges is proposed. To review the literature on entrepreneurship and innovation education courses, curriculum evaluation, and quality evaluation of entrepreneurship and innovation education courses, and to study the elements of entrepreneurship and innovation education course quality evaluation to extract influencing factors of education quality; combined with network analytic hierarchy process (ANP) Super Decision software calculates the weight coefficient of the quality evaluation index system for education courses. Develop and distribute questionnaires for the evaluation of course quality, collect relevant empirical data, and verify the scientificity of the questionnaire through reliability and validity tests. Based on the scoring results and the weight coefficient of the evaluation index system, the key factors affecting the quality of entrepreneurial innovation education courses are derived. Based on the survey data, descriptive statistics, analysis of variance, and Pearson's correlation coefficient method were used to verify the research hypothesis and valuable empirical results were obtained. In addition, the method of this paper is compared with the traditional method to prove the effectiveness of the model of curriculum quality system designed this time.

Keywords: Internet+ · Vocational college · Entrepreneurial innovation · Education courses · Quality system model

S. Liu et al. (Eds.): eLEOT 2020, LNICST 339, pp. 271–285, 2020.
https://doi.org/10.1007/978-3-030-63952-5_23

1 Preface

In order to make better use of the radiation effect of high-quality education resources and meet the increasingly individualized learning needs of learners, educational institutions at all levels in China have comprehensively carried out mixed teaching reforms of traditional courses and entrepreneurial innovation education courses [1]. Many colleges and universities have established entrepreneurship and innovation education courses centers to independently develop entrepreneurship and innovation education courses and carry out traditional digital work of teaching materials. There are also some well-known universities that cooperate with large MOOC platforms to introduce massive high-quality entrepreneurial and innovative resources directly into traditional courses. Since 2012, Udacity, Coursera and Edx have provided hundreds of high-quality entrepreneurship and innovation education courses to registered learners from all over the world. China's Peking University, Tsinghua University and other top universities also joined in in 2013, and have established cooperative relationships with foreign entrepreneurship and innovation education curriculum platforms, sharing the independently developed entrepreneurial innovation education courses on the platform [2]. In the context of Internet +, entrepreneurship and innovation education courses are not simply using Internet tools to transfer traditional courses to online platforms. We must organically combine the course attributes of the entrepreneurial innovation education course from the characteristics of the network environment in the course development and teaching design to promote the deeper integration of online and offline education resources.

Improving the quality of entrepreneurship and innovation education is an issue that cannot be ignored in the development of higher education. At present, many colleges and universities have launched a wide range of entrepreneurship and innovation education courses, and the number of students learning entrepreneurship and innovation education courses is increasing. However, many problems have been exposed in the development of entrepreneurship and innovation education courses, which have not yet been effectively resolved. Research on the quality evaluation of entrepreneurial innovation education curriculum has become an urgent problem to be solved [3]. At present, there are few empirical studies on the quality evaluation of entrepreneurship and innovation education courses, and more is to explore the quality of entrepreneurship and innovation education courses from a macro level, and there is no analysis of the quality evaluation of entrepreneurship and innovation education courses from a micro perspective. By constructing an indicator system for the quality evaluation of entrepreneurial innovation education courses, this paper conducts an empirical study on the quality of entrepreneurial innovation education courses, collects and analyzes relevant empirical data, and provides effective empirical materials and method references for the study of the quality evaluation of entrepreneurial innovation education courses. The improvement and development of the curriculum evaluation system for entrepreneurial innovation education has enriched the significance of the quality management theory of entrepreneurial innovation education curriculum [4].

High-quality educational resources are the core value of entrepreneurship and innovation education courses. Ensuring the quality of courses is the foundation for the sustainable and healthy development of entrepreneurship and innovation education. Therefore, the evaluation of the quality of entrepreneurship and innovation education courses is an important first step to improve the quality. In order to effectively promote the popularization and internationalization of higher education, bring into play the radiation effect of large-scale entrepreneurship and innovation education courses, and form a new way of lifelong learning system, it is necessary to place the improvement of the quality of entrepreneurship and innovation education courses in an important strategic position [5]. This paper uses questionnaire surveys and data analysis to study the current situation of the quality of entrepreneurship and innovation education courses, finds out the problems in the quality management of entrepreneurship and innovation education courses through statistical analysis, and gives practical suggestions for the key influencing factors of entrepreneurship and innovation education courses. The quality of entrepreneurship and innovation education courses and the promotion of mixed teaching reforms provide effective evidence and policy references.

2 Cross-Strait Vocational Schools Entrepreneurship and Innovation Education Curriculum Quality System Model Design

2.1 Analysis of the Elements of the Quality System Model of Entrepreneurial Innovation Education

The selection based on core elements should have the principles of guidance, timeliness, entrepreneurial innovation, practicality, and acceptability. At the same time, the preliminary selection of survey results should be based on the rules that the level of selection results should be consistent. The core elements of the system model in this paper are The core elements of space, regional cognition, human-land conception, time perspective, comprehensive thinking, entrepreneurial innovation practice ability, map skills, globalization awareness, survivability, scale correlation, entrepreneurial innovation expression, entrepreneurial innovation tools and technologies, etc. [6].

The results of the preliminary selection of the core literacy elements of this article are combined with the connotation of the entrepreneurial innovation education curriculum standards of the vocational colleges across the Taiwan Strait to combine the connotations of the four major elements and the connotations of the main performances (Fig. 1).

Analyze the connotation and significance of the five entrepreneurial innovation core literacy embodied in the core literacy of entrepreneurial innovation, and clarify their respective priorities in constructing the core literacy system model of entrepreneurial innovation, and clarify the system element relationship for the construction process.

As can be seen from the above figure, based on the survey results, the elements that have been preliminarily selected to build a model of the core literacy system for entrepreneurial innovation can be incorporated into the four core literacy.

Entrepreneurship and innovation educators have pointed out that "all entrepreneurial innovation phenomena, all entrepreneurial innovation events, all entrepreneurial innovation effects, and all entrepreneurial innovation processes on the surface of the earth all take place on the basis of the entrepreneurial innovation space. The entrepreneurial innovation The systematic research of space, or the connotation of the distribution, form, structure, laws and other connotations of the entrepreneurial innovation space, the rest of

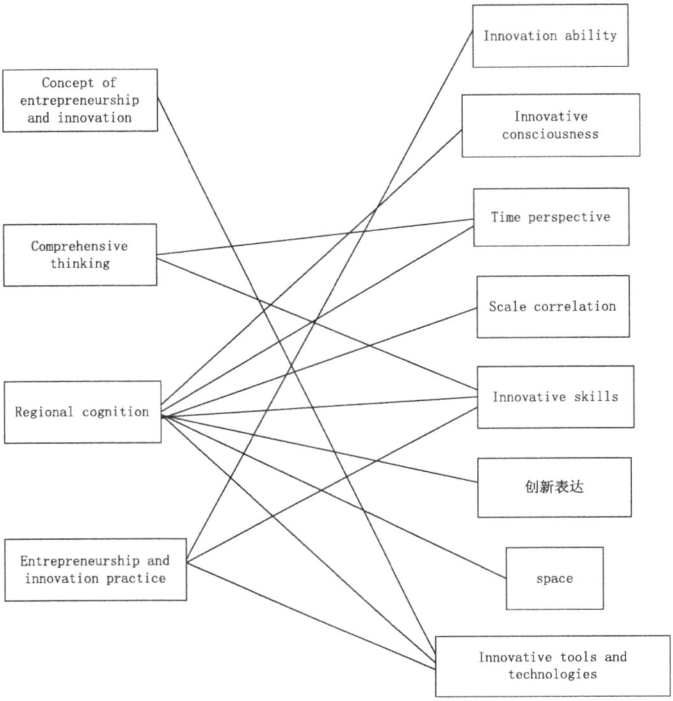

Fig. 1. Consolidation of the core elements of the preliminary selection

the theoretical principles related to entrepreneurial innovation, without exception, will lose their existence. "Entrepreneurship and innovation emphasizes regionality. Regions are divided according to certain standards from a spatial scale. From the perspective of space, everything is an entrepreneurial innovation perspective of entrepreneurship and innovation education. It is the basic idea of entrepreneurship and innovation education. The four literacy connotations given by the group are not appropriate in the simple integration of entrepreneurial innovation space into regional cognition. Therefore, the core elements for constructing the core literacy system model of entrepreneurial innovation in this paper are the four elements of core literacy and the spatial perspective, that is, the human-land concept, spatial perspective, comprehensive thinking, regional cognition, and entrepreneurial innovation practice.

2.2 Set the Weight Coefficient of the Quality System Index for Entrepreneurial Innovation Education

Considering that the entrepreneurial innovation education curriculum is an organic combination of teaching activities and network environment, the construction of a curriculum quality system must cover all influencing factors. And there are many factors influencing the quality of entrepreneurial innovation education courses. Judging from the characteristics of the curriculum activities, the possibility of maintaining independent existence among indicators is very small, and there may be a certain interdependence and interaction relationship. Therefore, in the selection of methods, we must consider the impact of this correlation between indicators on the quality evaluation results of entrepreneurial innovation education courses. At present, the construction of the evaluation index system for the quality of entrepreneurship and innovation education courses is mainly based on the AHP method, which cannot take into account the dependencies and feedback relationships between the factors that influence the quality of entrepreneurship and innovation education courses. Weighting factor for quality indicators. Calculate the unweighted supermatrix. The unweighted supermatrix can choose the criteria of the judgment matrix and the element set of which the judgment matrix is constructed. The association of all elements in all element sets will be quantitatively reflected in the way of this judgment matrix. After the unweighted super matrix is established, the super matrix can be weighted. Finally, in order to reflect the dependency relationship of the elements, the stability of the weighted matrix is calculated by calculating the limit super matrix of the weighted matrix [7].

According to the calculation results of the Super Decision software, the global weights of the quality evaluation indicators of entrepreneurial innovation education courses are obtained. The results are shown in Table 1.

Through the combination of qualitative and quantitative methods, a quality evaluation index system for entrepreneurship and innovation education courses was established and weights were determined for each indicator, making sufficient preparations for the construction of the entrepreneurship and innovation education course quality system.

2.3 Constructing a Quality System Model for Entrepreneurship and Innovation Education

The construction of the core literacy system model of vocational colleges' entrepreneurship and innovation is the unification of guiding ideology, operating methods, construction principles, model frameworks, and specific filling index systems, and requires coordinated operations.

There are two basic methods for constructing a model of the core literacy system of entrepreneurial innovation: the first is the discipline-based thinking, based on the characteristics of the entrepreneurial innovation discipline, selecting core and key elements from the constituent elements of the entrepreneurial innovation literacy to build a system; Thinking, starting from social needs, and seeking contributions to the cultivation of future qualified citizens in the discipline of entrepreneurship and innovation, involves the selection of key elements [8]. The "Opinion" points out that cultivating students' core literacy system is to enable students to have the necessary characters and key abilities to meet the needs of lifelong development and social development. It is a learning result that trains students according to social needs and is a socially-oriented need Based on this, this article adopts the second idea to build a core literacy system for entrepreneurship and innovation in vocational colleges.

The core literacy system model of entrepreneurship and innovation in vocational colleges is the main content of the academic quality standards reached by students after the completion of the higher education stage. The level division of each element constitutes the main part of the system model and should be hierarchical. In the process

Table 1. Global power of quality evaluation indicators for entrepreneurial innovation education

Control layer	Two level index	Three level index	ANP weight
Curriculum quality of entrepreneurship and innovation education	Curriculum preset	Course description	0.060090
		Environment creation	0.014004
		Goal setting	0.031365
		Interest arousing	0.121398
	Curriculum interaction	Student interaction	0.047685
		Media presentation	0.154391
		Target collaboration	0.084266
		Interface design	0.033207
		Teacher-student interaction	0.264721
	Course support	network transmission	0.030863
		Operational assistance	0.039793
		Content linkage	0.012347
		Download mode	0.027683
	Curriculum analysis	Data analysis	0.011360
		Achievement evaluation	0.006441
		Intelligent learning	0.045928
		Duration of course	0.006085
		Language standard	0.008374

of level-specific division of the index system, the thematic method of interpretation, the method of screening elements, etc. are mainly used; the reference teaching goal statement process includes the Majestic behavior statement method, Glenland internal and explicit behavior combination statement method, Eisner performance Declarative method. The model construction process in this paper mainly adopts a flexible declarative method combining three technologies, supplemented by literature reference method.

The core literacy system model of entrepreneurship and innovation in vocational colleges is the concrete implementation of the core literacy system in the discipline of entrepreneurship and innovation in China's higher education stage. The construction process should follow the following principles: first, it must reflect the future entrepreneurial and innovative needs of qualified citizens; It is necessary to highlight the unique educational value of the entrepreneurial and innovative discipline; thirdly, to lead the direction of entrepreneurial and innovative curriculum reform and teacher professional development; fourthly, to undertake effective vertical connection with other academic levels; fourthly, to closely follow international Under the premise of the reform trend of entrepreneurial innovation education, we should pay attention to the current situation of China's basic national conditions. Sixth, we should pay attention to the integration of horizontal lines between different disciplines.

Entrepreneurial innovators point out that looking at everything from space is the basic perspective of entrepreneurial innovation. The American National Entrepreneurship and Innovation Curriculum Standard states that a spatial perspective enables students to participate in human, regional, and environmental issues related to the world around them; it helps students answer important questions such as past, present, and future spatial organizational structures, and can predict events in different regions The results and predictions of what might happen under certain conditions underscore the importance of a spatial perspective for training qualified future talents in the country. Based on this, the spatial perspective should run through the entire process of cultivating high school students' entrepreneurial innovation core literacy. Based on this, based on the four major elements of the standard group of entrepreneurship and innovation courses in vocational colleges, this article builds a model of the core literacy system for entrepreneurship and innovation of higher vocational students as shown in Fig. 2.

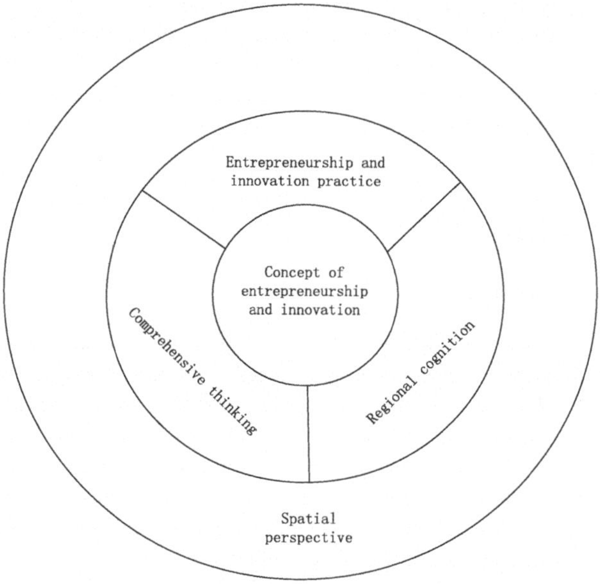

Fig. 2. Model of core literacy system for entrepreneurship and innovation of higher vocational students

The model is viewed from the inside to the outside. At the innermost level is the concept of entrepreneurship and innovation, which is essential for the study of entrepreneurship and innovation. The correct concept of entrepreneurship and innovation is the ultimate goal of cultivating the core literacy system of entrepreneurship and innovation for higher vocational students. Located on the second layer are comprehensive thinking, regional cognition, and entrepreneurial innovation practice: the discipline of entrepreneurial innovation has two characteristics of comprehensiveness and regionality. Based on this, two major factors of regional cognition and comprehensive thinking of the core literacy of entrepreneurial innovation are proposed; In addition to these two characteristics, entrepreneurship and innovation is still a highly practical discipline. The scientific process of establishing a scientific concept of entrepreneurship and innovation, cultivating comprehensive thinking, and regional cognitive literacy cannot be separated from human practice. Higher vocational education should be cultivated more. Students' practical ability, instead of doing problems every day in the classroom; the three together constitute a way to cultivate the correct concept of human and land [9]. At the outermost level is a spatial perspective. Comprehensive thinking, regional cognition, and entrepreneurial innovation practice are inseparable from the spatial scale. It is like fish cannot be separated from water. The entrepreneurial innovation learning process cannot be separated from the perspective of spatial perspective. The phenomenon of innovation is the prerequisite for cultivating the three core elements of entrepreneurial innovation in the second tier.

Based on the composition and connotation of the five core literacy, construct a core literacy model for entrepreneurial innovation, as shown in Table 2:

From a horizontal perspective, the model is divided into core literacy, components, and specific connotations from left to right, following the construction idea of dividing core literacy by components and elaborating the content of each component. From a vertical perspective, the five core literacy are juxtaposed, the levels of each component are kept consistent, and the connotation interpretation focuses on operability and measurability [10].

3 Empirical Analysis

3.1 Questionnaire Analysis

This survey researches different types of student groups in science and engineering, social sciences, and art design disciplines in vocational colleges across the Taiwan Straits, respectively, and collects and collects data. The distribution of samples is shown in Tables 3 to 5 below. The number of boys participating in the survey accounted for 28.4%, and girls accounted for 71.6%. Among them, the number of seniors is the largest, with 132, and the number of seniors is the smallest, 104. The number of people classified by subject category is as follows: humanities and social sciences, science and engineering, agriculture, medical science, and art design (Table 4).

The average score of each indicator can be calculated through data calculation, see Table 6.

It can be seen from Table 6 that overall, the course interaction score is the lowest, and the course support score is the highest. The scores in descending order are course support, course analysis, course preset, and course interaction. The average scores for course description, goal setting, content connection, and course duration are relatively high; the average scores for environment creation, interest stimulation, interface design,

Table 2. Model of core literacy system of entrepreneurship and innovation education for higher vocational students

Five qualities	Component	Concrete connotation
Entrepreneurial innovation	The impact of entrepreneurship and innovation on Students	Correctly stating that entrepreneurship and innovation are the basis of human existence, and establishing scientific outlook on innovation, learning and education
		Rational view on the impact of entrepreneurship and innovation on human activities, and take reasonable measures
	The influence of students on entrepreneurship and innovation	Explain the process of students' activities adapting to entrepreneurship and innovation
		On the basis of following the learning law, we should transform the learning environment reasonably
		Analyze the impact of transforming learning environment
	Students' coordination of entrepreneurship and innovation	A correct understanding of the evolution of entrepreneurship and innovation education
		In the process of practice, we should follow the concept of coordinated development of entrepreneurship and innovation, and establish a science and technology department Entrepreneurship and innovation of learning
Spatial perspective	Feature space location	Be good at observing research objects and forming awareness of overall spatial pattern
	Feature space analysis	Integrate spatial related elements and analyze their interrelations comprehensively
Comprehensive thinking	Object innovation	Study regional integration and analyze its leading factors

(*continued*)

Table 2. (*continued*)

Five qualities	Component	Concrete connotation
	Comprehensive analysis	Comprehensive analysis of the leading factors according to the problem orientation, including the integration of elements, space-time and education
Innovative cognition	Organization area	Region objectification, frame space position
	Learning area	Horizontal and vertical scanning, overall perception of the main characteristics of entrepreneurship and innovation
		Analyze the learning environment and conditions that form the main characteristics of the region
		Rational evaluation of regional policies to promote regional sustainable development
Entrepreneurship and innovation practice	Innovation and technology consciousness	Be good at using science and technology to describe the characteristics of learning environment
	Practical ability and quality	Using the knowledge we have learned to explain and reason the innovation around us, and making use of it to form a comprehensive thinking of attention perception explanation of innovation
		To survive under the condition of learning and maintain the solid and optimistic character of accumulation

and performance evaluation are relatively low. The environment creation score is the most serious in the course preset, and the interest stimulation score is also relatively low. The scores of student interaction, goal collaboration, and teacher-student interaction in the course interaction are relatively high; interface design scores are the worst. The content support part of the course supports the highest scores in connection, and the lowest download score. The order from highest to lowest is content contact, network transmission, operation assistance and download method. In the course analysis, scores were severely lost. From the analysis and comparison, it can be seen that the interactive part of the course with a low score is the key aspect that we need to pay attention to

Table 3. List of sample gender distribution

	Male	Female	Total
Number	130	328	458
Percentage	28.4	71.6	100
Effective percentage	28.4	71.6	100
Cumulative percentage	28.4	100	

Table 4. List of sample grade distributions

	Number	Percentage	Effective percentage	Cumulative percentage
First grade	106	23.1	23.1	23.1
Second grade	116	25.3	25.3	48.5
Grade three	104	22.7	22.7	71.2
Fourth grade	132	28.8	28.8	100
Total	458	100	100	

Table 5. List of sample disciplines

	Number	Percentage	Effective percentage	Cumulative percentage
Science, technology, agriculture and medicine	184	40.2	40.2	40.2
Social science	196	42.8	42.8	83
Art design	78	17	17	100
Total	458	100	100	

when formulating the recommended strategy. At the same time, environmental creation, interest stimulation, interface design and performance assessment are also key factors in improving the quality of our entrepreneurial innovation courses.

Since the weight coefficient of each indicator has been determined in the foregoing, we calculate the weighted comprehensive score based on the survey data scoring situation. The results are shown in Table 7 and Table 8 below.

From Table 7, we can see that the number of valid observations is 229, of which the first grade is the highest, and the fourth grade is the lowest. The comprehensive scores for grades one through four increase in order: 4.0285, 3.9291, 3.9148 and 3.9090. The averages of the sample average 95% confidence interval estimates include the total averages. We know that students in all grades have no significant difference in the overall scores of the entrepreneurial innovation courses and the overall comprehensive scores.

Table 6. List of average scores of various indicators

Control layer	Two level index	Average score	Three level index	Average score
Curriculum quality of entrepreneurship and innovation education in vocational colleges across the Straits	Curriculum preset	3.98	Course description	4.07
			Environment creation	3.83
			Goal setting	4.16
			Interest arousing	3.87
	Curriculum interaction Course support	3.91	Student interaction	3.93
			Media presentation	3.90
			Target collaboration	3.94
			Interface design	3.84
			Teacher-student interaction	3.93
		4.02	network transmission	4.05
			Operational assistance	3.98
			Content linkage	4.07
			Download mode	3.96
	Curriculum analysis	4.01	Data analysis	4.01
			Achievement evaluation	3.87
			Intelligent learning	3.94
			Duration of course	4.15
			Language standard	4.08

From Table 8, we can see that the comprehensive score of the science, technology, agriculture and medical group is the lowest, and the overall score of the art design group is the highest. The comprehensive scores in order from low to high are science and technology, agriculture and medical science, humanities and social sciences, and art design. The intervals formed by the 95% confidence interval estimates of the sample averages in the table include the total averages. We know that the students' scores on the

Table 7. List of comprehensive grades for different grades

		First grade	Second grade	Grade three	Fourth grade	Total
Number		106	116	104	132	458
Average value		4.0285	3.9291	3.9148	3.9090	3.9431
Standard deviation		0.5023	0.5583	0.5444	0.5250	0.5316
Standard error		0.0690	0.0733	0.0755	0.0646	0.0351
95% confidence interval of mean	Lower limit	3.8901	3.7823	3.7632	3.7799	3.8738
	Upper limit	4.1670	4.0759	4.0663	4.0380	4.0123
Minimum value		2.18	2.39	2.47	2.67	2.18
Maximum value		4.88	5.00	4.97	4.98	5.00

Table 8. Summary scores of different subject categories

		Science, technology, agriculture and medicine	Social science	Art design	Total
Number		184	196	78	458
Average value		3.8322	3.9786	4.1152	3.9431
Standard deviation		0.5578	0.5150	0.4584	0.5316
Standard error		0.0582	0.0520	0.0734	0.0351
95% confidence interval of mean	Lower limit	3.7167	3.8754	3.9666	3.8738
	Upper limit	3.9477	4.0818	4.2638	4.0123
Minimum value		2.18	2.47	2.98	2.18
Maximum value		4.98	5.00	4.88	5.00

entrepreneurial and innovative courses are not significantly different from the overall scores.

3.2 Comparative Analysis

The questionnaire survey and corresponding analysis above prove the effectiveness of this method. Next, the method is compared with the traditional method, and a class in a vocational college is selected as the comparison object. The design model and traditional method are used to evaluate the teaching quality., The comparison results are shown in Table 9:

Table 9. Comparative analysis table

	Traditional method	This article method
System integrity	60%	95%
Teaching evaluation accuracy	55%	92%
Student satisfaction	70%	98%

Through comparative analysis, it can be seen that the quality system model of entrepreneurship innovation education curriculum designed in this paper is superior to the traditional methods in student satisfaction and integrity, which proves the effectiveness and practicality of the design model in this paper.

4 Concluding Remarks

This article puts forward a model of the quality system of entrepreneurship and innovation education courses based on the Internet + across straits vocational colleges. The construction of the evaluation index system for entrepreneurship and innovation education has always been the focus of domestic research on the quality of entrepreneurship innovation education courses. However, there are few empirical studies on the evaluation index system that has been constructed. A questionnaire survey on the quality evaluation of entrepreneurship and innovation education courses collected relevant empirical data and conducted empirical analysis in order to provide effective empirical materials and practical experience for further research.

Fund Projects. Internet plus occupation project innovation research project FBJG20190139.

References

1. Xiaotang, L.: Research on the construction of innovation and entrepreneurship education curriculum system in higher vocational colleges in the internet era. China Inf. Technol. Educ. **12**, 98–101 (2017)
2. Xiuli, L.: The construction of innovation and entrepreneurship education system in vocational colleges. Educ. Vocat. **16**, 57–61 (2019)
3. Juanhui, D.: Construction of innovation and entrepreneurship education system in higher vocational colleges from the perspective of strategic management. Vocat. Techn. Educ. **38**(2), 52–54 (2017)
4. Xianjie, B.: The construction of innovation and entrepreneurship education system for college students majoring in archives. Arch. Manag. **5**, 53–55 (2017)
5. Yi, Q., Luwen, Z., Geng, F.: SWOT analysis of entrepreneur and innovation education in medical colleges. Chin. Health Serv. Manag. **36**(06), 452–455 (2019)
6. Yongxiang, W., Yijun, L., Xueli, H.: Exploration and construction of the curriculum system for the cloud computing technology and application specialty of higher vocational education—based on the investigation on the national first scheme of higher vocational demonstration colleges. Vocat. Tech. Educ. **38**(8), 29–32 (2017)

7. Jing-yi, W.: Research on the mechanism of innovation and entrepreneurship education to enhances college students 'opportunity-identification ability. Technoeconomics Manag. Res. **08**, 32–38 (2019)
8. Xiaozhou, X., Hao, N.I.: Towards 2050: vision and strategies of building an innovation and entrepreneurship education ecosystem. China High. Educ. Res. (01), 53–56 + 103 (2018)
9. Xueying, Z.: Research on promoting mechanism of innovation and entrepreneurship education in American higher education institutions. Vocat. Tech. Educ. **38**(9), 66–71 (2017)
10. Liewei, X., Hongmin, R., Jianshe, W.: Study on the relationship between Tao Xingzhi's education thoughts and innovation and entrepreneurship talents training in higher vocational colleges. Vocat. Tech. Educ. **38**(07), 63–68 (2017)

Design of General Integrated Teaching System for Operational Research

Jing Liu[1], Jun-feng Qiao[1], and Sha Yu[2(✉)]

[1] School of Mathematics and Statistics, Nanyang Institute of Technology, Nanyang 473000, Henan, China
liujign3133@163.com

[2] Sports Department, Shaanxi University of Traditional Chinese Medicine, Xianyang 712046, China
yusha4431@163.com

Abstract. In order to solve the problems of fixed teaching mode and limited learning content, this paper puts forward the design method of general integrated teaching system for split class oriented to operational research. In order to improve the operation effect of the system and improve the hardware configuration of the system reasonably, the 64 MB video card of VRAM and AMD Athlon processor are selected to provide the hardware operation effect of the system, further optimize the software operation process of the integrated teaching system, and finally realize the reasonable design of the system. Finally, the experimental results show that the detection curve of the proposed system is higher than that of the comparison method, and it is maintained above 89%, which is more practical than the traditional teaching system.

Keywords: Operations research · Divided class · Integrated teaching · Teaching system · Hardware configuration

1 Introduction

In order to solve the problems of fixed place and limited learning content of traditional teaching mode, arouse students' interest and cultivate students' ability of independent learning and independent thinking, teaching institutions all over the world are trying to make use of the latest technology, such as multimedia technology and network technology to establish new teaching mode [1]. But for many kinds of courses with loose knowledge structure, rich knowledge points and wide knowledge scope, multimedia and network teaching still can not meet the needs of teachers and students. Based on this design and development of a set of teaching system based on the presentation and interaction of the sub-class, operations research as an example of this course teaching design and implementation [2]. It is necessary to consider the characteristics of the subject teaching in order to select the teaching content of the subject to be taught. The common physics classes are mainly divided into concept class, regular class, exercise class

S. Liu et al. (Eds.): eLEOT 2020, LNICST 339, pp. 286–297, 2020.
https://doi.org/10.1007/978-3-030-63952-5_24

and review class. Because there are many physical models involved in co-ordination, paradigm selection in lectures is critical and should be flexible, simple or complex, but not too complex. Students can learn some basic knowledge, including basic concepts, basic laws and basic methods, through the analysis of examples, and students can be inspired by the original examples to think of some details or more in-depth and breadth problems, which can be taught to students to explore independently as a blank content [3]. To learn basic concepts, laws, or methods by observing or operating an experiment. It provides a new solution to improve the existing classroom teaching mode by the ability of real-time 3D spatial representation and human-computer interaction. The general integrated teaching mode of the divided classroom arouses the students' initiative with the visualized teaching content and the game-like learning mode. The students can look for the interest points and expand the knowledge from the points and areas. The general integrated course space of the divided classroom can be used for teaching and playing.

2 Universal Integrated Teaching System for Divided Classes

2.1 System Hardware Configuration

The general function design structure of the system refers to the composition of the whole system and the physical and logical relationship between the parts and elements of the system [4]. The main task of the overall structure design is to define each function module, the system combines Windows XP operating system and later version or Mac OS X10 operating system and later version. System requirements for running Maya 2013 (64-bit); Windows: 7 SP1 operating system or XP x64 SP2 operating system; Mac OS X 10. 7. x operating system; Red Hat Enterprise Linux 6. 0 WS operating system. AMD Athlon processors (or later) supported by Windows and Linux Intel Pentium with the SSE3 instruction set.

Macintosh: A Macintosh computer with an Intel 64-bit processor. Certified hardware accelerator OpenGL graphics card. Microsoft Internet Explorer 8 Internet Browser or later, Apple Safari Web Browser, or Mozilla Firefox Web Browser. Properly handle the internal relations of modules and the call relationship and data connection between them, and define the internal structure of each module to display the hardware configuration of the integrated teaching system as follows (Fig. 1):

In the integrated teaching system hardware configuration, the system requirements to run Unity3D 3. 5. 5 are: Windows: XP SP2 or later; Mac OS X: Intel CPU & "Leopard" 10. 5 or later (note that Unity3D is not tested on Windows or OSX server versions).

VRAM 64 MB graphics card and pixel shader and 4 texture units [5]. Any video card should apply [6]. Using occlusion culling requires GPU occlusion queries (some Intel GPUs do not support this). The rest only depends on the complexity of the project.

System requirements for Unity3 D content: Windows XP operating system or later. Mac OS X 10. 5 operating system or later [7]. Computer platform configuration requirements:

Core Duo Intel Core Duo processors or higher end models. 1 GB of memory and above. NVIDIA GeFore GTX_560 graphics card and higher configuration or ATI Radeon HD_58_50 graphics card and higher configuration (desktop); NVIDIA GeFore

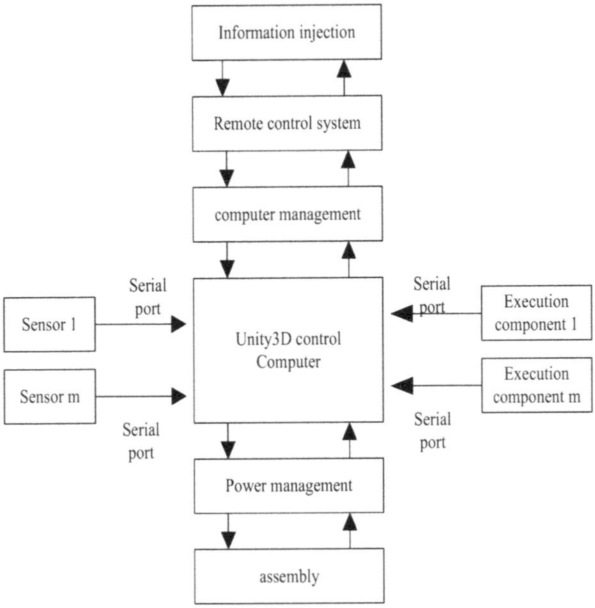

Fig. 1. Hardware configuration of integrated teaching system

GTX460 graphics card and higher configuration or AMD Radeon HD 7730M and higher configuration (laptop).

Unity3D iOS production system requirements: an Intel-based Mac. Mac iOS X Snow Leopard 10. 6 or later [8]. The rest only depends on the complexity of the project. Based on the above hardware structure, further optimize the system sensor interface circuit, the specific structure is as follows (Fig. 2):

Based on the above equipment, the system hardware configuration is optimized to improve system operation efficiency.

2.2 System Software Steps

Based on the above hardware structure, the software flow of the system is optimized. Because the sub-teaching mode is the teaching mode that completes the teaching task through teacher's lecturing, internalization, discussion and exchange. Its core philosophy is to allocate half of the classroom teaching time to lectures and half to interactive learning for discussions among students, so that each student can improve and achieve diversity at his or her previous level [9]. Therefore, in the process of system design, the teaching cycle is divided into three processes: teaching, internalization, and discussion. The sub-class teaching system requires students not to do the preview before class. It not only includes the characteristics of traditional classroom teachers teaching students before class, but also has the characteristics of student-student interaction, teacher-student interaction and promoting autonomous learning in the discussion class [10]. Combining with the

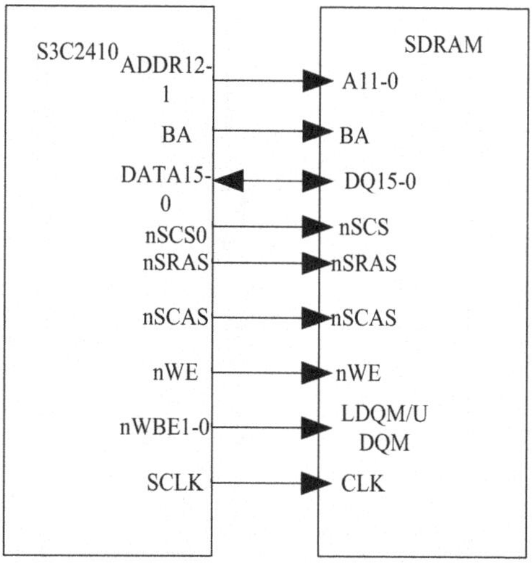

Fig. 2. Circuit diagram of sensor interface

teaching content of Operations Research, this paper optimizes the present integrated teaching mode of divided classes as follows (Fig. 3):

In the course of discussion and communication, students should have a full understanding of the information before teaching it to others. This requires students to go beyond simple repetition and process the information carefully. Fine processing of learning content, so it is easy to grasp the meaning of learning content, so as to enter the long-term memory, improve the retention time of information in the brain, thus improving the learning effect. Action research in education mainly refers to the research carried out by the actors themselves in order to improve their own practice [11]. System optimization has at least three key features: participation, improvement, and system disclosure. Participation means that the teacher is not only the practitioner but also the researcher, and the teacher should participate in the whole research process; improvement means that the aim of action research is to improve the teacher's educational practice and concept, and not only the researcher's tool; system and openness means that the action research differs from the solution of random problems, needs scientific research methods, and is carried out in a planned, systematic and self-critical manner, and the research process should be open to the public and enter the field of public criticism [12].

In the initial stage of implementing the design of the sub-classroom teaching system, the new class teaching is mainly adopted, and the students are assigned to finish the homework after class. According to the feedback from the students, the school requires the students to study the subjects of the College Entrance Examination first, which makes it difficult for the students to finish their physics homework. Then changed to use the classroom on the points, strict division of a class can be completed in the classroom learning content, so that students do homework in the classroom for internalization absorption. In the course of teaching, students should read the whole textbook according to the contents of the lectures, mark the key points on the textbook and make proper notes. Then they should think over the reference questions further. Over time, the number

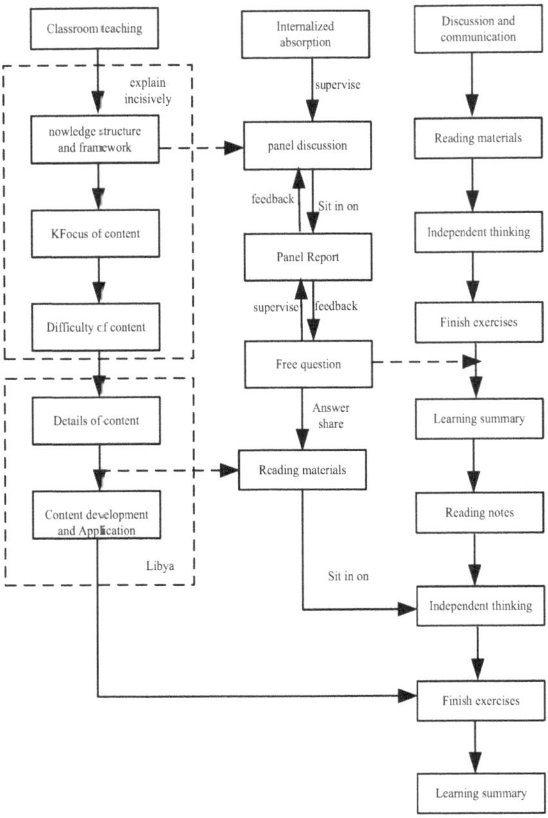

Fig. 3. Integrated teaching model with divided classes

of people with access to integrated learning systems has increased over a given period of time [13]. Some students fill in the knowledge frame by reading the textbook at the end of the lecture, and some students don't finish the arrangement of knowledge points, but do the title directly, and find the knowledge points again when they meet the title they won't do. Less than half of the students use the integrated teaching system seriously after finishing the knowledge points and practice. More than half of the students only mark or simply mark in the textbook or the original text.

In the application and communication of classroom teaching mode, students should fully understand the knowledge before teaching others, which requires students to go beyond simple retelling and fine processing of information. Such processing often involves the significance of information and deep processing such as analysis, comparison and judgment of information [14]. The specific processing steps are as follows (Fig. 4):

Based on the above steps, the knowledge base of teaching content is selected. The knowledge base is a regular aggregation to mine different effective data. In the process

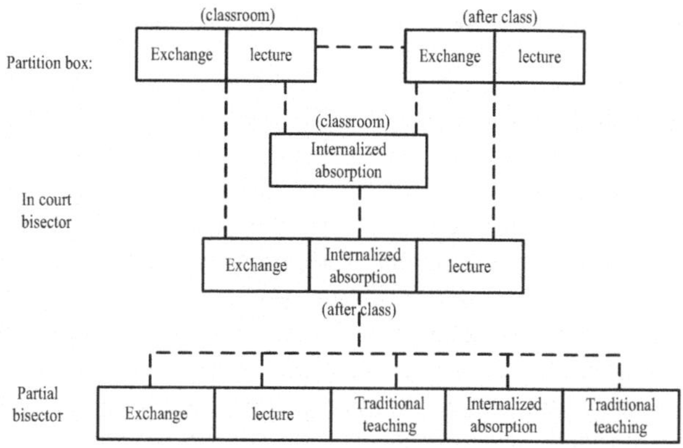

Fig. 4. Teaching information processing steps of co-ordination

of system design, considering that the model is ultimately imported into Unity for programming, we try our best to reduce the number of models, save computer resources, and reduce the hardware requirement of the teaching system, so as to improve the running speed of the system. In order to make the scene of the exhibition hall look more real, let the learners have a stronger sense of experience, and have a feeling of immersion, it is necessary to draw a map for the model, so that the teaching system can achieve a relatively perfect visual effect.

Data mining algorithm based on data entropy is used to optimize the system operation [15]. Let N = $(Q,\ E,\ R,\ T)$ be the characteristic value of the information of the integrated database, and if the outliers $\frac{Q}{E} = \{a_1, a_2, \cdots, a_m\}$ and p are the entropy coefficients of the data, then:

$$H_a(E) = -\frac{N\{Q-(a_m)\}}{E}\sum_{i=1}^{m}\log[p(a_i') - 1] \tag{1}$$

Furthermore, the characteristic values of research object a are mined. If $H(E)$ is the information entropy of $E, H_a(E)$ is the information entropy of m after data mining object E. Let the collected data information be T, and the teaching content is classified as V and x as the students' learning progress. Then we can get the attributes of information a, b, c:

$$\Delta w = \prod \frac{x(a+\mathrm{b}+\mathrm{c})^m}{2\lim\limits_{x\to\infty} VH(E)}\sum \log H_a(E) - Nm \tag{2}$$

Based on the above algorithm, the corresponding integrated teaching model function is established. In order to ensure the smooth design of the system, the classification of teaching content is designed according to the model function, and the system software running flow is improved by combining various coding mechanisms of the real agent to realize the optimization of the general integrated teaching system in the sub-classroom.

2.3 Realization of Integrated Teaching in Different Classes

Compared with the traditional teaching system, the general integrated teaching system does not require students to preview, and emphasizes the importance of teaching, but the content of teaching is different from the traditional teaching form. Classroom discussion is a well-prepared discussion based on the construction of the individuation of knowledge. Therefore, the biggest difference between the general integrated teaching system and the traditional teaching system is that it does not rely on teaching to make students make progress. To some extent, the teaching system provides students with learning situation, subject knowledge structure and direction of construction, but depends more on students' autonomous learning and group discussion to complete learning. Compared with the latter three teaching modes, the general integrated teaching in different classes does not need preview, and the students can learn directly from listening to the lectures, the lectures reflect the knowledge structure, provide the scaffolding for the students, and let the students learn independently after a certain height. There is a difference between the internalized absorption of general integrated teaching and the self-study process of efficient classroom. First, students are required to carry out independently. Secondly, allowing students to think individually can go beyond textbooks, syllabuses and even disciplines, not only for knowledge, but also across the realm of thought and emotion.

In the process of systematic teaching, administrators need to make PPT courseware and introduce the materials of the sub-class in advance, and introduce the general integrated teaching system to students during class time. First of all, the system does not encourage students to learn new content in advance in the classroom before the new content to reduce the burden of after-school work, not preview can reduce the occupation of students' after-school time. Second, improve the teaching module, tell the students that the teaching is different from the traditional teaching, the teaching content is only the framework of physical knowledge, key points and difficulties, do not introduce details, do not ask questions, do not discuss in the teaching process, the teaching style does not have the performance, leaving room for students to understand through independent learning. Thirdly, it introduces the module of doing homework, which is different from the traditional form of homework. Most of the traditional physics homework is in the form of exercises. This paper mainly introduces the connotation and significance of the homework of integrated teaching system, and gives some suggestions on how to complete the integrated teaching system. Fourth, optimize the discussion module, the discussion of the sub-class is prepared to discuss, after the completion of the homework process, for their own integrated teaching system within the group communication and discussion. At the end of the group discussion, some of the groups will report the results of the discussion. The group will not have a leader. A group member will be randomly selected to report the results of the discussion and the existing problems. For a group of existing problems, the other group can be resolved on the spot to give an answer, if the other group did not answer or the answer is not perfect by the teacher to give additional answers, but the speech and answer do not comment. Finally, you can give a certain amount of time for the whole class to ask questions freely. The answers to the questions can be classmates or teachers. Then the teachers make some summaries according to the discussion.

Based on the above steps, the original teaching software, teaching content and teaching modules are further integrated, and the error handling process in the system operation is investigated. In the process of system design, it is necessary to detect the user's identity, and authenticate the user when he logs on the system, so as to avoid logging failure and loss of information. Based on this, the user's course content browsing information and other learning information are recorded and stored. In order to reduce the problems caused by the ineffective operation of the teaching system, a new online message module and an online question answering module are added in the system link. When a user leaves a message or answers a question, he will be alerted that the message or the question answering connection fails. Combined with C+ language to optimize the system running code, to improve the teaching system running process, based on the teaching system running basis table for specification, as follows (Table 1).

Table 1. Flow chart of teaching system

Parameter type	Data	Field length	Meaning
Single precision	Int	8	Main key position
Floating-point	U-Int	4	Login account
Multi precision	Nvarchar	97	User status
Multi precision	Nvarchar	97	User password
Floating-point	U-Int	4	Remarks information
Multi precision	Nvarchar	199	User information

Based on the above table data, make the UV-Unfold utility do not overlap UVs. Be sure to put all the UV on the 1: 1 grid, as far as possible to occupy 1: 1 UV full box, but do not go beyond the edge of the box. Expand the UV. The last step is to export UV, select Polygons-UV Snapshot, export UV, and then according to need to be able to adjust the path, size, color of UV export and export UV image format, etc., as required, after these parameters are adjusted, export images, so that in other editing software in accordance with UV mapping, such as Photoshop can be mapping.

The original teaching software system backstage administrator work flow, take the teaching goal as the point of departure which needs to analyze, applies to all has the network study demand crowd, through watches the study video frequency, the correlation study picture way, consolidates the elementary knowledge. In order to ensure the efficiency of mass information transmission, the system and backstage management module are set up inside the system. The whole management module workflow includes: managing users' history browsing records, managing users' personal information and so on. The improved integrated teaching software system, the background administrator workflow, add the management of online message and online question answering module, the administrator in the background processing stage, according to the specific content of the message, analysis and processing, and then based on the user's questions, in-depth analysis, to get the satisfactory answer, and then through the formal translation software, translation into English to reply to the questioner. Complete the improved background administrator workflow as shown in Fig. 5 below.

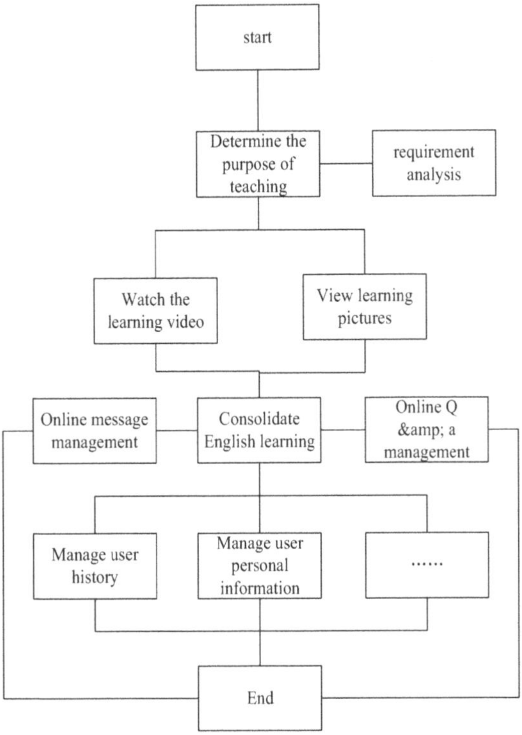

Fig. 5. Integrated teaching system background management process

Based on the above process, the optimization design of the general integrated teaching system must follow the standard system, data number and table information in the process of system optimization. Each student's learning progress can only be affected by the evaluation of the online system after the system memorandum, which stores the data of the student's learning progress and mines the data; the mined data is standardized to some extent, traced back to the data source, and the initial value of the online evaluation is obtained after analysis; and the final value is determined for online evaluation.

3 Analysis of Experimental Results

In order to verify the effectiveness of the general integrated teaching system in separate classes, a comparative detection experiment was conducted. Experimental research in the general sense is scientific Experimental research, consisting of three elements: the research questions and assumptions, the design of the research (including the control of unrelated variables), and the testing and presentation of experimental results. Experimental research as part of educational reform and scientific Experimental research also include the same elements mentioned above. The difference is that experimental research on educational reform controls unrelated variables and does not test experimental results too rigorously, and aims to promote the new methods pursued by researchers. Most educational experiments are not standard experiments, but quasi-experiments, because they do not have all the elements of a standard experiment. For example, for the sake of not interfering with the experimental results, only a post-test is conducted for the experimental group, which can be implied in some previous routine tests. Sometimes the control group is not specially arranged to avoid the Henry effect, and the control group is implicit in the surrounding unreformed class or school, and can be compared in a certain way. Therefore, the quasi-experimental research is not a loose experimental research, but more in line with the characteristics of the educational phenomenon of experimental research. Based on this, the experimental environment is uniformly set up as follows:

3.1 Experimental Environment

Experiments using three-dimensional software and Unity3 D game engine design and production. The main content is from the course content of film history. Photoshop, Final Cut Pro, Adobe Premiere are used to complete the content and layout of pixel mapping and video mapping in the system. Maya is used to build a model to import into Unity 3D to realize interaction. After optimization, the program of virtual teaching system is exported. The teaching system of film history is divided into different classes. By adapting and reproducing the teaching content, the students can find their own interest points to study and understand the teaching content. After importing and opening Final Cut Pro, click on the file options in the toolbar, create a new event, customize the name, locate the import, click on the file, select the selected material, and Final Cut Pro imports the file. Click File Options, select New Project, and drag the imported movie material to the New Project bar. Click on the tool to select the item, use the cutting tool to cut the video material, slide over, find the part you want to keep, select where to start, and click Finish. When the cut is complete, click on the unwanted section and delete. Export Material: Select Share in Toolbar - Export Media. Export mode for video and audio, video encoder select H. 264, so that the encoding can be played on different players smoothly, click next, select the export location.

3.2 Experimental Results

Based on the above data, the operation effects of the two systems are judged and the inspection results are recorded as follows (Fig. 6):

3.3 Experimental Conclusions

It is not difficult to observe the test results in the above figure. Compared with the traditional operation research teaching system, the general integrated teaching system designed in this paper is oriented to operation research. In the practical application

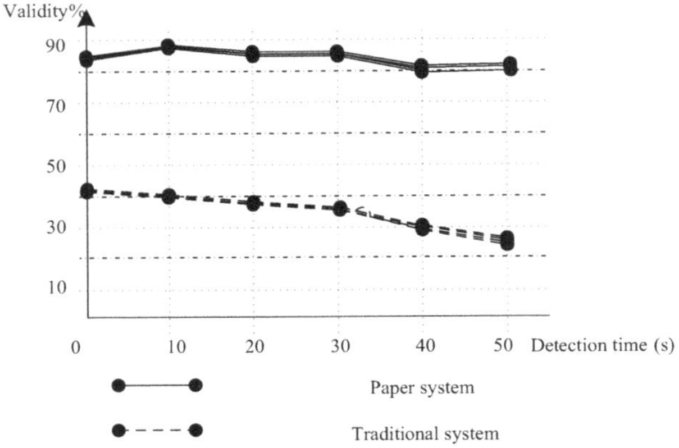

Fig. 6. Comparative experimental results

process, the operation effect test curve is significantly higher. And the validity was maintained above 89%, which was higher than 42% of the highest validity of the comparison method. It shows that the system designed in this paper has higher effectiveness and practicability, and fully meets the research requirements.

4 Closing Remarks

In our country's education, the traditional teaching method continues for many years, the people already gradually realized its malady and the insufficiency. In recent years, after the introduction of multimedia teaching methods, teachers are no longer limited to the blackboard, but can rely on computers, projectors, audio-visual equipment, through the visual, auditory, tactile and other ways to assist teaching, thus achieving excellent results. From the above findings, it is not difficult to predict: the split class will become an important tool of the teaching system, which provides a certain scientific basis for the teaching of operational research, and is conducive to improving the teaching efficiency.

References

1. Fattahi, M., Govindan, K.: Integrated forward/reverse logistics network design under uncertainty with pricing for collection of used products. Ann. Oper. Res. **253**(1), 193–225 (2016). https://doi.org/10.1007/s10479-016-2347-5
2. Devlin, M., McKay, J.: Teaching inclusively online in a massified university system. Widening Particip. Lifelong Learn. **20**(1), 146–166 (2018)
3. Ming, G., Gang, X., Liu, T.Y., et al.: Development of teaching training and assessment system for warming acupuncture. Zhongguo zhen jiu = Chin. Acupunct. Moxib. **39**(9), 1021–1023 (2019)
4. Almohammadi, K., Hagras, H., Yao, B., Alzahrani, A., Alghazzawi, D., Aldabbagh, G.: A type-2 fuzzy logic recommendation system for adaptive teaching. Soft. Comput. **21**(4), 965–979 (2015). https://doi.org/10.1007/s00500-015-1826-y

5. Bayati, S., Bastani, P., Sagheb, Z.M., et al.: The performance implications of pharmacy information system at the university teaching hospitals of Shiraz, Iran: cluster approach. J. Adv. Pharm. Technol. Res. **8**(4), 125–130 (2017)
6. Doherty, A., Bracken, M., Gormley, L.: Teaching children with autism to initiate and respond to peer mands using picture exchange communication system (PECS). Behav. Anal. Pract. **11**(4), 279–288 (2018). https://doi.org/10.1007/s40617-018-00311-8
7. Phillips, A.E., Walker, C.G., Ehrgott, M., Ryan, D.M.: Integer programming for minimal perturbation problems in university course timetabling. Ann. Oper. Res. **252**(2), 283–304 (2016). https://doi.org/10.1007/s10479-015-2094-z
8. Zhao, Y.F.: Research on the diversified evaluation index system and evaluation model of physical education teaching in colleges and universities. J. Comput. Theor. Nanosci. **14**(1), 99–103 (2017)
9. Bai, J., Fügener, A., Schoenfelder, J., Brunner, J.O.: Operations research in intensive care unit management: a literature review. Health Care Manag. Sci. **21**(1), 1–24 (2016). https://doi.org/10.1007/s10729-016-9375-1
10. Marjorie, K.N., Ricardo, A., Maria, T.A.S.: Automotive industry line board optimization through operations research techniques. IEEE Lat. Am. Trans. **16**(2), 585–591 (2018)
11. Vieira, B., Hans, E., Vlietvroegindeweij, C.V., et al.: Operations research for resource planning and -use in radiotherapy: a literature review. **72**(1), S129 (2017)
12. Tayal, A., Gunasekaran, A., Singh, S.P., Dubey, R., Papadopoulos, T.: Formulating and solving sustainable stochastic dynamic facility layout problem: a key to sustainable operations. Ann. Oper. Res. **253**(1), 621–655 (2016). https://doi.org/10.1007/s10479-016-2351-9
13. Seth, J., William, M., Michael, B.: Released for public comment: space weather benchmarks and operations-to-research plan: public comment on benchmarks and O2R plan. Space Weather **15**(2), 282 (2017)
14. Thorsen, A., Yao, T.: Robust inventory control under demand and lead time uncertainty. Ann. Oper. Res. **257**(1), 207–236 (2015). https://doi.org/10.1007/s10479-015-2084-1
15. Chen, Ya., Cook, W.D., Du, J., Hu, H., Zhu, J.: Bounded and discrete data and Likert scales in data envelopment analysis: application to regional energy efficiency in China. Ann. Oper. Res. **255**(1), 347–366 (2015). https://doi.org/10.1007/s10479-015-1827-3

Analysis of the Conflict Model of Education and Culture in China and Britain Based on Deep Learning

Xia Wang(✉)

School of Foreign Languages, Mianyang Teachers' College, Mianyang 621000, China
WangXia3476@163.com

Abstract. In the process of the development of modern education, the conflict between Chinese and British education and culture is increasingly fierce. In order to carry out sufficient research and control of cultural conflict, this paper constructs a model of Sino-British educational cultural conflict. In the process of using the model, the problem of abnormal analysis results is often caused by improper selection of index range. Therefore, a model of Sino-British educational culture conflict based on deep learning is designed. Based on the analysis of educational differences between China and the UK, the index of the model is set up, and the deep learning algorithm is used to construct the model. So far, the design of Sino-British educational culture conflict model based on deep learning has been completed. Compared with the original model, this model has a wider index range. In summary, this model is better than the original model.

Keywords: Educational model · Cultural conflict · Causes of conflict · Chinese and English culture

1 Introduction

Under the complex background of economic globalization, cultural diversity and knowledge economy, many Chinese enterprises have begun to actively participate in the world division of labor system, from domestic operation to transnational operation, and Chinese-foreign equity joint ventures have emerged. In order to adapt to such enterprises, a Sino-British integrated education system has emerged [1, 2]. In the process of the continuous development of Chinese and foreign education, the objective existence of cultural differences will inevitably become a realistic problem to face and solve. Cross-cultural conflict management has also become a common concern in academic and practical fields. Based on the theories and methods of cross-cultural management, corporate culture, organizational behavior, management and sociology, this paper tries to combine theoretical analysis with case study and a few data to systematically analyze the development of Sino-British education and the practical problems encountered, and to introduce representative Eastern and Western countries to analyze the cultural

S. Liu et al. (Eds.): eLEOT 2020, LNICST 339, pp. 298–307, 2020.
https://doi.org/10.1007/978-3-030-63952-5_25

mechanism, using practical cases to try to reveal the deep problems of cross-cultural management.

The materials obtained above are generally classified by skimming, and the articles or bibliographies explaining the same problems are classified together. Finally, a point of view is formed on a problem by reading the same kind of problems. In previous studies, conflict model is often used to study the differences between Chinese and British education and culture, but in the process of using the model, there are errors in the analysis results.

Deep learning is the learning of the intrinsic laws and presentation layers of sample data, and the information obtained in these learning processes can be of great help in interpreting data such as words, images, and sounds [3, 4]. Its ultimate goal is to enable machines, like humans, to analyze and learn, and to recognize data such as words, images, and sounds. Deep learning is a complex machine learning algorithm, which has achieved much better results in speech and image recognition than previous related technologies. The analysis and controllability of the design method can be improved effectively by using this technique.

2 Construction of Sino-British Educational Culture Conflict Model Based on Deep Learning

In the process of using the old model, the error of the analysis result is more serious because of the narrow range of the analysis index, so the analysis method and structure of the old model are optimized. To ensure that the research process has a basis, the design process is set as follows (Fig. 1).

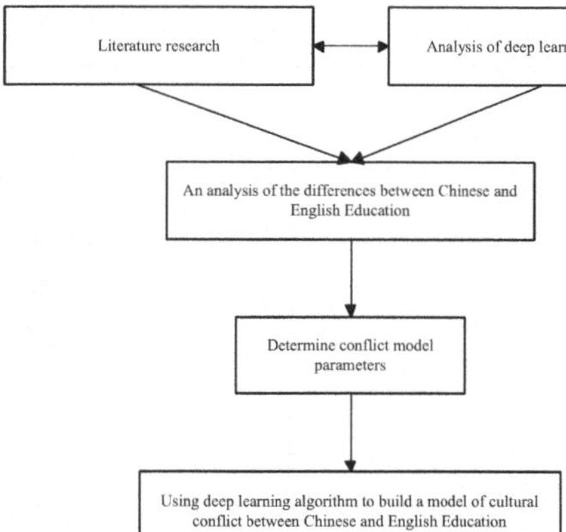

Fig. 1. Design process of analysis method of Chinese-British educational culture conflict model based on deep learning

Using the above process, we can improve the stability and reliability of the model and make sure that the design results can be fully analyzed and understood in the daily use of Sino-British cultural conflicts.

2.1 Analysis of Educational Differences Between China and Britain

In this part, in order to understand the Sino-British education in detail, and apply it to the selection of model parameters, using literature research and questionnaire survey data to explore the Sino-British educational and cultural differences. In this section, the design studies are shown below.

First of all, both in the Sino-British education of teachers and students, teachers have attached great importance to the role model of education. Because the teacher is not only the model of the students, but also the pioneer of the students' mind, which plays an important role in shaping and leading. In the West, teachers and students in teaching, but also on the role of their own teachers made a unique and detailed explanation.

Moreover, in China and the West, both teachers and students have a profound national character [5]. Because the teacher-student teaching mode, as a way of cultural transmission, should reflect the essential characteristics of national culture from a single important aspect. Nationality is a national characteristic different from other nationalities, that is, a national characteristic or characteristic [6]. It includes many aspects, such as national spirit, national temperament, psychology, character, habits, traditions, ideals and the way of understanding things and way of life and so on. These are similarities between Chinese and British education. There are many differences between Chinese and English education. In this part, we compare the differences between Chinese and English education and culture in the form of Table 1.

Table 1. Information table of cultural differences between Chinese and English

	Education in China	Western Education
Student status	Pay more attention to yourself	Pay more attention to achievements
Teacher Perspective	Attach importance to the development of students' specialty	Pay attention to the development of students' achievements
Teacher-student relationship	Equality	With relative hierarchy
Education mode	Students and teachers learn together	Teachers pay more attention to lectures
Focus of Education	Students' personality development	Whether students can meet the performance standard
Student development specific	Professional talents are easy to appear and students have strong independence	It's easy to have all-round talents, and the independence of students is weak
Student creativity	Students are creative	Students' creativity is weak
Direction of Education	Two way teaching	One way teaching
Discipline emphasis	Natural science	Humanities

Based on the above table, the paper analyzes the educational differences between China and Britain, integrates the contents of the table, obtains the index of educational differences between China and Britain, and applies it to the construction of conflict model.

2.2 Determine Conflict Model Parameters

Finally, the parameters of the conflict model are selected and set according to the above differences. In this part, using the game analysis technology, conflict analysis strategy and other theory [7] conflict analysis method to complete the model parameters acquisition.

Based on the theory of game analysis technology and conflict analysis strategy, the scope of index acquisition is expanded. This method is widely used at present. In this study, the conflict model is constructed as the F-H conflict analysis model [8]. Such models use sociology, psychology, logic and other knowledge, and based on game theory, set theory and other mathematical techniques, using analytical methods, experimental methods, simulation methods and other methods to build a mathematical model of conflict problems, analyze the possible outcome of conflict, study the psychological reaction and behavior of the main conflict, and simulate the development process and law of conflict.

In the setting of the model parameters, the hierarchical evaluation algorithm is used to carry out the analysis results of the Chinese and English education obtained in the above part. In the process of conflict model construction, there are a indicators, numbered $b_1, b_2, b_3, \ldots, b_n$, by comparing b_1 with b_n, the order of importance is obtained, the coefficient of importance is Q, and the result of the above analysis is set in the form of a two-dimensional matrix, which can be expressed as:

$$Z = Q(b_1/b_n) \tag{1}$$

Through the calculation results of the important coefficient formula for the above indexes, the classification results of the importance of the above analysis results can be obtained as follows (Table 2).

Table 2. Division of the importance of the results of the analysis of cultural differences between Chinese and English

Information importance number	Information importance number	Information characteristics
1	Teacher-student relationship	Direct cause of conflict
2	Education mode	Indirect causes of conflict
3	Focus of Education	Direct cause of conflict
4	Student status	Direct cause of conflict
5	Teacher Perspective	Direct cause of conflict
6	Student development specific	Indirect causes of conflict
7	Student creativity	Indirect causes of conflict
8	Direction of Education	Indirect causes of conflict
9	Discipline emphasis	Indirect causes of conflict

Through the contents of the table, the selection results of conflict model parameters are obtained. In order to ensure the reliability of the model parameters, the fuzzy evaluation algorithm [9, 10] is used to set the parameters in other directions of the design model. The specific calculation process is as follows (Fig. 2).

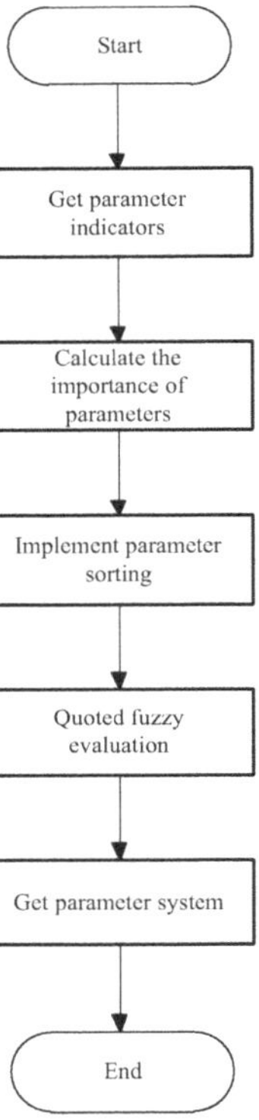

Fig. 2. Other aspects of the model parameters calculation process

Based on the fuzzy evaluation theory and the actual situation involved in chinese and english education, this paper establishes a whole and omni-directional index system, which belongs to the model of chinese and english education and culture conflict.

2.3 Applying the Deep Learning Algorithm to Construct the Conflict Model of Chinese and English Educational Culture

Generally speaking, the conflict analysis graph model mainly includes three parts: modeling, stability analysis and post-stability analysis. In the process of conflict modeling, firstly, it is necessary to describe the important event nodes, causes, development process, focus of conflict, mutual relations of conflict bodies, motivation of conflict bodies, conflict strategies that may be adopted by conflict bodies and other issues, and then determine conflict bodies and conflict strategies, so as to generate conflict situations (feasible states), and determine the preference information of conflict according to the relevant information of conflict bodies, so as to abstract physical models in actual conflicts into mathematical models; while stability analysis is mainly used to calculate the stability of various conflict bodies to obtain the global equilibrium point, i.e., to stabilize the conflict situation; and post-stability analysis generally includes structural stability analysis and path evolution analysis. To sum up, the model design process in this design is as follows (Fig. 3).

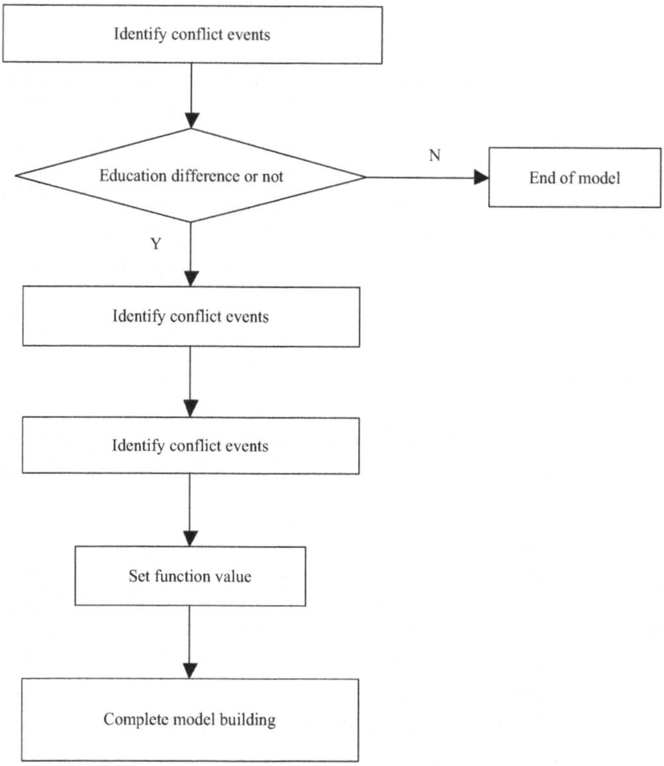

Fig. 3. Process of constructing the Chinese-English model of educational culture conflict

According to the above procedure, the collision is set to $E = (Z, Y, X, f)$, if $Z = (Z_1, Z_2, Z_3 \ldots, Z_n)$ is a set of non-empty finite conflict bodies, Z_n denotes the n conflict event; $Y = (Y_1, Y_2, Y_3, \ldots, Y_n)$ is a collection of limited non-empty conflict events, Y_n is the n conflict event. $X = \cup X_j$ is the range of the conflict system, $Y_n \in Y, X_j = \{-1, 0, 1\}$ is the range of conflict event Y_n, and -10,1 is the voting value, representing the opposition, neutrality and approval of a conflict event by a conflict body respectively.

$$f : Z * Y \rightarrow X \tag{2}$$

Through the above calculation, set $E = (Z, Y, X, f)$ as conflict information system. The deep learning algorithm is used to deal with the conflict information system, and the conflict information system is set as $E = (Z, Y, X, f)$. The scores of the Chinese educational culture s and western educational culture r on the conflict situation E_t arising from the Sino-British educational culture conflict event X_j are Y_{sj}^t and Y_{rj}^t, respectively.

$$\wp_j(s, r) = \begin{cases} 1\ if\ Y_{sj}^t Y_{rj}^t = 1\ or\ s = r \\ 0\ if\ Y_{sj}^t Y_{rj}^t = 0\ and\ s \neq r \\ -1\ if\ Y_{sj}^t Y_{rj}^t = -1 \end{cases} \tag{3}$$

The above formula is the conflict model of education and culture between China and Britain, and the conflict information system is set as $E = (Z, Y, X, f)$ according to the original. $\forall X_j \in X$ is a model function of the Conflict Information System and, if $\wp_j(s, r) = 1$, is referred to as Conflict s and r as the Alliance for Conflict Events X_j, recorded as $p_j^+(s, r)$; In the case of $\wp_j(s, r) = 0$, conflict s and r are referred to as conflict events X_j; neutral relations are recorded as $p_j^u(s, r)$; If $\wp_j(s, r) = -1$, then the conflicts s and r are referred to as conflict events X_j; they are hostile relations and are recorded as $p_j^-(s, r)$. Through the analysis of the conflict between Chinese and English education and culture, the model of conflict between Chinese and English education and culture based on deep learning is completed.

3 Test Experiment

In order to make up for the deficiency in the original model, this paper constructs the experimental link, and compares the original model with the design model in this paper.

3.1 Experimental Content

In the experiment, the original model and the design model are used to analyze the current Sino-UK educational and cultural conflicts, and the parameters of the two models are compared. To ensure the effectiveness of the experimental process, the experimental environment is setting as follows (Fig. 4).

Using the above experimental environment, the experimental links to the original model and the design models are completed.

3.2 Design of Experimental System

In order to ensure that the original model and the design model can be calculated and run in the same platform, the experimental system is set as follows (Table 3).

The above experimental system is installed into the experimental environment, and the analysis process is completed by using the set software to obtain the experimental results.

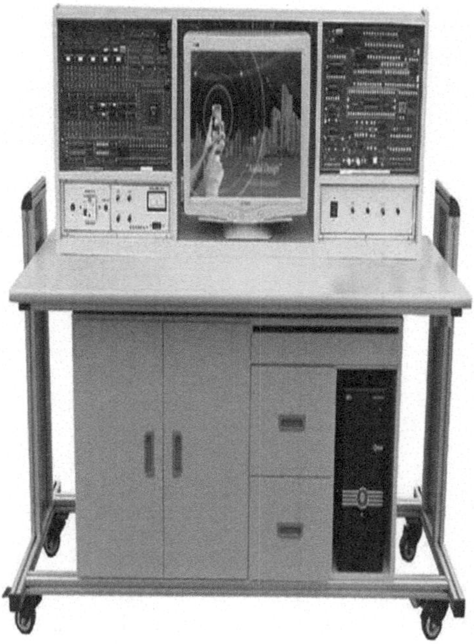

Fig. 4. Experimental environment

Table 3. Experimental system

Parameter direction	Parameter contents	Model
System hardware	CPU	Intel
	Hard disk	3T
	Memory	16G
Systems software	Data base	SQL2013
	Control system	Win10
	Control platform	Office

3.3 Experimental Result

Using the above experimental environment and experimental system, the original model is compared with the design model in this paper. In the part of the experimental results, the indexes that may be involved in the analysis are listed, and the index range of the original model and the design model in this paper is obtained (Table 4).

In the above experimental results, for example, the index included in the model is expressed in terms of T, but not in terms of F. From the above experimental results, it can be seen that the index range of the designed model is wider than that of the original model. And the designed model has a wider range of indicators in terms of education

Table 4. Comparison results between the original model and the index range of the design model in this paper

Index name	Original model index range	Index range of design model in this paper
Student status	T	T
Teacher Perspective	T	T
Teacher-student relationship	T	T
Education mode	T	F
Focus of Education	F	F
Student development specific	F	F
Student creativity	T	T
Direction of Education	T	F
Discipline emphasis	T	T
Other indicators	T	F

model, education direction and other indicators than the original model, it can be seen that the index range of the designed model is wider, which can more comprehensively analyze the Sino-British educational and cultural conflicts. Through this comparison, it can be seen that the reliability of model analysis results can be improved with a wide range of indicators. Therefore, the reliability of the analysis results of the design model is better than that of the original model. In conclusion, the application effect of the design model is better than the original model.

4 Conclusion

Today, on the one hand, the increasing cultural exchanges between China and the West, China's performance in the international arena has become increasingly self-confident; Therefore, In order to fully study and control cultural conflicts, a Chinese-British education cultural conflict model based on deep learning is proposed. By analyzing the results of differences in education between China and Britain, setting model indicators, and citing deep learning algorithms to build a model of cultural conflict between China and Britain. The experimental results show that the index range of the designed model is wider than that of the original model, which can effectively improve the reliability of the analysis results. The conflict between Chinese and British education and culture should also be based on our own historical development, and lead the trend in the international exchange and cooperation of education globalization. The power construction of contemporary university culture is a problem that we need to rethink and solve.

Fund Projects. Special project to build Mianyang Normal University in 2019: Theoretical research and practical exploration of foreign language teacher education (project number: 2019 mysytdz11) college.

References

1. Li, J., Yang, X.R., He, B.: Research on RGB-D depth completion with deep learning. J. Henan Inst. Sci. Technol. (Nat. Sci. Ed.) **46**(06), 35–42 (2018)
2. Li, Xi.Y., Song, W.: Image semantic segmentation research process based on deep learning. Sci. Technol. Eng. **19**(33), 21–27(2019)
3. Hou, Y.S.: A new clustering analysis algorithm based on deep learning. J. Xinxiang Univ. **35**(12), 21–24 (2018)
4. Han, J.W., Zhang, D.W., Cheng, G., et al.: Advanced deep-learning techniques for salient and category-specific object detection: a survey. IEEE Signal Process. Mag. **35**(1), 84–100 (2018)
5. Shu, Q., Huang, J.C., Zou, J., et al.: Analysis of cloud deep learning experiment based on NanoNets. Ind. Control Comput. **31**(11), 87–89 (2018)
6. Fan, L.H., Ni, M., Xu, H.P.: Focusing on the differences of mathematics education between China and England: findings from The Shanghai Maths Project for English Primary Schools. J. Math. Educ. **27**(04), 1–6+67 (2018)
7. Wang, Y.: Reflections on the difference of education between China and UK in higher vocational colleges. Value Eng. **37**(09), 164–165 (2018)
8. Pan, T.L.: On deep learning in high school Chinese classroom. J. Qiannan Normal Coll. Natl. **38**(06), 60–64 (2018)
9. Zhou, Q.S., Fan, X.R.: Study on the short text sentiment classification based on stacking fusion deep learning model and traditional machine learning model. Wuxian Hulian Keji **15**(24), 63–65 (2018)
10. Wang, H.Z., He, K.K., Fang, L.: Application of deep learning in motor fault diagnosis. Comput. Simul. **36**(10), 423–428 (2019)

The Information Grading Management System of College Students Based on Deep Learning

Tao Jiang and Ye Song(✉)

College of Humanities and Information,
Changchun University of Technology, Changchun 130122, China
yyg00321@163.com

Abstract. In view of the traditional student information management system can not maintain a certain system response speed under a large number of concurrent users, this paper designs a hierarchical management system of college student information based on deep learning. First of all, we use RFID technology to build the hardware module of student information collection, and design the software part of the management system. Then it constructs the structure of student information hierarchical management system, and determines the model of the system for student information hierarchical management. At last, we build the deep neural network model, and use the student information data set to train the neural network, realize the hierarchical management of university student information, and complete the design of the management system. By comparing with the traditional management system, it is proved that the management system based on deep learning can keep high response speed and superior system performance under a large number of concurrent users.

Keywords: Deep learning · Student information · Hierarchical management · System design

1 Introduction

Deep learning is a branch of machine learning, which aims at analyzing and interpreting data by establishing and simulating the operation process of human brain neurons. Neural network of deep learning is composed of multi-layer artificial neural network, through which the abstract knowledge expression can be learned automatically. Deep learning has the ability to automatically learn from the data to extract features, but also more scalable, by adjusting the training set data can identify more types. Using the method of deep learning, the training task and classification task can be separated when the application is realized, so as to achieve the effect of rapid classification of objectives [1].

Student information management is an important part of school office affairs management. Making full use of information technology, network technology and computer technology in student information management, the student information management system is constructed into an application system integrating information processing,

S. Liu et al. (Eds.): eLEOT 2020, LNICST 339, pp. 308–317, 2020.
https://doi.org/10.1007/978-3-030-63952-5_26

business process and knowledge management. Through the construction and use of student information management system, teachers and students can share information conveniently, communicate efficiently, change the traditional complex and inefficient way of work, achieve efficient, high-quality and all-round information processing, business process and knowledge management, and provide strong help for the modern college student information management, greatly improve work efficiency and management quality, and promote the college information construction [2, 3]. Through this system, the university teachers can use the network student information management, the curriculum information management and the student result management and so on; The student can carry on the result inquiry and the on-line choice and so on; The school administrator can carry on the batch student information management and the maintenance and the management and so on through this system. Student information management system through the network, space-time separation of the two sides can work together to achieve the information exchange between various departments, work coordination and cooperation, and this interaction and coordination can be completed almost instantaneously in the network environment, a great convenience to work. Therefore, this article will design the university student information grading management system based on the deep study.

2 Design of Hardware of College Student Information Grading Management System Based on Deep Learning

The hardware part of the student information hierarchical management system is composed of RFID data acquisition module and several servers. The following is a detailed description of RFID data collection module design.

Students' names, student numbers, majors, colleges, grades and other information are manually entered and stored in student cards. Students' school information, facial information and social information are collected by using radio frequency transceivers, high-definition cameras and ID card reading devices. The HD camera and ID card reader will input some information into the system software through the serial port, while the RF transceiver will read the relevant information from the student card and input it into the system software for processing.

The RF transceiver chip used in this paper is CC2540F256RHAR, the output power is 4 dBm, the maximum transmission rate is 1 Mbps, and the operating voltage is 2–3.6 V. Its flexible and efficient development tools, support KEILC, ISP download [4]. The appearance of the actual picture is shown in Fig. 1.

The programming environment of RF transceiver is KileC51, the programming language is C+, the information transceiver module is embedded with high-speed MCU and RF transceiver, its MCU is equipped with special SPI interface on chip, MCU operates and configures the register of RF transceiver through SPI interface, which can realize the control of RF transceiver working mode, and then control the data transmission and reception. Before sending data, initialization configuration and working mode configuration of RF transceiver need to be completed respectively.

The initialization and configuration of RF transceiver is mainly completed in rf init() function. Its main work is to configure channel, channel address, number of bytes sent each time, whether with CRC verification, power, etc. through RF = 1. Turn on the

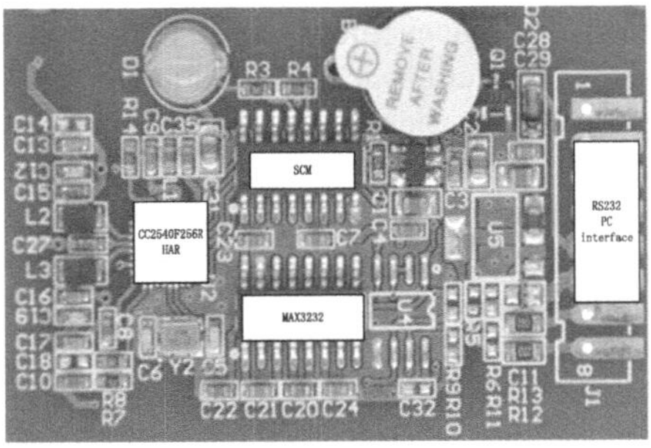

Fig. 1. Physical figure of RF transceiver

RF interrupt, set the transmission and reception address width of the RF transceiver through the SPI write buf() function, and initialize the RF transceiver by specifying the transmission power, transmission rate and received packet length. The transmission mode configuration of RF transceiver is completed in TX mode() function, and the data to be sent is written to transmission buffer through SPI Write buf() function, enabling CE to start transmission. For packet processing, ShockBurstTM mode is adopted. In shockbursttm mode, RF transceiver will use IRQ interrupt mode to inform MCU whether data transmission is completed, that is, when RF transceiver enters transmission state. MCU waits for the data to be sent out. When the data is sent out, IRQ interrupt will inform MCU that the data is sent out. When the data is sent out, the interrupt flag bit TX _DS of data transmission is changed to high level, which will interrupt IRQ pin and clear the status register, thus reducing the query time of MCU [5, 6]. The above is the hardware part of the system.

3 Software Design of College Student Information Grading Management System Based on Deep Learning

Based on the software part of the system, the software part of college student information grading management system based on deep learning is designed to realize the related functions of the management system.

3.1 Design the Architecture of Student Information Management System

The student information hierarchical management system established in this paper is divided into two levels as a whole, the first level management is school level management, the second level management is hospital level management. In order to update the student information data in time, the courtyard level management is divided into two levels according to grade and specialty.

MEAN Stack is the program framework development mode of the hierarchical management system, which is divided into front-end component AngularJS and back-end component, including ExpressJS skeleton engine, Node.js service running environment and database, in which the database design mode is nested by C/S and B/S. The front-end component is implemented by the AngularJS framework, which provides the front-end MVVM pattern, controller modularization, automated bi-directional data binding, semantic tags, and so on. Back-end components include the ExpressJS skeleton engine, the Node.js service runtime environment, and the MongoDB database [7]. The back-end server environment is provided by Node.js, and the ExpressJS provides the entire back-end framework by relying on different node template engines, including error controllers, caches, routing controls, and a database for data persistence. Through the mapping between database and component, it realizes the management of user's operation on system information and user's call on system information. After determining the hierarchical architecture of the management system, the database of the information management system is designed.

3.2 Information Management Database Design

Considering the system security, the foreground system software is installed at the node of the user with high operation authority. Only the operator with high operation authority has the right to access the operation, and the general user has no right to access it. The other type is installed on a specific server in the form of a backend, which stores the students' information that can be disclosed, and the relevant personnel can submit the modification within their own legal operation authority. The access architecture of student information management database designed in this paper is shown in Fig. 2.

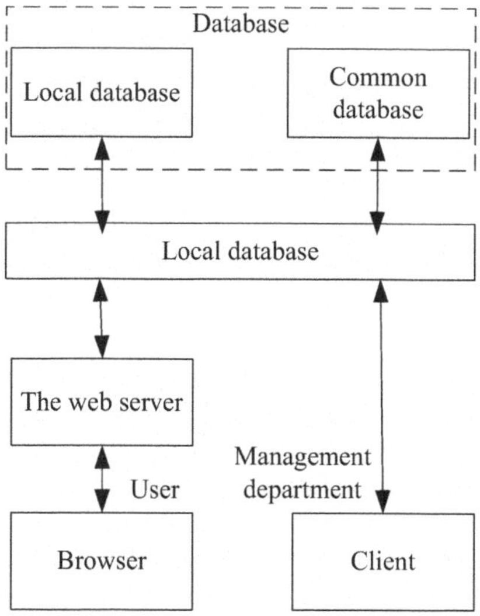

Fig. 2. Database access architecture

Table 1 below lists some of the data table's sub segment structure information.

Table 1. Sub segment structure information of some data tables

Field code	Project	Type (length)
BH	Serial number	CHAR(24)
XM	Name	CHAR(12)
XM2	Former name	CHAR(12)
XB	Gender	CHAR(2)
NL	Age	CHAR(4)
XH	Student id	CHAR(12)
BJ	Class	CHAR(12)
ZY	Major	CHAR(24)
YXDM	Department code	CHAR(6)
YXMC	Department name	CHAR(24)
CSRQ	Date of birth	CHAR(12)
JG_SSDM	Native city code	CHAR(2)
JG_DQDM	Native code	CHAR(6)
JT_TXDZ	Home address	CHAR(64)
DM	Social relationship code	CHAR(6)
SHGXMC	Name of social relations	CHAR(24)
TX	Image symbol	CHAR(1)
PHOTO	Image	BLOB(4000)
KM	Course	CHAR(16)
KMDM	Course Code	CHAR(24)
CJ	Grade	CHAR(8)

According to Table 1 above, the system database structure designed in this paper adopts the mode of combining C/S mode and B/S mode, and uses the advantages to make up for the disadvantages and uses them in a cross way. During the development, the functions of C/S mode will be made into client application programs, and the functions of B/S mode will be developed according to the format of web service programs, then each user application program will be installed on the appropriate client, and then the web service program will be installed on the web server, and browser software will be installed for all clients [8]. When using, users can use different ways (start client application or run browser) to realize the interactive function with database according to their needs. After designing the database of the student information management system, we use the principle of deep learning to build a hierarchical model of deep neural network.

3.3 Establishment of a Depth Neural Network Model

Deep neural network is an important branch of deep learning. In this paper, deep neural network is used to improve the hierarchical management efficiency of management system. The GoogLeNet network structure model shown in Fig. 3 is needed.

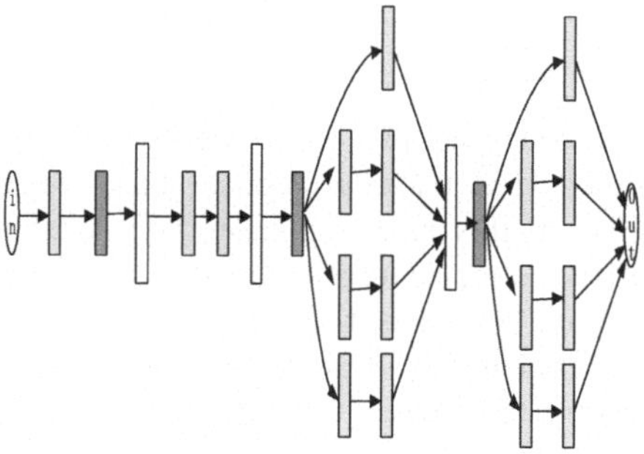

Fig. 3. GoogLeNet network structure model

GoogLeNet adopts a modular structure for easy addition and modification. Select a part of student information data set as the training set of neural network, through the training of neural network, get the specific parameters of neural network, realize the hierarchical management of student information.

The training process of neural network is described as follows: input sample data in the lowest layer of the network, through which the feature vectors are extracted and sampled to get some feature vectors. These eigenvectors are input into several join layers, and then the outputs are input into a classifier. Finally, the classification results of sample data, i.e. the probabilities of each classification, are obtained.

The computational expression of the entire neural network layer can be expressed as follows.

$$f(x) = s(b + Wx) \tag{1}$$

Where x represents the original input eigenvector. W represents the transformation mode of x, that is, the transformation matrix. b represents the offset adjusted after transformation, s is a nonlinear activation function, and the transformation is nonlinear [9]. As the output of the neural network layer, $f(x)$ represents the new eigenvector after transformation.

The training process is actually to input the sample data x, through a layer of calculation, get the final calculation result $f(x)$. Then, by adjusting the network parameters of each layer, that is, the transformation matrix W and the offset b, $f(x)$ is as close to the input x as possible, and finally the closest parameters of the neural network are obtained. The following formula is the updated gradient calculation formula of neural network parameter weight.

$$\frac{\partial c(\theta)}{\partial \theta} = -\frac{1}{m}\sum_{i=1}^{m}(y_i - h_\theta(x_i))x_j \tag{2}$$

In the above formula, y_i is the output of the middle layer of the deep neural network, θ represents each weight parameter, and $h_\theta(x_i)$ is the output value of the activation function of the last layer [10]. θ represents each weight parameter, and the partial derivative obtained is taken as the adjustment value of the weight parameter, i.e. offset b. The calculation formula of weight parameter θ is as follows.

$$\theta^{k+1} = \theta^k - \eta \frac{\partial c(\theta^k)}{\partial \theta^k} \tag{3}$$

In the above formula, η is the learning rate of the deep neural network, which represents the multiple of the adjusted deviation for each update. Its value generally decreases with the increase of training times. In this paper, it is set as 0.02. After training, the deep neural network is used to process the collected information data, and the processed data is stored in the system database, waiting for the user to send a call request to the database and call the data. So far, we have completed the design of the information grading management system of college students based on deep learning.

4 Experiment Results

This paper studies the students' information grading management system based on deep learning, in order to test the performance of the system, the following will be a comparative experiment. Through the analysis of experimental data, the relevant conclusions are drawn.

4.1 Experimental Content

In order to scientifically and effectively test the performance of the management system designed in this paper, this experiment adopts the form of comparative experiment. The contrast group of the experiment is the traditional student information management system, and the test group of the experiment is the college student information grading management system based on the deep learning. The contrast index of the experiment is the response time of the system under different user concurrency, and the response speed of the system is evaluated by comparing the response time.

4.2 Experimental Preparation

In the laboratory, build the test network environment with physical architecture as shown in Fig. 4.

The configuration parameters of each server in Fig. 4 are shown in Table 2.

Before the beginning of the experiment, the test group and the comparison group were tested to make sure that the relevant functions of the system could be realized. The detection software is used to monitor the response time of the two groups of systems to user requests under different user concurrency. Analysis of experimental data, evaluation of the test group and comparison group management system.

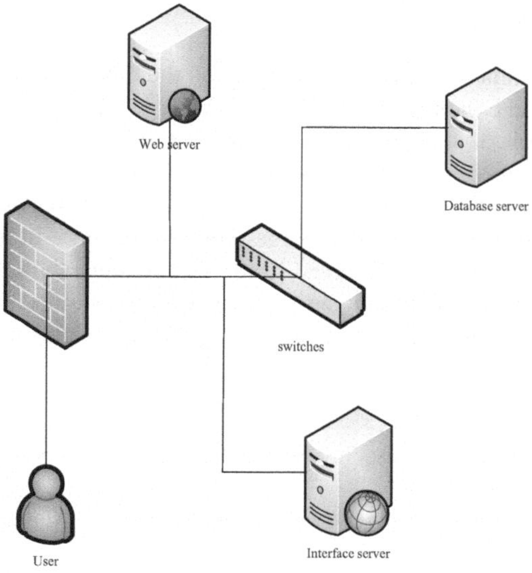

Fig. 4. Physical architecture of test environment

Table 2. Server configuration parameters

The serial number	Equipment	The hardware configuration	The software configuration
1	Client	CPU, Intel I5 9400F 2.4 GHz, memory, 8G, The hard disk, 500G, The network card: 100M	Windows 10 operating system, Office 2013, IE 10
2	Web server	CPU, Intel I9 9900K 3.6 GHz, memory, 16G, hard disk, 1 TB ordinary hard disk, 500 GB Solid state drives, Double gigabyte Ethernet card	Windows Server 2008 R2 operating system, Apache server
3	Database server	CPU, Intel i7-9700K 3.6 GHz 16 memory, 16G, hard disk: 1 TB ordinary hard disk, 500 GB Solid state drives, Double gigabyte Ethernet card, UPS power supply	Linux Cent OS 4.0 operating system, My SQL Database 5.6
4	Backup server	CPU, i7-9700K 3.6 GHz 16, memory, 8G, hard disk, 1 TB ordinary hard disk, Double gigabyte Ethernet card	Windows Server, 2008, R2 operating system

4.3 Experimental Results

The experimental results are shown in Table 3, and the data in the table are analyzed to draw the experimental conclusion.

According to Table 3, with the increasing number of concurrent users, the response time of both systems increases. When the number of concurrent users is less than 350, the difference between the two groups of systems is small, but when the number of concurrent users is more than 350, the increase rate of response time in the comparison group is much faster than that in the test group. The results showed that the response speed of the control group was significantly slower. In conclusion, under the large number of concurrent users, the management system designed in this paper can maintain better response rate and performance.

Table 3. System response time of different concurrent users/S

Serial number	User concurrency	Test group system	Contrast group system
1	50	0.1	0.7
2	100	0.1	1.1
3	150	0.2	1.4
4	200	0.5	1.9
5	250	0.7	2.2
6	300	0.9	2.7
7	350	1.1	3.0
8	400	1.4	3.6
9	450	1.5	4.2
10	500	1.5	5.0
11	550	1.7	5.7
12	600	1.8	6.4
13	650	1.9	7.1
14	700	1.9	8.0
15	750	2.1	8.9

5 Conclusion

Promoting information management is the focus of the current work of colleges and universities. In order to improve the efficiency of the management of College Students' information, this paper studies the hierarchical management system of College Students' information based on deep learning. Through the contrast experiment with the traditional student information management system, it is proved that the management system designed in this paper can bear a large amount of user concurrency and keep normal operation under a large amount of user concurrency. That is to say, the performance of the information management system designed in this paper is better.

References

1. Chen, J., Wang, Z., Chen, J., et al.: Design and research on intelligent teaching system based on deep learning. Comput. Sci. **46**(1), 550–554+576 (2019)
2. Huang, Y., Wang, H., Cheng, F., et al.: Design and performance test of USV information management system based on time-series database. Chin. J. Ship Res. **14**(04), 161–166 (2019)
3. Cao, B., Chen, W., Wei, S.: Stereoscopic monitoring and management information system of riverbank dynamic changes. J. Yangtze River Sci. Res. Inst. **36**(10), 28–33 (2019)
4. Xiao, X.: Automatic classification of electronic documents based on deep learning: case study of electronic image documents. Inf. Res. (06), 78–82 (2019)
5. Wang, C., Xu, J.: Crew physioiogicai information management system based on Internet of Things. Electr. Autom. **41**(03), 7–9 (2019)
6. Zhang, Y.: Simulation of real-time management of orderly access information for urban traffic in big data. Comput. Simul. **35**(12), 139–142 (2018)
7. Qin, J., Qiu, L.: Design and development of a non-contact attendance system for College Students. Electron. Test (06), 58–59 (2019)
8. Zhu, J.: The design and implementation of the employment information system for students in higher vocational colleges. Autom. Instrum. (11), 141–143 (2018)
9. Zhang, W.: Research on data mining of the Internet of Things based on cloud computing platform. IOP Conf. Ser. Earth Environ. Sci. **113**(1), 49–53 (2018)
10. Wei, Y., Li, W., Zhou, L., et al.: Construction and application of geological information management system in karst hydrogeological environment. Carsologica Sinica **37**(01), 146–153 (2018)

Teaching Quality Evaluation Method Based on Multilayer Feedforward Neural Network

Ye Song(✉) and Tao Jiang

College of Humanities and Information, Changchun University of Technology, Changchun 130122, China
ghy69520@163.com

Abstract. In order to promote the development of education, multi-layer feedforward neural network is applied to the teaching quality evaluation process, and a new evaluation method is proposed. The evaluation model based on multilayer feedforward neural network is established. The experiment data is used to compare the results of the experimental group and the control group. The results show that the application of multilayer feedforward neural network to the evaluation of teaching quality can reduce the error between the target output and the actual output, and make the quality evaluation result more in line with the actual situation.

Keywords: Multilayer feedforward neural network · Teaching quality · Evaluation method

1 Introduction

Since 1999, the scale of enrollment in colleges and universities has been enlarged, which is unprecedented in the history of China's higher education, and unprecedented in the history of the world's higher education. On the one hand, the enrollment expansion of higher education has promoted the adjustment of our country's economic structure and played an active role in realizing the sustainable development of our country's economy; on the other hand, the school-running ability and educational quality of institutions of higher learning have undergone tremendous tests under such extraordinary expansion. The quality of running colleges and universities will directly affect the development of higher education in our country. The quality of teaching in institutions of higher learning is reflected by the quality of teaching in various specialties or departments, and the quality of teaching in institutions of higher learning is reflected by the quality of courses, and the quality of courses is reflected by the quality of teaching of teachers undertaking the courses [1].

Feedforward neural network is the simplest kind of neural network in which the neurons are arranged hierarchically. Each neuron is connected only to a previous layer of neurons. Receives output from the previous layer and outputs it to the next layer. There is no feedback between layers. It is one of the most widely used and rapidly developing artificial neural networks. Since the 1960s, the theoretical research and practical

S. Liu et al. (Eds.): eLEOT 2020, LNICST 339, pp. 318–328, 2020.
https://doi.org/10.1007/978-3-030-63952-5_27

application have reached a very high level [2]. The feedforward neural network adopts a unidirectional multilayer structure. Each layer contains a number of neurons. In this kind of neural network, each neuron can receive the signal of the first neuron and produce output to the next layer. Layer 0 is called the input layer, the last layer is called the output layer, and other intermediate layers are called hidden layers (or hidden layers, hidden layers). The hidden layer can be one layer or multiple layers. Teaching quality evaluation in colleges and universities is a complicated problem. Multi-layer feedforward neural network is used to evaluate teaching quality.

2 Materials and Methods

2.1 Teaching Quality Rating

The evaluation of teaching quality in colleges and universities is a complicated problem. It includes many factors, such as teaching conditions, course difficulty, teachers' teaching and learning effect, which interact with each other.

(1) Research on the subject of teaching quality evaluation: there are many ways or methods to evaluate teaching quality, such as teachers' self-evaluation, peer evaluation, administrative leadership evaluation, expert evaluation and students' evaluation of teachers, etc. Because of the different roles of evaluation subjects, their roles in the evaluation should be different. Each evaluation method and its results are only a part of the evaluation of teaching quality, and cannot be equated with the whole of teaching quality [3]. Because of the large number of college teachers and frequent evaluations, it is not only time-consuming and laborious for leaders and peer experts to adopt the evaluation method of general survey, but also difficult to operate because of the influence of interpersonal relationship and unfamiliarity with the teaching process. Therefore, the method of student-centered evaluation of teachers' teaching quality is widely adopted by most colleges and universities. Since the eighties of last century, colleges and universities in our country have gradually carried out student evaluation of teaching, which has played a certain role in improving the teaching quality. As the direct object of teaching, students have the right and ability to evaluate the teaching of teachers. Because of the diversity of types, complexity of majors and the uneven level of students, the requirements for the evaluation of teachers' teaching quality are also different [4].

(2) Determination of the content of the evaluation of teaching quality: when designing the content of the evaluation system of teaching level, considering that the learning and development are a continuous process and the environment for learning and growth are diverse, it is very difficult to quantify the role of a certain teacher in a certain course or a certain learning stage, and generally, the evaluation content is placed on the teaching process instead of taking the course performance as the main indicator or teaching effect as the main indicator. From the point of view of process management, the teaching process of school is a combination of many factors and links. It is difficult to compare the teaching of different subjects, different courses, different teaching links and different teaching objects. Therefore, the system of teaching quality evaluation is designed mainly from the aspects of the most basic

factors which can directly reflect the teaching level and have common characteristics [5]. According to the present evaluation system of teaching level, the design of the index is mainly embodied in the following aspects: ① Teaching attitude: whether the teaching is serious and responsible, whether the spirit of class is full, whether the preparation of lessons is sufficient, whether the tutoring, answering questions and correcting homework are serious. ② Teaching content: whether the selection and handling of content are appropriate, whether the concept is accurate and clear, whether the focus is prominent, whether the difficulty and depth are appropriate, whether the theory is closely connected with the practice, and whether the content is rich. ③ Teaching ability: whether the organization is clear, the language is vivid and concise, attractive, focus, difficult to elaborate accurately, whether the writing is neat. ④ Teaching methods: whether to teach students in accordance with their aptitude, whether the method is flexible, whether to focus on inspiring students to cultivate innovative awareness and ability, whether to focus on exchanges with students, interaction [6]. ⑤ Teaching: whether rigorous scholarship, exemplary, strict and fair requirements for students. ⑥ Teaching effect: Whether can promote the student to think positively, whether student's result promotion, whether the student grasps comprehensively to the knowledge spot. Because different schools have different understandings and emphases on teaching quality, there are some differences in the content of evaluation.

(3) The current teaching quality evaluation methods: after the establishment of each index system in the teaching quality evaluation system, it is necessary to process these data with certain methods so as to obtain the final teaching quality grade. This paper summarizes the research on this aspect. ① Traditional teaching quality evaluation methods: the results of traditional teaching quality evaluation depend on: first, the scoring of evaluation indicators; second, the formulation of grading criteria. The evaluation results of each index of the evaluation object are expressed by A, B, C, D , and the proportion of evaluation contents in the evaluation system is determined, 10% for teaching and education; 20% for professional level; 35% for classroom teaching; 20% for organized teaching; and 15% for students' learning quality. Then determine the importance coefficient (proportion) of each content sub-index. When the evaluation subject makes A, B, C, D for each content's sub index, according to the reasonable procedure and scoring method, the quality grade coefficient Xa, Xb, Xc, Xd of each content is obtained, and then according to the proportion of the evaluation content, the grading standard coefficient Ka, Kb, Kc, Kd of the total index is synthesized, and a grading plan is drawn up, For example, excellent is $\mathrm{Ka} \geq 70,\ \mathrm{Kd} = 0$, good is $\mathrm{Ka} + \mathrm{Kb} \geq 70,\ \mathrm{Kd} = 0$, etc.

Fuzzy comprehensive evaluation method: This method uses the theory and method of fuzzy mathematics to deal with each index grade given by the evaluation subject, so as to get the comprehensive evaluation of teaching quality. The specific steps are as follows:

Step 1: Establish factor set U. Take the evaluation content in the evaluation system as factor set $\mathrm{U} = \{U_1, U_2, \ldots U_n\}$, and the sub indexes of each evaluation content constitute set $\mathrm{U_i} = \{U_{i1}, U_{i2}, \ldots U_{is}\}$, $i = 1, 2, \ldots n$. Determine the weight distribution

$a_i = (a_{i1}, a_{i2}, \ldots a_{is})$ and $\sum_{j=1}^{s} a_{ij} = 1, a_{ij} \geq 0$ according to the function of each sub index, and give the weight of U_i as $A = (A_1, U_2, \ldots A_s)$ and $\sum_{i=1}^{n} A_i = 1, A_i \geq 0$.

Step 2: Set up evaluation set V. In fact, V is to determine the grade of teachers' teaching quality. $V = \{v_1, \ldots, v_m\}$, element $v_j (j = 1, 2, \ldots m)$ are all possible total evaluation results, which can be either numerical value or qualitative description, which can be fuzzy or non fuzzy. For example, in the evaluation level of ten system, $V = \{v_1, v_2, \ldots, v_m\} = \{10, 9, 8, 7, 6, 5, 4, 3, 2, 1\}$.

Step 3: Carry out fuzzy evaluation. A single factor evaluation matrix R is established to evaluate each indicator u_{ij} in U_i, so as to determine its membership degree $r_{ij}(j = 1, 2, \ldots m)$ to evaluation set element $v_j (j = 1, 2, \ldots m)$, From this, a single index evaluation matrix R_i can be formed, so that the comprehensive evaluation $B_i = a_i * R_i$, of U_i can be normalized for each B_i, and the matrix $B = (B_1, B_2, \ldots B_n)^T$ can be obtained, then the comprehensive evaluation of U can be obtained: $B = AR = A(B_1, B_2, \ldots B_n)^T = (A_1, A_2, \ldots A_n)(B_1, B_2, \ldots B_n)^T$, then it can be normalized to B, and the score grade of the teacher is $M = BVT$.

③ Markov chain evaluation method: Markov chain is one of the important processes in probability theory. When evaluating the teaching effect of different teachers, the differences in the students' original knowledge base and other aspects may be eliminated, and the grades of the students in a class (or grade) in a certain examination may be assessed as follows:

Excellent (more than 90 points), good (80–89 points), medium (70–79 points), passing (60–69 points) and failing (less than 60 points), and then, taking this result as the initial state, examine the changes of the second examination results (for multiple examinations, the method is the same) to explain the teaching effect of the teachers during this period, so as to compare the teaching quality of different teachers.

At the beginning of the term, the number of N students in the class with excellent, good, medium, pass and fail in the examination is n_i, respectively, and the state vector at the beginning of the term is $i = 1, 2, 3, 4, 5$:

$$R(1) = \left(\frac{n_1}{N}, \frac{n_2}{N}, \frac{n_3}{N}, \frac{n_4}{N}, \frac{n_5}{N},\right) \tag{1}$$

After the final examination, among the original n_1 students with excellent scores, n_{11} students are still excellent, and n_{12}, n_{13}, n_{14}, n_{15} students are reduced to good, medium, pass and fail, respectively. Therefore, the transfer of students with excellent scores at the beginning of the semester is as follows:

$$\left(\frac{n_{11}}{n_1}, \frac{n_{12}}{n_1}, \frac{n_{13}}{n_1}, \frac{n_{14}}{n_1}, \frac{n_{15}}{n_1}\right) \tag{2}$$

Similarly, the transfer of scores of students who have obtained good grades, medium grades, passed grades and failed grades is:

$$\left(\frac{n_{i1}}{n_i}, \frac{n_{i2}}{n_i}, \frac{n_{i3}}{n_i}, \frac{n_{i4}}{n_i}, \frac{n_{i5}}{n_i}\right)(i = 2, 3, 4, 5) \tag{3}$$

This gives the transition probability matrix:

$$p = (p_{ij}) = \left(\frac{n_{ij}}{n_i}\right)(i,\ j = 1, 2, 3, 4, 5) \tag{4}$$

The transition probability matrix P is the transition change on the original basis, independent of the original basis. According to the properties of Markov chain, the stable distribution $(x_1, x_2, x_3, x_4, x_5)$ can be obtained. If the agreed scores of excellent, good, medium, pass and fail are 90, 80, 70, 60 and 50 respectively, the teaching effect will be quantified as follows:

$$s = 90x_1 + 80x_2 + 70x_3 + 60x_4 + 50x_5 \tag{5}$$

The above teaching quality evaluation methods play a positive role in improving teaching quality and promoting teachers' teaching level. Based on this, a multi-layer feedforward neural network is established.

2.2 Establishment of Evaluation Model Based on Multilayer Feedforward Neural Network

Multilayer feedforward neural networks depend on initial weights and thresholds, which are given randomly. Genetic algorithm searches for the optimal solution in the whole space, which can improve the shortcomings of neural networks based on gradient descent method, such as falling into local minimum and slow convergence. The flow chart is shown in Fig. 1:

A biased network can approximate any rational number if it contains an S-shaped implicit layer and a linear output layer. Among them, the more layers, the more accurate the results obtained, but the increase in the number of layers, the calculation will increase, therefore, the training cycle will increase. The feedforward neural network with single hidden layer can map all continuous functions, and only need two hidden layers when learning discontinuous functions, so the multilayer feedforward neural network only needs two hidden layers at most [7]. When designing a multilayer feedforward neural network, generally speaking, a hidden layer should be considered first. If the number of nodes in the hidden layer is large enough and the network performance is not improved, the training cost will increase with the increase of the number of hidden layers. The input layer receives data from external inputs, so the number of nodes depends on the dimensions of the input vector for the specific problem. The transfer function used in the input layer is generally linear, that is $f(x) = x$. The trial and error method is one of the methods to determine the number of hidden layer nodes. After the initial value is determined, the optimal number can be analyzed by experiment. The initial value of the trial and error method shall be determined in three forms, as shown in formula (6) to formula (8), and the number of nodes of the initial hidden layer shall be determined using empirical formula (6).

$$m = \sqrt{n+1} + a \tag{6}$$

$$m = \log 2^n \tag{7}$$

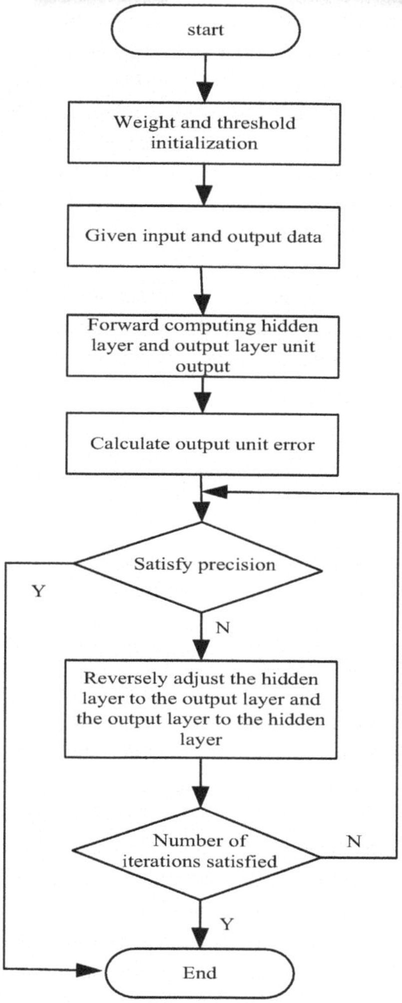

Fig. 1. Flow chart of multilayer feedforward neural network

$$m = \sqrt{nl} \tag{8}$$

Where m is the number of hidden layer nodes, n is the number of input layer nodes, l is the number of output layer nodes, and a is a constant between 1–10.

The number of nodes in the output layer depends on the dimension of the objective variable in the actual problem. The nonlinear transfer function is used. The more commonly used nonlinear transfer function is hyperbolic function formula:

$$f(x) = \frac{1}{1 + e^x} \tag{9}$$

Obtain data samples and preprocess the data. In general, the more experimental samples, the more accurate the results of the reaction, but when its number reaches a certain amount, the accuracy is fixed in a range, there will be no change. The larger the size of the network, the more complex the mapping relationship. Generally speaking, the number of training samples is 5–10 times the total network connection weights. Generally, there are two ways to select the initial weights of a network: the first way is to select a small enough initial weights, and the second way is to make the weights of 1 and −1 equal. Learning rate is an important factor affecting the variation of weights in cyclic training. If the value is large, the system will be unstable; if the value is small, the training time will be increased, but the error range can be guaranteed. There are two ways to stop training, one is through error range control, the other is to achieve the maximum number of iterations, two conditions as long as there is one can stop training [8–10]. It is usually possible to train multiple networks and ultimately select the appropriate network based on the analysis results.

3 Results

In order to verify the effectiveness of the above teaching quality evaluation methods, a control experiment is proposed and the test results are obtained.

3.1 Preparatory Process

Setting up the index of students' evaluation of teaching, the students of the college evaluate the practical teaching of teachers, and get the neural network learning and forecasting dataset. After the sample data is screened and processed preliminarily, it is normalized. According to the evaluation index, the number of neurons in input layer and hidden layer and the output layer are determined, and the action function, learning function and performance function are determined. The number of learning iteration, learning rate and error precision are determined, and the sub-neural network is studied by using the training sample data set. Using the corresponding sub-neural network system generated after learning, the prediction data are simulated and calculated by using the prediction sample data set. According to the result of network operation, the effect and feasibility of evaluation are evaluated. In view of the classroom evaluation result of each student in the hospital is only one, the number of output neurons of the neural network subsystem is set at 1. According to the formula for determining the number of neurons in the hidden layer:

$$n = \sqrt{n_i + n_0} + a, 0 \leq a \leq 10 \tag{10}$$

Where, n_i represents the number of neurons in the input layer, n_0 represents the number of neurons in the output layer, a represents the constant, and the value range is $0 \leq a \leq 10$. In the experiment, the number of neurons in the input layer is 10, and the number of neurons in the output layer is 1. According to the formula (10), $n = 4 - 14$ is obtained. According to the experimental results, the optimal number of neurons in the hidden layer is 7.

3.2 Experimental Sample

Training sample data set is a necessary and sufficient condition for network simulation, and the quality of training sample data set directly affects the simulation effect of multi-layer feedforward neural network. Therefore, the selection of training samples needs to grasp the size and quality of the sample data on the basis of analysis and summary. Based on the statistical analysis of the students' teaching evaluation index system, a checklist of practical teaching evaluation is drawn up, and students are organized to evaluate and grade 6 secondary indexes of teaching teachers in an orderly manner. At the end of the assessment process, the student's classroom teaching assessment form will be retrieved.

3.3 Analysis of Results

The evaluation data of the reclaimed classroom teaching evaluation form shall be treated as follows: (1) Since each classroom teaching evaluation requires students to score separately, that is, it is equivalent to having multiple judges. Therefore, this subject adopts the average value of student evaluation after removing the five most scores and five least scores, that is, the data of input neuron indicators of practical teaching evaluation of instructors, so as to exclude the adverse effects of individual subjectivity and other factors. (2) After selecting the suitable sample data, according to the proposed method of multi-layer feedforward neural network evaluation data preprocessing, the sample data is normalized, that is, the student's evaluation data [0, 100] is normalized to the data within the range of [0, 1], so as to reduce the differences between different evaluation data as much as possible, which is convenient for multi-layer feedforward neural network processing. Take the evaluation data of a course teaching student of the college as an example, the processed sample data is shown in Table 1.

Table 1. Student evaluation data

Sample serial number	Secondary evaluation index				Evaluation target		
	X1	X2	X3	X4	X5	X6	
1	0.55	0.61	0.73	0.58	0.76	0.58	0.630
2	0.61	0.60	0.65	0.62	0.71	0.82	0.608
3	0.83	0.88	0.84	0.68	0.61	0.77	0.814
4	0.79	0.60	0.74	0.85	0.61	0.81	0.653
5	0.85	0.87	0.91	0.77	0.8	0.78	0.895
6	0.73	0.72	0.68	0.81	0.66	0.78	0.692
7	0.61	0.63	0.67	0.78	0.83	0.55	0.646
8	0.87	0.92	0.84	0.51	0.62	0.77	0.872

(*continued*)

Table 1. *(continued)*

Sample serial number	Secondary evaluation index						Evaluation target
	X1	X2	X3	X4	X5	X6	
9	0.51	0.62	0.67	0.69	0.72	0.87	0.571
10	0.65	0.61	0.54	0.67	0.81	0.83	0.720
11	0.73	0.71	0.45	0.52	0.76	0.5	0.699
12	0.78	0.66	0.64	0.87	0.81	0.65	0.714
13	0.58	0.60	0.67	0.49	0.7	0.5	0.639
14	0.84	0.78	0.65	0.82	0.87	0.56	0.714
15	0.69	0.54	0.49	0.52	0.85	0.79	0.639
16	0.65	0.61	0.94	0.91	0.85	0.87	0.830
17	0.57	0.45	0.54	0.88	0.75	0.57	0.602
18	0.84	0.90	0.64	0.61	0.87	0.68	0.726
19	0.42	0.75	0.94	0.58	0.78	0.56	0.686
20	0.61	0.60	0.35	0.85	0.57	0.84	0.780
21	0.82	0.63	0.15	0.72	0.81	0.85	0.601
22	0.74	0.78	0.46	0.59	0.78	0.74	0.602
23	0.56	0.64	0.46	0.92	0.81	0.87	0.690
24	0.78	0.82	0.15	0.54	0.79	0.86	0.821
25	0.80	0.88	0.64	0.85	0.53	0.55	0.859

The first 20 groups of data in the table are regarded as the training sample data set, and the last 5 groups of data are regarded as the prediction sample data set. The simulation results of the neural network subsystem model formed after the learning process are verified (Fig. 2).

Compared with the results of the control group, the convergence speed of the multi-layer neural network subsystem used in the teaching quality evaluation is faster. After several iterations, the system error has reached 0. 000273773, and the error between the target output of the training sample data set and the actual output is consistent with the set value ($\leq$0.001). The output value of the system is close to the actual teaching evaluation data, which shows that the neural network subsystem can approach the teaching quality evaluation rules of the training sample data.

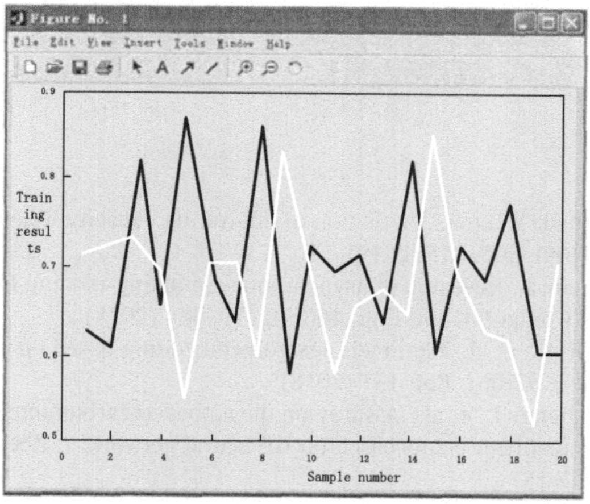

(a) Control group

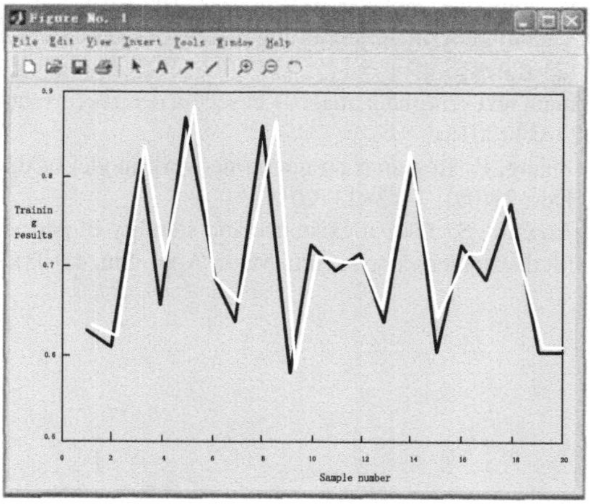

(b) Experimental group

Fig. 2. Experimental control results.

4 Conclusions

Teaching evaluation of college teachers is of great significance to improve teaching quality, teachers' quality and students' learning effect. The evaluation system of college teachers' teaching quality is a kind of high dimension nonlinear relation. After studying some methods of teachers' teaching evaluation and analyzing their advantages and disadvantages, a new method of teachers' teaching evaluation based on multi-layer feedforward neural network is proposed. Different evaluation systems are adopted for different subjects and different specialties, which makes the evaluation more reasonable, scientific and objective.

References

1. Ma, W., Li, W., Zhao, Y., et al.: Prediction of hot rolling capacity based on deep learning. J. Iron Steel Res. **31**(09), 805–815 (2019)
2. Li, Y., Xie, G., Guan, J.: Research of asynchronous imitating-reading BCI based on extreme learning machine. Comput. Digit. Eng. **46**(03), 479–484 (2018)
3. Xu, L., Lin, H., Qi, R., et al.: Sentiment lexicon embedding based on radical and phoneme. J. Chin. Inf. Process. **32**(06), 124–131 (2018)
4. Fang, R., Shi, Y., Jiang, T., et al.: A study on the activated carbon intelligent dosing system for urban sewage treatment plants based on BP neural network. J. Zhejiang Univ. (Sci. Ed.) **45**(04), 468–475 (2018)
5. Li, W., Chen, B., Li, J., et al.: Surface scratch recognition method based on deep neural network. J. Comput. Appl. **39**(07), 2103–2108 (2019)
6. Wang, Z., Zhang, H.: A fast image retrieval method based on multi-layer CNN features. J. Comput. Aided Des. Comput. Graph. **31**(08), 1410–1416 (2019)
7. Liu, W., Xie, H.: Generation of intelligent fitting pattern based on BP neural network. J. Text. Res. **39**(07), 116–121 (2018)
8. Yu, C.: A cross-domain text sentiment analysis based on deep recurrent neural network. Libr. Inf. Serv. **62**(11), 23–34 (2018)
9. Cao, J., Gong, J., Zhang, P.: Research on neural network model of data-to-text generation. Comput. Technol. Dev. **29**(09), 7–12+23 (2019)
10. Meng, Y., Huang, L., Guo, S.: Global existence and stability of periodic solutions of BAM neural networks with distributed delays. Acta Math. Appl. Sin. **41**(03), 369–387 (2018)

Research on Planning Methods of Students' Professional Development Trajectory Based on Big Data Forecast

Ming-jun Cen and Zhu-zhu Li(✉)

Nanning University, Nanning 530200, China
mjdgdd@163.com, lzz443291045@163.com

Abstract. The traditional student professional development trajectory planning method has low accuracy in student behavior prediction. To this end, a method for student professional development trajectory planning based on big data prediction is designed. Mining students' professional behavior information, cleaning and transforming the data, and establishing student behavior description indicators. Based on this, the student behavior indicators are subdivided, and student professional development trajectory planning is planned based on the predicted student behavior. Experiments have proved that the design of the professional development trajectory planning method based on big data prediction is more accurate than traditional methods for student behavior prediction, and it can meet the needs of student professional development trajectory planning.

Keywords: Big data prediction · Specialty · Development trajectory · Planning · Mining

1 Introduction

With the development of information technology, big data has brought a new turning point for the bottleneck of higher education exploration and personalized training of students, especially for colleges and universities with massive, available and high-quality education data, which provides the possibility for in-depth data mining and academic evaluation [1]. With the continuous increase of various service management platforms in the campus, the amount of accumulated data is also growing. In order to realize the efficient management and sharing of campus data, make full use of students' behavior data in school, build a digital campus and an intelligent campus, and improve the level of campus information, we need to use the method of data mining to optimize student management, according to the characteristics of students' behavior, analyze their behavior rules and guide them to develop in an all-round and healthy way. Therefore, mining and analyzing students' behavior has become the key problem of students' professional development trajectory planning. Aiming at the problems existing in the traditional methods, this paper designs a method of students' professional development trajectory planning based on big data prediction. By mining the information of students' professional behavior,

S. Liu et al. (Eds.): eLEOT 2020, LNICST 339, pp. 329–340, 2020.
https://doi.org/10.1007/978-3-030-63952-5_28

establishing the indicators of students' behavioral characteristics, according to the differences between the quantitative level and data dimension of the indicators of students' behavioral description, the development track of students' professional development is planned. The validity of this method is verified by experiments.

2 Students' Professional Information Mining

The key elements of education data mining include the modeling of students' academic knowledge, daily behavior and work experience, the filing of students' natural information, the modeling of subject knowledge, and the modeling of students' development trend analysis. Among them, academic information modeling mainly collects students' learning information, which can be at the level of curriculum, knowledge points, and students' learning initiative. Behavioral information modeling mainly collects information generated by students in daily life and social work, including accurate investment, activity effect, experience, academic impact, reward acquisition and other data. Data mining refers to the process of extracting hidden information with potential use value from massive data and providing people with decision-making function through analysis. Data mining is a process of continuous reciprocating optimization, mainly including data preprocessing, data mining and model evaluation. Its process is shown in the following Fig. 1:

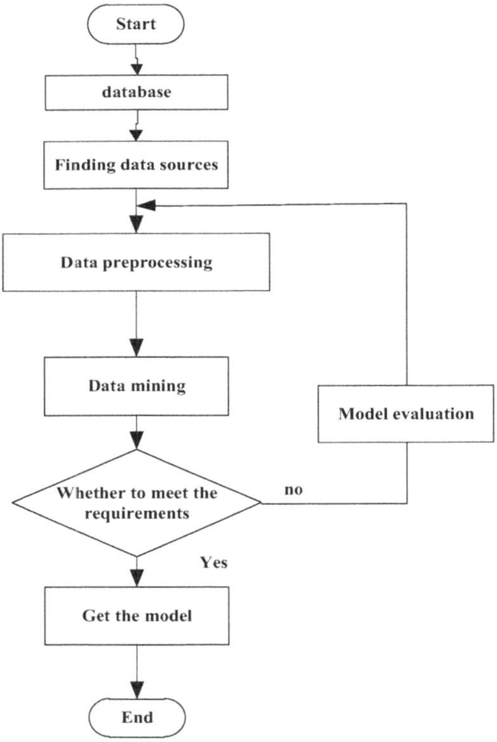

Fig. 1. Data mining process

In view of the course performance data from the student educational administration management system, due to the early construction of the system, coupled with the system update in recent years, the data structure is chaotic, resulting in the collection of data including the students' performance data who have left school, and some students' data lack due to the uncertainty factors such as suspension of school, absence of examination, etc. The main collected information is as follows (Table 1):

Table 1. Key data sheet

Index	Project	Content
1	Student basic information	Student number, name, place of origin, nationality
2	Student major and course information	Major, course, grade, etc.
3	Student card information	Consumption time, consumption place, consumption amount, operator serial number, etc.
4	Student access control information	Library access control, bathhouse credit card access, dormitory access control, computer room access control, etc.
5	Student online log information	Network access time, logout time, IP address, MAC address, URL, etc.

In order to ensure the integrity of the data, clean the data, and remove the redundant and partially missing data [2]. The cleaning formula is:

$$F = \sum_{i=1} f * \frac{d}{g} \tag{1}$$

Where, F represents all student data information collected; $\sum_{i=1} f$ represents noise data in student data; $\frac{d}{g}$ represents data cleaning parameters.

Because the data comes from different systems, there are many duplicate data attributes, and many attributes are not related to the mining target of this paper. For this kind of irrelevant data attribute [3], in this paper, the data specification is eliminated in the preprocessing stage, so as to reduce the data dimension. The calculation formula is as follows:

$$G = l * \frac{f}{M * n} \tag{2}$$

In the formula, G represents data attribute; l represents data source; $M * n$ represents data specification parameter; f represents data dimension.

In the mined student data, a large number of data are user's historical record data. Therefore, the data mined is transformed, and the data is compressed, generalized and standardized by statistics, clustering and classification methods. The calculation formula is as follows:

$$|k| = \int_{i=1} e * h \tag{3}$$

In the formula, $|k|$ represents the frequency of students' consumption time period; $\int_{i=1} e$ represents the data form of students; h is the data conversion parameter.

3 The Establishment of Student Behavior Description Index

Students' basic information is mainly collected by collecting students' natural information, family information, campus environment information and related data of students' participation in network activities. The knowledge modeling of the discipline and professional field of the school includes the information of the professional course setting, professional course learning, professional practice activities, academic research, innovation and entrepreneurship development, etc. The analysis and modeling of students' development trend includes individual academic initiative, knowledge mastery, interest and interest, innovation achievements, etc. Through the analysis of data availability [4] and the evaluation of students' behavior in school, we build a database of students' behavior characteristics, as shown in the following Table 2:

Table 2. characteristics of students' behavior in school

Consumption law	Learning situation	Living habit
Semester consumption	Class attendance	Physical exercise indicators
Average monthly consumption	Book borrowing	Rest time
Consumption frequency	Library access	Surfing time
Consumption level	Final average grade	Diet index
Maximum single consumption	Number of scholarships won	Frequently
Consumption habits	Number of attached courses	
	Study duration	

The consumption behavior of students in school is analyzed, and the consumption records in school, including students' consumption habits, monthly average consumption, semester consumption, single highest consumption and consumption frequency, are extracted as data feature sources, so as to find out the consumption law and consumption level of students; in order to analyze students' efforts and learning achievements, the class attendance rate, book reading amount and learning rate are used Learning time, learning habits and course passing rate are analyzed as data feature sources, so as to understand students' learning situation and grasp learning dynamics [5]; in order to effectively evaluate students' living habits, students' work and rest time, physical exercise, online time and activity location are used as evaluation indicators to analyze the collected data, so as to Understand the law of students' daily life habits. On this basis, students' academic performance is evaluated, and the key contents are as follows (Table 3):

Table 3. Link design and key content of developmental academic evaluation

Serial number	Evaluation link	Important content
1	Evaluation purpose	What purpose is the evaluation information used for, and the evaluation can meet expectations
2	Evaluation goals	Evaluation of the feasibility of the goals, and which development goals the assessment points to
3	Evaluation method	Acceptance of evaluation methods
4	Evaluation rules	Controllability of the evaluation process and participation of relevant personnel
5	Results presented	Credibility of evaluation results, how to define evaluation results, generalization of rating results
6	Final evaluation	Individual student evaluation report, student group development trend report

One of the goals of big data analysis on campus is to subdivide and reasonably classify students' behaviors, provide personalized management and services for different types of students, and improve the accuracy of student management and services [6]. According to the characteristics of students, the segmentation of students is the basis of personalized management for different students.

4 Planning of Students' Professional Development

According to the above analysis, there are big differences in the size and dimensions of the data indicators in the student behavior description indicator table. Part of the data includes the mixed data set composed of numerical type, enumeration type and text attribute [7]. Clustering analysis will seriously affect the analysis results. In order to eliminate the interaction between indicators, we need to standardize and normalize the data [8]. Numerical attribute: numerical data refers to the characteristics of attributes expressed by numerical size [9]. Numerical attributes are divided into discrete and continuous types. Continuous attribute is one-to-one correspondence with real number in given value range, while discrete attribute can only take some specific values in given value range. The normalization method is as follows:

$$x = m * \frac{f}{\max - \min} \tag{4}$$

In the formula, F represents multiple options representing different orders of magnitude; f represents the similarity between multi-dimensional attributes;x is the standardized processing parameter of high-dimensional attributes.

The similarity between attributes is calculated as follows and expressed by distance. The distance calculation of continuous numerical attributes is shown in the following formula:

$$s(i,j) = \frac{vd}{\max * n} \tag{5}$$

In the formula, $s(i,j)$ represents the discrete attribute of data size difference; n represents the number of student behavior indicators; vd represents the distance parameter of continuous numerical attribute [10].

In view of the large amount of clustering and subdividing data for students, and in order to ensure the scalability of the system in the future, we design and implement the algorithm. The parallelization process is shown in the following Fig. 2:

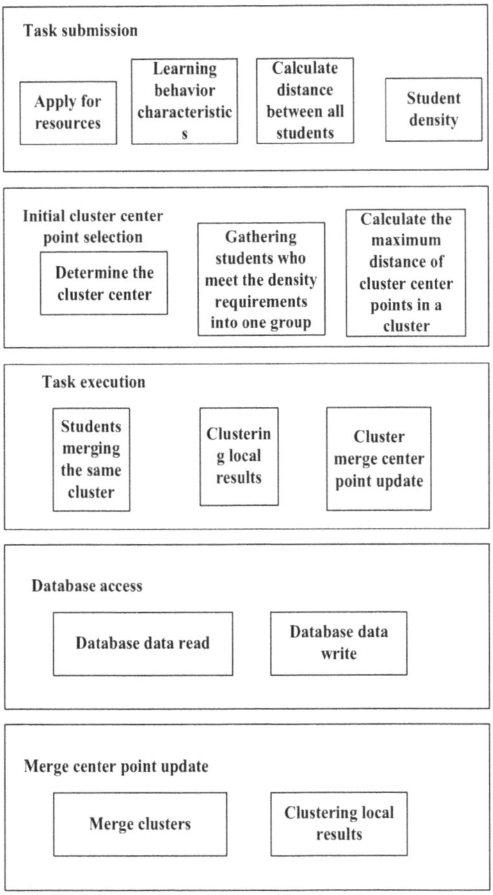

Fig. 2. Clustering of student segmentation indicators

Based on the above extracted Student Behavior Characterization indicators and personal information such as student age, gender, college, etc., a set of student behavior characteristics is constructed:

$$s = \{c_1, c_2, c_3, \cdots, c_n\} \tag{6}$$

In order to construct the hierarchical model of students' behavior, we need to give different weights to different features in the student feature set in order to distinguish the contribution degree of different features to the model, and meet the following requirements:

$$\sum_{i=1}^{n} w = 1 \tag{7}$$

On this basis, the weight of each student's behavior characteristics is determined for the above-mentioned characteristics. Entropy weight method obtains the weight after data processing through statistical method. The calculation process of entropy weight method is as follows:

Firstly, the original behavior characteristic matrix of students is formed

$$X = \begin{bmatrix} x_{11} & \ldots & x_{1n} \\ \vdots & \ddots & \vdots \\ x_{1m} & \cdots & x_{mn} \end{bmatrix} \tag{8}$$

Then the original student behavior characteristic matrix is standardized, and the calculation formula is as follows:

$$n = \frac{s}{\sum_{x}^{s} f} \tag{9}$$

In the formula, n represents the weight of student behavior index; $\sum_{x}^{s} f$ represents the behavior index of target student in target semester; s represents the classification parameter of student behavior.

According to the above calculation, the early warning of students' behavior is classified. The general framework of the early warning model of students' behavior prediction is shown in the Fig. 3 below:

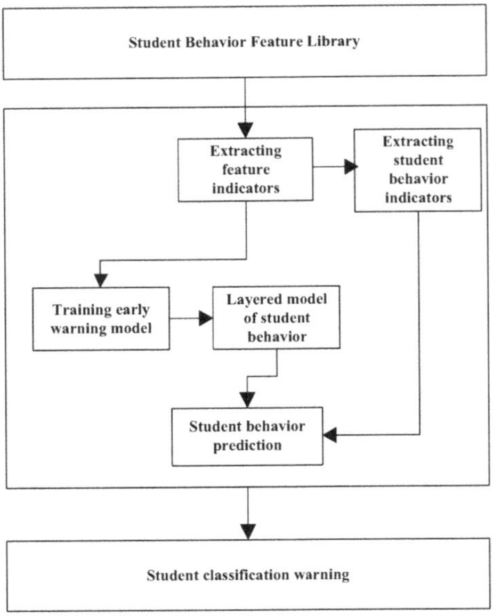

Fig. 3. Prediction of students' behavior stratification

Based on the hierarchical model of students' behavior, the grade of students is determined according to their personal information, and the samples of senior students participating in the prediction of students' behavior are extracted accordingly. Then, based on the hierarchical model of students' behavior, the similarity between the target students and senior students is calculated. In order to improve the accuracy of prediction, the data is standardized before the similarity calculation of the two students' behavior. The main steps are as follows:

First, according to the grade of the target students and the term to be predicted, the historical data of the behavior characteristics of the senior students are loaded;

Second, input data is divided into several parts and distributed to each computing node in big data prediction cluster;

The third is to obtain the characteristic weight of the hierarchical model of students' behavior;

Fourthly, in each node, the similarity between the historical data and the behavior characteristics of the students to be predicted is calculated in parallel;

Fifthly, the results of the similarity calculation of each node's eigenvector are summarized and sorted, and the nearest senior students' history data which is closest to the test data's eigenvector is extracted;

Sixthly, the calculated value based on the weight of the behavior characteristics of the neighbor historical data is taken as the prediction value of the target students.

According to the above process, the study characteristics of students are analyzed to plan their professional development track according to their behavior characteristics, so as to complete their professional development track planning.

5 Experiment

The experimental data source of this paper is the data in the digital campus shared database of a university, and the original data includes 18, 586 undergraduates from March 2015 to March 2017 The data of consumption records of all-in-one card on campus of students in August 2015, library book borrowing records from August 2015 to February 2017, automatic class attendance records from February 2016 to March 2017, access control records from August 2015 to March 2017, as well as school student performance data, physical exercise records, campus wireless network access records, etc. In the experiment, we select some important indexes in the feature database of students' portraits to establish the model of students' behavior prediction and early warning.

This experiment is mainly to verify the effectiveness of the design method of student professional development trajectory planning based on big data prediction, and compare the design method with the traditional method to compare the prediction accuracy of the two methods for student behavior. The prediction accuracy of students is calculated by the following formula:

$$R = \frac{1}{M} / \sum_{B} b \tag{10}$$

In the formula, R represents the predicted value in the dimension; $\frac{1}{M}$ represents the real value in the attribute of the predicted index; $\sum_{B} b$ represents the average value of the relative error after the prediction.

5.1 Establishment of Experimental Environment

The distributed cluster system of the experimental platform consists of one master node and three workers. The master node is also used as the worker node. The main control node and the computing node are interconnected by Ethernet. The specific hardware configuration of the experimental platform is shown in the Table 4 below:

Table 4. Configuration of experimental hardware environment

Node name	Quantity	Parameter
Master	1	IBM, 32 GB RAM, 2.1GHZ *core4, 1 TB
Worker X	4	IBM, 32 GB RAM, 2.1 GHZ *core4, 1 TB
Master		10.50.28.221
Worker1		10.50.28.222
Worker2		10.50.28.223
Worker3		10.50.28.224

The specific configuration of the software environment of each machine in the spark cluster is shown in the Table 5:

Table 5. Configuration of experimental software

Serial number	Software Environment	Configuration information
1	OS	Ubuntu12.04
2	JDK	Jdk1.7.0_67
3	Scala SDK	Scala 2.11.8
4	hadoop	hadoop-2.7.3
5	Spark	Spark-2.0.1

In this experiment, the traditional method and the design method are mainly used to predict the situation of students' professional courses.

5.2 Analysis of Experimental Results

The key point of the planning of students' professional development track is to predict students' behavior. Therefore, the accuracy of the prediction of students' behavior in the first and second grades is taken as the experimental object in this experiment. The comparison results of the two methods are shown in the following Fig. 4:

Analysis of the above figure shows that the experiment has carried out a total of 5 content analysis, and the actual situation of the students is known. The comparison shows that the prediction accuracy of the design method for students in grade one and grade two is high, because the design method fully applies big data prediction technology, and carries out the behavior characteristics of students from multiple perspectives analysis. However, the prediction accuracy of the traditional method is low, and the prediction accuracy of the five contents is lower than that of this design, so it can be proved that this design method has practical application significance.

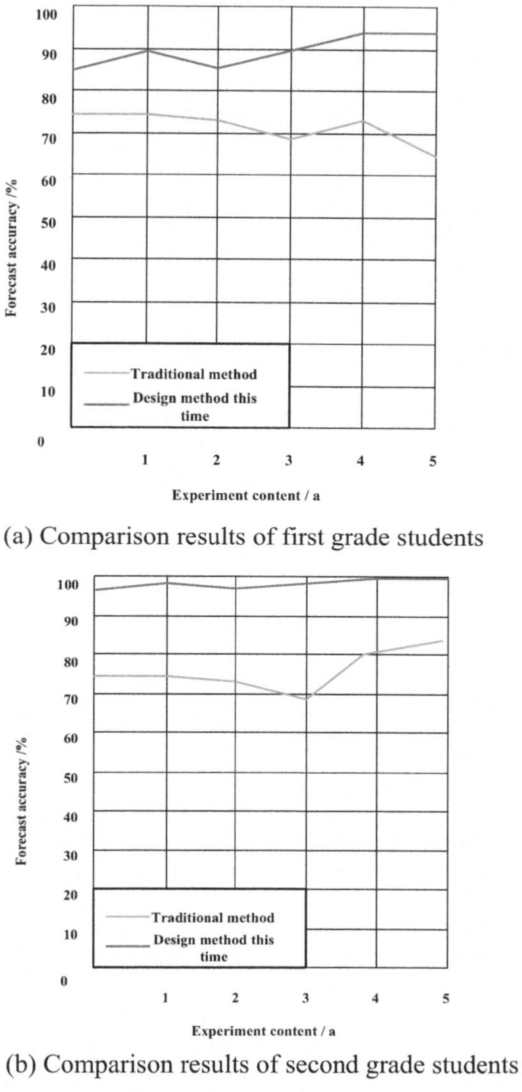

Fig. 4. Experimental comparison results

6 Concluding Remarks

The method of this research designs and constructs the characteristic database of students' portraits, which provides the basis for students' behavior analysis and prediction model. The clustering data mining algorithm is studied. According to the characteristics of students' behavior, the students' behavior is subdivided and the behavior characteristics of all kinds of students are analyzed. This paper constructs a hierarchical prediction model of students' behavior, through which students' behavior is predicted and forewarned according to the inheritance relationship between grades. However, there are still some deficiencies in the design method. In the process of analysis and prediction of students' behavior characteristics, due to the limitations of data sources, the evaluation indicators of students' behavior characteristics can not fully reflect students' behavior in school. In the future, it is necessary to improve the data sources and refine the description indicator system of students' behavior. Because the platform of student behavior analysis and prediction deals with off-line data, there are some disadvantages in data updating and model online learning.

7 Fund Projects

Research and Practice on the Construction of "Mixed Types" Teaching Staff Based on School Enterprise Cooperative Education–Taking ZTE Communication Engineering College of Nanning University as an Example 2016JGB441

References

1. Guangya, S., Fei, W., Yang, L.: System analysis method based on simulation big data. J. Syst. Simul. **31**(3), 511–519 (2019)
2. Dan, L.: The value and cultivation of teachers' positive emotion to the student and teacher development. Teach. Educ. Res. **29**(6), 23–28 (2017)
3. Li, Z., Jianyu, W.: Analysis of satisfaction for the teaching quality based on fuzzy data mining. **48**(18), 106–116 (2018)
4. Yan, L., Nan, Z.: On pathway to innovation of student file management of applied university based on "Internet+" thinking. Vocat. Tech. Educ. **38**(14), 13–15 (2017)
5. Huang, L., Wang, X., Wu, F., et al.: Research on public perception of innovation policy based on network information mining: a case study on new energy vehicle policy. Sci. Sci. Manage. S.&.T. (Monthly) **40**(6), 21–36 (2019)
6. Zhang, R., Haifeng, L.: Associated factors of physical exercise participation among primary and middle school students in Jiangsu. Chin. J. Sch. Health **38**(12), 1793–1795 (2017)
7. Luo, C., Sun, L., Qu, S., et al. Academic performance and physical exercise among high school students in Shanghai. Chin. J. Sch. Health **38**(12), 1804–1806 (2017)
8. Huichao, L.: Research on physical exercise behavior of student pilot based on social cognitive theory. J. Guangzhou Sport Univ. **39**(3), 125–128 (2019)
9. Wang, W., Dong, Y., Hu, Y.: Research on evaluation factors of the students' learning ehavioral engagement based on interpretation structure odel. Math. Pract. Theo. **49**(9), 107–116 (2019)
10. Fayu, W., Yan, J.: Learning interest analysis of users in campus wireless network based on self-organizing neural network and fuzzy C-means clustering algorithm. Appl. Res. Comput. **35**(1), 186–189 (2018)

Interactive Design and Application of Preschool Education IH5 Web Page Based on Cloud and 2–3.5-Year-Old Children's Psychology

Zhu Tiejun(✉), Ma Wenqing, and Zheng Yue

Anhui Polytechnic University, Wuhu 241000, China
ztj@ahpu.edu.cn, 763174353@qq.com, 1971322085@qq.com

Abstract. Due to the influence of traditional concepts, the fierce competition in a large population, the rapid development of China's economy, the increasing improvement of people's living standards and the one-child policy for more than 30 years, Chinese society and families generally attach great importance to the comprehensive education of preschool children. However, through in-depth investigation and research, preschool education resources are unbalanced and scientific education knowledge propaganda is inadequate, which leads to the many misunderstandings and inappropriate educational methods in current China, especially in the stage of 2–3.5-year-old preschool education. In addition, China has rapidly entered the era of online education. IH5, as a design tool to support various mobile devices and mainstream browsers, has the characteristics of short time-consuming, information gathering and clear information transmission. Therefore, based on a thorough study of the physical and mental development characteristics of children aged 2 to 3.5 and thematic education methods, through a cloud-based IH5 page design with strong interaction, high cognition, easy operation and wide popularity, it integrates scientific and authoritative preschool education knowledge, practical and interesting interactive content and simple and easy operation interface. This paper aims to improve the lagging situation of the network propaganda and promotion of preschool education between 2 and 3.5 years old in China, at the same time, to provide targeted, accurate and valuable preschool education information for the public and families of preschool children, so as to meet the realistic needs of the market.

Keywords: IH5 · Cloud · Interactive design · Preschool education · 2–3.5-year-old children's psychology

1 Introduction

Nowadays, China's education is more and more in line with the international community. Besides, because of the One Child Policy in the past decades, Chinese people are paying more and more attention to preschool education. For preschool children, education at the age of 2–3.5 is crucial. However, although preschool education is generally valued

S. Liu et al. (Eds.): eLEOT 2020, LNICST 339, pp. 341–350, 2020.
https://doi.org/10.1007/978-3-030-63952-5_29

by Chinese society and families, the educational resources are not balanced enough, education methods are inadequate. Professional, authoritative, scientific and effective educational knowledge has not been widely disseminated and propagated, especially in preschool education at the age of 2–3.5, the public still has a bigger one-sided educational awareness and misunderstandings, and their demands are not satisfied.

According to the statistical data of China's online education market outlook and investment strategic planning analysis report published by China Prospective Industry Research Institute, it shows China's online education market has exceeded 300 billion Yuan in 2018, and in 2019, China's online education market is expected to reach 387 billion Yuan [1]. Another group of data from "China Smart Mobile Terminal Software Industry Market Operation Situation and Development Prospect Forecast Report 2018–2024" shows The number of mobile terminals in the world has exceeded 10 billion in 2018, and the number of mobile Smartphone has reached 2.8 billion, [2] of which the number of mobile Smartphone in China alone has exceeded 50% of the global number [3]. Therefore, it is of great significance and expected effect to combine mobile devices and mainstream browsers to carry out the dissemination and promotion of scientific cognition of 2–3.5-year-old preschool education.

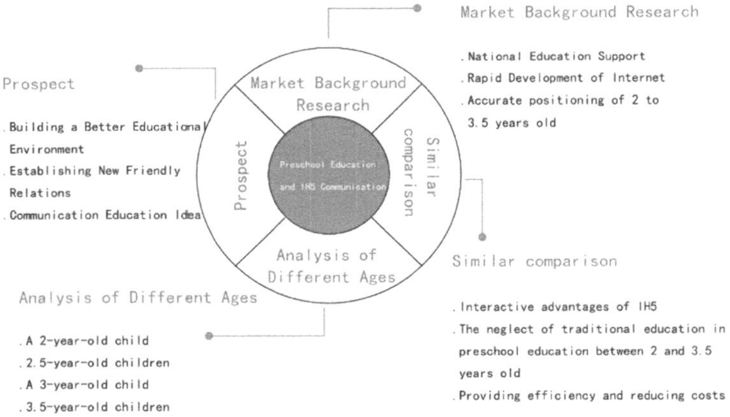

Fig. 1. Framework of social and market investigation

With the help of IH5 web page interactive design tool based on cloud, internet traffic classification [4] and Internet of Things information processing technology, [5] this paper develops web page design for preschool education of 2–3.5 years old, and produces many kinds of interactive content such as PPT, atlas, games and videos. On the one hand, users can realize online editing function by visualizing the information of preschool education for 2–3.5-year-old children and multimedia elements, such as dragging, discharging and setting, without coding, so as to effectively meet the diverse needs of different users. On the other hand, this research and design aims to provide educational consultation based on thorough and meticulous investigation (Fig. 1), help and guidance to the public and parents of young children with IH5 rich mobile interaction design style and professional

2–3.5-year-old early childhood education system, and to build a sharing platform to realize the positive interaction among the government, society, educational institutions and children's families.

2 Analysis of IH5 Pushing Utility of Preschool Education Information from 2 to 3.5 Years Old

Through time, we have seen mobile phones transform into multifaceted devices, adapted to meet and exceed our everyday needs [6]. With the rapid development of the network era, more and more applications have leaped into people's vision [7]. The rising popularity of mobile social media enables personalization of various content sharing and subscribing services [8]. In such a prosperous situation, people are no longer satisfied with the amount of information expressed, or there is no way to handle the huge social network information, [9] so more and more people would like to pay more attention to whether they can get the information they need at a glance. In this situation, what is needed is to attract the users' attention. If it is a long story, it may not grasp people's desire for acquiring information and knowledge. In addition, according to the findings of the survey, in China, K12 (from kindergarten, usually 5–6 years old, to twelve grades, usually 17–18 years old) is the most promising market, while ignoring the education of 2–3.5-year-old children. At the same time, the traditional online education has the drawbacks of dullness, lack of communication and learning atmosphere. Therefore, this paper conforms to the rhythm of the times and takes IH5 as the carrier to promote the traditional online education of 2–3.5-year-old children. The combination of preschool education and ih5 page design can well convey the interaction of education. As shown in Fig. 2, IH5 is more interactive than MAKA, RABBITPRE and other online creative tools. The IH5 page design and information push can effectively enhance the interaction and interesting of user learning and communication.

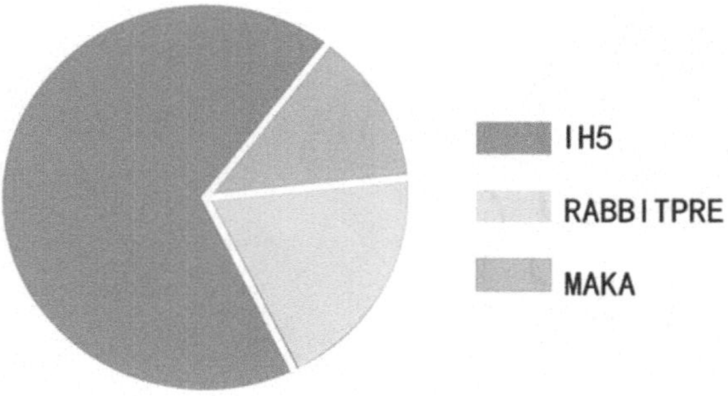

Fig. 2. Interactive percentage of ih5 with Maka and Rabbitpre online creative tools

IH5 is a design tool that supports various mobile devices and mainstream browsers. It can design and produce PPT, application prototype, digital greeting cards, albums, profiles, invitations, advertising videos and other types of interactive content [10]. Its main characteristics are simple, cross-platform, involving a wide range. This form can effectively promote people's active learning [11]. Like today's very popular short video APP such as Trembler, Fast Hand, and so on, in addition, wedding companies and others also use IH5 technology to promote the network to the extreme. As for why these APP based on IH5 is so popular, on the one hand, it is because of the short display time, attractive content and theme, on the other hand, it is because of the information gathering, so that people can see it at a glance, without spending too much thought, and it can also easily trigger transfer learning [12]. IH5 has the characteristics of short time-consuming, information gathering and clear information transmission.

However, there is no product directly related to 2–3.5-year-old preschool education in IH5 application on the Chinese market. In order to better let everyone know about scientific and systematic knowledge preschool education, a mobile phone push and jump project has been made in IH5. Unlike the usual IH5 application, there are usually only advertisements and promotional products to be pushed [13], but the education aspect is not effective involved. Seeing the fast dissemination of ih5 and the convenience of customers' use, this IH5 push with preschool education is designed to enable users to simply and clearly obtain information on 2–3.5-year-old preschool education, and to get the content they need without any obstacles, as well as link queries on the website. Graphs have been widely used for social network, [14] especially in children education field. The ideas of page design in Fig. 3 are mainly yellow and blue colors, creating a happy atmosphere. Place the yellow-blue triangle around indirectly, the triangle has the directional function, is conducive to gathering the viewer's line of sight, can better

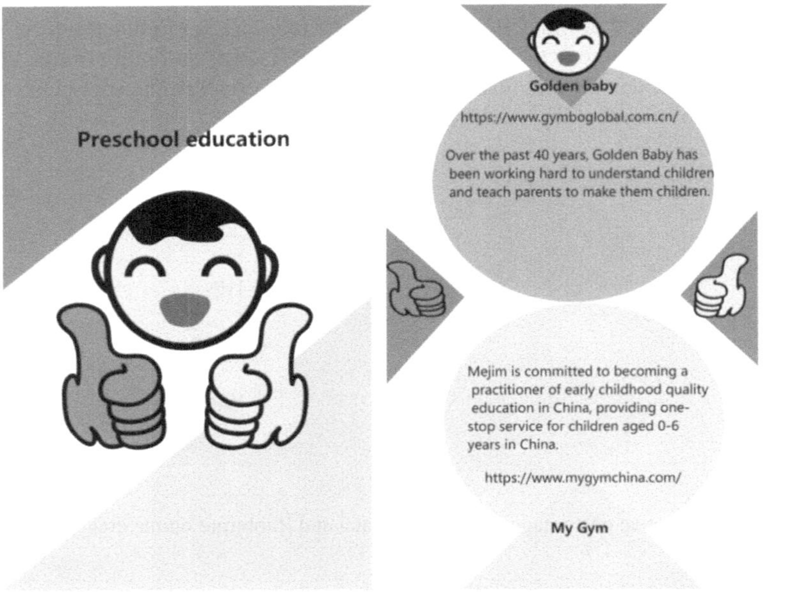

(a)First Page (b) Authoritative Website Recommendation

Fig. 3. Push page of IH5 application of 2–3.5-year-old preschool education

highlight the content to be displayed. The smiling face expression is placed in the upper triangle and the yellow and blue hands are placed in the left and right triangles, so that the three forms the action of embracing or praising, which reflects the reassurance and security.

In the early stage of design, a lot of information about 2–3.5-year-old preschool education was collected and investigated. Early childhood education and adult education are completely different thinking patterns. 2–3.5-year-old preschool education lies in directional education. It does not require them to acquire much knowledge, but needs to let them better understand the outside world. It is an enlightening role. As the first teacher of a child, how do parents educate their children? Different children have different personality manifestations. We do not emphasize the unity of educational methods. Instead, parents are required to have a baseline to measure right and wrong and a baseline to guide them. Many people are in a relatively vague state about early childhood education [15], especially as a novice mother, may be in a state of haste in children's education. Of course, in the network information age, what kind of questions can be found satisfactory answers on the Internet, and there is also knowledge about early childhood education on the Internet. But because of too much information, people's choices will become confused, and people will be uncertain, cannot tell the good from the bad. Information push based on IH5 of preschool education between 2 and 3.5 years old children formally solves this problem.

At this stage, the main task is to make educational strategies for the age group of 2 to 3.5 years, including the analysis of children's understanding at different stages, and the analysis of what kind of attitude they should hold. If you don't know how to educate and communicate with children, it doesn't matter. This project can tell you how to educate and guide children, how to make them more knowledgeable and better.

3 Analysis of Psychological Behavior of Children Aged 2 to 3.5

At present, early childhood education pays attention to "conscious" education after 4 years of age, but neglects the "habit" education formed by "unconscious" of children from 2 to 3.5 years old. For example, in the eyes of adults, children always rely on something. In fact, in young children, they need something to support their psychological needs [16]. The problem with traditional early childhood education is largely adult ignorance. This stage of children's cognitive style is also the most unique, should receive the attention of adults, parents need to learn together.

2-year-old babies begin to like to play with small partners, communication opens the door to a new world for them, and their perception has changed greatly in all aspects [17]. For different age groups of children, through data research, made the following simple analysis.

(1) 2-year-old children actively explore the world and try to learn the world. Their learning ability will grow stronger with their growth. The platform of combining 2-year-old preschool education with IH5 will provide targeted guidance to let parents know why their children in this age are becoming less obedient, and even more domineering. This phenomenon is because they have their own consciousness, willingness and intention.

(2) 2.5-year-old children have a preliminary understanding of the outside world, can feel some differences around them, but their world is mostly self-centered [18]. When they see something interesting and they like it, they all think it's their own. This is a normal phenomenon. In this case, how to communicate with children can be found and learned in the IH5 push of 2–2.5-year-old preschool education.
(3) 3-year-old children are the age stage that they like to share with others. They will not be as tough as before. At this time, they will have their own communication circle, they will find new things, they will have things they like most, they will learn to cooperate. As the saying goes, the performance of a three-year-old child can be used to predict his performance as an adult [19]. Children in this period will gradually form some basic personality factors. How to guide, IH5 push platform for 3-year-old preschool education can lead users and children to explore together.
(4) Children aged three and a half are relatively insecure. They don't know how to handle their relationship with others correctly. How to give children a sense of security, let children know their relationship with others, IH5 push information can be faster to let parents know. Furthermore, this stage of children's performance has a certain continuum, and will continue to form their personality performance. If there is no correct external influence and guidance at this stage, there will be personality defects in the future. Therefore, parents should pay attention to the psychological development of 3.5-year-old children.

Let parents participate. Let them experience, judge and make decisions about the way children grow up, and build up similar psychological feelings with children [20]. As shown in Table 1, in order to show the bright prospects of early childhood education, the

Table 1. Physical and mental characteristics of 2–3.5-year-old children

No.	Age group	Physical and mental characteristics
1	2 year old children	Begin to care about others, and actively study and explore the world. Learning ability and acceptance range are increasing day by day. At this time, we need to pay attention to providing children guidance with language skills and communication skills
2	2.5 year old children	Psychologists call the period the "first resistance period" of life. The self-consciousness including strong need for independence, a willingness to act and sense of possession is mainly expressed
3	3 year old children	In the period, the children's attention cannot be last and usually shifts from one this to another. However, once a child encounters something that attracts them, he or she will devote himself to it and repeat or mimic. Therefore, in some sense, their concentration ability is amazing
4	3.5 year old children	Compared with above three periods, this period children are more clever and naughty. Therefore, we cannot ignore the early education and psychological nursing including physical, intellectual, moral and aesthetic aspects and so on

physical and mental performance of children in each stage is designed in blue strips, rising step by step, forming a ladder to highlight the cognitive growth process of 2–3.5-year-old children.

On the other hand, blue has a sense of science and technology. Based on the blue background, it implies the orderly presentation of educational content and the extraction of concise information. Let the user's visual center be clear, but also let the mind be clear. Functionality and practicality coexist, which conforms to the public's aesthetics.

4 IH5 Interface Design for Preschool Education from 2 to 3.5 Years Old

Through the investigation of the data about early childhood education in recent years, we find that parents in China want their children to learn knowledge or have a happy childhood. They also want the early birds to eat insects, win at the starting line, and let their children's enlightenment education take the lead. In fact, 2 to 3.5 years old is also a crucial period for young children [21]. They are like explorers, who are willing to explore their own way of life, and they will have a completely different way of accepting things from the future. The most effective education for children is interest. Children with strong action and practical ability learn more than their counterparts.

For this reason, two IH5 interface schemes of 2 to 3.5 years old preschool education are designed.

Scheme 1: The scheme is designed for is designed for children's cognitive psychology and habits, as shown in Fig. 4. Bright color, simple layout and cartoon design. It embodies interestingness, so as to cultivate children's temperament and interest. Doll's smiling face represents the process of children's happy growth and a bright future; Round, rectangular and triangular forms a simple geometry and block surface, showing inclusiveness and dynamic. On the other hand, arrows are instructive and can play a better guiding role. The simple abstraction of the content makes the impression more profound.

The use of color is made up of yellow and blue, which has a sense of youth, relaxation and tidiness. Watching it, the mood will be pleasant. Among them, the color transparency will be somewhat different in depth, which will open up some space and make the viewing more hierarchical.

Scheme 2: The scheme is designed for parents of 2–3.5-year-old children and the public, as shown in Fig. 5. Mainly from four aspects to reflect the advantages and focuses: First, the Internet interaction platform, using a concise vector diagram, blue background reflects the blueprint of educational prospects, the middle of the white paper to convey the IH5 interactivity, let users interact and communicate better while getting information; Second, objective and comprehensive analysis, using three different transparent blue tones and a three-dimensional surround interpolation to show the rich and diverse content of education; Third, the precise positioning of the service group, also using the vector of the blue tone vector diagram, color from light to deep, and there is a ladder shape from right to left, which reflects the continuous growth of children aged 2 to 3.5 years; Fourth, the strong support of the national policy, the opening up of the Internet + strategy and the education policy, has stimulated the new development of online education, of course, including early childhood education.

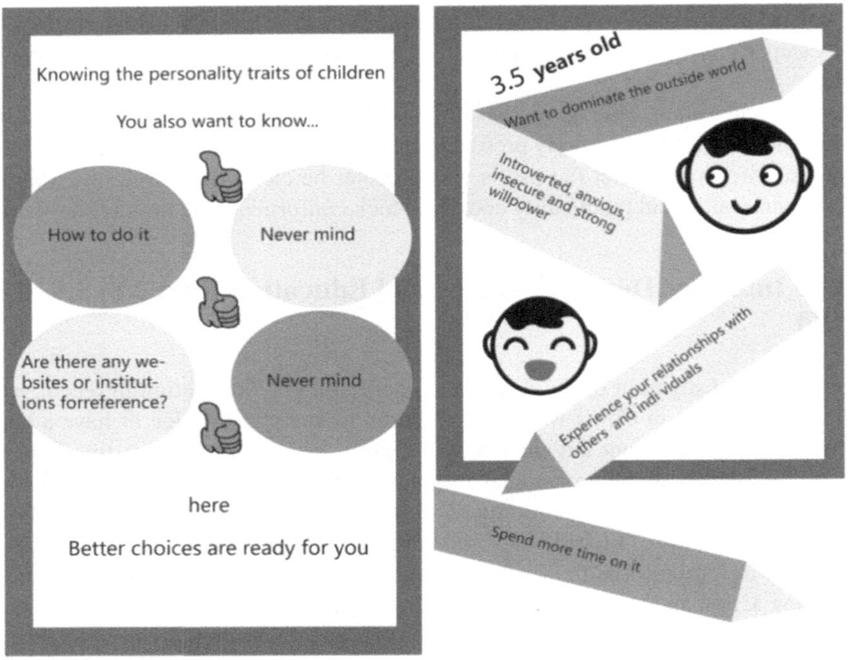

(a) Classified Selection Design (b) Psychological and Behavioral Characteris tics of 3.5-year-old Children

Fig. 4. IH5 interface design display of scheme 1

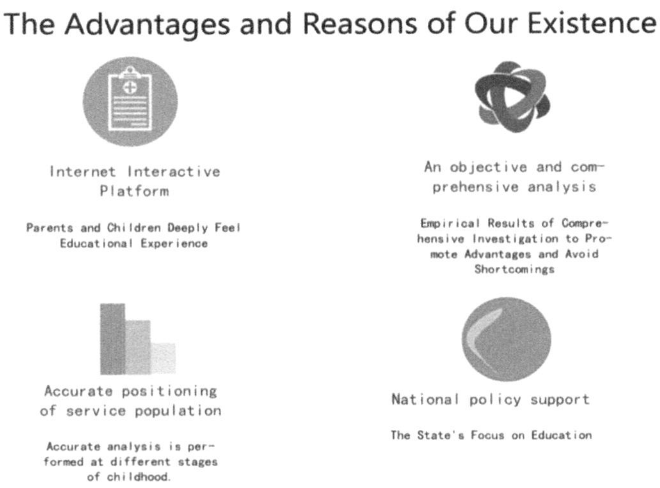

Fig. 5. IH5 interface design display of scheme 2

5 Conclusions

Education is the cornerstone of a country, and information is an important resource nowadays. Interactive design and application of 2–3.5-year-old preschool education ih5 web page based on cloud, through in-depth research, on the one hand, this paper carries out targeted design in content and form from the cognitive habits and characteristics of 2–3.5 years old children's growth stage. On the other hand, it effectively utilizes the advantages of IH5 to create a scientific media that conforms to the development of children's mind, and strives to make the public better accept and popularize the scientific knowledge of preschool education between 2 and 3.5 years old, so as to better improve the quality of education.

At present, the rapid development of online education is more than any other industry. In the future, IH5 and 2–3.5-year-old preschool education will popularize mobile terminals. Users can receive the scientific knowledge of 2–3.5-year-old preschool education anytime and anywhere. The combination of network information and education can better promote the growth of 2–3.5-year-old children, create a better educational environment for them, and let more adults respect children. To understand children and establish a new kind of friendly relationship with them.

In the future, the platform can be attached to other Apps without taking up precious space on the phone, and in the competitive world of tomorrow, parents will be even busier about their children's futures, there will be less communication between parents and children, resulting in more children being sent to the Care Center. However, children aged 2–3.5 years old are not able to take care of themselves and have poor psychological endurance. This platform will be the bridge between parents and the Care Center, always pay attention to children's behavior and psychological situation; children aged 2–3.5 years in some families will ask a nanny to take care of their children, this platform can not only be used for the guidance of children's psychological conditions, but also make nannies more targeted to take care of children. If implanted into the future robot nanny, it will bring more convenience to parents and children.

The popularity of this platform will enrich China's 2–3.5-year-old children application software and fill in the relevant vacancies, the platform of some psychological guidance so that children and parents get along more comfortable, so that children have a good physical and mental development. On the basis of children's psychology, simple graphics, rich colors, will attract more children users to use; at the same time, parents can better understand their children according to the platform. Therefore, children aged 2–3.5 and their parents need such a platform especially in the future.

Acknowledgment. This work is supported in part by quality engineering supports special project of online teaching in colleges and universities during epidemic prevention and control(Anhui Polytechnic University) "Research on the online implementation and management of international students' intelligent classroom and practice teaching under large-scale epidemic outbreak" (2020xsjyxm08) and Zhongjiang scholar talent project.

References

1. Liu, W.: 2018 China Mobile Communication Terminal Equipment Industry Research Report. China Market Research Online (2018)
2. Yan, Z.: Current Situation and Trend Analysis of Online Education Industry in China in 2018. Prospective Industry Research Institute (2018)
3. You, M.: 2018 Global Mobile Internet Market Research Series Report. Research Center for Electronic Commerce (2018)
4. Sun, G., Chen, T., Su, Y., Li, C.: Internet traffic classification based on incremental support vector machines. Mob. Netw. Appl. **23**(4), 789–796 (2018). https://doi.org/10.1007/s11036-018-0999-x
5. Sun, G., Li, J., Dai, J.: Feature selection for IoT based on maximal information coefficient. Future Gener. Comput. Syst.-Int. J. Escience **89**, 606–616 (2018)
6. Han, Q.L., Liang, S., Zhang, H.L.: Mobile cloud sensing, big data, and 5G networks make an intelligent and smart world. IEEE Netw. **29**(2), 40–45 (2015)
7. Chen, W., Liu, N.: Internet + Education. China Economic Publishing House (2015)
8. He, Z., Cai, Z., Han, Q., Tong, W., Sun, L., Li, Y.: An energy efficient privacy-preserving content sharing scheme in mobile social networks. Pers. Ubiquit. Comput. **20**(5), 833–846 (2016). https://doi.org/10.1007/s00779-016-0952-6
9. Shi, Q., Wang, H., Li, D., Shi, X., Ye, C., Gao, H.: Maximal influence spread for social network based on mapreduce. In: Wang, H., Qi, H., Che, W., Qiu, Z., Kong, L., Han, Z., Lin, J., Lu, Z. (eds.) ICYCSEE 2015. CCIS, vol. 503, pp. 128–136. Springer, Heidelberg (2015). https://doi.org/10.1007/978-3-662-46248-5_16
10. Montessori, M.: Montessori's Education. Beijing University of Technology Press (2015)
11. Sun, G., Li, S., Chen, T., et al.: Active learning method for chinese spam filtering. Int. J. Performability Eng. **13**(4), 511–518 (2017)
12. Sun, G., Liang, L., Chen, T., et al.: Network traffic classification based on transfer learning. Comput. Electr. Eng. **69**, 1–8 (2018)
13. Liu, Z.M.: Exploration and analysis of product growth design. Decoration **54**(6), 145–159 (2012)
14. Wang, Y., Wang, H., Li, J., Gao, H.: Efficient graph similarity join for information integration on graphs. Front. Comput. Sci. **10**(2), 317–329 (2016). https://doi.org/10.1007/s11704-015-4505-3
15. Yang, S.M.: Exploring the design innovation of outdoor articles for infants and young children. Prod. Des. **20**(5), 33–36 (2018)
16. Montessori, M.: Secrets of Childhood. People's Education Press (2004)
17. Li, C.Y., Yang, H.: Exploring the application of modular design method in children's furniture. Ind. Des. **8**(3), 56–58 (2016)
18. Adler, A.: Child Growth Psychology. China Rule of Law Press (2018)
19. Zhou, Z.K.: Modern Child Development Psychology. Anhui People's Publishing House (2000)
20. Yin, J.: Innovative Strategy of Game-based Education to Change Internet Education. People's Posts and Telecommunications Publishing House (2018)
21. Carl, H.G., Carl, W.: Education. Harbin Publishing House (2009)

Research on the Dimensions of Art Design Education in Taiwan Shih Chien University

Zhu Tiejun(✉) and Zhang Linlin

Anhui Polytechnic University, Wuhu, China
ztj@ahpu.edu.cn

Abstract. With the increasing frequency and deepening of cultural and educational exchanges between the two sides of the Taiwan Strait and the proposal of the latest requirements given by the social era of the optimization of the professional quality and practical ability of senior art and design talents, the cultivation of art and design talents in Mainland Colleges and universities should adhere to the tradition, open up and innovate, learn from the practical characteristics and new talent cultivation mode of art and design education in Taiwan Colleges and universities, and through focusing on Taiwan the art and design education of bay practice university is analyzed and elaborated from the aspects of curriculum, teachers' construction, campus culture, capital investment, etc., and shows its value and Enlightenment of art and design education, so as to provide innovation and reform of art and design education in mainland China and linkage and complementarity of Art and Design Education Exchange and talent training mechanism between the two sides, and finally realize the art and design between the two sides. The high quality and optimization of the education and development of technical design senior talents.

Keywords: Art design major · Education dimension · Higher education in Taiwan · Educational characteristics · Innovative practice

1 Background

Taiwan Shih Chien University is an institution of higher learning with more than 60 years of experience in running schools. It was founded in 1958. "It is a comprehensive university with two campuses in Taipei and Kaohsiung, and five colleges including design, people's livelihood, management, business and information, culture and creativity. Its school of design has been rated as one of the 60 top design schools in the world by business week. In recent years, many universities in the mainland have sent people to investigate and observe, and many universities have cooperated with them in running schools" [1]. With the continuous deepening of cross-strait exchanges, it will become an important way for mainland universities to improve the quality of art talents training to jointly train art talents with Taiwan universities, including Taiwan practical University. Based on the in-depth investigation and observation during his time as a visiting scholar

S. Liu et al. (Eds.): eLEOT 2020, LNICST 339, pp. 351–361, 2020.
https://doi.org/10.1007/978-3-030-63952-5_30

in the Shih Chien University, this paper focuses on his art education practice and highlights his art education concept and value from the practice orientation and operation path of curriculum, teacher construction, campus culture, capital investment and other dimensions.

2 The Structural Dimension of Curriculum

2.1 Specialized Courses and Basic Courses with Independent Ecology

According to statistics, about 70% of Taiwan's colleges and universities have art majors and 80% of them in mainland China. This proportion highlights the importance and urgency of the reform and innovation of art talents training, and at the same time, it is more necessary to build a systematic and harmonious art design education state. In terms of art and design education and personnel training, Taiwan University of practice attaches great importance to the refinement and convergence of art education ideas and design thoughts, and actively creates independent art education ecology suitable for the development of Taiwan's art thoughts and the promotion of design industry. Its design institute integrates art, design, culture, humanistic aesthetics, creativity, life style and other knowledge fields in a short period of time. In the course of more than ten years' development, we have broken through the obstacles of Taiwan's education system, and "In teaching, focus on learners, emphasize the practical characteristics of 'hand as eye', and cultivate students' independent creative thinking and design execution ability" [2]. Now it is reflected in the basic curriculum, more showing the understanding and understanding of the design spirit and creative methods and ideas, while its design institute's positioning in the professional curriculum is "professional interaction and integration", professional cross-border, multi-dimensional interaction and exchange and learning together have become the soft environment of its professional curriculum teaching, and its art design education professional curriculum and basic curriculum independent ecology. The successful construction of the model has become a benchmark and epitome of the development of art education in Taiwan. Due to the lack of language and cultural barriers, the mainland art majors studying in Taiwan can not only integrate into this benign art education system and ecology without barriers, but also combine and use better art education methods and learning means in the mainland to achieve the optimal state of art major learning and self-improvement of comprehensive literacy.

2.2 A Practical Course for Cultivating the Temperament and Self-restraint of Humanities and Arts

"The design work of art is composed of numerous distinctive artistic individuals, which integrates a variety of artistic images and cultural connotations", [3] art and design, as an ideology reflecting social life, are an important part of human culture, so the effective expression and creative design of art must have profound cultural connotation, while the cultivation of art talents to foster, we should put cultural ideas and cultural literacy into art education. In addition to the general education courses offered by the Liberal Arts Department, the Taiwan University of practice realizes the student-centered experiential practical teaching based on the real situation through the deployment and integration of cross field courses and in combination with the social and cultural guidance and trend of the Taiwan industry, aiming at offering drama, performance, film, literary classics reading and art appreciation to the students of the design institute analysis, cultural lectures, cultural and creative industries, cultural and art management and other courses and series of activities can provide students with a wider range of contacts and deep understanding and experience of cultural connotation while learning professional technology, with humanistic and artistic temperament and self-cultivation, while Taipei City Art Museum, World Trade Center, Songshan Airport, Taipei Contemporary Art Museum and other art design based on the closely fitting social practice base, it also provides students with the humanistic orientation and design execution ability to adapt to the society, which has become a firm education direction for the cultivation of contemporary, social and practical art and design talents in practical universities.

To realize the quality monitoring and evaluation of practical courses and effectively ensure the quality of practical teaching is another feature of art design education in practical universities. It pays attention to the creation verification of students, emphasizes reflection and criticism, and highlights design services. At the same time, combined with the evaluation activities of practical courses and in-depth participation in the annual joint exhibition of graduation design in Taiwan's colleges and universities, it is designed to bring young students. At the same time of the enlightenment and experience of the opening of the brain hole of the planner, it also makes the students learn the real ability from the practice course and acquire the real social application ability.

2.3 Liberal Arts General Course with the Concept of All-Around Art Design

Art can be said to be a discipline that draws on the strengths of all, but also a comprehensive discipline. The traditional training courses for art and design talents are simple, old-fashioned and contain limited knowledge horizon, which cannot meet the standards of high-quality and all-round comprehensive art and design talents. Taiwan's colleges and universities attach great importance to liberal education and general education in addition to the professional knowledge of art students. Liberal education, also known as "liberal education", originated from ancient Greece, mainly refers to the establishment of an educational concept that cultivates people with a wide range of knowledge and elegant temperament, and carries out a wide range of inclusive practical teaching. As for general education, "generally speaking, A. Levine's general education the definition of general education has been generally accepted. Levin points out that general education refers to the common part of the undergraduate course with a certain range of contents. It usually includes the study of courses related to several disciplines, trying to provide a kind of undergraduate training that should be shared by all students in a school. The core of general education is to emphasize the balanced development of people so as to lay a comprehensive foundation for future work" [4]. Both liberal education and general education require students to have a broader vision, knowledge and more comprehensive quality. Taiwan practical university has done a good job in this respect. Its liberal arts department was founded in 1997, formerly known as general education center. It can be seen that liberal arts education and general education in Taiwan have certain commonality. "The general education system of Liberal Arts Department of Taiwan practical university has the following characteristics: (1) the primary goal of talent training is to cultivate students' mind and temperament and create happiness Life. (2) The general education curriculum is planned comprehensively, covering a wide range of fields; (3) focusing on the professional background of teachers, emphasizing the academic ability training of teachers and students; (4) attaching importance to language ability training, increasing the proportion of Chinese learning; (5) attaching importance to social services, quality training, and encouraging teachers and students to participate in social services; (6) the natural science curriculum focuses on health care, eco-tourism, scientific life application, and learning It's easy to learn" [5].

Although most colleges and universities in mainland China have gradually popularized general courses, the distinction between art and design majors and other liberal arts majors is not obvious. The liberal arts general courses offered by Taiwan practical university are more "art" and "design" with more elements. The first semester of 2018–2019 academic year of Kaohsiung Campus of practical university is liberal arts. For example, as shown in Fig. 1, the courses of interest directly related to art account for 32%. In addition, other courses related to humanities and society are also related to art design, and even natural courses can fully realize cross-border accommodation, achieve a global understanding based on art design, so as to promote the improvement of their art level and social cognit (Table 1).

Table 1. The first semester of 2018–2019 academic year in Kaohsiung Campus of Shih Chien University

Course No.	Course Name	Credit	Teaching Hour	Course type
1273	(130) Marriage and family	2	2	Social type
1274	(871) Career development and planning	2	2	Social type
1276	(J1Y) Handicraft Aesthetics	2	2	Humanistic type
1277	(J2B) Behind the scenes news and social operation	2	2	Social type
1278	(J2D) Leadership and communication	2	2	Social type
1279	(J2K) First aid knowledge and Application	2	2	Natural type
1280	(J2R) Gender and social culture	2	2	Social type
1281	(J2U) Globalization and gender equality	2	2	Social type
1282	(J3S) Appreciation of calligraphy art	2	2	Humanistic type
1283	(J45) Music and life	2	2	Humanistic type

(continued)

Table 1. (*continued*)

Course No.	Course Name	Credit	Teaching Hour	Course type
1284	(J5R) Ecological environment and sustainable development	2	2	Natural type
1287	(J75) Film and music	2	2	Humanistic type
1288	(J76)Visual arts	2	2	Humanistic type
1289	(J79) Psychology and life	2	2	Social type
1290	(JB9) First aid and prevention of sports injury	2	2	Natural type
1291	(JF1) Music appreciation	2	2	Humanistic type
1292	(JN8) National parks and ecological conservation	2	2	Natural type
1293	(K28) Chinese medicine and life	2	2	Natural type
1295	(LK2) Film and culture	2	2	Humanistic type
1299	(Q95) News process and social operation	2	2	Social type
1300	(XB4) Nature and life	2	2	Natural type
1301	(XB5) Introduction to environmental protection	2	2	Natural type
1302	(XB7) Ecotourism	2	2	Natural type
1303	(XG3) Elegant etiquette and life image	2	2	Humanistic type
1304	(XH2) Service learning course	2	2	Social type
3121	(JN6) Brain and mind	2	2	Natural type
3122	(J4T) Biodiversity and sustainable development	2	2	Natural type
3124	(J6L) Gender and psychology	2	2	Natural type
3126	(J1M) Aboriginal literature in Taiwan	2	2	Humanistic type

3 The Cross-Border Dimension of Teachers' Construction

The diversity of teachers in Taiwan's colleges and universities has become a major feature and highlight of Taiwan's higher education. Most of Taiwan's private colleges and universities have already entered a period of intense student resources. In order to gain a place in the fierce competition and attract more students to apply for the examination, most of Taiwan's private colleges and universities recruit people with practical experience and top professionals as part-time teachers of the school. Meanwhile, a large number of overseas experts and scholars are employed to practice the Design College of the University. For example, during 2012–2017 alone, more than 100 professors and senior executives from universities and companies from the United States, Germany, Japan, South Korea, Britain, Denmark, Finland, Singapore, Malaysia, Australia, the Netherlands, Switzerland and other countries were employed. Among the full-time teachers, not only the academic qualifications are generally high, but also most of them are overseas returnees. "The school of design of practical University also attaches great importance to the multiple characteristics of curriculum teachers, so that students can simultaneously contact different creative ideas and different professional demands. At the same time, through the long-term contact mechanism and cooperative relationship with the international community, we have selected internationally renowned design experts and scholars as guest teachers to give systematic instruction. On the one hand, we have expanded the international vision of students, and also invited teachers and students from overseas sister schools to participate. This will not only improve our international reputation, but also show the design momentum of teachers and students to the international community" [2]. The teachers are avant-garde in concept, active in thinking, creative and passionate. They not only have the knowledge and skills to "practice", but also most of them have their own companies or studios, rich management experience and social experience. They understand the market dynamics of today's society, what kind of talents enterprises need, and how to prepare for entrepreneurship, etc.

According to the survey and statistics made by the author during the visit to the practical University, the students of the University have more opportunities to contact the society. For example, the "entrepreneurship and innovation lecture" course offered by the university has a total of 18 weeks of courses. The lecturer has contacted 13 Social executives of different companies in different fields to give lectures directly to the students. One and a half hours of lectures plus one and a half hours of in-depth interaction. The remaining five weeks there will be three off campus visits, and students will visit relevant companies in person. If students intend to join their company after graduation, they will also be given opportunities after evaluation. "Combine the professional theoretical knowledge with the practical ability of the industry effectively, so that students can learn practical experience in Teachers' projects. Teaching is not limited by form, emphasizing the combination of product design and industrial development needs, focusing on the cultivation and expression of innovative design thinking, and strengthening the training of practical skills" [7]. Such a large number of teachers directly introduced into the society, combined with the teaching and practice content closely related to the society and reality, is exactly what the current mainland students, especially the students majoring in art and design, urgently need and look forward to.

To sum up, the teachers' construction and teaching characteristics of Taiwan practical university can be summarized as follows: first, cross boundary at home and abroad; second, cross boundary between school and enterprise; third, cross boundary between industry and research; fourth, cross boundary in multi-dimensional classroom; fifth, cross boundary in learning, practice, training and business operation, which is a kind of ability building and vision expansion, while the education and teaching based on cross boundary will inject. It is a continuous stream of innovative applications and quality improvement.

4 Practical Dimension of Campus Culture

Art and design talents need a wide vision, broad knowledge and broad stage, and all these needs to be obtained in accordance with the times and the deep practice of social development. Therefore, the practical education and teaching of art and design specialty should be promoted to a higher level and occupy a larger proportion. Since the establishment of the University, the main feature of the practical university has been adhering to is "creative practice", and its operation The idea of learning is also "practice by force, repair the whole and govern the peace", hoping to promote wisdom to emerge by practice, and then exert strength by wisdom, benefit people's livelihood and "practice the ideal of world harmony". "The main goal of design education in Colleges and universities is to form an all-round and diversified education mode, that is, on the basis of improving students' ability in the professional field, paying attention to the strengthening of quality-oriented ability, and finally making students become compound professional talents conforming to the social development" [8]. With the increasingly close cooperation and exchange of higher education between the two sides of the Taiwan Strait, studying in Taiwan has become a new way, new measure and new channel for mainland art students to carry out professional practice and reform and innovation of art talents training mode in mainland universities. Taiwan practice university is named after "practice". The characteristics and highlights of its "practice" education are self-evident. As shown in Fig. 1, the practical training courses and arrangement account for 33.2% of the total number of courses offered. It's the reason why it can grow rapidly in a short time and become a more active and well-known university in the world is that it adheres to a different philosophy and implementation of running a school Effective practical education and teaching activities cannot be separated" [9].

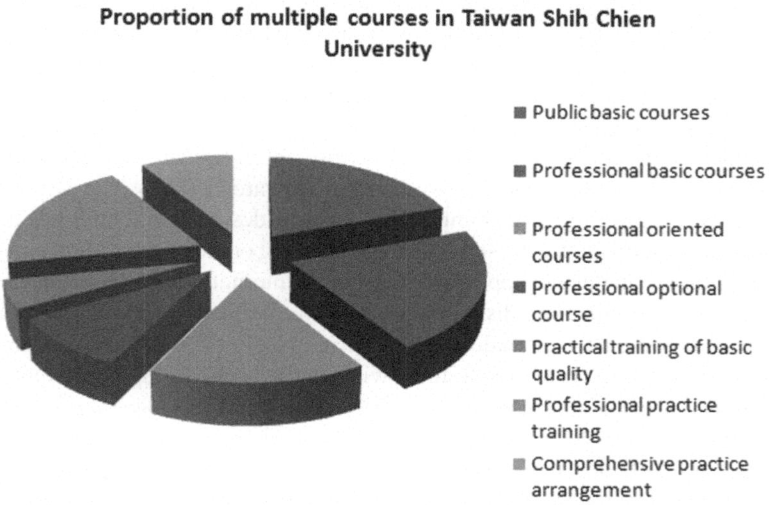

Fig. 1. Proportion of multiple courses in Taiwan Shih Chien University

Shih Chien university not only pays attention to practical education in the course system, education and teaching system and talent training program, such as vigorously expanding the flexible learning of major, encouraging students to practice in summer, strengthening creative design education, organizing all kinds of development design activities, promoting perfect and guaranteed practice system, etc., but also in students' daily life education, ideological education and moral education, etc. It also integrates the concept of "practice" everywhere, forming the practice fashion of the integration of body and mind, inside and outside the campus, such as the implementation of labor education, participation in the school environment renovation, the implementation of teaching assistant action, the opening of moral lecture, behavior norms and ideological and moral education series activities, etc., aiming at the art design major, it also creates the cultivation of design management practice and innovative management ability, design academic and creation. In the process of practice discussion and transposition teaching, the school running characteristics and Strategies of this kind of infiltrative practice will eventually establish the concept of campus culture based on practice and create a campus culture atmosphere characterized by practice.

5 The Guarantee Dimension of High Capital Investment

"At present, colleges and universities have limited funds, insufficient equipment and equipment, and the supply of raw materials can not meet the practical needs of students. Part of the teaching equipment in schools is old, and the off campus practice space provided for students is insufficient, which restricts the transformation of practical teaching and teaching mode, and is not conducive to the cultivation of innovative and applied talents" [10]. Although the education sector continues to increase investment in education every year, the absolute amount of investment in education continues to increase, and the proportion of financial education funds to GDP is more than 4%, but the relative amount remains at a low level, not only lower than the level of developed countries and regions, but also lower than the level of some less developed countries, compared with Taiwan's investment in higher education. In particular, there is still a considerable gap in investment in art education.

In addition to the above-mentioned soft investment in teachers and talents, Taiwan practical University also has a large investment in hardware facilities. The whole campus of Kaohsiung Campus of practical university is a well-designed and built teaching and living environment, no matter the style of single building or the harmony and unity of the whole building, no matter the appearance design or internal design Humanized design and functional positioning and distinction, have achieved originality, unique. Teaching facilities and equipment for art majors are also available. For example, the classroom for fashion photography is a professional studio with complete photographic equipment. The graduation show for students majoring in fashion design also has a special T-shaped performance platform and related professional facilities. There are professional large-scale wood processing factories, metal technology factories and digital manufacturing laboratories that cooperate with practice teaching, Art majors study and live in an environment full of art atmosphere and breath, and art spirit will be born from within.

Compared with most colleges and universities in mainland China, the running funds of Taiwan practical University, as the first domestic school and private school in Taiwan, are mainly funded by the government, and the sources of its high-value running funds are diversified, mainly including the regular income of students' miscellaneous expenses. According to the research of the author in Taiwan practical University, the income of this department only accounts for the running funds of the whole university About 56%; the second is the income from industry university cooperation, which is especially worth studying in most mainland universities, accounting for about 15%; the third is the income from promoting education, that is, non academic education, which is also an important part of flexible and diversified funding sources for running schools; the fourth is the income from donation. In recent years, the work of Alumni Association in mainland universities has been deepening, and alumni donation has gradually entered the normal state, while Taiwan's Taiwan's private colleges and universities, such as Shih Chien University, have a long history of obtaining school running funds due to private or team donations, and have also become an important source of school running funds; fifth, government subsidies, tax concessions and other income or relief.

6 Conclusion

The multiple dimensions of art design education in Taiwan's practical universities have brought many inspirations to the education and teaching of art design major in mainland universities.

No matter the specialized courses and basic courses with independent ecology, or the practical courses that are expected to cultivate the temperament and self-cultivation of Humanities and arts, or the liberal arts and general courses with the concept of all-around art design, they all focus on the independence, characteristics, novelty and cutting-edge, constantly enrich the implicit and enlightening art design aesthetic education activities, vigorously carry out the divergent and standing art practice and Design service activities, pay attention to the cultivation of cross-border accommodation, liberal arts and beauty, and have a sense of social responsibility, innovation awareness and pragmatic spirit of talents, its reasonable and diverse cross-border interactive curriculum structure dimension features.

Teachers' socialization and socialization. Although mainland universities also pay attention to the diversity of teachers and the combination of production, teaching and research, the cross-border dimension of the construction of teachers in Taiwan practice universities is not only to introduce policies to encourage and promote the professional teachers of art and design to integrate into the society and connect with the world, but also to pay more attention to the spiritual cross-border and temperament cross-border based on the improvement of teachers' ability and quality. Only teachers who have experienced and understood can realize "situational teaching" and bring students a thorough understanding of both body and mind.

The construction of the practical dimension of the campus culture of the practical university brings not only the all-round and all-round infiltration of the practical activities, but also the influence of the students from the small and large practical spirit and innovative practice. The cultivation of the practical culture is worthy of the deep reference of the universities in mainland China, even though the universities in mainland China run the University For lack of learning funds, it can also be carefully set up in details, focusing on small areas, so that the form of "art micro practice" can trigger each student's "dream big practice", at the same time, "reasonable allocation and use of teaching and practice resources", give full play to professional characteristics, and make full use of winter and summer holidays and some holidays, organize and carry out primary school and centralized "Art + life", "art" The practice of "Art +" featured fashion such as "Art + culture" and "Art + morality" enables students to develop the art practice fashion of unity of knowledge and practice, integration of body and mind, and access to both inside and outside.

Although most of the public colleges and universities in mainland China fail to reach the goal, their ideas and ways, especially the promotion of production and research income, promotion education and donation income, should be the direction of the development of colleges and universities in mainland China. The multiple and smooth sources of funds bring not only sufficient funds, but also the school running strength, social reputation and the comprehensive performance of service capacity improvement for local economic construction.

Under the in-depth exchange of art and culture education between the two sides of the Taiwan Strait, the characteristics, innovation and practice mode of art and design education in Taiwan's universities represented by Taiwan practical University provide a platform for the innovation and reform of art and design education in mainland China, as well as the exchange and talent training mechanism of art and Design Education between the two sides of the Taiwan Strait, so as to realize the development of art and design senior talent education across the Taiwan Strait High quality and optimization.

Acknowledgement. This work is supported in part by 2018 Anhui provincial quality engineering project "Sino-foreign cooperation training project" (2018zwpy001) and Zhongjiang scholar talent project.

References

1. Qiang, X., Yang, L.: Building the curriculum system of clothing specialty with practice and innovation as the main line – the characteristics of clothing specialty of Taiwan practice University. Text. Clothing Educ. **03**, 226–229 (2017)
2. Introduction to the school of design of Taiwan practical University. https://www.usc.edu.tw/zh_tw/academics/academic02/academic0201. Accessed 20 May 2020
3. Jianting, W.: The application and importance of Chinese painting in Art Design Teaching. Fujian Tea **04**, 122–123 (2020)
4. Xiangyang, F.: The development of general education in China should pay more attention to elegance. J. S. Chin. Univ. Technol. (Soc. Sci. Ed.) **04**, 105–108 (2010)
5. Zhongyan, L.: Research on general education system of Taiwan's undergraduate institutions from the perspective of Liberal Arts. Jiangsu Soc. Sci. **3**, 253–256 (2012)
6. Yang, L.: The characteristics and reference of fashion studio teaching form in Taiwan Universities – Taking Taiwan practical University as an example. Text. Ind. Technol. **z1**, 58–60 (2018)
7. Yidong, S., Yilan, S.: Enlightenment of design teaching in Taiwan's colleges and Universities – taking environmental design as an example. Archit. Cult. **01**, 82–83 (2020)
8. Qingshou, Z.: Educational characteristics and experience of Taiwan practical University. J. Minjiang Univ. **4**, 125–159 (2011)

9. Na, Y.: Research on the construction of talent training mode of art and design major in local universities. Ind. Des. **05**, 60–62 (2017)
10. You, W.: A glimpse of the new measures for the development of art education in Taiwan and Its Enlightenment. J. Chongqing Electron. Eng. Vocat. Coll. **6**, 84–86 (2017)

Study on Teaching of Engineering Design Course with 3D Modeling Software and 3D Printer in International Training Course

Rui-can Hao(✉), Hua-gang Liu, and Shang Wang

Beijing Polytechnic, No. 9 Liangshuihe First Street, Yizhuang, Beijing, China
haoruican@bpi.edu.cn

Abstract. Engineering design is one of the most important major courses for students in international training course. The goal for them is mastering professional comprehensive knowledge and applying it into the professional work projects. The content of engineering design and the international requirements was introduced. In order to improve the shortcoming of traditional teaching, novel teaching integrated with 3D modeling software and 3D printing technology was studied. For specific designing task, 3D modeling could make it more convenient to calculate the parameters of the designing. 3D printing could get the designed products rapidly and directly to help students to measure the precisions of the products. It is helpful to evaluate the designing scheme and to improve the quality of the products. The new teaching methods make it improved that the designing quality and efficiency. The comprehensive ability of students has been improved by combining 3D printing technology with the engineering designing work in the practice of the students.

Keywords: Engineering design · 3D modeling · Teaching · Internationalization

1 Introduction

Engineering design is an important course for students majoring in electromechanical specialty in international training course. The course includes two parts of knowledges. This first part of the course in engineering design introduces the students to concepts, procedures, data, and decision analysis techniques necessary in modern design applications. Power transmission components including gears, belts, chains, bearings, couplings, and shafts are studied in detail, and incorporated into a significant term-end project. The second part of the course continues the directions started in the first part, using similar methods to introduce new topics. A major project, including calculations and production drawings, will involve a linkage mechanism and a welded structure. The teaching methods were researched on the basis of the traditional teaching methods and study [1, 2].

S. Liu et al. (Eds.): eLEOT 2020, LNICST 339, pp. 362–369, 2020.
https://doi.org/10.1007/978-3-030-63952-5_31

In the processing of the design work, 3D modeling software is necessary for students to understand the designing model. 3D modeling was a popular research topic in design fields [3–9]. Integrating 3D modeling established with a software into the designing process is a helpful teaching method to get better effect in class. 3D modeling is to build a model with three-dimensional data through virtual three-dimensional space through three-dimensional production software.

While 3D printing technology is a novel manufacturing technology which is rapid and direct to get the designed real parts, and it is facilitate to evaluate the design scheme. 3D printing could be applied in many engineering fields [10–14]. The 3D printing technology will be more and more popular and is researched by many methods [15–17]. The principle of 3D printing is that the materials needed such as metal or plastic are overlaid and bonded layer by layer through printer. The technology could help students to get the designed products rapidly from the 3D printer instead of numerical control machining of multiple processes.

Integrating the international knowledges with the 3D modelling and 3D printing technology is a novel teaching method for teachers and an interesting experience.

2 Requirements and Teaching

For students in international training course, the knowledges they mastered should adapt to the internationalization. The comprehensive ability corresponding to the specialty knowledges is important for students to continue the study and work in Canada or Britain. So the internationalization and the combining knowledges are both necessary key requirements for students.

2.1 Internationalization of Knowledges and Abilities

Internationalization is a way of designing and producing products that can be easily adapted to different locales. This requires extracting all language, country/region and culturally dependent elements from a product. In other words, the process of developing an application whose feature design and code design do not make assumptions based on a single locale, and whose source code simplifies the creation of different local editions of a program, is called internationalization.

With the developing of the globalization, the knowledges for students should be generalization and internationalization to meet all of the job positions in the specialty.

Engineering design is an important specialty course for students in mechanical major. The mainly contents of the course are composited of two parts. The first part of the course includes concepts, procedures, data, and decision analysis techniques necessary in modern design applications. Power transmission components including gears, belts, chains, bearings, couplings, and shafts are studied in detail, and incorporated into a significant term-end project. The skills required are shown in Table 1.

Table 1. Skills required in Engineering Design 1

Employability	Essential Employability Skills addressed in this course
Communication	• Communicate clearly, concisely and correctly in the written, spoken, and visual form that fulfills the purpose and meets the needs of the audience • Respond to written, spoken, or visual messages in a manner that ensures effective communication
Numeracy	• Execute mathematical operations accurately
Critical Thinking and Problem Solving	• Apply a systematic approach to solve problems Use a variety of thinking skills to anticipate and solve problems
Information Management	• Locate, select, organize, and document information using appropriate technology and information systems • Analyze, evaluate, and apply relevant information from a variety of sources
Interpersonal	• Show respect for the diverse opinions, values, belief systems, and contributions of others • Interact with others in groups or teams in ways that contribute to effective working relationships and the achievement of goals
Personal	• Manage the use of time and other resources to complete projects • Take responsibility for one's own actions, decisions, and Consequences

Computer aided design is encouraged in the processing of solving the problems in homework for students. Figure 1 is a calculation example for students to solve problems in the processing of designing project.

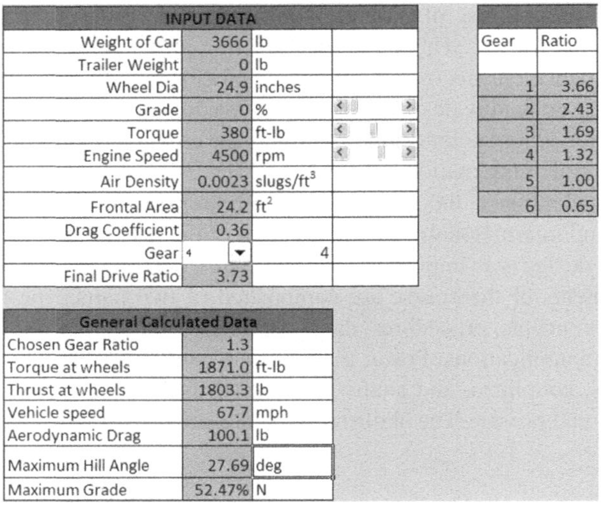

Fig. 1. Calculation software example for students

The second part of the course will enable the student to: 1) Describe the wide range of mechanisms already designed and be able to research for suitable means of obtaining a required motion. 2) Construct linkage displacement diagram to determine overall motion. 3) Develop force analyses for linkages. 4) Select suitable hydraulic, pneumatic, or electric linear actuator. 5) Check column strength of actuator. 6) Design plain bearings and select suitable propriety units. 7) Select suitable brake and clutch units for given loads and acceleration. 8) Design welded joints. 9) Define the considerations of strength and rigidity in welded frames and structures. 10) Integrate the design of the above elements into an overall machine design and produce assembly and detail drawings.

Figure 2 is an example for students to get design an mechanism. The question enhanced the calculation ability and broaden the design thinking of students.

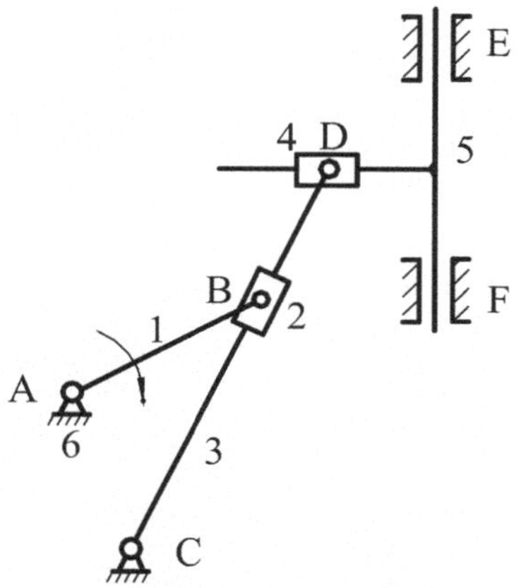

Fig. 2. An example for designing to get the required motion

2.2 Integrate 3D Modeling Software

The designing projects in the course is an important part for students to attain the designing ability. The designing projects are required and arranged in teaching plan for students to practice the software. At school, the designing homework were required to apply 3D modeling software for modeling and other software for calculating. It is also encouraged for students to use office software to write the design specification.

In the processing of designing mechanism, the mechanical drawing is the key work. While in the mechanical drawing, 3D modeling is a necessary work for understanding the designing objects except 2D drawing. Integrate 3D modeling software into the designing work is a helpful work.

With 3D modeling software, we could evaluate the products from each view to help the designing projects. Figure 3 shows the 3D models of parts and assemble drawing made by 3D software which could help students to check the feasibility of the design. (a) shows a shaft of a reducer designed for outputting the rotation. (b) shows a gear designed by a 3D software to match with a shaft. (c) shows the assemble reducer. Assembling by using the 3D modeling software could check that whether the assembly between parts is reasonable. From the example, integrating 3D modeling software with the designing could help students to practice designing the required model directly and visually.

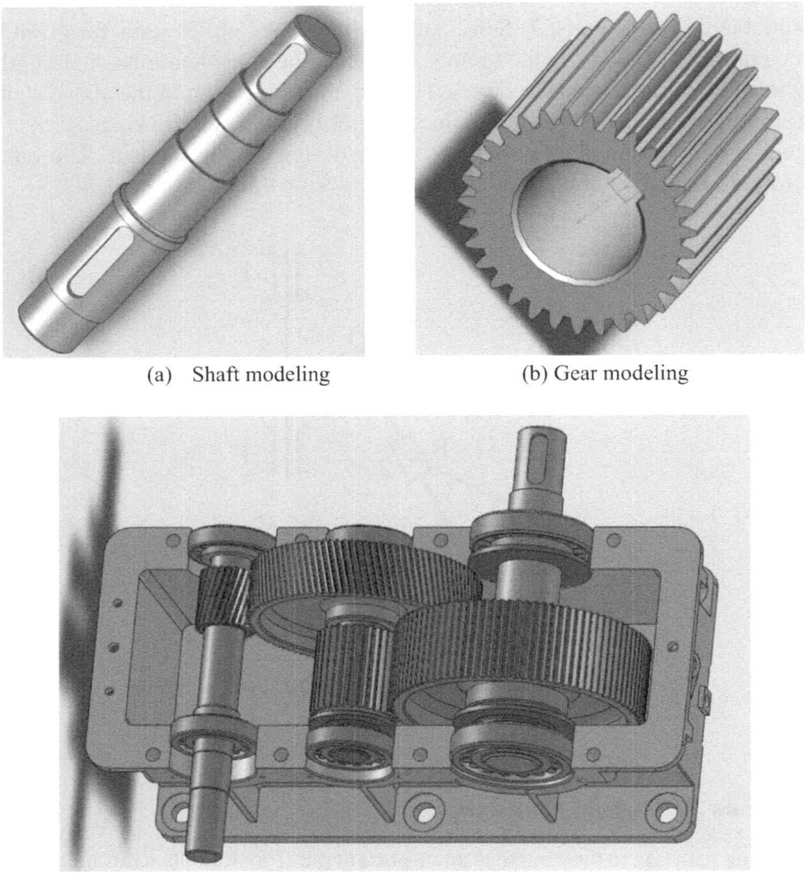

(a) Shaft modeling (b) Gear modeling

(c) Assembly modeling

Fig. 3. 3D modeling for designing example

2.3 Integrating 3D Printing

3D printing is novel manufacturing technology which could convert the data in the computer designed by software to the signals in the printer, to overlaid and bond the metal or plastic materials layer by layer through the printer. In the course of Engineering Design, 3D printing technology could follow up the 3D modeling to realize the transfer from the modeling to the real products. It could help students to understand the designing model and evaluate the real quality of the products designed in the process. In the 3D printing class, students could realize their designed plan by 3D printer which could initiate their innovation ideas and innovative thinking. Then the interesting of designing and innovation could be inspired in the class.

Students could study from the modeling library and design their objective by their innovative ideas by talking with their teammate. The group cooperation could train students' ability of teamwork. Figure 4 shows the models and products for students to practice and design.

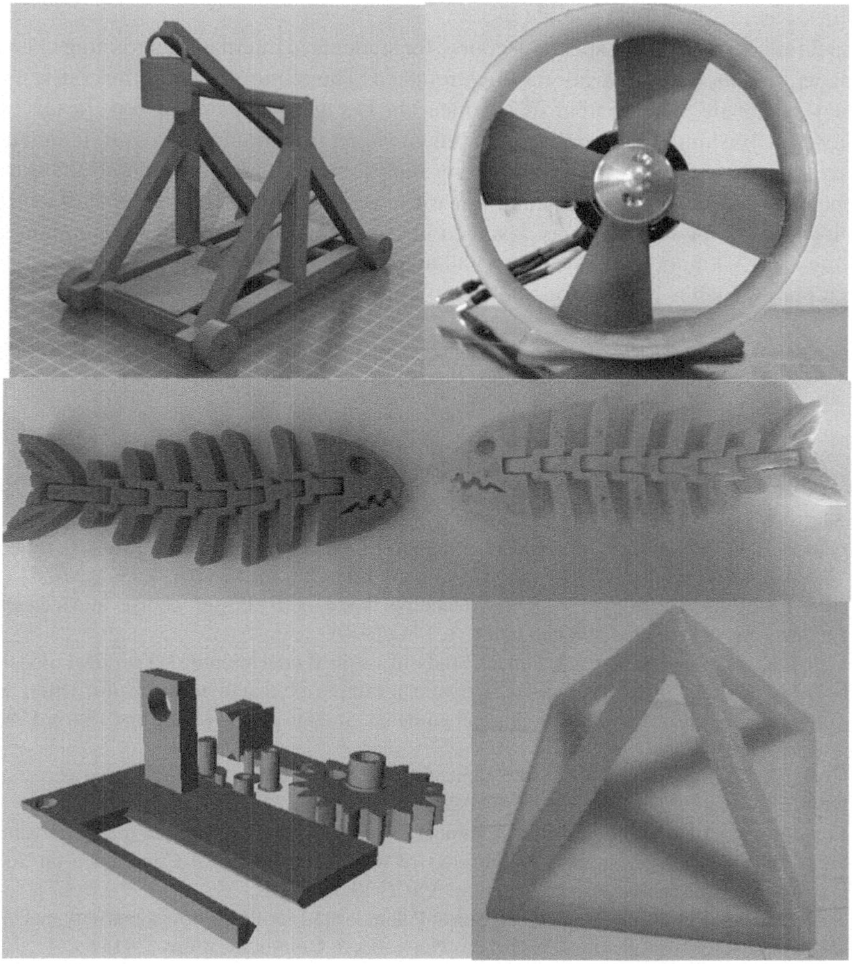

Fig. 4. Modeling and products for students to practice

In the 3D printing class, the divergent thinking is important for students to generate innovative ideas. So combination of free play in thinking and group cooperation in realizing the design is necessary. Teacher statements the requirement conditions and the other time leaved for students to free thinking, talk and cooperate with the teammates.

Combining 3D printing and 3D modeling could attain good teaching effect in the studying process of the course. Integrating 3D printing technology and 3D modeling software into the teaching class is an effective and popular teaching mode for students in the international training class.

3 Summary

Engineering design is a key specialty course for students in international training class. In the paper, the internationalization was introduced. The requirements of the course were studied and made. The content of Engineering Design was summarized. In teaching method, establishing 3D modeling for students is an important progress to understand and express their design ideas. Integrating the 3D modeling software into the course is necessary and helpful for students. 3D printing technology is a novel manufacturing which could get the real products designed in class rapidly and directly. Combining 3D printing with 3D modeling is effective and helpful for students to view and evaluate the design plan, which is helpful for students to improve the designing work.

Acknowledgements. Thanks to the fund and support from the general program of Beijing Municipal Edu-cation Commission (KM201910858005).

References

1. Qingwen, D.: Discussion on the diversification of teaching content and teaching mode of "mechanical design basis". Ind. Inform. Technol. Educ. **11**, 59–62 (2018)
2. Jing, L., Lihui, S., Daijun, S.: A new teaching mode of 3D design course in Mechanical Engineering. Mech. Electr. Educ. Innov. **1**, 176 (2020)
3. Ganry, L., Hersant, B., Bosc, R., et al.: Study of medical education in 3D surgical modeling by surgeons with free open-source software: example of mandibular reconstruction with fibula free flap and creation of its surgical guides. J. Stomatol. Oral Maxillofac. Surg. **119**(4), 262–267 (2018)
4. Cross, D.E., Bauer, T.M., Tchantchaleishvili, V.: 3D organ modeling with open-source software. Artif. Organs **43**(6), 596–598 (2019)
5. Fuman, L.: 3D modeling design and simulation processing of complicated surface ashtray based on CATIA software. In: Proceedings of the 8th International Conference on Social Network, Communication and Education (SNCE 2018) (2018)
6. Technical and System Software Companies; Patent Issued for Passive Associativity in Three-Dimensional (3D) Modeling. Computers, Networks & Communications (2015)
7. Han, K., Zhang, D., Chen, J., et al.: Presurgical visualization of the neurovascular relationship in trigeminal neuralgia with 3D modeling using free Slicer software. Acta Neurochir. **158**(11), 2195–2201 (2016)
8. Chung, T.-T.: 3D modeling and software created for human coronary artery. In: Abstracts of 2015 International Conference on Structural, Mechanical and Materials Engineering (ICSMME 2015). IETP-Association, vol. 40 (2015)

9. Li, L., Qin, S., Peng, J., et al.: Engineering gelatin-based alginate/carbon nanotubes blend bioink for direct 3D printing of vessel constructs. Int. J. Biol. Macromol. **145**, 262–271 (2020)
10. Ho, W.H., Tshimanga, I.J., Ngoepe, M.N., Jermy, M.C., Geoghegan, P.H.: Evaluation of a desktop 3D printed rigid refractive-indexed-matched flow phantom for PIV measurements on cerebral aneurysms. Cardiovasc. Eng. Technol. **11**(1), 14–23 (2019). https://doi.org/10.1007/s13239-019-00444-z
11. Zastrow, M.: 3D printing gets bigger, faster and stronger. Nature **578**(7793), 20–23 (2020)
12. Kühnel, C., Seifert, P., Mulik, C., et al.: 3D printing of fillable individual thyroid replicas based on nuclear medicine DICOM data used as phantoms for gamma probe calibration. Nuklearmedizin. Nucl. Med. **59**(1), 12–19 (2020)
13. Choi, J.-H., Leeghim, H., Ahn, J.-H., et al.: Fracture surface of 3D printed honeycomb structures at low temperature environments. J. Nanosci. Nanotechnol. **20**(7), 4235–4238 (2020)
14. Wang, C., et al.: 3D printing of bone tissue engineering scaffolds. Bioact. Mater. **5**(1), 82–91 (2020)
15. Sun, L., Liu, H., Xu, C., et al.: 3D printed navigation template-guided minimally invasive percutaneous plate osteosynthesis for distal femoral fracture: a retrospective cohort study. Injury **51**(2), 436–442 (2020)
16. Rungrojwittayakul, O., Kan, J.Y., Shiozaki, K., et al.: Accuracy of 3D printed models created by two technologies of printers with different designs of model base. J. Prosthodont. Official J. Am. Coll. Prosthodont. **29**(2), 124–128 (2020)
17. Schwartz, J.K., Fermin, A., Fine, K., et al.: Methodology and feasibility of a 3D printed assistive technology intervention. Disabil. Rehabil. Assistive Technol. **15**(2), 141–147 (2020)

The Integrated Design of 'Industry-University-Research-Application-Cultivation' Based on the Course of 'Mechanical Design Foundation' in Higher Vocational Colleges

Qing-song Zhu and Rui-can Hao(✉)

Beijing Polytechnic, No. 9 Liangshuihe First Street, Yizhuang, Beijing, China
Qingsong111@163.com, haoruican@163.com

Abstract. Mechanical design foundation is a key major course for students in major of mechanical design. The integrated design reform of industry-university-research-application-cultivation was studied and the corresponding reform measures have been implemented, which includes breaking the discipline framework and design the knowledge ability content with the project as the carrier, building a multi-level and three-dimensional course module system for social needs, breaking through the time and space of classroom, and create a MOOC resource library, constructing the intelligent interconnection between teachers, students and teaching resources by means of information, keeping pace with the development of the times and integrate multi-standard, reforming the teaching mode and exploring the form of promoting learning, promote innovation and entrepreneurship education and building a platform for innovative design and product promotion. The reform is meaningful and feasible for higher vocational colleges to build an 'industry-university-research-application-cultivation' learning environment.

Keywords: Mechanical design foundation · Higher vocational colleges · Integrated design

1 Introduction

Mechanical design foundation is a professional basic course of most engineering courses in higher vocational colleges. It is boring and obscure, and few people are good at it. At present, this course is only at the teaching level in many higher vocational colleges, which means that theoretical teaching and experiment have little formal innovation and application expansion. Therefore, it has far from fully played its role in supporting the foundation of the major. This paper starts from teaching, scientific research, social services and cultural inheritance of higher vocational colleges; combines with the actual situation of BEIJING POLYTECHNIC; deepens the cooperation between college and enterprise; integrates industry and education; expands and reforms content, form and application of the original course of mechanical design foundation to a great

S. Liu et al. (Eds.): eLEOT 2020, LNICST 339, pp. 370–375, 2020.
https://doi.org/10.1007/978-3-030-63952-5_32

extent; faces different audiences in the society; considers action-oriented as the main teaching form; develops the three-dimensional course module system of innovation and application of mechanical design; forms the overall advancement route of non-standard mechanical product design as shown in Fig. 1; and integrates culture, innovation, competition, entrepreneurship, scientific research, promotion and other elements in the process of advancement, thus building the industry-university-research-practice-cultivation architecture of mechanical innovation and application design, and giving full play to the strong supporting role of the course of mechanical design foundation in enlightening vocational education, innovating entrepreneurship education, guiding career and improving scientific research ability.

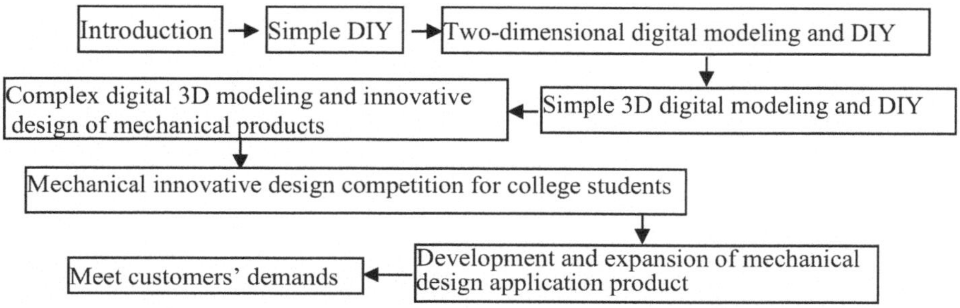

Fig. 1. The overall advancement route of non-standard mechanical product design

2 Integrated Design Reform of Industry-University-Research-Application-Cultivation

In order to deepen the cooperation between college and enterprise and integrate industry and education, this paper explores and reforms the integrated design of industry-university-research-application-cultivation in the following seven aspects based on the course of mechanical foundation.

2.1 Break the Discipline Framework and Design the Knowledge Ability Content with the Project as the Carrier

We should break the original subject knowledge system framework of mechanical design foundation, and integrate the content according to the project approach. Each project takes practical activities as the main line, and the amount and difficulty of project design content depend on the existing knowledge structure and internal demand of the overall learner, focusing on the improvement of comprehensive quality. Each project in the course is composed of several tasks. Each task organically combines relevant knowledge and practice process, and strives to embody the teaching philosophy of "learning by practicing" and "practicing by learning". The selection of project content centers on practical application, and cultivates students' practical ability, innovation ability, independent learning ability and practical working ability to solve problems. Figure 2 shows an example of a project in the course. Students should select a motor with a speed torque curve. A typical one is shown below is in the Fig. 2.

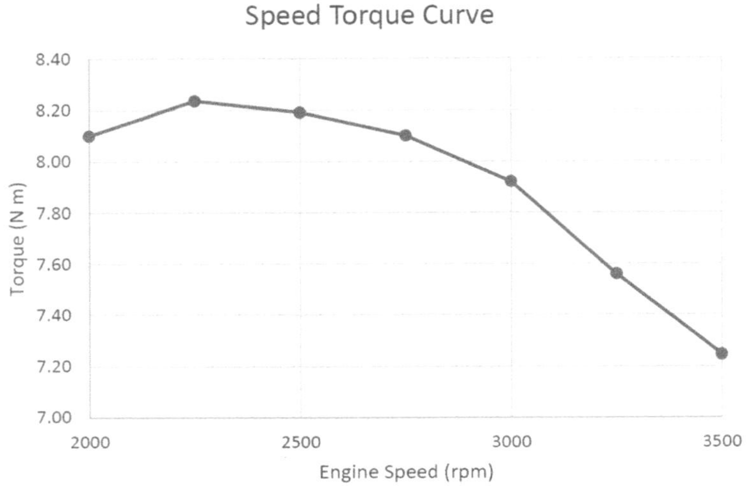

Fig. 2. A typical speed torque curve

2.2 Build a Multi-level and Three-Dimensional Course Module System for Social Needs

For enthusiasts of mechanical design among teenagers, professional enlightenment education of primary and secondary school students, demand of theory-practice integration of mechanical design for students of higher vocational colleges, and enthusiasts, users, developers of mechanical innovative design in the society, according to the prior knowledge and cognitive law of audiences, a set of mechanical innovative design course modules which adapt to elementary school, junior high school, high school, vocational college, college competition and development and application, and have moderate difficulty and progressive levels, are developed. In each course module a number of projects are designed. The distribution of knowledge points and difficulty of different levels of course modules will continue to increase, so as to build a three-dimensional course module system with wide knowledge and skills and deep levels.

2.3 Break Through the Time and Space of Classroom, and Create a MOOC Resource Library

Students can focus attention for only 10 min on average. According to this rule, the original traditional paradigm of 45 min for each class is broken. Each task in the project is a small unit. The MOOC video not longer than 10 min is designed, the MOOC resource library with different levels of course modules is established, and the function of social interaction between teachers, students and learners is provided, such as online discussion board, so that learners can communicate about and share learning resources online. MOOC for primary and secondary school students and social workers mainly adopts the mode of independent learning, while MOOC for vocational college students mainly adopts the mode of flipped classroom, which means that the watching of course teaching video is arranged by students independently after class, while in class the teacher answer questions and peers communicate and discuss with each other.

2.4 Construct the Intelligent Interconnection Between Teachers, Students and Teaching Resources by Means of Information

In order to promote the ubiquitous learning of the course of mechanical design foundation, an APP based on mobile terminals is developed to facilitate teachers and students to access course resources. Yisaotong is developed. By setting QR codes in textbooks and devices, the interconnection between teaching information resources such as textbooks and devices is established. Based on the existing VR and AR technology platforms, the latest equipment and technology frontier are integrated. Students can experience the interest and charm of high-end mechanical design products through virtual space. At the same time, an online learning evaluation system is established to record students' online learning status and learning effect. A comprehensive evaluation and comparative analysis are made on students' learning process on a regular basis, and learning suggestions are given to help students acquire knowledge and skills of mechanical design faster and better.

2.5 Keep Pace with the Development of the Times and Integrate Multi-standard

The newly issued relevant national standards and professional teaching standards promulgated by the Ministry of Education are integrated into the course teaching content, and the international industry standards are also referred to, so that standards must be followed. At the same time, the technological progress and industrial upgrading of the society are kept pace with, and relevant knowledge and skills of new technology, new process, new materials and new products (referred to as "four new") are timely integrated into the teaching content of the course of mechanical design foundation, so as to keep pace with the times. The classic mechanical design, invention and creation cases of ancient China are introduced into the teaching content to show the wisdom and civilization essence of Chinese ancestors. Meanwhile, the craftsman spirit of cherishing pos and devoting wholeheartedly to work, keeping improving, cooperating and making progress together and pursuing excellence in the new era is integrated into the teaching content to inherit and carry forward the culture.

2.6 Reform the Teaching Mode, and Explore the Form of Promoting Learning

The concept that class time must be in the classroom is reformed, and the classroom constraints are broken. According to their learning situation and personality characteristics, students can be divided into ordinary, competition and scientific research types.

Ordinary students study in the form of flipped classroom, while students of competition and scientific research types replace the original classroom teaching by promoting learning through competition and helping with learning with research. At the same time, after class according to their ability to learn and targets they can freely choose different levels of mechanical design MOOC for autonomous learning. The scope and difficulty of mechanical design project content involved in the competition and scientific research are bigger and higher than that of ordinary students, so as to achieve personalized teaching. The final results of the competition and scientific research will be regarded as new teaching case.

2.7 Promote Innovation and Entrepreneurship Education and Build a Platform for Innovative Design and Product Promotion

A mechanical innovation and design organization is set up, the selection and cultivation mechanism of members of the organization is improved, an innovation and entrepreneurship base for mechanical product innovation and design is established, and the equipments, facilities and corresponding software and hardware conditions of the base are constantly improved. The organization aims to solve the actual problems in life and production. Through the mechanical innovative design, the standardization of development of mechanical and electrical products and parts, and application for national patents, the independent intellectual property rights are formed, a company is established, and products are promoted on some domestic and foreign mature crowd funding platforms. At the same time, product program will also be developed and placed into MOOC as a new teaching or cultivation case. In free autonomous learning, social and primary and middle school learners can purchase the company's standard parts for innovation of works and assembly of innovative design. Figure 3 shows the design example for students to practice.

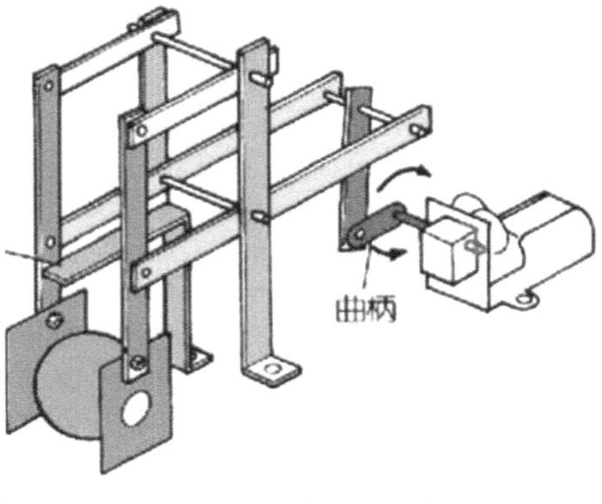

Fig. 3. An design example for students to practice

3 Summary

This paper explores and reforms from building a multi-level and three-dimensional course module, creating MOOC resource library, building the smart interconnection among teachers, students and teaching resources, integrating many standards, "four new" and craftsman spirit, exploring to promote learning with competition and help with learning with research, and building an innovative design and product promotion platform. The industry-university-research-application-cultivation architecture of mechanical innovation application design was set up. A solid foundation for further deepening the cooperation between college and enterprise was laid.

Acknowledgement. Thanks to the fund and support from the general program of Beijing Municipal Education Commission (KM201910858005).

References

1. Ke, Z.: On the practice of the integration of industry, education and research in mechanical teaching. Cont. Educ. Res. **4**, 153–154 (2013)
2. Zhang, G., Hong, Z.: Curriculum construction of foundation of mechanical design. J. Mach. Des. **S2**, 213–215 (2018)
3. Yi, L.: Project-based teaching reform of mechanical design foundation in higher vocational colleges. Sci. Technol. **26**, 9–59 (2018)
4. Jing, T., Lei, J., Chen, X., et al.: Research on the teaching methods for the foundational course of mechanical design. J. Mach. Des. **S2**, 330–332 (2018)
5. Sun, G., Xu, D., Shang, D., et al.: Study on blended teaching for course of mechanical design basis. J. Mach. Des. **S2**, 174–175 (2018)
6. Liu, H., Cheng, Z., Yang, J., et al.: Study on SPOC blended teaching mode in course design for fundamentals of mechanical design. Educ. Teach. Forum. **19**, 140–141 (2018)
7. Jinliang, C., Feng, Z., Hao, D.: Study on the teaching reform of fundamentals of mechanical design in industrial design. Ind. Des. **1**, 25–26 (2018)
8. Wang, F., Ni, J., Zhang, X., et al.: Exploration of mechanical basic courses based on expanding CAD teaching mode. J. Yuncheng Univ. **37**(6), 51–54 (2019)

An Investigation of Intercultural Communicative Competence Among Master's Graduate Students of Non-English Major in the Context of Content-Based English Instruction

Qingling Wang and Qingying Zhou(✉)

School of Foreign Languages and Literature, Yunnan Normal University, Kunming 650500, YN, China
316411187@qq.com

Abstract. Intercultural communicative competence (ICC) is the ultimate goal of teaching and learning of English as a foreign language (EFL). Content-based English Instruction (CBEI) refers to the teaching of the content or materials of a field in English, enabling students to acquire English while learning specialized knowledge. This study tries to investigate the cultivation of ICC among Master's graduate students (MGS) in a cultural content-based English course. A questionnaire was distributed to 300 MGS for the survey before and after the CBEI course was conducted. And the results do reveal that CBEI course can increase students ICC in five dimensions, namely, language competence, intercultural knowledge, intercultural attitude, intercultural awareness and intercultural strategy. Classroom observation on the process of teaching was conducted to find out the way it improves the ICC of MGS.

Keywords: Intercultural communicative competence (ICC) · Content-Based English Instruction (CBEI) · Master's graduate students (MGS)

1 Introduction

Intercultural communicative competence (ICC) is the ultimate goal for teaching and learning of English as a foreign language (EFL). As English has become an international lingua franca for communication and been widely used around the world, all graduate students in China are required to study English, and English course is compulsory in China's graduate education. As early as 1992, the National Education Ministry has issued the Non-English Major Gradates English Instruction Syllabus, which claimed that the aim of graduate English teaching is to cultivate students' ability to use English as a tool to learn disciplinary knowledge, to do academic research and to cultivate their competence in international communication. Hence, colleges and universities have developed various curricula and syllabuses of graduate English course for improving students' international

S. Liu et al. (Eds.): eLEOT 2020, LNICST 339, pp. 376–386, 2020.
https://doi.org/10.1007/978-3-030-63952-5_33

communicative capability either in their academic study or in general interactions. However, the traditional language-driven model of graduate English teaching for cultivating students' English skills neglects the actual use of English in the international communicative context of the globalizing world. Moreover, as master graduate students (MGS), most of them have learned English for more than 14 years from primary school through their undergraduate education, and have accumulated vocabularies, acquired grammatical structures as well as language skills before they took graduate English course. As a result, in graduate English teaching context, content-based English instruction (CBEI) is much more accepted, and more suitable for the needs of students. In CBEI course, English is used as a tool to learn subject matter, with the learning and teaching happened in an authentic context. Such content-driven model integrating language learning into subject matter learning by using authentic materials in a certain field and creating real communicating context is a suitable way to develop students' ICC. This study attempts to investigate the correlation between graduate students' ICC improvement and the CBI model, and to find how this model improves MGS' ICC.

1.1 Content-Based English Instruction and Intercultural Communicative Competence

Content Based Instruction (CBI) refers to teaching of the content or materials of a field in the target language (mostly a second or foreign language), in which students acquire the language while learning specialized knowledge [1]. Language is the carrier of content, and the content reflects specific applications of language. This teaching concept advocates the teaching of a second language or foreign language by means of subject content, which is effective, authentic and combines the learning of language and content [2]. In CBI, learners acquire the second or foreign language while learning the contents in authentic language communicative context through which their language ability and ICC are improved, and such improvement makes it easier for them to learn subject knowledge. CBI language course is strongly discipline-oriented. It combines language learning with subject matter study, shifting the focus from language itself to the subject materials. And in Content-based English Instruction (CBEI), English is used in the teaching and learning of the content materials. This teaching mode is also function-oriented, in which students learn subject material in English through activities that can not only improves their English capacity, but also cultivates their ICC. CBEI emphasizes the learning of subject content, the authenticity of language materials, the novelty of information and the needs of students. Language teaching under this concept improves learners' English competence on the premise of fully meeting their learning needs and stimulating their learning enthusiasm. In this process, students learn professional knowledge, understand the latest trend of the discipline, and cultivate their ICC.

The concept of ICC is variously defined by scholars resulting from their different views on intercultural communication and conceptualization of competence. Spitzberg [3] state that intercultural communication competence, cross-cultural communication competence, and trans-cultural communication competence are interchangeable concepts referring to the ability to effectively and appropriately communicate with people who are from different countries, different regions and different communities with different cultural backgrounds. Samovar & Porter [4] declare that ICC is a kind of behavior that individuals behave properly and appropriately who are able to successfully communicate with people from other cultural backgrounds. For TESL scholars, ICC refers to the ability which enables one to effectively and appropriately interact in a second or foreign language with others from different linguistic and cultural backgrounds [5]. As a result, developing leaners ICC and helping them to successfully communicate with people from other cultures whose mother toughs are different becomes the goal of language education.

As for component of ICC, Byram [6] holds that ICC should include linguistic competence, sociolinguistic competence and discourse competence, including elements such as attitudes, knowledge, skills of interpreting and relating, skills of discovery and interaction, and critical cultural awareness. Fantini [7] proposes a similar model which consists of knowledge, awareness, attitudes to different cultures, and language skills. Both of them emphasize the cultivation of intercultural as well as linguistic competence. Byram further [6] points out that the purpose of language education is to foster intercultural competences of language users, so as to help language users be open to views or ways differ from those of them, to be able to communicate with people speaking different languages from different cultures. Hence, integration intercultural knowledge into language education should be a feasible way to develop learners' ICC.

CBEI has been a significant approach for teaching English as a second or foreign language. And in most cases, the contents are cultural materials or subject knowledge. It aims to develop learners' English proficiency and subject matters in an authentic learning context. Stryker & Leaver [8] state that CBEI can be a "new paradigm" in second language education that centers on developing students' communicative competence—the ability of communicating with others from different cultures in real communication context.

1.2 Research Purposes

As a group of advanced English learners, MGS has urgent needs for ICC. CBEI integrates language learning into content learning which is widely used in second/foreign language settings. However, few studies research on ICC among graduate students in a CBEI course. As a result, this study is to explore whether the CBEI course can improve students' ICC, and how does it improve their ICC through investigating MGS' ICC before and after the take CBEI course.

2 Research Methods

2.1 Research Subjects

The investigation was done in a university in southwest of China. This is a typical provincial university which can trace back to 1938 when China was in Anti-Japanese War. In this university, the English course is compulsory for all non-English major MGS which has 108 credit hours with 4 credits lasting 2 semesters in the first year of their graduate education. From 2013, this university implemented content-based English instruction approach in the course of "American Culture". In 2017 academic year, the university enrolled 1362 MGS among whom 1027 are full-time students, and 335 are part-time ones), ranging from liberal art, education to science and engineering. And among 1027 full-time MGS, 72 are English majors who are not required to take the graduate English course, for most of their course are full English ones. As a result, the total number of full-time MGS of non-English major is 955.

In this investigation, 300 MGS of 2017 were randomly chosen as research subjects, accounting for more than 3% of the total full-time non-English major MGS who take the graduate English course through 2017–2018 academic year.

They are first-year graduate students of 2017 and most of whom have learned English for about fourteen years. Among them, 167 graduate students are in liberal art, including literature, sociology, linguistics, philosophy and history, 133 graduate students are in science, majoring in mathematics, chemistry, physics, engineering, and biology. 176 subjects are female students, accounting for 59%, while 124 are male students accounting for 41% of the total (see Table 1).

Table 1. Demographic information of the research subjects.

	Major		Gender	
	Arts	Science	Male	Female
Number	167	133	124	176
Percent	56%	44%	41%	59%

Among them, only 42% and 14% students respectively have passed (CET4) (N = 127) and CET6 (N = 42) (see Table 2), which indicates that as graduate students, their English level is not good as we expected. [Note: CET4, the abbreviation of College English Test Band 4, is a national English proficiency test mostly for the first and second year college students, while CET6, the abbreviation of College English Test Band 6, is mostly for the third and fourth year ones.]

Table 2. English proficiency of the research subjects.

	You passed CET4		You passed CET6	
	Yes	No	Yes	No
Number	127	173	42	258
Percent	42%	58%	14%	86%

2.2 Research Methods

Questionnaires and classroom observation are used as the primary research methods in this study to analyze the status quo of graduate students' ICC and the effects of CBEI course on their ICC in the Chinese graduate English context. The statistical package for social science 18.0 (SPSS 18.0) and excel 2007 are applied to export results of the collecting data.

2.2.1 Questionnaire

This study utilizes one questionnaire with 5-Likert scale to investigate whether the CBEI has positive effects on students ICC improvement. "Questionnaire of Intercultural Communication Competence Inventory for Chinese MGS" was made by integrating Zhong et al.'s [9] scale "The Intercultural Communication Competence Self Report Scale (ICCSRS)" and Gao's [10] "Intercultural Communication Competence Inventory for Chinese College Students (ICCICCS)". This questionnaire includes two parts, first part is subjects' demographic information including major, gender and English proficiency (whether passed CET4 and CET6). Part two includes 42 items classified into five parts – language competence, intercultural knowledge, intercultural attitude, intercultural awareness and intercultural strategy (see Table 3).

Table 3. Structure of questionnaire one.

Dimension	Name	Items
1	Language competence	From 1 to 6
2	Intercultural knowledge	From 7 to 18
3	Intercultural attitude	From 19 to 27
4	Intercultural awareness	From 28 to 33
5	Intercultural strategy	From 34 to 42

The questionnaire was distributed to the subjects before and after they took the CBEI course among the same subjects to survey whether CBEI course has improved their ICC, and how does it help in the improvement. Their CBEI course lasts two semesters.

2.2.2 Classroom Observations

Classroom observations are conducted among five CBEI teachers' class through two semesters. It was observed that the teaching in CBEI course is mostly student-centered and task-based, and students are frequently asked to do presentations, to discuss questions in groups assigned in the previous week. And the instructors mostly acted as guiders and controllers who designed class activities, controlled steps, inspired students' interests in the content and language, making some explanation on the language and some comparisons between American and Chinese cultures. Observation on students mainly includes their language choose in carrying the task, activity participation, confidence and anxiety of L2 use. Observation on program is centering on linguistic appropriateness, content learning, and ICC developing.

2.3 Teaching Materials

CBEI integrates language learning into content learning and its teaching materials should be authentic subject matter information appropriate to specific needs.

The content of this CBEI course mainly focuses on learning subject matters (American culture) (see Table 4) which are authentic texts written by Russell Duncan & Joseph Goddardthe, an original version published by China's Renmin University Press. This graduate English course is open to all graduate students who are from different majors and different subjects, so their major is different. The main themes of this textbook are presented in Table 4.

Table 4. Structure of the textbook.

Lesson	Topics
Lesson 1	History (The Rise of Nation, The Rise of Power, From Isolation to Superpower, The Cold War, The 1990s)
Lesson 2	Land and People (The land, The People, Regions, Immigration)
Lesson 3	Government (The Constitution, The Federal System, The Branches of Government)
Lesson 4	The Political System (The 2004 Election, Political Parties, Politics)
Lesson 5	Society (The American Family, women, Race, Crime and Punishment)
Lesson 6	Education and Social Policy (Education, Social Services)
Lesson 7	Culture (Diversity, The Rise of American Culture, Leisure Time, Print Media, Mass Entertainment, Government Activities, The World Wide Web, Sports, The Arts, Popular Music)
Lesson 8	The Economy (The US Domestic Economy, Labor Unions, Business and Industry, The Global Marketplace, The Dollar and the Trade Deficit)
Lesson 9	Foreign Policy (Separation of Powers and Foreign Policy, The Administration of Foreign Policy, History of Foreign Policy, The Cold War, 1945—1991, The New World Order, The Bush Administration)
Lesson 10	Conclusion (The Home Front, Foreign Affairs)

In CBEI course of this study, graduate students' do not waste much time on studying grammar rules that they have learned before, but give much efforts to gain what they does not know or what they are unfamiliar with. Additionally, on account of students' task different, information gap will be emerged in this course, which creates good opportunities for students' exchanging information. That is to say this is a process of learning new information or gaining information gap rather than review what they have learned.

For appropriateness to specific needs, the teaching materials in CBEI course is not limited by the textbook, students are able to choose original materials that they really interested in around the given topic to share with their classmates.

3 Results and Discussion

3.1 Comparison of ICC in Pretest and Post-test

The questionnaire was done twice (pretest and post-test) among the 300 research subjects before and two semesters after they had the CBEI course. Table 5 and 6 demonstrate the results of the pretest and post-test of the questionnaire.

Table 5. Descriptive statistics of total means ICC in pretest and post-test.

	N	Min	Max	Means	SD
ICC in pretest	300	1.76	4.43	3.319	0.336
ICC in post-test	300	1.52	5.00	3.647	0.472

Table 5 shows a general description on students' ICC before and after they took the course. In pretest, the mean score of ICC among the 300 research subjects is 3.319, while in post-test, it has increased 3.364. After one-year CBEI course, students' ICC has improved in general.

The questionnaire surveys students ICC from five dimensions including language competence, intercultural knowledge, intercultural attitude, intercultural awareness and intercultural strategy. The statistics are illustrated in Table 6. Students' means scores of the five dimensions of ICC in post-test have increased a lot. Students mean score of language competence has increased 0.1473 from 3.3933 to 3.5406, and the maximum has increased from 4.67 to 5.00; the means of their intercultural knowledge is 0.4957 higher, from 2.9222 to 3.4169; the means of their intercultural attitude has been raised 0.2093, from 3.8281 to 4.0374; their intercultural awareness increases by 0.3578, from 3.2233 to 3.5811; their intercultural strategy raises by 0.3250, from 3.3544 to 3.6800. Their improvement can be described as intercultural knowledge > intercultural awareness > intercultural strategy > intercultural knowledge > English competence. Students have the lowest score ($M = 2.9211$) in pretest in intercultural knowledge, but improves most in post-test, which is the best example to illustrate the sharp contrast in the traditional English instruction and that of CBEI. In traditional instruction, the teaching materials are articles about different topics, and instructors mostly focus the teaching on language itself by explanation of words, sentence structures and the practice of them, neglecting the cultural knowledge the implied in the materials. While in CBEI course, the content is cultural materials of America, and in teaching process, the instructors frequently compare American culture with Chinese culture and extend into other cultures in the world. In such a way of teaching, in the comparison and study of culture, their cultural knowledge has greatly improved. And in this teaching process, their culture awareness has also greatly improved. In both pretest and post-test, they have highest scores in culture attitude, revealing that China's MGS has a positive attitude to diversities cultures, and they are open to the differences among peoples in the world. However, the English competence is relatively low and the progress is narrow, which is only 0.1473. In the teaching, in order to express clearly sometimes the instructor speak Chinese, and in the discussion and question & answer part, in order to express complicated thoughts about cultures students may speak Chinese. Nevertheless, they do have made progress in the CBEI course.

Table 6. Descriptive analysis of ICC in pretest and post-test.

		N	Min	Max	Means	SD
In Pretest	Language competence	300	1.33	4.67	3.3933	0.52855
	Intercultural knowledge	300	1.00	5.00	2.9211	0.64986
	Intercultural attitude	300	1.78	5.00	3.8281	0.54858
	Intercultural awareness	300	1.50	4.67	3.2233	0.45264
	Intercultural strategy	300	1.44	4.56	3.3544	0.42157
In Post-test	Language competence	300	1.00	5.00	3.5406	0.6435
	Intercultural knowledge	300	1.00	5.00	3.4169	0.7441
	Intercultural attitude	300	1.00	5.00	4.0374	0.6908
	Intercultural awareness	300	1.33	5.00	3.5811	0.6089
	Intercultural strategy	300	1.44	5.00	3.6800	0.5358

As seen from Table 7, findings reveal that in pretest 254 students have the mean score higher than 3, which account for 84.6%, and only 4 are accounting for 1.3%. In post-test, the number increases to 284, accounting for 94.6%, a 10% growth in their ICC. For those who get the high score between 4 and 5 ($4 <= M <= 5$), the number has increased from 4 to 55. And number of students' means scores lower than 3 has decreased from 46 to 26, the percentage changes from 15.3% to 5.35. These results demonstrate that through studying CBEI course, students' ICC has apparently improved a lot, but developing students' ICC is a process of continuous learning and practicing in authentic context.

3.2 Teaching Mode of the Instructors Through Classroom Observation

This is a comprehensive graduate English course, which is required for all MGS. This university use materials of American culture as the content of instruction. The objectives of this course are as follows: (1) to require students have a comprehensive understanding of the history, politics, society and culture of the United States through the study; In the study, students should expand their knowledge from American culture to western culture and its origin. Furthermore, instructors should guide them to make comparison and explore the differences between Chinese culture and American culture, the oriental and

Table 7. Frequency analysis of students' ICC means scores between pretest and post-test.

	The range of the means scores	N	Percent	Valid percent	Cumulative percent
In Pretest	M < 2	1	0.3%	0.3%	0.3%
	2 <= M < 3	45	15%	15%	15.3%
	3 <= M < 4	250	83.3%	83.3%	98.7%
	4 <= M <= 5	4	1.3%	1.3%	100%
In Post-test	M < 2	3	1.0%	1.0%	1.0%
	2 <= M < 3	13	4.35	4.3%	5.3%
	3 <= M < 4	229	76.3%	76.3%	81.7%
	4 <= M <= 5	55	18.3%	18.3%	100%

Note: M < 2 means that the means score of ICC is lower than 2
2 <= M < 3 represents the means score of ICC is 2 (M = 2) to 3 (M < 3)
3 <=M < 4 refers to the means score of ICC is 3 (M = 3) to 4 (M < 4)
4 <= M <= 5 is about the means score of ICC is 4 (M = 4) to 5 (M < 5)

western cultures, in the effort to cultivate their confidence and pride in Chinese culture, and to develop their awareness of cultural relativity. (2) to improve students' English language skills, and to cultivate intercultural communicative competence (Table 8).

This is a design of one hour's class. The teaching and learning are carried out mostly in cooperative study in groups, and classroom discussion, while the instructor makes the general explanation and supervise students to involve in classroom interactions. The instructor assigns students to learn the material before the class. And the assignments are in the form of question. In the chapter of American Civil war, the questions concerns about the reasons and causes, the details, and what the American chose by and from the war, the significance of the war. One question is about the comparison between the civil war between the Kuomintang and Communist Party in 1945–1949 which led to the complete victory of Communist Party in China. In the classroom, the instruction carries out in discussion around these questions in class. After the discussion, the instructor analyzes the chapter and makes conclusion of the chapter.

Such mode of teaching is mostly student-centered. They need to study the content of text book and consult relevant materials in order to answer the questions assigned by the instructor. And in classroom, they need to participate in class activities of discussion, make presentation, and other group activities. After class, in addition to finishing some written assignments, they have to prepare for the new chapter for next week. In this model of teaching and learning, students learn intercultural knowledge, and in this process of learning, they develop intercultural awareness, learn intercultural strategy, cultivate a positive intercultural attitude, and acquire English competence.

Table 8. One class period of the instruction: American civil war.

Task: reading the chapter of the Civil War in the text book and preparing for the questions given by the instructor by consulting relevant materials	Reasons	Significance	Comparison	Cooperative learning
	Northern development road Southern development road Causes of civil war 1. States' rights vs. federal rights 2. Social contradictions 3. Economic benefits ……	Safeguarding national unity; Abolition of slavery; Solving the land problems; Developing Capitalism…	1945–1949 civil war between China's Kuomintang and Communist Party	Group cooperation to complete tasks, and to participate in class discussions
	Details	Choices		
	Capitalism vs. slavery Lincoln Road for development the Western states Major battles of the civil war Gettysburg The Emancipation Proclamation. Homestead Act	The right of the union over the right of the states, The United States is well on its way to liberal capitalism, Freedom, equality, no slavery		
Intercultural communicative competence				

4 Conclusion

Through surveying and analyzing, we have found that after participating in CBI English course for one year, most students' ICC has improved, and a few have made great progress, indicating that the CBI English course is an effective and feasible way to enhance students' ICC. The CBI English course can promote students' ICC development in all dimensions, and their intercultural knowledge can be greatly improved.

This study is of immense significance to promote the potential shift of traditional graduate English teaching to CBI course in the upsurge of current foreign language education reform in China. Specifically, it differs from traditional language teaching for integration of language learning into content learning and it is able to simultaneously enhance students' ICC, academic knowledge and language proficiency rather than merely emphasize language skills acquisition.

References

1. Snow, M., Brinton, D.: Content-Based Classroom. Longman, New York (1997)
2. Stoller, F.: Content-based instruction: perspectives on curriculum planning. Ann. Rev. Appl. Linguisti. **24**, 261–283 (2004)
3. Spitzberg, B.H.: A model of intercultural communication competence. In: Samovar, L.A., Porter, R.E. (eds.) Intercultural Communication: A Reader, 9th edn. Wadsworth Publishing Company, Belmont (2000)
4. Samovar, L.A., Porter, R.E.: Communication Between Cultures, 7th edn. Beijing University Press, Beijing (2012)
5. Tran, T.Q., Duong, T.M.: The effectiveness of the intercultural language communicative teaching model for EFL learners. Asian-Pacific J. Second Foreign Lang. Educ. **3**(1), 1–17 (2018). https://doi.org/10.1186/s40862-018-0048-0
6. Byram, M.: Teaching and Assessing Intercultural Communicative Competence. Multilingual Matters, Philadelphia (1997)
7. Fantini, A.E.: A central concern: developing intercultural competence. SIT Occas. Pap. Ser. Addressing Intercult. Educ. Train. Serv. **1**, 25–42 (2000)
8. Stryker, B., Leaver, L.: Content-based instruction: some lessons and implications. In: Stryker, B., Leaver, L. (eds.) Content-Based Instruction in Foreign Language Education: Models and Methods 282–310. Georgetown University Press, Washington, D.C. (1997)
9. Zhong, H., Bai, Q.H., Fan, W.W.: Study on the intercultural communication competence self report scale among China's college students. Foreign Lang. Circle **2**, 47–56 (2013)
10. Gao, Y.C.: Investigation and analysis on the current situation of intercultural communication competence of Chinese college students. Foreign Lang. Foreign Lang. Teach. **2**, 71–78 (2016)

Author Index

The manufacturer's authorised representative in the EU is Springer Nature Customer Service Centre GmbH, Europaplatz 3, 69115 Heidelberg, Germany. If you have any concerns regarding our products, please contact ProductSafety@springernature.com

Printed and bound by CPI Group (UK) Ltd, Croydon, CR0 4YY
30/09/2026
02225688-0008